The Connected Home: The Future of Domestic Life

Richard Harper

Editor

The Connected Home:
The Future of Domestic Life

 Springer

Editor
Richard Harper
Microsoft Research Ltd.
J.J. Thomson Avenue
CB3 0FB Cambridge
United Kingdom
r.harper@microsoft.com

ISBN 978-0-85729-475-3   e-ISBN 978-0-85729-476-0
DOI 10.1007/978-0-85729-476-0
Springer London Dordrecht Heidelberg New York

British Library Cataloguing in Publication Data
A catalogue record for this book is available from the British Library

Library of Congress Control Number: 2011943013

Printed on acid-free paper

Springer is part of Springer Science+Business Media (www.springer.com)

Acknowledgements

All books depend upon their completion on the forbearance of various good souls. This forbearance is often required in the undertaking of the research and in the writing up of it: this book is no exception. First, thanks are due to the editors at Springer, Beverley Ford and Helen Desmond, both of whom kept encouraging me to 'get it done'. Meanwhile, various of the chapters were funded by different agencies and were undertaken in different institutions, all of whom merit acknowledgement. These are hopefully correctly listed in the footnotes. Some thanks are also due personally, to those who contributed beyond what can be expected. Dave Randall, author of Chapter 7, would like to thank Billy, Camille, Danny, Heather, Liz, Mary, Nichola, Nick and a couple of anonymous contributors for their invaluable insights. Siân Lindley, author of chapter 9, would like to thank myself and our colleague Abi Sellen here at MSR, and Peter Taylor and Simon Lewis from The Technology Partnership, for their insight, their work in developing Wayve, and their contribution to the running of the field trial she reports in her chapter. Jofish Kaye, author of chapter 10, would like to thank his current and former colleagues and collaborators in the Connected Reading projects at Nokia Research Center North America and Sesame Workshop, particularly Mirjana Spasojevic, Hayes Raffle, Tico Ballagas, Koichi Mori, Hiroshi Horii, Glenda Revelle, Morgan Ames and Janet Go. Will Odom, author of chapter 12, would like to thank Intel for partly funding the research reported, as well as colleagues Jared Cole, Brandon Frambes, and Dave Rocco for their assistance in data collection in the project reported. He would also like to thank all of the participants across both studies that took the time and effort to contribute to the research. James Barlow and colleagues, authors of chapter 13, draw on research partly funded by the Engineering and Physical Science Research Council (UK) through its Health and Care Infrastructure Research and Innovation Centre (HaCIRIC). Parts of the chapter draw on and develop work carried out by Tim Venables and James Barlow (2004) & Barlow J and Venables T, (2004). Doubtless there are others too who have aided in the preparation of this book: thank you, despite your anonymity.

Cambridge, UK   Richard Harper

Contents

Contributors

Richard Banks Microsoft Research, Cambridge, UK

Louise Barkhuus University of California, San Diego, CA, USA

James Barlow Imperial College, London, UK

Steffen Bayer Imperial College, London, UK

Barry Brown Mobile Life VINN Excellence Center, Stockholm, Sweden

Debora Dunkle University of California, Irvine, CA, USA

Jodi Forlizzi Carnegie Mellon University, Pittsburgh, PA, USA

Lynne Hamill University of Surrey, Guildford, UK

Richard Harper Microsoft Research Ltd., Cambridge, UK

Joseph "Jofish" Kaye Nokia Research, Palo Alto, CA, USA

Dave Kirk University of Nottingham, Nottingham, UK

Simon C.R. Lewis Conceptual Simplicity, Cambridgeshire, UK

Siân Lindley Microsoft Research, Cambridge, UK

William Odom Carnegie Mellon University, Pittsburgh, PA, USA

Tiago Cravo Oliveira Imperial College, London, UK

Dave Randall University of Siegen, Siegen, Germany; Manchester Metropolitan University, Manchester, UK

Stephen Robertson Microsoft Research, Cambridge, UK

Mark Rouncefield Lancaster University, Lancaster, UK

Abigail Sellen Microsoft Research, Cambridge, UK

Peter Tolmie Nottingham University, Nottingham, UK

Alladi Venkatesh University of California, Irvine, CA, USA

William Webb Neul Ltd, Cambridge, UK

Amanda Wortman University of California, Irvine, CA, USA

John Zimmerman Carnegie Mellon University, Pittsburgh, PA, USA

Part I
Setting the Scene

Chapter 1
From Smart Home to Connected Home

Richard Harper

Introduction

Until quite recently, the development of smart homes as a new form of housing, combining both novel computer applications within and network access without, seemed appealing and imminent. The expectation was that new smart home technologies would alter how families entertain themselves with mum's and dad's sharing 'lean forward' interaction experiences on the internet enabled TV, for example (See Taylor & Harper, 2003: pp115-126); it was thought too that kids would be provided with revolutionary educational tools that would alter the relationship they had with homework (and with the institution of school) (Randall, 2004: pp227-246). Perhaps most commonplace – and thus hardly worth citing any instances of this view - was the assertion that those individuals who chose to work at home would find all the networked access they required delivered to their door: only old fashioned habit and the occasional face to face meeting would force them to leave and actually go to work. Work would come home; travel would reduce.

Underneath these apparently persuasive aspirations was the thought that smart homes would alter the lives of those who lived within them by providing technologies that took on some of the responsibilities that had hitherto been the sole responsibility of the human. As Taylor *et al* noted in a critical review of the idea (2007: 383-393), the smart home agenda turned around the expectation that smart homes would let the occupants be dumb by taking on some of the responsibility for managing their entertainment, health, education and even eating. Smart homes would alter the relationship between the human and the technology since technology would take on some of the burdens of 'intelligence'. Examples of such aspirations could be found in work reported by Mozer and his *Adaptive House* (2005), by Intille *et al's House-n* at MIT (2002) and more recently, the efforts reporting on Georgia Tech's *Aware Home* (2008: 3675-3680).

R. Harper (✉)
Microsoft Research Ltd., Cambridge CB3 0FB, UK

R. Harper (ed.), *The Connected Home: The Future of Domestic Life*,
DOI 10.1007/978-0-85729-476-0_1, © Springer-Verlag London 2011

Much of this early research on smart homes, instantiated by these projects, suggested that, although some of the particular manifestations of this overarching aspiration might turn out to be exaggerated and some even misdirected, overall, a shift in the role of person and machine would materialize. All that was required was time, sufficient investment, better design and usability. People would eventually find that the smart homes they would begin to occupy would contain technology that took on more responsibility; life at home would be more relaxed by dint of there being less labor for them, the human; and less for them, the human, to reason about. The smart home could take on all the labor, mental and physical.

This is to put the view strongly, perhaps too bluntly for some who held it; but this does encapsulate it. This view, however expressed, was commonplace ten years ago, perhaps five years ago. So do we find smart homes like this, now, some years on? Despite the fact that some researchers persist in this ambition, in general, the measure of time would seem to suggest that the vision has not and will not materialize. This bold agenda for smart homes seems to have lost its vigor. Whereas at the time I published *Inside the Smart Home* in 2003, a UK mobile phone operator, Orange plc, was willing to build a smart home to demonstrate what it thought would be the future, a future that was in accord with this vision, now this seems extremely unlikely. Indeed I can think of no current instance. The Orange-@-home establishment (See Harper, 2003) contained a remarkable range of computers that were intended to monitor, aid and support everything that occupants did in such a fashion as to take responsibility away from them: the Orange-@-home smart home was intended to be servant for the labors of home and butler for the reasoning required to make home. Now, as I say, some ten years later there are virtually no large communications companies (or for that matter computer technology companies) building such homes. Though my former boss, Bill Gates, might have a home in Redmond, Seattle, that would appear to offer smart home-like functions, this is achieved by having a full time support staff: the smartness here is delivered through Wizard of Oz techniques. Indeed, real butlers walk around the building (albeit not with that title), not machine proxies. Meanwhile the company he co-founded, Microsoft, has its own smart home 'demo suite' (some miles from Gate's home) and this presents a very different vision. This home is designed to demonstrate how technologies can help the occupants reason, letting them choose from more alternatives than they might have had in the past, encouraging more choice in the kitchen, when consuming media, or when contacting friends and family. Microsoft, just like Orange, no longer thinks that the future is in making homes that are smart. These companies do not think that technology can alter the balance between the intelligent human and the intelligent machine. For these (and other companies) the phrase *smart home* has lost its appeal.

Within academe, in various institutions in the US and in Europe, there are still some undertaking smart home inquiries of this early kind. Researchers at MIT, for example, have continued to devise kitchen systems that monitor the occupant's behavior, their cooking and eating, even the frequency with which they open the fridge. With this information it is hoped that applications can be devised that will shift the balance between technology and the human, not so much by taking on some of the chores of the kitchen, but by taking on some of the decision-making about what to cook. In other words, this agenda is still about making homes smart so as to allow the occupants to be dumb. But such research is much less common than it was; the view it espouses less commonly held. Even within academic research, where aspirations are sometimes even more outlandish than those in commercial life, the likes of the MIT researchers are rare. It seems reasonable to say that the smart home agenda is now on the wane both within academe and the corporate research world.

This doesn't mean that it has abated altogether. A thoughtful review by Brush *et al* (2011) suggests that the urge towards smart homes as defined above has slowly been replaced with a concern for the more prosaic antecedent that would allow for such smart homes: namely, with a concern for ubiquitous sensing and routine automation technologies. After all, for lights to come on and off, for doors to lock or open and, for another example, for heating to operate without human intervention, then some kind of system of sensors and monitors is required. Such systems would be much less advanced than those that might monitor other, 'higher level' aspects of human affairs in the home setting, such as an occupant's dietary needs, their 'edutainment' requirements and so on, but certainly would need to come before any such systems, at least Brush *et al* propose. They go on to suggest that this stepping stone concern has replaced the vitality and brash ambition of the early smart home agenda: indeed, they imply that the stepping stone is now becoming the target, the end point: the place where smart homes technologies will go. Given the excitement of ten years ago one might respond by saying that this seems a little disappointing - surely more ought to be held out for. Nevertheless, some of this research, even if it is less ambitious, is still curiously novel: Cohn *et al's* use of electromagnetic fields produced by the human body to control light switches is a case in point (2011). This novelty hardly hides the reduction in ambition that is conveyed however.

A Changing World

Be that as it may, those working within the smart home agenda, even those who have admitted that they need to be more pragmatic in their concern, have in any case found themselves oddly sidestepped by the world at large. For homes have altered in ways that has largely passed them by – and these changes have nothing much to do with the more outlandish smart home ambitions or the more everyday sensor technologies that Brush *et al* discuss. The research undertaken and reported in the smart home literature has not been reflected in what has happened in the world at large. There, one finds that homes haven't altered; the built environment has not got intelligent nor do most homes have more embedded cabling. Nevertheless, what people do in homes with technology has altered a great deal. Key to these changes has been both a willingness on the part of people to develop new practices and the introduction of new technology. Leaving aside the willingness of people for the moment, what is for sure is that some of this technology was of concern to the smart home researchers. But it has turned out that many of the expectations placed on technology can now be seen to have been misplaced and ill-fitting; sometimes technology has even ended up being used to do things that researchers had never imagined.

All of us are familiar with these changes – the technical and the social. They are now so ubiquitous as to be commonplace: wi-fi networks are now the norm in homes, for example; thus PCs are networked. We are all of us used to plugging into the internet on our couches, even in bed. But what history is showing is that the important lesson from this (and other changes) is not quite as expected. That PCs are networked to other PCs or other devices in the home and to the internet was assumed and predicted in the smart home literature, for example. The lesson is not in this, however. Rather, in being connected to the world outside, the PC itself has become merely a vehicle of sorts. Home users don't think of the PC when they engage with computing, they think of the *browser*, or more likely what the *search engine* they use will do for them. It is not so much that the PC and its connection to the internet has been domesticated then, but that in this domestication, the *search engine* has become tamed: it is *that* that is the primary tool for domestic life. And, further, in taking on this role, the search engine has become a tool for human intelligence in the domestic sphere and not a tool for substituting that intelligence (leaving aside arguments about how search engines work for the moment). As it happens curiously little was written on search engines in smart homes literature ten years ago; even less on how the search engine would come to augment the domestic mind.

One consequence of the form of these changes, changes in what technology is used for and changes in what people do, is that one has to approach them carefully, and avoid misinterpretation precisely because they have had these often highly nuanced forms. Careful dissection is required.

According to some measures people now spend more time on the Web than they do watching broadcast television, for example. The significance of this is not that 'web viewing' is now the norm (this was expected); it is rather that a narrative about the future of television has turned out to be wrong – a narrative we mentioned at the outset. This held that television content would merge into the internet content and, as a consequence, people would alter the relationship they have to content. They would not sit back and passively consume 'internet TV' like they had consumed 'broadcast TV', in a lean back mode, it was argued. Rather, because use of the web-content demands engagement, clickthroughs and positive acts, so would the new form of TV content, the internet-enabled TV content. A future of 'lean forward television entertainment' was going to emerge. But this has simply not happened. As we shall see in chapter 6, lean forward TV entertainment has not taken over from what was dismissively called, when this narrative first aired, lean back experiences, the ones afforded by traditional broadcast media. In contrast, television watching still has some of the properties that were discernable ten years ago. As it happens important elements of those properties were largely disregarded by smart home researchers. Television watching is often neither about lean forward or lean back experiences; oftentimes it is about having a *family experience*. TV watching is then about being sociable, doing something as a family. The doing here might consist of watching or it might consist of simply being together with a TV as the pretext.

Just as the impact of the internet needs care in addressing, and similarly the social consequences of using (or accessing) content provided through the internet need care, equal sensitivity is required when thinking about sociability – as this last example indicates. Most people now have access to email at home. Email eases communication, especially in comparison to the written letter, and is certainly cheaper than, say, telephone. One might expect therefore that people will socialize more now than, say, ten years ago. And indeed they do socialize more, but not because it's cheaper. As we have just noted, people socialize in all sorts of ways and use computer mediated experiences in all sorts of forms to do this. But their forms of sociability are many and varied; some are new, to be sure, but many can be discerned in practices existent before new computational and networked technologies became commonplace. One has to be diligent when one seeks to dissect them.

Some of these new forms highlight practices that were not properly recognized before. We have already noted the sociability of the TV which had not been recognized hitherto. Aspects of sociability with games are being highlighted which also might have been neglected. It is a platitude to say that people socialize when playing on-line games, of course. It is similarly obvious to say that just as they used to socialize when playing games face to face, now they would appear to play games more than ever and so are more sociable. But one should not forget that people sometimes socialize through games with others elsewhere, outside the home, say, so as to be unsociable with those they share their home with – to get away from mum and dad, or brothers and sisters – even sometimes 'to get away from oneself' as we shall see in chapter 7. What socializing and being sociable means, how it is mediated by connecting technologies, is then subtle, surprising, requiring care in understanding.

Relatedly, and as we mentioned in the opening paragraph, ten years ago there was an expectation that network connectivity would let people work at home. But careful analysis will show that the networks in question are being used for sociability rather more than they are for work. Social lives at home have altered more than the geographic locale of where paid employment occurs. Networked access has not allowed work to come home as it has allowed friends to come home, or allowed those within the home to go out and be with friends.

The Purpose of the Book

In this regard, technology use has sometimes ended up inverting expected trends: if work-home contrasts provide one set of examples, many others can be brought to mind. To take one: instead of smart fridges automatically ordering food, as an illustration, the technology of search engines has allowed people to choose more diverse and eclectic substances, whilst still keeping the fridge full of the boring staples. As it happens, this change has occurred at the same time as there has been a move away from technological substitution of human labor in the kitchen towards a return to craft and delight in the art of cooking. It's human hands that are now being sought over the stove, not digital substitutes (See for example Grimes & Harper, 2008).

Of course, whether some of these changes continue to show themselves in years to come or whether, as a case in point, the desire to cook in the kitchen ever progresses beyond a current fad led by intoxicating TV shows and celebrity chefs is another matter. But what is sure is that homes are now different places than they were just ten or fifteen years ago. How they are different, why they are different and how they might continue to alter, is the topic of this book. The book has a title that reflects the move from the smart home agenda to a new agenda, or one might say to an agenda that has become a *fait accompli*: the connected home. The technologies that make these connections are remarkable in their range and in their consequences; they are remarkable too for being commonplace in living rooms, kitchens and bedrooms. They include the online games technologies just mentioned; video connections, via Skype, as another example (discussed in chapter 10); and even technologies that don't seem about connection, but which rely on connection to function adequately: such as e-readers. Without connection to book content such devices are, needless to say, as useless as blank pages.

Connecting technologies are not necessarily limited to the home, though naturally our concern with such here is their role within the home. So, for example, smart phones (such as Apple's I-Phone or Windows 7 Mobiles), like early generation mobiles, allow people to engage with others wherever they might be, but unlike early phones, the latest smart phones also allow people to connect via social networks, letting them post on their Facebook accounts even as they watch TV. Meanwhile, these social networks allow the internal relations of households to alter even as they allow external relations to remain the same. Current research on social networking shows that most teenagers use these sites to keep in touch with buddies from school, for instance. Facebook is not about going out to the digital world and meeting strangers, then, it is about hanging out with friends from down the road (Harper, 2010). Likewise in research report here: as we shall see in chapter 9, new messaging technologies for family life end up not so much allowing families to bridge the distances to those who are far away, grandparents, say, or aunties in distant places. Rather these technologies help solve the problems of distance to some degree but more significantly give greater vitality to relations nearby. The wayve device described in that chapter was primarily used to communicate with neighbors and friend up the street, not with loved ones far away, for example.

All of this is further evidence for the claim that the way that the connected home is manifesting this new emphasis, on connection, requires some subtlety to understand. One needs to recognize that this connection has to do with the local as much as with the remote, to do with connections to those near-about as with those who are far away. At the same time, and as we see through the chapters in the second section, sociality always goes hand in hand with associability, with restrictions and aversions to being in touch. As I have shown in my book *Texture* (2010) social network sites have a peculiar power that is only now being made visible: for if bedroom doors have always been insufficient to keep prowling mum's and dad's at bay, teenagers have found that they can inhibit their parents from accessing their *Facebooks*. In domestic settings, social networks might be about being in touch, but they are also about being out of touch, as in this instance, through keeping mum and dad outside of the network.

There are other technologies too that are altering the landscape of the home on the second decade of the 21st Century. New forms of sociality affect the relations between family members just as they allow new connections between strangers in virtual game lobbies. And some technologies that were originally designed for work settings and professional use, such as search engines, have now become every day tools in the kitchen and on the couch. This use has affected these tools and is now beginning to alter how they are designed, with 'domestic motives' being embedded in the functioning of the latest search tools and engines alongside professional information search requirements.

One could go on. There is much to comment on in the landscape of the current home. Given this it is curious that there are so few in-depth collections or monographs that report on the human computer interaction (HCI) aspects of the connected home, or indeed its earlier version, the smart home. Nor is there much in those HCI related disciplines that emphasize the social in HCI, such as CSCW (sometimes defined as collaboration, sociality, computation and the web – an evolution of what was originally coined as computer supported cooperative work). Most of the research that has appeared is to be found in small papers at various conferences – at CHI, for example, the annual gathering of the HCI community in North America, or in Ubicomp, a more technofiliac conference. The topic of the connected home has, as it were, no home.

This is despite the fact that the home is a domain that is and has been for some years the topic of more general social scientific inquiry. There are several books from a sociological perspective, for example – such as Shove *et al's The Design of Everyday Life* (2007). This and other texts tend to derive their inspirations from one or two early pieces which were not about home per se but about social organization in general, such as Mary Douglas's book *Purity and Danger* of 1966. The anthropological tradition, of which Douglas was also a part even if she remains influential in sociology, offers its own – such as Miller's *The Comfort of Things* (2008). This, like other similar books, tends to address essentially theoretical concerns to do with anthropology and its apparent indifference to material forms. Shove's work is, meanwhile, similarly concerned not with the lived experience of home life but what home life says about the primary topic of the sociology Shove and her colleagues are concerned with: a sociology with a predilection for power.

There is nothing wrong with different disciplines focusing on their seeding topics; of course they must. But in doing so, such studies do not offer insights into the topics we have here: how home life, the doings and patterns of behavior at home, are developing new forms and this is a result of the interplay of these patterns and the technology at hand. The result is that a number of new questions are emerging that ought to be central to a future looking HCI or CSCW.

First of all, they might include investigations of whether studies of 'home life' need to reconsider whether that should include only those things done in the *physical space of home* and only at home, or whether it should include those activities that meld the space of home with other spaces. A failure to do so would prohibit, for example, internet gaming. If this were to be accepted, what role then should one give to the space that is oftentimes used as a synonym for the home if the things constitutive of the home, like online gaming, are done in a way that blurs that space? Following on from this line of argument, one might also want to ask whether 'home' as a spatial domain is a salient category if the things done in it can be done elsewhere. Clearly, the term home is a category that pertains, but is it the most important, the dominant category, as the sociologists might say? Think of phrases like 'power-space geometries' so popular in sociology a few years ago (Massey, 1993; for a review of this concept and the use of connecting technologies in the home at that time, see Harper, 2005). Does a future-looking HCI need to consider the conflicts of space that manifest when work comes home, for example, or more likely, when street culture comes through the Xbox screen? By way of contrast, could home proprieties infect gaming culture, for example?; it might happen. Similarly, a future looking HCI will need to understand the evolution of the moral order of the home and its relation to space in regard to other, apparently less demonstrative activities: e-books might allow new ways of gathering and consuming text, but the reading of books at home still has its social context of due propriety; and this context is massively about space, about the where and when and how of reading, for instance.

In other words, a question for a future-looking HCI is what are the dynamics of power-space geometries when they are interleaved by connecting technology? Without wanting to prejudge research findings, it certainly seems that the term 'home' as a combinatory category for a space, a social domain and so forth, will continue to have vitality: what is done at home might alter because of what is done elsewhere and how this elsewhere and home connect. These are the concerns that make the modern home what it is. Changes will continue – evolving the concept of home, or rather the nested concept that the word represents.

A second concern ought to be with the *idea of home*, the possibility that people have a notion of what home is, what it ought to be, and how this is linked to ideas about family and social connection, and how this is linked to that first topic, the idea of a space, a domain called home. One automatically thinks about love and affection and the family when thinking about the idea of the home, as if that is what the term family means. This is certainly something that is explored in chapter 10. But home is also an idea that some people view as a target they should break or shatter. They may do so for good reasons, because they are leaving the nest so to speak. Consider what couples do when they meet and fall in love: they start a home that they move into. Their home is the physical embodiment of the idea that they have of each other and their relationship: that they choose to settle down and make a family. And then what do many couples therefore do? They make babies, and these babes eventually grow up and, as they move towards adulthood, seek to *leave* that home. The trajectories of different members of a home have almost opposite concepts of what a home is:

for one set it is the place to end up; for another, the place to escape from. How are connecting technologies going to affect these and other trajectories? Will some of the powers of connecting technology allay the desire to leave home? Or will those same technologies lead parents to more robustly encourage their Xbox-obsessed offspring to fly the coup?

Leaving home when one ventures to adulthood seems a well-known and accepted practice. But families break up for all sorts of other reasons and some cannot be labeled natural and to be expected; even 'good' for those involved. Consider those caused by death, and when this is unexpected, due to car crash or similar, the effect on the idea of home can be catastrophic. And then sometimes homes are broken through volition: broken up by those who started the home in the first place: feuding husbands and wives. After all, divorce is now commonplace; breaking up is very much part of what family life is, and thus it is a part of home life. So why should not a forward looking HCI look at this topic too: if home is an idea (as much as it is a space) then it is one that can be smashed to pieces even if doing so takes more effort and produces more anguish than the breaking up of real walls. People suffer the hurt of a broken relationship much more profoundly than they do the moving away from a building they have come to call a home, for example. In this instance, they simply move into another space and label that home. But relationships cannot be repaired through renaming.

There is much research to be done under the auspices of the connected home agenda. Though the smart home may have been a dead end and the use of a *Ubicomp* vision as the backbone of that agenda ill-judged, the world that has emerged with new computational and networked technologies is certainly worth investigating. It is worth investigating to discover its form, explicate its trajectory and to design its future forms: through technology, through new services and concepts and through new social possibilities. It is to that we now turn.

Overview of the Chapters

The theme of this book then is manifold and is essentially one that is pointing away from what we have called the smart home agenda. The new agenda pointed towards opens up a raft of possibilities as well as begs the question as to what is within scope of such inquiries and what is outside. The structure of the book is designed to help navigate an answer to these concerns. Bringing together 24 researchers from the USA, UK and Europe, the book consists of 14 chapters divided into three sections: Setting the Scene, Experiencing the Connected Home – the bulk of the book – and then, Remaining Aspirations.

Setting the Scene is an exploration of what was thought to be the future of home life some years ago, the actuality of what has come into being at the current time, and suggested trends that are beginning to appear. It will present this, in the opening chapter, in terms of scenarios, before presenting, in the second two chapters, various quantitative measures. The first chapter starts by recapitulating what were some of the hopes of the smart home agenda and what are by way of contrast the current hopes for the future of home living: it does this by evoking a scenario used ten years ago and then offering a revized one, given current thinking. This revized scenario, the one the chapter ends with, is not meant to be a summary of the findings that the rest of the book chapters present but one that is likely to represent the vision from technologists concerned with the future home.

The subsequent chapter, chapter 3, brings hard evidence on such things as time usage patterns of home life, and highlights how it would appear that much time usage is unlikely to change – being given over to eating and sleeping, for example, things that smart and connected homes might not affect. The chapter will go on to show that the evidence suggests that there have been shifts in time usage within these bigger constraints, with changes in the proportions of time households give to various chores altering as well as shifts in what attention is given to within the home. Key to this is the contrast between the amount of money people have and their lack of time – they are money rich and time poor, it will be argued. Chapter 3 is particularly concerned to analyze how families work their way through this conundrum given differences in choice, in income, in preferences. All families face time limits equally but families are remarkably diverse in the solutions they come up with: it depends on how they spend their money.

The next chapter presents a longitudinal study of the take-up of the PC and the internet in homes in the USA and the resulting consequences of this well-advertized change. Here we will discover that economics is not the primary driver of PC and internet usage at the home, but the existence of children. The argument here is not one that alludes to the idea that older generation people are resistant to the computer and the internet; it is rather that the culture of games and homework surrounding kids affects the way computers become normalized. It is having children that is the important factor in this normalization process, not age nor income nor education. The chapter also shows that, with the increasing use of computing at home, women further their dominance in the social organization of that setting: as John Strain noted some years ago (2003), just as the internet bank allowed women to take over domestic finance, so the internet is allowing women to take over other responsibilities today. The power-space geometry of the home, for want of a phrase, is being driven by two agencies: feminization and the internet-enabled computer (for a background to this, see not only Massey already mentioned, but also Martin, 1984).

The second section, Experiencing the Connected Home, consists of in-depth qualitative and design studies of the changing intersection of technology and human habit in the connected home. It opens discussions with an analysis of how search engine use has evolved over the years. Whereas search engines were designed for work settings, current domestic behaviors are infusing search engine design and development. As remarked, this is surprising: search engines were developed as the result of a combination of (a) security agencies wanting to find content in large data sets and (b) efforts by librarians to make their work easier: yet the domestication of search engines has resulted in them being used to find things to buy. Domestication has not made people at home information-rich or better at domestic surveillance;

it has made them more avid consumers. Nevertheless, this consumption is being used to develop and enhance the efficacy of search engines so that 'what the consumer wants is what the consumer gets'. This is not quite what the US government wanted when they originally sought to search content, nor was it what the information retrieval researchers had in mind when Alto Vista (search engine) was released. It was even less so, one would think, what the founders of Google had in mind when they devized their first algorithm.

The search engine may seem almost the most visible manifestation of new technology in the home, albeit that it is mediated by other more elementary ones – the browser to access one, and the PC to host it. But the next chapter argues that it is the TV that is really the centerpiece of the home. But not just technologically – it really is the centerpiece for much of the *mis-en-scène* of home life. Although there are a range of interactive entertainment and broadcast contents affecting the domestic hearth, this chapter will explore the dominance television, in its changing forms, has and is likely to continue to have. It will show how some patterns of television consumption have remained the same over the years, with the sociability of TV watching being an important if hitherto neglected aspect of it. The emergence of new set-top box technologies combined with the internet has not altered this, one finds. What these technologies are doing is allowing new forms of giving and sharing, as well as altering domestic consumption patterns around the same elemental phenomena: family entertainment, the telly.

A chapter on gaming will then follow. The topicality of this has to do with the introduction and widespread up-take of on-line games. But the chapter will want to assert that although this aspect of connectivity is altering some of the landscapes of home life, one must not neglect the power and all-pervasiveness of the home as a place for social propriety and longstanding social patterns of distinction, separation and togetherness, all of which have manifested themselves around old fashioned games based on paper boards and cards as much as they do with new-fangled ones relying on IP protocols. The chapter explores how new games technology has altered and deepened some of the patterns of juvenile sociality, for example, whilst creating opportunities for social connection between juveniles that paradoxically reinforces the long-held distinction between juveniles and adults. The chapter will also demonstrate how on-line games fit into a very robust and powerful social context where morals of behavior still intrude both on terms of play and use of the shared space that is the home. Play and gaming is not the only way that the domestic landscape of entertainment and distraction is altering and yet confronting resistance.

The next chapter reflects on the changing role of text in the home setting and in particular on the evolution of reading given the emergence of e-books, I-Pads and other technological competitors to traditional technologies of reading. E-books and television are all about connection to content; to content provided by people from far away. But the chapter shows that the social connections they affect are ones in the home – by the bedside or in front of the TV. It shows too that the codes associated with these social relations impose themselves upon reading practices in particular ways that make it quite clear that e-books are simply one instantiation of a way of reading and, in the home, there are several ways of reading: some required, some sought for, some never quite achieved. Sunday papers entail a different order of engagement to the daily papers, for example, and this is illustrative of the differences in the day of the week that affects reading. Designers of Kindles and owners of publishing houses really ought to look at what reading entails as a socially nested activity before they start fretting about the end of the book.

The next two chapters, meanwhile, will report on the relationship between digital messaging applications and real geography. The first seeks to tease apart an all too easy error that can occur when the term connected home is coined. This is the error of thinking that connections dissolve space. The chapter confirms the idea that the nearness of families in real and virtual senses are being altered through digital connection but it goes on to highlight the paradox that this same digital connection deepens local connection while often not alleviating the problems of long distance relations. And indeed, the digital can give real geographic distance new virtual forms that serve to attest the remoteness in question, not reduce it through novel means. Connecting technologies do not, as it were, solve the sense of great distance, and can sometimes only serve to highlight it even as they apparently offer means to overcome it. But these same technologies can make nearbyness, if that is a word, more effectively equate to social and moral nearness: the digital can make the geographically near nearer in other senses too. The chapter will go on to show that connected homes are not homes whose virtual diaspora is greater than the diaspora of past homes. Rather, it will show the tempo and the vitality of the connections that constitute neighborhood is altering: with connection, people connect more to those they are already close to and it turns out these are mostly people nearby.

The next chapter reports on matters that have less to do with geographic community and more to do with emotional ones. In *Love, Ritual and Videochat*, we will be presented with an analysis of the appeal of the video call for distributed families, particularly over skype-type video connections, free ones. The contrast between the use of video for family affairs and the evident lack of take-up of video connection in the workplace will be remarked upon. One point made is that this difference is surprising given that work settings often have much better network connections than are provided for the home. But it will come to be seen as less surprising when it is shown that the appeal of 'seeing' has to do with the visual display of physical tenderness of family life. Such displays would seem wholly inappropriate in the work setting, particularly on the West Coast of the USA where the research was undertaken: the aura of the nineteen sixties notwithstanding, Silicon Valley embodies organizational proprieties that are much more severe and conservative than elsewhere - certainly in comparison to Europe. Tenderness in the workplaces of London might be viewed in an altogether different light from San Jose. Nevertheless, the main concern is not work-home contrasts, but exploration of what can be called the work of love, work undertaken in messaging, visual messaging in the case of the domestic sphere, in home. This is the work that brings grandparents and kids, mum and dads together. Love's work, so the chapter will argue.

Both these chapters will report connections in real time, between people in the here and now. But the here and now can bleed into messages left for a future visitor or created as a reminder for a forgetful self. The next chapter, consequently, looks at nearness and distance over time: here the question is not about messaging but evoking. And the thing being evoked is, naturally, the home. What is proposed is that the home is more than a set of walls or built spaces populated by human bodies that have some sort of relation. A home is, in addition to this, a history, a future, a recollection and a showing. Home and family is produced in artful work: in things kept and things thrown away; in things curated to honor what has been done and in things kept to ensure that something else will be done. Home, family, is an idea that is beyond time, the chapter will argue, because it includes practices that deal in time. The chapter will show how technologies are altering the sense people have of their past, their memories and their histories; and it will explore also how this constructed past helps create a determinable future. It reports, in particular, on how new digital means are enabling families to take a more didactic approach to these concerns. The digital can let them think of themselves and what they use to represent their histories and direct their futures in new ways. Networked forms of archive can alter the bonds between place and familyhood, for example. At the same time, these new forms can highlight some of the affordances of the non-digital.

The next chapter, the last in this section, shows how it is that if homes are based on an idea, an idea populated by another idea, the idea of family, then these phenomena, if ideas can be so labeled, are also something that can break up – and one example of this are fights over the past as well as fights over material possession in the here and now, both of which behaviors can be guaranteed to break the thing in question: the idea constitutive family and family possession. Given the commonplaceness of divorce, and to a lesser extent, the experience of unexpected bereavement, it is all the more surprising how little attention has been given to this topic in research on the contemporary home and indeed in HCI more generally. It turns out that connecting technologies are as much a tool to help manage the difficulties of divorce and death as they can be grounds for further dispute; as much an opportunity for recall as a way of forgetting undesired events. This chapter shows how much effort is putting into using technologies to meld the family and its home together when it stretches to breaking point, and how those same technologies can be used to force that breaking in the first place. If families, homes, entail an idea of solidarity and place, then they also entail their opposite: fragmentation, departure, leaving.

The third and last section, Remaining Aspirations, offers discussion of how some of the sensing technologies that Brush *et al* think the future of smart home research will evolve: these possibilities are but pale in comparison to what was expected some years ago, but nevertheless are still sought for. The first chapter in this section will discuss, for example, the history of attempts to introduce lightweight medical technologies into the home setting, thereby allowing people to linger in their homes longer and with more contentment. When this is achieved, the move towards the modern geriatric ward can be delayed. We use this phrase since this move is normally the last a person will make, and is hardly ever reversed. The geriatric ward is typically unspoken about, a place that remains unknown since it is unnamed, but is nevertheless there, waiting for all.

Hospitals are not just terminals in this sense; they also provide expensive, inefficient dorms for those who need an interlude within them: those whose sickness is not terminal but do require 'hospitalization'. The chapter will also discuss why a move out of home into hospital for these reasons can be so undesirable and so costly. It will explain that there is ever increasing pressure by government and the medical establishment to reduce hospitalization. But the difficulties confronted by efforts to exert this pressure are great. These derive from problems to do with economics, with technology itself, its costs and size; and even to do with basic HCI – usability levels of medical systems are often strikingly poor. Using technology to keep people out of hospitals does not always succeed, therefore. There is also resistance from the ailing themselves, who may not always be persuaded that remote care is as good as hospital care: they fear that the hospital will end up being their grave but going there for a short stay will postpone that fateful moment, they believe: care at home, meanwhile, might kill them prematurely. Nevertheless, the chapter is essentially optimistic – the importance of improving matters in this area perhaps being too great to allow it to remain an unfinished ambition.

The last chapter is, however, all about unfinished ambitions. It is concerned with things that seemed, some years ago, technologies that would definitely come to pass. It was a taken-for-granted in the smart home agenda, more particularly, that heating and power consumption would be *automated*. If Brush *et al* are right that the building sensors and automatic systems for the prosaic aspects of the home will be the future of smart home research then this chapter shows that even heating and power consumption is not something that can be readily tamed through, say, the use of intelligent algorithms that enable better sensors. For the relationship people have to their heating and power systems, their view of justifiable consumption and conspicuously unnecessary consumption, their view of the reasonable use of light and heat and their view of the untoward as regards these matters, is far too complex and rich for any binary code to encapsulate: sensors cannot sense the morally ambivalent. The problem is not about measuring, sensing, automating; it is, as the author Simon Lewis notes, as much to do with the moral categories of 'what-matters-at-home-now' as it has to do with any demonstrable measure of air temperature or ambient light. It is about the complex delicate art of making home feel like home.

If the chapter shows anything, it is that the aspirations of the smart home agenda really were often placed on subject matters that turn out to be enormously more intractable to computer mediated change than had been thought. The lesson from this is not simply that the problems were misjudged; it is certainly not that the research in this area cannot be done. The lesson is that there may well be many a wrong path in research on home life. What this and prior chapters will show is that it is connections that ought to have been and ought to be the topic of this research area. But in saying this, one cannot therefore say that the resulting research will be easy. The move from smartness to connectedness does not make the researcher's life straightforward. As the last chapter shows: though, in the case of smart heating, there is a connection to the heating and power supplier, the real connection at issue is not that: it is the connections that people within the home have with one another. But that connection, though recognizable, is not therefore easy to dissect, to grapple with for the purposes of design and HCI. People in the connected home might choose heat to achieve one social end and coolness another but unfortunately these are barely physical matters; more profoundly moral ones. And to understand those sorts of matters is a task of category analysis, like a species of philosophy, and is hence a hard business, perhaps the hardest of all. It turns out that questions about heat and power are at once about a geographical category, a space heated and lit up, and a moral category, a disputed and fragile category: a domain called home with a gang of people within called a family who have views about what should be paid for and what not, what is a disruption and what is not. And it is this same gang who have a view about how chilliness can stop more important things being done and what, in contrast 'is the level of heat beyond which heat is unnecessary'. Even gangs make a stand when ethics come in to play. In sum, smart research should look at the connections between these categories, not at the connections that link computers. Only once that is understood can the ties of computing be made, for then and only then can the texture of home life be replicated with the digital in any useful and beneficial way. The purpose of this book is to suggest that doing that research, looking at that texture, grasping it, is not such an easy thing to do. But it needs to be done.

Cambridge, Spring, 2011

References

Brush, A.J., Lee, B., Mahajan, R., Agarwal, A., Saroiu, S. & Dixon, C. (2011) 'Home Automation in the Wild: Challenges and Opportunities', *Proc. of CHI 2011*, ACM Press, Vancouver.

Cohn, G. Morris, D. Patel, S. & Tan. D (2011) 'Your Noise is My Command: Sensing Gestures Using the Body as an Antenna', *Proc. CHI 2011,* ACM Press Vancouver.

Douglas, M. (2002): *Purity and Danger*, (originally published 1966), Routledge, London.

Grimes, A. & Harper, R. (2008) 'Celebratory Technology: new directions in food research for HCI', in *Proceedings of CHI'08*, ACM Press, Florence.

Hamill, L. & Harper, R. (2006) 'Talking Intelligence: a historical and conceptual exploration of speech-based human-machine interaction in smart homes', *Proceedings Intelligent Environments Symposium,* Homerton College, Cambridge, April.

Harper, R. (2010) *Texture: human expression in the age of communications overload*, MIT Press, Boston.

Harper, R. (2005), 'The Moral Order of Text: Explorations in the social performance of SMS' in *Mobile Communication – Perspectives and Current Research Fields*, Hoflich, J. & Gebhart, J. (eds), Peter Lang GmbH – Europäischer Verlag der Wissenschaften, Berlin, pp199-222.

Intille, S. 'Designing a home of the future', *IEEE Pervasive Computing* 1, 2(2002), 80-86.

Kietz, J., Patel, S., Jones, B., Price, E., Mynatt, E., Abowd, A. 'The Georgia Tech Aware Home', *Ext. Abstracts CHI 2008*, 3675-3680.

Martin, B. (1984): 'Mother Wouldn't Like It!' Housework as Magic'. *Theory, Culture & Society*, Vol. 2, no. 2, pp. 19-35.

Massey, D (1993) 'Power-geometry and a Progressive Sense of Place', in Bird, et al, (eds) *Mapping the Futures: Local Cultures, Global Change*, Routledge: London.

Mozer, M.C. (2005) Lessons from an Adaptive House. In D. Cook and R. Das (eds.) *Smart Environments: Technologies, Protocols, and Applications* (pp. 273-294). J. Wiley & Sons, Hoboken, NJ.

Randall. D. (2003) 'Living Inside a Smart Home: a case study' in Harper, R. (Ed.) (2003) *Inside the Smart Home,* Springer, London, pp227-245.

Taylor, A. & Harper., R. (2003) Switching on to Switch Off, in Harper, R. (Ed.) (2003) *Inside the Smart Home*, Springer, London, pp115-124.

Taylor, A. Harper, R. Swann, L. Izadi, S. Sellen, A. Perry, M. (2007) 'Homes that make us Smart', The *Journal of Personal Technologies*, Springer, London, 11(5), 383-393.

Strain J. (2003) 'Households as Morally Ordered Communities', in Harper (Ed) *Inside the Smart Home*, Springer, London, pp41-61.

Chapter 2
The Networked Home: The Way of the Future or a Vision Too Far?

William Webb

A Day in the Life of a Connected Home

It is some time in the distant future – perhaps 20 years or more away. John lives near Cambridge with his wife Julia and daughter Lisa. John works in London most days while Julia is a district nurse and Lisa attends a nearby school.

At 5:16am their home clicks into life. The home server has access to all their diaries and knows that John will need to get up at 5:40 to catch his train. It has accessed the local weather forecast to determine the outside temperature when he wakes up and thermostats in each room in the house tell it the current temperature. It then determines how long it will take to warm up the rooms of the house used in the morning to John's preferred temperature and activates the heating at exactly the right time.

After John has had his shower he clips his phone to his belt. This turns the phone on and in turn the home uses this to register John's presence around the home. It automatically deactivates the intruder alarm and as it tracks John in his movements around the home it turns the lights on or off in the various rooms.

In the kitchen the coffee machine is already on and warmed up and as John approaches it, the machine detects his presence and selects the settings he prefers – all he has to do is put a cup under it and press "Go". John gets himself a bowl of cereal and picks up the kitchen tablet, browsing through his favorite internet sites and a pre-assembled selection of news and items of interest put together for him by the home server overnight.

After finishing his coffee he heads out, holding his phone against the front door to unlock it - it will lock itself again as he closes it. The home registers that he has left and puts itself back into an idle mode, awaiting the next inhabitant to rise.

Julia is working a late shift that day so she is around in the home in the morning doing some housework. On the kitchen tablet she starts to plan the meals for the coming week. The tablet knows who will be in for dinner on which days by consulting the central diaries and makes some meal suggestions for each night based on preferences. Julia selects from the choices offered and the tablet compiles a shopping list based on its knowledge of what Julia has in her kitchen and how much there is likely to be left. It asks her to check on the cinnamon – it thinks she may be running low. The tablet presents the shopping list which Julia approves – the tablet then sends the list to a range of on-line stores along with the times that it knows someone will be in the home to collect it, and selects the store with the lowest price and best delivery schedule.

W. Webb (✉)
Neul Ltd, Cambridge, UK

R. Harper (ed.), *The Connected Home: The Future of Domestic Life*,
DOI 10.1007/978-0-85729-476-0_2, © Springer-Verlag London 2011

There is a sound of gentle laughter – it is the sign that there is a message from Lisa. Julia glances at the whereabouts clock, it shows that John is in the office and Lisa at school, and touches Lisa's avatar. The message pops up that Lisa will be late home – she has been invited round to a friend's after school. She has updated her calendar accordingly.

Later in the evening all the family are at home. Julia and Lisa are watching a talent show on television in the family room. They can see the faces of some of their friends in the bottom part of the TV who are also watching the show (and their friends can see them) and interact with them, chatting about each act and voting interactively. A separate part of the screen shows what John is up to – although the family like to do different things most evenings, being able to see each other even when they are in different rooms makes them feel more connected. John is practising the piano, with a virtual teacher showing him the musical score on a display above the piano and offering hints as to how his playing could be enhanced.

Later picking up a tablet in the lounge, John notices the "home icon" glowing gently – something needs some non-urgent attention. He touches the icon which shows him that sensors in the indoor plant pots have detected they need watering. Sadly, the home can't water them itself yet!

When the family head up to bed they do not need to check around the house that the doors are locked and everything is turned off – the home will do all that automatically, setting the intruder alarm and turning most of its own systems off for the night as it enters sleep mode too.

Such a vision of the future sounds seductive to many – but is it ever likely to be realized? Such visions have been commonplace for decades but have failed to materialize in the form envisaged. We ask why this is, looking at problems specific to the home and more general to forecasting, before drawing some conclusions on whether predictions such as the one above will ever happen, or indeed whether they are even worth making. We start with a prediction made in 2000 to illustrate the issues.

What We Predicted in 2000 That We Would Use in 2010

Those who predict the future rarely get it right. Smart-homes with plenty of futuristic applications have long been predicted – and indeed demonstrated in prototype form over the years. Before moving on to discuss whether the future really will be as John experienced it at the start of this chapter we look back at predictions made 10 years ago to see whether they are accurate and what can be learned from them. These predictions were made in "The Future of Wireless Communications", written in 2000. The predictions covered a wide range of wireless communications services both in the home and outside. Here we concentrate on those relevant to the home.

Back in 2000 we thought that by 2010 homes would have wireless networks based on BlueTooth with a number of nodes distributed around the home. These would interwork not only with devices in the home but also with the mobile phones of the inhabitants. Video communications would be used occasionally within the home, making up perhaps 1-2% of communications. Machines in the home would start to communicate with each other and humans would use speech recognition to communicate with machines.

As at the start of this chapter, in our view of 2010 we had a vision of what a day in the life of a user (also called John) might look like. The sections relevant to the home are as follows, though we have slightly altered the details so as to better understand the claims being made:

> At 5.20am the communicator utilizes its BlueTooth capabilities to communicate with the in-home network. The in-home network provides power to a special socket into which the coffee maker has been plugged, slowly brings on the lighting in key parts of the house and changes the temperature in various rooms, warmer in the bathroom, cooler in other parts of the house.
>
> At 5.25am the communicator talks to the cellular network to which John subscribes and requests traffic information for the journey to the airport. The communicator sends the start and end address to the network which returns the optimal route, provided by a third-party internet traffic service, affiliated to the network operator. The communicator stores this information for download to the navigation system in John's car once the communicator is in proximity to the car. The communicator also requests flight information, checking departure times and gate information.
>
> At 5.30am the communicator plays wake-up music that John has set as his preference until it hears John say "alarm off". It then presents John with his itinerary for the day. John gets ready to leave the house, drinks his coffee and then climbs into his car. The car has downloaded the journey details from the communicator and provides John with directions on his journey to the airport.
>
> On route John remembers that he will miss a key television program that evening, however, as yet, there is no simple link into his home network once his communicator has left the house. Instead he leaves a message for his wife, still asleep, to set the video when she wakes.

If we consider which of these predictions are accurate we can see that wireless has been provided throughout many homes, albeit using WiFi rather than BlueTooth. (Back in 2000 WiFi was thought too power hungry for mobile phones and hence BlueTooth was seen as a better home networking standard.) The error in the standard adopted actually makes little difference to the outcome. We thought that in-home networks would allow the mobile phone to be used within the home. This has not really happened, only recently have femtocells provided a viable solution. That this has not occurred is not due to technology – standards have been developed to allow mobile phones to hand over to home WiFi systems. It is more because it was not in the interests of the mobile operators and because users saw little benefit. Indeed, there were some advantages in keeping a personal mobile phone as well as a communal home phone. Phones are now starting to make use of home WiFi but more to carry data than voice calls.

The predictions for video communications were probably not far off. It is used by some households, some of the time, notably for Skype calls to distant relatives. However, the prediction that machines would communicate to other machines was optimistic as was the use of speech recognition to communicate with machines.

John's day started with his phone (or "communicator") talking to the in-home network. This sort of functionality has not been implemented. While a phone in a home today could use WiFi to communicate to the home PC it is far from clear what this would be for – at present most interaction of this sort is purely to synchronize content. Even if it could, virtually no homes have electricity sockets or lighting systems controlled by the home PC. The home then downloaded routing information to the navigation system in the car. Again this is barely possible today – only a few car navigation systems accept downloads (it is an option on BMW's expensive "Professional Multimedia Package"). Perhaps the only prediction that can be achieved is for the phone to act as the alarm clock!

Segmenting Home Use

In considering the accuracy of these predictions it is helpful to segment smart home applications. Previous authors have provided a helpful split between "time saving" and "time using". Time saving applications allow tasks to be completed with less human input – e.g. a washing machine. Time using applications provide entertainment within the home – e.g. Internet gaming. In considering our predictions, a further degree of segmentation is helpful:

- Time saving – enables existing tasks to be completed more quickly or with less human input.
- Environment enhancing – makes the home a nicer place by controlling heating, lighting, etc., more intelligently.
- Money saving – saves money by reducing energy consumption, water usage, etc.
- Entertainment or time using – provides mechanisms to make leisure time more enjoyable.

Regarding time saving, most of the "low hanging fruit" was picked from around 1920 to 1960 when vacuum cleaners, washing machines, dishwashers, etc., were introduced. Further meaningful gains have proven hard to deliver effectively. For example, the robotic vacuum cleaner has not been widely adopted – it is expensive, less effective than "real" cleaning, requires complex set-up and is viewed with scepticism given all the previous claims for robotic advances. Kitchen cupboards are often full of "labor saving machinery" that has failed to live up to its promise from the electric carving knife to the automatic ice-cream maker. Further advances in this space seem unlikely and few predictions now mention robots that do the ironing.

The area of enhancing the environment seems initially one where progress could be made. As suggested in the predictions above, aligning the heating and lighting more closely with user needs, managing home security better and so on could be implemented. However, there is a range of problems here. Firstly, implementation is often difficult – adding a thermostat to each room that can be remotely read and altered requires substantial wiring and plumbing work which could have a large cost. Secondly, the benefits are often seen by users as minimal. Thirdly, the added complexity is unwelcome and users worry that they will not be able to operate it correctly or that it will malfunction and require costly and inconvenient visits from specialists. Experience has shown that users prefer the occasional inconvenience of a cold home than the cost and complexity of one that is optimized to their every movement. This explains why environmental enhancements have long been predicted but have almost completely failed to materialize.

Money saving is a relatively new area for the smart home. In the past, smart home initiatives have been targeted at those who have the least need to save money. It is an area gaining increased prominence through rapidly rising energy costs and Government initiatives to implement "smart grids". Saving money through lower energy costs is of interest to home owners – energy saving light-bulbs are widely implemented and consumers are increasingly concerned with the energy consumption of appliances. It may be that Governments or energy companies increasingly require home owners to have a home network that allows control of their appliances. Home owners that purchase appliances that can be controlled remotely might see a saving on their energy bills, in the same way that car owners that fit security alarms can see a saving on their insurance costs. Remotely controlled appliances may not sound like much of an advance for the smart home, but it may be, that once appliances can be communicated to over the home network, other applications might emerge, such as the fridge that understands more about its contents.

It is in the area of entertainment that the biggest changes have occurred in the home in the last decade. Homes now often have broadband connections to the internet, wireless networks, multiple TVs around the house, hard disk recorders and even tablet computers. Much of this was predicted – as illustrated earlier. However, a subtle but very important distinction has occurred. Earlier predictions imagined a managed home network which stored information, coordinated entertainment devices around the home, managed family diaries and more. Instead, most devices are personal and see the home as simply another wireless access point – the only difference with one in Starbucks being that the home can be trusted to a greater extent. Even non-personal devices such as TVs are being designed to connect directly into the internet for their content using initiatives such as YouView. Newer operating systems such as Windows7 allow for file sharing between laptops further removing any need for a home network. This approach makes sense for users. Their devices then work equally well both in the home and outside, and there is no need for complex IT management in establishing and running a network. Indeed, as users increasingly rely on personal devices, the need for home telephones, home gaming systems and other legacy electronics actually decreases. Regarding entertainment, instead of a smart home, users will simply want a wireless broadband zone. Perhaps, then, the smart home was an idea without merit – users actually want a dumb home and smart devices?

Is It Worth Predicting?

With previous predictions of smart homes discredited in many respects, what hope is there that any future predictions will be useful? It may be that finally we understand enough about home usage to be able to make accurate predictions but we cannot be sure about this.

Prediction is generally valuable in directing research and industrial activity, in encouraging the development of standards and in engaging in structured debate.

It can work particularly well where there is some degree of central planning – for example cellular technology and networks are determined and implemented by a relatively small number of companies and here prediction can be reasonably accurate. A problem with prediction in the home is that there is no central entity that performs such planning and hence homes tend to "evolve", adding new products and technologies with little overall strategy.

Perhaps predictions for the smart home have been incorrect because the wrong question was asked initially. Asking "what will the smart home of the future look like?" presupposes that homes will become smart and encourages researchers to think about how technology might change the home. Alternative questions might be "will homes of the future be smart?" or "how will homes of the future support personal devices?"

Predictions are invariably affected by experience. For those now aged 40 and above, their experience of the home has been the introduction of many new devices including, for example, home cordless phones, home internet and home security systems. Perhaps a younger generation making predictions might be more inclined to focus on personal devices and applications rather than home or family applications.

In fact, the safest way to predict over the last 20 years has been to "under-predict" – to generally assume that no change will occur. This has been particularly true in the home environment. So a cynical forecaster might, at this point, suggest that a prediction of the future of the home is that it will broadly continue to look and function as it does now.

Our Observations

Time and experience has shown that:

1. Adding any new application to the fabric of the home is very difficult. Wiring homes, providing power to devices and installing central control points is almost invariably too expensive to justify any benefits. Even when building new homes, builders choose not to install complex wiring since end-users see little value in it and it is not clear what wiring should be installed and where.
2. All home systems are stand-alone. The heating system has its own wiring and plumbing. The security system has its own sensors, wiring and control panel. The lighting system has dedicated wiring and switches. The entertainment system has its own wiring or wireless connections and so on. Users generally prefer the simplicity this provides.
3. Complex control systems are fragile. PCs regularly need rebooting or more detailed attention. Home networks are occasionally unavailable. Viruses cause concern. Few users would wish to trust critical home systems to such an unreliable network. Despite years of work by the computer industry this has not improved over time and there is little expectation that it will get any better in the future.

4. Devices are increasingly personal. As a result, the concept of the home is of little interest to them. The home is just another network they can use to access information.

All of this suggests that the smart home is the wrong concept. Instead users will embrace smart devices within a dumb, but well-networked home.

What We Predict Now That We Will Use in 2020

Given what we have said in the previous section, we can now look at what technologies and services we can realistically expect to be using a decade from now.

As we have noted, entertainment is an area of change with a move away from physical storage media such as CDs and DVDs towards electronic storage and with the advent of new entertainment devices such as IPTV connected screens. It seems likely there will be increased desire to share content across multiple screens, sound systems or photo display devices. This sharing could take place via one of two mechanisms. The first would be for all content to be placed on a home server which would be accessed by all the devices in the home using the home network (probably WiFi). The second is for all the content to be stored in the cloud and for devices in the home (and elsewhere) to access the internet using the home network and from that access cloud information. Both solutions could exist, with some homes opting for one and some for the other – or indeed both co-existing within the same home. The cloud solution seems more likely at this point. This is because it is much simpler. Installing a home server and configuring home devices such that they can work with it is likely to be a complex task beyond the abilities of most who struggle to upload their photos to their home PC. Pointing a device to an internet site is much simpler. Storing material in the cloud also has the benefit that it is available when outside of the home.

Hence we predict that within the next 10 years user will store audio and video material and photos in the cloud and that entertainment devices in the home will use WiFi to access the internet and to download this content, synchronizing themselves with it where applicable. So an MP3 player or digital photo frame might check the cloud on start-up and synchronize with any new material. A TV might have a menu option of "my videos" alongside the conventional channel list which would list titles stored in the cloud and the TV would stream material selected.

Telephony seems an area where change might finally happen. Convergence between the fixed phone and the mobile phone has long been forecast, but as mentioned above has not occurred. Part of this is due to the structure of the industry which tends to act to compete between fixed and mobile telephony rather than converge. Part of it has been tepid user demand for convergence – for many it is convenient to be able to have a phone for the home as well as individual phones. Part of it has been pricing where calls from home phones have often become free and critically where calls to mobile phones can be expensive.

Change is happening in some of these areas but not all. New solutions in the form of femtocells are enhancing mobile coverage indoors, while many more phones are gaining the ability to use WiFi networks for voice and data calls. Younger users especially are more reliant on their mobile and see less need for a home phone and the price differential between calls is falling with regulatory action bringing down the termination charge paid to mobile operators to almost nothing. The area where there is less sign of change is integration between fixed and mobile operators. The result of this may be that the simplest solution is to dispense with the home phone and use the mobile both outside and within the home – and indeed this is what an increasing number of users are doing. We predict that this trend will continue with increasing numbers dispensing with their home phone (or using it less and less, keeping it "just in case"). The mobile will make use of a mix of external cellular networks, home femtocells and home WiFi depending on the user and the operator they are with.

We noted earlier that the key difference between the predictions of the future and what transpired was the assumption that the "fabric" of the home would be connected. By the "fabric" we mean functions such as lighting, heating and security as well as the major appliances such as fridges, ovens and coffee machines and by "connected" we mean linked to the home network such that they can be controlled remotely from the home PC, the internet or elsewhere. Our view now is that change in this area is slow and difficult. Costs are high and benefits relatively low. Complexity is a real challenge with every home being different and the chance of home controllers crashing or getting a virus.

There are some possibilities. Lighting control could be achieved by replacing the existing switches with ones with built-in wireless connectivity so that they could be remotely controlled as well as manually. This might not be too expensive (a few dollars a switch) nor too difficult since it only takes a few minutes to replace a switch. The heating control unit could be replaced by one with wireless connectivity when an upgrade is necessary, or potentially sooner if energy savings could justify the cost. High end appliances already have some WiFi connectivity and this might be expected to gradually extend down the range so that over the next decade or so, as appliances are replaced, networking gradually becomes possible. But none of this is easy or certain.

Tablet computing devices are likely to make a wider appearance in the home. With a few scattered around various rooms, this will make it simple to pick one up and complete a task such as ordering the weekly shopping or changing settings on various systems.

Even if only part of these changes happen, then managing the home will become more complex. We have already observed that many users see the home PC as a fragile machine that they could easily break if they did something wrong. As systems become more integrated and home networks more important the risk of failure becomes greater. Home IT will have to become like home plumbing, with users having a 24 hour helpline number that they can call in emergencies to get support. Because many IT problems can be resolved remotely it may be that visits from the IT support team are rare but users will need confidence that problems can be resolved quickly and cost-effectively. At present, experience in this area is poor with support often being off-shore and ill-qualified. We predict that over the next decade most homes will have an IT support contract and that installing, maintaining and upgrading home IT systems will become an increasingly big business.

Life at Home

We now return to our vision of life some 20 years in the future. It is clear from the discussion in this chapter that this was a vision that was technically possible but that there are many commercial realities that will prevent aspects of this happening. In this closing section of the chapter we restate the vision as it seems more likely given all the analysis. We reverse the roles of the adults involved so as to help highlight the differences between the two scenarios.

At 5:20am the home clicks into life. The heating normally comes on at 6am but knowing that she had to get up earlier Julia modified the setting the night before. She can do this from his laptop now that she has installed a WiFi-equipped heating controller and can select 5:20am just for the next day – it will revert to the previous settings tomorrow. Julia has set the target temperature for the house to be colder in the mornings than the evenings to save energy now that gas costs are so high.

After Julia has had her shower she turns her mobile phone on. This is recognized in the femtocell unit in the house and presence information is passed to the home PC. This knows to activate the coffee machine and sends a message via the WiFi network for the machine to come on and warm up. The machine reports a lack of coffee beans which the home PC ignores since it does not know how to deal with it.

At least the coffee machine is warm as Julia approaches it and adding some extra beans does not take too long to brew. Julia presses her favorite setting button and the coffee arrives. Julia gets herself a bowl of cereal and picks up the kitchen tablet, browsing through her favorite internet sites and a pre-assembled selection of news and items of interest put together for her by her cloud provider overnight who makes use of a profile Julia entered some time before and which it updates based on how long she dwells on each item.

After finishing her coffee she heads out, unlocking the front door with her house keys. The femtocell registers that she has left and deactivates her home presence but this does not trigger any function from the home PC.

John is working a late shift that day so he is around in the home in the morning doing some housework. On the kitchen tablet he starts to plan the meals for the coming week. First he checks everyone's diaries and tells the tablet who will be in for dinner on which days. It then makes some meal suggestions for each night based on preferences. John selects from the choices offered and the tablet compiles a shopping list based on its knowledge of what John has in his kitchen and how much there is likely to be left. It asks him to check on the cinnamon – it thinks he may be running low. John also knows that Julia got through rather more cheese than normal this week so he adds it to the shopping list. The tablet presents the shopping list which John approves – the tablet then sends the list to a range of on-line stores. It presents John with the list of options on prices and delivery times and John checks his diary to see which will work best before selecting the preferred option.

There is a sound of gentle laughter – it is the sign that there is a message from Lisa. John glances at the whereabouts clock, it shows that Julia is in the office and Lisa at school, and touches Lisa's avatar. The message pops up that Lisa will be late home – she has been invited round to dinner at a friend's after school. So much for the automated menu system – looks like Julia will get an extra portion of lasagne tonight!

Later in the evening all the family are at home. Julia and Lisa are watching a talent show on television in the family room. They can see the faces of some of their friends in the bottom part of the TV who are also watching the show (and their friends can see them) and interact with them, chatting about each act and voting interactively. John occasionally pops his head into the room to see what is going on. He is practising the piano on their new electronic keyboard which features a virtual teacher showing him the musical score on a display which pops up out of the piano and offering hints as to how his playing could be enhanced. Unfortunately it is not very diplomatic in its feedback and John gets exasperated and shuts it down.

Wandering into the conservatory John spots that the houseplants are looking rather dehydrated. He had put little wireless sensors into their pots which should have alerted him via a message to his phone that they needed watering. He digs out a sensor which does not seem to be working – John surmizes it needs another change of battery. Sometimes he wonders whether he spends more time seeing to the sensors than the plants.

At bedtime Julia takes a quick look round the house to check all the doors and windows. She takes a look at the screen on the home PC to check it is OK to put it into a sleep mode where it will shut down most of its functions but continue to monitor traffic on the home network. She notes that there is an update available for the Home Server software and clicks on accept, hoping that it will not result in the network going down overnight. Thankfully, if it does, all that will suffer is her coffee in the morning.

References

Webb, W. (2001) *The Future of Wireless Communications*, Artech House, London.

Chapter 3
Changing Times: Home Life and Domestic Habit

Lynne Hamill

Introduction

Why should this book include a chapter on time? Because how people use time tells us much about the prevailing social and economic conditions. In opening his book, *Changing Times,* Gershuny (2000: 1) argued that "if we can measure how the members of a society spend their time, we have the elements of a certain sort of account of how that society works". Thus, in a sense, this survey of time use sets the scene for the later chapters.

Wacjman (2008) suggested that "the temporal perspective in sociological theory" has been neglected and "there is an urgent need for increased dialogue to connect social theory with detailed empirical studies". However, this chapter deals not with social theories but with empirical evidence. There are many ways to look at time use. Nansen et al (2009) argued that when looking at the pattern of domestic life it is important to distinguish between "chronometrics (time-measured), chronaesthetics (time-felt) and chronomanagement (time-ordered)". Fine (1996: 55) identified five dimensions of time:

Periodicity refers to the rhythm of the activity; tempo, to its rate or speed; timing to the synchronization or mutual adaptation of activities; duration, to the length of an activity; and sequence, to the ordering of events.

The evidence discussed below focuses on just one of Fine's dimensions, duration, collected though large surveys, to which thousands of respondents contributed. With such large scale surveys, it is impossible to collect details of who did what with whom when and whether they felt hurried for instance. For such analysis small scale studies have to be used, such as Southerton's (2006) interviews with 27 people or Nansen et al's (2009) in depth study of just five families. The evidence presented in this chapter is largely drawn from UK Government sources: the Office for National Statistics (ONS) and Ofcom, the UK communications' regulator.

L. Hamill (✉)
University of Surrey, Guildford, UK

R. Harper (ed.), *The Connected Home: The Future of Domestic Life,*
DOI 10.1007/978-0-85729-476-0_3, © Springer-Verlag London 2011

This chapter focuses on how British people spend their time and how this has changed since the mid-1990s. During this period the technology found in homes changed and new technology means new activities. In particular, the internet arrived and the internet is now used for a range of domestic activities from entertainment to maintaining social relationships and shopping. Yet there are only twenty-four hours in the day: time, said Juster & Stafford (1991), is the ultimate scarce resource. So, putting aside multi-tasking, a new activity can only be undertaken by giving up an old activity. This chapter therefore examines both the changes in domestic technology and the changes in what is done at home. In passing, it also considers the so-called work-life balance and why we feel pressed for time.

I start by briefly discussing the problems of measuring time use. I then present some basic data and examine the division of time between paid work, including telework, and other activities. Next I focus on how time is used at home, which is of course affected by the adoption of new domestic technology, and in particular, the arrival of the internet.

Measuring Time Use

Measuring how people spend their time is surprisingly difficult. There is a large amount of literature on the subject and this section does no more than to highlight some of the major problems.

We spend our time doing all sorts of things. Time-use researchers have to try to classify these many and various activities and often end up with a list of hundreds. For example, in ONS's 2000 survey, 250 activities were coded; for the 2005 survey, the number of activity descriptions were reduced to 30 (ONS, 2006a: 74). But to make sense even of 30 activities we have to reduce these categories further. There are, of course, many ways this can be done. The first cut is to divide time use between paid work and other activities. Differences tend to arise between how those other activities are further divided. (See Kaufman-Scarborough (2006)'s list for example.) I have chosen Gronau's (1977) approach. As usual, Gronau divided time between paid work and other activities, but then divided those other activities between those which a third party could be paid to do, or a machine could be used to shorten the time required – such as washing the dishes – and those for which third party production is conceptually impossible, such as sleeping or enjoying leisure. So, for example, child care, or pet care, becomes domestic work because you could pay someone else to do it even though you may enjoy the activities.

But there is a fundamental problem of defining what people are doing at any given point in time due to polychronicity or, more colloquially, multi-tasking. For example, if you are doing online shopping, are you shopping or using your computer? If you are doing the ironing while listening to the radio, are you doing housework or enjoying leisure? Or if you are watching a DVD with your kids, does that count as childcare or leisure? Different surveys treat this polychronicity in different ways and this is discussed further later in the chapter.

Then there is the issue of how best to collect the data. For instance, respondents can be asked to recall the previous day – as in the ONS's 2005 *Time Use Survey* that is extensively quoted in this chapter – or by use of diaries, as in the ONS's previous time survey (ONS, 2006a: 74). How finely time use is reticulated can vary too: the 2005 ONS *Survey* used ten minute slots for instance.

All these difficulties need to be borne in mind when interpreting survey results, and in particular, when comparing results from different surveys.

Time Use in Britain in the First Decade of the 21st Century

The Average Day

According to ONS's 2005 *Time Use Survey* (2006a) about half of the average day was spent in personal and biological maintenance (such as eating and sleeping), a quarter was spent in leisure and the remaining quarter was equally divided between "paid work, study and commuting" and domestic work. But these figures are averages: averages over those in paid work and those who are not, averages taken over weekdays and weekends (ONS, 2006a: x). It is unlikely that anyone actually experienced this average day. So as well as showing the time spent on each of the 30 activities identified in the survey – plus travel allocated according to its related activity – Table 3.1 also shows what proportion participated in the activity and the average time spent by these participants. There is no difference between the overall average time spent sleeping and the average for participants because everyone slept. There is little difference in the time spent watching TV and the like because four out of five people did that. But for those activities where the participation rates were low, there is a large difference. For example, overall on average only 11 minutes were spent using a computer, but only 11 percent did so and those that did, used it on average for about $1\frac{1}{2}$ hours a day. The fact that nine out of 10 spent no time at all on their computers has very different social (and policy) implications than if everyone spent 11 minutes.

Time use also varies over the day as shown in Fig. 3.1. What is striking is the large area that represents leisure: indeed, leisure accounts for almost half the time compared to a quarter in Table 3.1. This is because in this data set those who report multi-tasking are counted more than once. So that if someone was ironing and listening to the radio say, they would be counted as doing both activities.

Changes in Time Use

Identifying changes in time use is not straightforward due to the differences between surveys. Data is available for 1995 but is not strictly comparable with that for 2000 and 2005 (Table 3.2).

In broad terms using the five basic categories – personal maintenance, paid work and study, domestic work, travel, and leisure – the only major change between

Table 3.1 Minutes per day: average and by participants, UK, 2005

Activity	Participation rate (1)	Average minutes per day		Of which at home
		Participants (2)	All (3)	
Personal maintenance				663	618
Sleep	100%	491	491	
Rest	51%	89	46	
Eating & drinking	97%	85	82	
Personal care ie wash/ dress	92%	48	44	
Paid work, study and commuting				199	17
Paid work	39%	434	170	
Formal education	4%	269	11	
Commuting	29%	62	18	
Domestic work				193	132
Cooking, washing up	70%	59	41	
Cleaning, tidying	38%	82	31	
Shopping, appointments	37%	90	34	
Travel for shopping	26%	42	11	
Washing clothes	19%	61	11	
Caring for own children	16%	148	24	
Pet care	13%	52	7	
Repairs and gardening	13%	126	17	
Escorting someone	10%	50	5	
Caring for other children	6%	141	9	
Caring for adults in own household	2%	95	1	
Caring for adults other household	2%	120	2	
Leisure				371	233
TV & videos/DVDs, radio, music	80%	196	157	
Miscellaneous travel eg visits	58%	83	48	
At home with family/friends	33%	152	50	
Going out with family/friends	14%	172	24	
Contact with friends/family	15%	55	8	
Reading	28%	88	24	
Hobbies	14%	136	19	
Using a computer	11%	97	11	
Sport & outdoor activities	10%	100	10	
Travel for exercise/pleasure	7%	71	5	
Entertainment and culture	3%	153	5	
Attending religious meetings etc	3%	99	3	
Voluntary work	2%	153	3	
Recreational study	2%	177	4	
Other specified/not specified	10%	141	14	**14**	**4**
Total				**1440**	**1004**

Note: Average time by those who participated in the activity (col 3) = (average time per day for all people (col 2)/proportion of people who participated in the activity (col 1)) × 100
Source: ONS (2006a: 11, 13, 64)

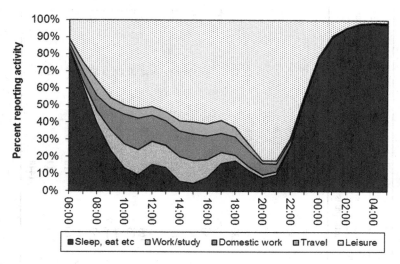

Fig. 3.1   Activity by time of day, 2010
Source: Ofcom (2010: 29)

1995 and 2000 was a doubling of time spent travelling. But whether this change is the result of differences in the survey techniques or reporting rather than a real difference in time use is not clear: in the reporting of the 1995 survey results, over an hour a day is described as "other".

ONS has itself compared the results from its 2000 and 2005 surveys (ONS, 2006a: 17) and two changes in the overall averages are striking. The average amount of time spent socialising increased by about half an hour a day while that spent on domestic work (excluding childcare) fell by a similar amount. Changes in the overall average can occur because the proportion reporting the activity changes or the amount of time they spend on it changes, or both change. For domestic work, not only did fewer report doing it in 2005, but those that did spent less time on it. Fewer reported socialising too, but those who did socialise spent longer in 2005 than in 2000. Indeed, participation rates for all the leisure activities fell while time spent by those who did participate increased. This suggests that leisure activities are becoming more specialized in the sense that people spend longer on fewer activities.

ONS (2006a: 47, 69) also noted the "considerable growth" in the use of computers over the 5 years 2000 to 2005. "On any given day in 2000, around 12 per cent of the population used a computer outside their workplace (workplace use is not recorded in the diaries). By 2005, some 16 per cent of the population were doing so each day". Also, those using computers spent longer doing so; thus overall, averaging over computer users and non-users, "computing time increased from an average of 12 minutes per day in 2000 to 20 minutes per day in 2005." (However, it is not clear how this 20 minutes a day fits with the 11 minutes shown in Table 3.1, which is based on a different table in ONS's report.)

Table 3.2 Detailed change in time use. GB. 1995 to 2005

Activity	1995	2000			2005			Change 2000–2005		
	Average mins/day	Participation rate	Average mins/day		Participation rate	Average mins/day		Participation rate	Average mins/day	
	All (Approx)		Participants	All		Participants	All		Participants	All
Personal maintenance	**627**			**664**			**663**			**-1**
Sleep & rest		100%	530	530	100%	537	537	0%	7	7
Personal care ie wash/dress		96%	49	47	92%	48	44	-4%	-1	-3
Eating & drinking		98%	89	87	97%	85	82	-1%	-4	-5
Paid work & study	**181**			**190**			**184**			**-6**
Employment		39%	446	174	39%	434	170	0%	-12	-4
Study (including recreational)		6%	267	16	6%	233	14	0%	-33	-2
Domestic work	**197**			**193**			**166**			**-27**
Care of own children		20%	100	20	16%	150	24	-4%	50	4
Other domestic work		91%	190	173	85%	167	142	-6%	-23	-31
Travel	**46**	88%	97	**85**	86%	102	**87**	-2%	5	**2**
Leisure	**310**			**297**			**325**			**28**
Social life		60%	93	56	50%	164	82	-10%	71	26
Hobbies & games		24%	88	21	24%	125	30	0%	38	9
Voluntary work & meetings		16%	100	16	12%	142	17	-4%	42	1
TV/video/DVD/radio/music		na	na	156	80%	196	157	na	na	1
Entertainment and culture		6%	100	6	3%	153	5	-3%	53	-1
Reading		43%	65	28	28%	88	24	-15%	22	-4
Sport & outdoor activities		15%	93	14	10%	100	10	-5%	6	-4
Other specified/not specified	**79**	29%	31	**9**	10%	141	**14**	-19%	110	**5**
Total	**1440**			**1440**			**1440**			

Source: ONS (1998: 216; 2006a: 17)

Work Life

Time Poor – Money Rich?

As people became better off, it was expected that they would enjoy more leisure. In his 1931 *Economic Possibilities for Our Grandchildren* – that's us! – Keynes suggested that "with no important wars and no important increases in population" by 2030 there would be a 15 hour working week with the main problem being how to use our leisure (Keynes, 1931: 369). There has, of course, been a major war – World War 2 – and the UK population has increased. So, it is perhaps not surprising that, although working hours have fallen, they have not fallen as much as Keynes predicted. From the time Keynes wrote, to 1979, the average hours worked per person fell by about a third, and since 1998, this trend to shorter hours appears to have continued (Matthews et al, 1982: 66-67; Castells, 2000: 469; Gallie, 2000: 306-7; ONS, 2007a). Yet we are much richer: real GDP per head, a common measure of how well off we are, has more than quadrupled since Keynes wrote (Feinstein, 1972: Table 42; ONS, 2010c). We could therefore afford to 'buy' more leisure but it appears that we, as a society, have chosen to take the benefits of economic growth in terms of more consumption rather than more leisure. Put another way, people have in effect chosen to be money-rich and time-poor.

In the previous section, it was noted that on average people spent one seventh of their time working, nearly 3 hours a day. This may seem surprisingly low. But not everyone works and for some of those who do work, the day on which the data was collected was not a working day. Thus only four out of 10 reported undertaking paid work, and on average this took up $7\frac{1}{4}$ hours of their day (Table 3.1): and for those who worked full-time and reported working on the survey day, work took up nearly one third of their day, as one would expect. Figure 3.2 compares the average day for everyone, for those who worked full-time and for those who were retired. Because the average day for the full-timers includes weekends and holidays, work accounted for only about a fifth of their time.

So why do we often hear that we have 'busy lifestyles', that we are somehow more rushed, more pressed for time than people were in the past? According to Glennie and Thrift (2009: 51) this idea that "the everyday world is intensifying and speeding up; becoming ever more frantic, and producing a general shortage of time" is not new, and has in fact been repeated "across several centuries". Even in medieval times, time was structured into weekly, lunar, seasonal and religious cycles: certain jobs, ploughing for example, had to be done by certain times (Thrift, 1996: 180-206). But while there may be nothing new in complaints of 'too little time', what in particular has prompted the current complaint? The answer appears to be the distribution of leisure.

Gershuny (2000: 5-7) argued that in "the developed world in the last third of the twentieth century", there has been "a reversal of the previous status-leisure gradient. Those of higher status previously had more leisure, and subsequently had less of it than those of lower social status". Partridge (2005) argued that it is because

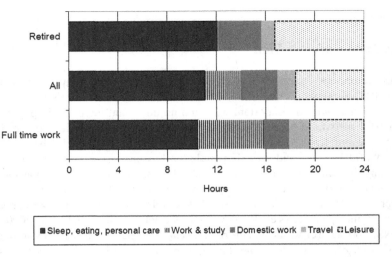

Fig. 3.2 Time use by economic status, 2005
Source: ONS (2006: Table D9501)

it is these "high status" individuals who write academic and media articles, that there is a perception that there is a shortage of time. Taking highest educational achievement as an indicator of status, in 2005 on average those with degrees did work much longer hours than those with no qualifications: nearly 4 hours a day compared to about 1½ hours. But half of those with degrees reported working compared to only a fifth of those with no qualifications and if we just compare these workers, those with degrees worked only half an hour longer on average than those who had no qualifications (ONS, 2006: online table D9505). Clearer support for Gershuny and Partridge comes from Tam's (2010) analysis of data from the Labour Force Survey (LFS). Tam looked at the proportion of workers who would prefer to work fewer hours for less pay, who she labeled "the overemployed". According to Tam since 2001, 1 in 10 of workers in the UK have been overemployed and, perhaps not surprisingly, this rose to almost 1 in 6 of those who were working more than 48 hours a week. In line with Gershuny and Partridge, the overemployed were older, better educated, better paid and more likely to do managerial and professional jobs. Overemployment reflects the inflexibility in the labour market; people cannot choose their hours, particularly at more senior levels where part-time work is simply not an option and there is a general expectation that you work far longer than your contracted hours. At the other end of the scale were the "underemployed" who wanted and were available to work longer. (Underemployment is in effect hidden unemployment.) The underemployed, too, accounted for about 1 in 10 of the workforce. Those in 'elementary occupations' (such as labourers) and those working part-time are most likely to be underemployed.

Since 1961, for men on average, there has been a reduction in paid work while for women, there has been an increase: but despite this, by 2000, women of working age had more leisure than in 1961 (Partridge, 2005; Gershuny, 2002). So why the reported time pressure? Partridge (2005) suggested that moving from single to dual income households has, by reducing the time that neither partner is working, created the perception of lack of leisure time. There is support for this idea too in Tam's data. Tam (2010) found that women, especially those of child-bearing age, were much more likely to be overemployed: 1 in 7 women working full-time were overemployed and "the gender difference was most evident in the age range 25-34, with women around twice as likely as men to be overemployed".

The Rise of Teleworking?

It is often argued that the industrial revolution resulted in paid work leaving the home for the factory, thus separating people's work lives from other aspects of their lives but that new technology has reversed this trend. In his 1967 seminal paper, *Time, Work-Discipline and Industrial Capitalism*, Thompson argued that "mature industrial societies. . . are marked by a clear demarcation between 'work' and 'life'" (although Thompson's view is now questioned by, for example, Thrift, 1996: 169-212). New communications technology, it is argued, reverses this. Forty years ago, in 1970, Toffler wrote in *Future Shock*:

> Machines and men both, instead of being concentrated in gigantic factories and factory cities, will be scattered across the globe, linked together by amazingly sensitive, near-instantaneous communications. Human work will move out of the factory and mass office into the community and the home (Toffler, 1972 edition: 402)

By the 1980s, it was being suggested that a large proportion of white-collar workers would in future work at home (Pratt, 1984). The arrival of "interactive technologies" have revived this argument: for example, according to Kaufman-Scarborough (2006) this demarcation between work and home can be "bridged once again". As I sit in my home-office, writing this chapter, looking out over the fields between accessing articles from journals, maybe held the other side of the world, then yes, it seems this has indeed happened. But how typical is my experience?

To measure something, we first have to define it. Is someone who works at home the occasional day a teleworker? Or is a teleworker someone who works entirely from home making intensive use of the internet? Haddon & Brynin (2005) concluded that "teleworking should be *defined* by technology and location but *qualified* by timing" (their italics). However, twenty years ago, in 1990, the ILO's definition of telework focused on new communications technology enabling people to work away from their co-workers with no reference to timing (Ruiz & Walling, 2005). In 1994, the UK is reported to have been ahead of other European countries in adopting telework, with some 1 in 20 workers "doing some kind of telework" (ECaTT, 2000: 6) although it is not clear whether this was based on the ILO definition.

In Britain in 2001, if doing any work at home was counted, then, just under half of workers were teleworkers (Haddon & Brynin, 2005). But on closer inspection, some of these are best regarded as mobile workers. Only one in five relied on the internet or personal computer to work at home, and this takes no account of how much time was spent working at home (although it did exclude occasional overtime).

In 2002, the EU produced a definition of telework that did at least cover the frequency with which people worked away from their employer's premises: telework was "a form of organizing and/or performing work, using information technology, in the context of an employment contract/relationship, where work, which could also be performed at the employer's premises, is carried out away from those premises on a regular basis" (EU Article 2 of the *European Framework Agreement on Telework of 2002* (Eurofound, 2009: 3)). In 2005 8 percent of UK workers – the same as five years previously – were teleworkers defined as an employee working "with a personal computer away from the employer's premises at least a quarter of the time" and 2½ percent teleworked "almost all of the time" (Eurofound, 2009: 4-6).

However, to observe long term trends we need a run of data based on consistent definitions and this is provided by the Labour Force Survey (LFS), a major national survey which has been conducted since 1979 (ONS, 2010d). The LFS first included a question about where people worked in 1981 and this showed that 4 percent of workers worked mainly from home or used their home as a base (Felstead et al, 2003). Unfortunately, the question was not repeated until 1992, by which time the figure had risen to 5½ percent. But in 1997 new questions were added allowing the identification of teleworkers (Felstead et al, 2003). Taking a broad definition of teleworkers, as those who work mainly in their own home, or use their home as a base, and who use a phone and computer, then 3½ percent were teleworkers in 1997. By 2009, this figure had risen to 10 percent and almost all of these could not telework without both a phone and a computer – so-called "TC teleworkers". However, about two-thirds of these TC teleworkers were using their home as a base while the popular conception of a teleworker is someone who actually works mainly at home. On this very narrow basis – TC teleworkers working mainly from home – the figure falls to only 2 percent of the British workforce – about ½ million people – in 2005 although the numbers have probably risen since. Details are shown in Fig. 3.3.

Who are these teleworkers? Haddon & Brynin (2005) noted that the wider the definition used, the more heterogeneous will be the groups labeled as 'teleworkers'. They found that in 2001 those who used the internet tended to be relatively well paid professional men while other teleworkers tended to be more typical of the working population as a whole. Similarly according to the LFS data, by 2005 homeworkers were more likely to be self-employed men than workers in general but had similar occupations. In contrast, those "TC teleworkers" who worked mainly at home were more likely to be self-employed women in the higher occupational groups as shown in Table 3.3. Thus rather than being adopted as a new way of managing staff in large corporations, the ability to work at home appears to have facilitated self-employment.

How do these findings relate to the 2005 time survey data quoted in Table 3.1 above? Of the 170 minutes in the average day spent working, 133 minutes were done away from home. Only 15 minutes of paid work was done at home but the

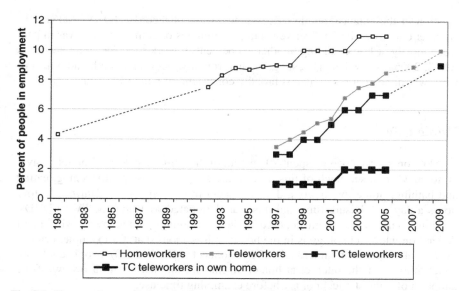

Fig. 3.3 Homeworkers and teleworkers as a proportion of people in employment, UK: 1981-2009
Note: "TC teleworkers" work at home or use their home as a base and could not do so without a phone and a computer. Data not available for all years
Sources: Based on LFS data from Felstead (2003), Ruiz & Walling (2005), ONS (2006), Randall (2010)

Table 3.3 Characteristics of homeworkers compared to the working population, UK, 2005

	All in employment	All homeworkers	TC teleworkers	
			Home as base	Mainly at home
Percent				
Men	53	68	78	44
Self-employed	13	64	60	60
Full-time	72	72	82	54
Occupation				
Managers & senior officials	16	16	23	24
Professionals	13	13	20	17
Associate professional/technical	17	17	22	27
Skilled trades	27	27	23	7
Estimated number (million)	28.0	3.1	1.5	0.5

Source: Ruiz & Walling (2005)

location of the balance, another 22 minutes, was not recorded (ONS, 2006a: 13). Another clue from the 2005 survey is that 18 minutes of computer time was in paid work mostly at home, adding another 10 percent to work time for computer users (ONS, 2006a: 47 & 70). This suggests that, roughly, between a tenth and a fifth of work was done at home, which is broadly consistent with the LFS data.

Home Life

In 2005, on average people spent 70 percent of their time – nearly 17 hours a day – at home. Of course, much of this time, some 10 hours, was spent sleeping, eating and bathing. Some two hours a day was spent in domestic work. But nearly four hours a day was leisure time and this was dominated by watching TV or DVDs, listening to the radio and music. (See Table 3.1.) Home-based activities will in part depend on what technology is in the home. It is obvious that, for example, prior to the arrival of broadband internet in 2000 (Connected Earth, 2010), people could not watch films over the internet at home. So this section starts with a review of the adoption of domestic technology before examining time use.

Innovators and Laggards

The diffusion of innovations of all kinds has been studied since the mid-twentieth century and a considerable literature has developed (see Rogers, 2003: 39-101). Adoption of new technology is essentially a social process, which can be only partly explained by economics (Douglas & Isherwood, 1996: xx-xxvii; Rogers, 2003: 289). Rising incomes and falling prices do not of themselves create demand for new domestic technology or anything else as, rather to their dismay, economists Deaton and Muellbauer (1985: 71-72) found. Economists can provide useful assessments of the short term impact of changes in prices and incomes but not the longer term question of why some goods come to be adopted by the majority of the population while others do not (Douglas and Isherwood, 1979: 99).

On the basis of many studies over many years of many different types of innovations, Rogers (2003: 281-2) divided adopters into five groups; innovators, early adopters, early majority, late majority and laggards.

- Innovators account for 2½ percent or 1 in 40 of the population. They have wide social networks, financial resources and technical knowledge but they are not necessarily respected within their social system. They can be likened to Simmel's stranger (ibid: 42, 290-1), i.e. people who are in a sense on the margins of the social system.
- Early adopters account for about 1 in 7 of the population. They are somewhat similar to innovators but are more embedded in the social system, being opinion leaders and respected role models for whom status is likely to be important (ibid: 251, 316-319). Early adopters are better educated, of higher social status, and more likely to be upwardly mobile and wealthy (ibid: 288).

- The early majority comprize about a third of the population. They interact frequently with their peers but are rarely opinion leaders.
- The late majority account for another third and are persuaded to adopt by peer pressure although they have limited resources.
- Laggards are the last sixth of the population to adopt, and they tend to interact with other laggards.

During the majority phases – both early and late – the rate of growth of adoption is usually fast while at the start and at the end, it is usually slow. This produces the well-known S-curve.

A good example of this pattern is the adoption of black-and-white television in Britain from when transmissions were resumed after the Second World War in 1946 to when adoption peaked at 93 percent in 1970, after which black-and-white TVs were replaced by colour sets. This is shown in Fig. 3.4.

Table 3.4 shows the length of Rogers' phases and the time needed to reach saturation (defined as 95 percent adoption) for various domestic technologies. Data on the length of the 'innovators' phase is rare because the adoption of new technology is usually not monitored until adoption has reached early adopters or even the 'early majority' so Table 3.4 combines innovators and early adopters. For instance, colour TVs were launched in 1967 and in four years, by 1971, had reached 16 percent of households and in another five years, had reached 50 percent, thus taking nine years in total. But it took another 15 years for adoption to reach saturation.

As noted in the previous section, we appear to live in a money-rich, time-poor culture. People prefer to earn more money and, it is argued, have less, but higher quality, leisure rather than having less money but more time. This apparent desire for high quality leisure time emerges from studies of consumption: it is claimed that

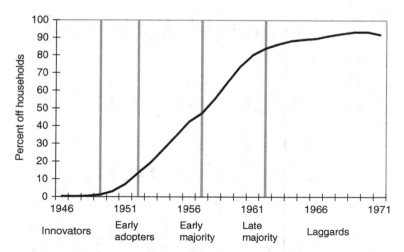

Fig. 3.4 Adoption of black and white television in England & Wales, 1946-1971
Source: Bowden & Offer (1994)

Table 3.4 Time taken for selected domestic technologies to reach key adoption levels

		Year adoption reached				Length of phase (years)			
	Year product launched	Early majority (16%)	Late majority (50%)	Laggards (84%)	Saturation (95%)	Innovators and early adopters (0 to 15%)	Early majority (16 to 49%)	Late majority (50 to 84%)	Laggards (85 to 95%)
TV: colour	1967	1971	1976	1985	1991	4	5	9	6
Video recorder	1979	*Early 80s*	*Late 80s*	1997-8		*Under 5*	*5-10*	*About 10*	
Home computer	*Early 1980s*	1986	2002-3			4	16	5	
TV: B&W	1946	1953	1958	1963		7	5	5	
Internet connection	1992	1999-0	2004-5			7	5		
Satellite receiver	1982	*Early 90s*	2004-5	2009		10	15	5	
Mobile phone	1985	1996-7	2001-2			11	5	7	
Fridge	1946	1960	1968	1975	1980	14	8	7	5
DVD player	1997		2003-4	2007				4	
CD player	1982		1995-6	2003-4				8	
Microwave oven	*Mid 1970s*		1990	2000-1				10	
Washing machine	1933	1955	1964	1987	2004-5	22	9	23	17
Tumble drier	1950	*Late 70s*	1994-5			*30*	*15*		
Dishwasher	1957	1993		1988	1998-9	*36*			
Telephone	1880	*Late 50s*	1974			*80*	*15*	*15*	*10*

Note: italics indicate estimates, rounded to nearest 5 years

Sources: Launch of Telephones: The Telephone Company (1880); Mobile phones: Agar (2003: 81); Others: OPCS (1995: Table 2.6); ONS (1997: Table A10); ONS (1999: Table 9.4); ONS (2010a and 2010e: Tables A50 & A51); Bowden and Offer (1994)

time-using goods that increase the quality of time spread much faster than time-saving goods that increase the quantity of free time (Bowden & Offer, 1994; Tellis et al, 2003). And Table 3.4 shows that it took more than 10 years for many time-saving appliances to reach the early majority – starting at 16 percent of households – while it took less than 10 for many entertainment technologies to reach that stage. But after that early majority is reached, the distinction between time-savers and time-users is not so clear.

What Has Changed Since 1998?

Why start with 1998? The short answer is the availability of consistent data. In 1998, the ONS revamped their method of calculating household adoption rates and started collecting data on household internet connections. So starting with 1998 facilitates comparisons both over time and between adoption of the internet and other household appliances.

Now even though economic growth does not guarantee increased adoption of any particular item of domestic technology, it does tend to make these technologies more affordable. By 2007, households were about one fifth better off in real terms (i.e. after inflation) than they had been 10 years previously, although by 2009, this had fallen to about one sixth[1]. While prices in general rose by almost a third, the prices of consumer durables fell by a fifth, and in particular the prices of "audio-visual equipment" and "information processing kit", fell dramatically: audio-visual equipment that cost £1,000 in 1998 cost only about £200 in 2009 and information processing kit that cost £1,000 in 1998 cost only £80 in 2009[2]. There are of course difficulties in measuring price changes when products are changing rapidly as technology develops (see, for example, Brand, 2001). Nevertheless, it is hardly surprising that the proportion of households owning domestic technology generally rose over the period given this growth in real incomes together with the fall in prices of these goods relative to other goods.

Three groups of domestic durables can be distinguished by the change in the proportion of households adopting them over the 11 years, 1998 to 2009, shown in Table 3.5:

- Falling adoption: those items for which the adoption rates were high in the late 1990s but declined due to some degree of technological obsolescence: video recorders, which were superseded by DVDs, and fixed line phones, superseded by mobile phones;

---

[1] As measured by the growth in real GDP per head, IHXW on the ONS database (ONS, 2010c).

[2] "Prices" measured by the all items RPI (CHAW on the ONS database); "Consumer durables" (CHBY), "audio-visual equipment (DOCZ) and "information processing kit", which includes personal computers, by CPI 9.1.3 (D7EP) (ONS, 2010c).

- Moderate risers, for which adoption increased by less than 20 percentage points: washing machines and tumble driers, microwaves, dishwashers and CD players. Except CD players, these are all time-savers.
- Fast risers, for which adoption rates increased by more than 40 percentage points: home computers, mobile phones, satellite receivers, internet connections and DVD players. With, arguably, the exception of mobiles, all these were all time-users.

But the averages shown in Table 3.5 hide the sometimes large difference in adoption between rich and poor households. Figure 3.5 shows how the difference in adoption between the poorest and richest households has changed in the last 11 years. The left edge of each bar shows the percentage of households adopting in the lowest income decile – the poorest – while the right edge shows the percentage in the highest, richest, decile. This is a rather unusual presentation and some explanation may help.

- The longer the bar, the greater the difference between the richest and poorest households: the longest bars are for internet connections and dishwashers.
- The shorter and further to the right the bar, the closer is adoption to saturation: as for microwaves and washing machines in 2009.
- The less the overlap between the pair of bars for each item, the more the change between 1998 and 2009: for example for satellite and cable TV, where there is no overlap at all!

Table 3.5   Adoption of domestic technology by British households, 1998-2009

	Percent of households adopting			Percent change 1998-2009
	1998-99	2002-03	2009	
Video recorder	85	90	61	-24
Telephone	95	84	88	-7
Washing machine	92	84	96	4
Tumble drier	51	56	58	7
Microwave	79	87	93	14
Dishwasher	23	29	39	16
CD player	68	83	84	16
Home computer	33	55	75	42
Mobile phone	27	70	81	54
Satellite receiver	28	45	86	58
Internet connection	10	45	71	61
DVD player	(1)	31	90	90

(1) Data starts 2002-3
Source: ONS (2010e: Table A50)

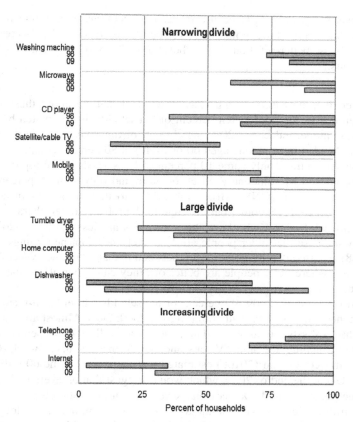

Fig. 3.5 Change in adoption among poorest and richest households: 1998-9 to 2009
Sources: ONS (1999, 2010a)

This presentation allows us to distinguish between three broad groups:

- First, where there was a narrowing of the difference in adoption rate between rich and poor households – the length of the bars shortened – washing machines, microwaves, DVD players, CD players, satellite/cable TV and mobiles.
- Second, where the length of the bars did not change much between 1998 and 2009 although they tended to shift to the right as more households in all income groups adopted: tumble driers, dishwashers, and home computers.
- Third, where there was an increase in the difference in adoption rate between rich and poor households, the length of the bars increased: fixed-line phones and internet connections. For fixed-line phones, the increase in the gap between rich and poor was small, and the overall adoption rate fell as poorer households substituted mobile phones. For internet connections, the difference increased dramatically as the overall adoption rate rose. The gap between rich and

poor households increased because internet connections were found in only a third of the richest households in 1998, but 11 years later they were almost ubiquitous in better-off households but found in only one third of poorer households.

However, it is necessary to introduce a word of caution about these figures. The bottom decile, the poorest ten percent of households, is dominated by retired people living alone: indeed, in 2009, nearly half of the households in the bottom decile were headed by someone aged 60 or over and 80 percent comprized of just one person. In contrast, only some 10 percent of households in the top decile, the richest, are headed by someone aged 60 or more and only some 5 percent comprised just one person (ONS, 2010e: Table 54). So the differences in adoption rates do not just reflect income, but also age (and probably other characteristics). Nevertheless, while those who have lower incomes are less likely to adopt, it is not simply the case that older people are less likely to adopt new things. Rogers (2003: 288) reported that the relationship between age and "innovativeness" is not clear because where older people are better off, they can better afford the risks of innovation.

To sum up, by early 2009, 99 percent of households had either a fixed line or mobile phone, and 4 out of 5 had both (Ofcom, 2009: 248). Almost all households probably had TV sets too, although data is no longer collected: 98 percent of people reported watching TV on a TV set sometime during the survey week (Ofcom, 2010: 38). Indeed, Ofcom (2010b) estimated that there were some 60 million TV sets in the UK at the end of 2009, which would suggest that on average there were about three per household. Devices that save time on domestic chores were very common: fridges were probably ubiquitous although again, data is no longer collected and over 90 percent of households had washing machines and microwave ovens. More than four out of five households had CD and DVD players and satellite (or cable) TV; and more than seven out of ten, home computers and internet connections (Table 3.5).

Impact on Time Use

But how has this affected time use? Today's luxuries tend to become tomorrow's necessities (Douglas & Isherwood, 1979: 99, 121-2): "the poor", Douglas and Isherwood argued, are "periodicity-constrained" and have to spend more time doing chores while the rich can afford new technology to free them. In a similar vein, Urry (2000: 10) argued that money is time: it is "access to money which enables time to be put to good use". In other words, the rich buy time.

What evidence is there about the money-rich time-poor? Although the 2005 survey did ask about respondents' income, 40 percent declined to provide any information (ONS, 2006: online table D9503). Given this poor response, data on time use by highest educational qualification is arguably a better indicator. Of course a high educational qualification does not ensure a high income, nor lack of

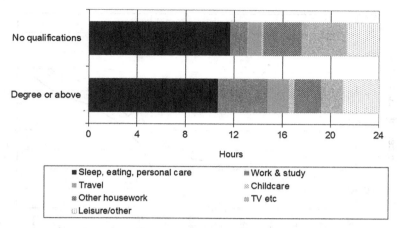

Fig. 3.6   Time use by highest qualification. GB. 2005
Source: ONS (2006: online table D9505)

qualifications a low income. Nevertheless, the results (not published in the report but available online) are interesting. The quarter of the sample with degrees spent more time working and travelling than the quarter with no qualifications; and those with degrees spent less time on housework (other than child care) and had less leisure time than the unqualified. Furthermore, that leisure time was less dominated by TV and associated media: fewer of those with degrees reported watching TV and those who did watch did so for less time. (See Fig. 3.6.) The findings are consistent with the idea that the better off 'buy' leisure time reducing the time needed for housework.

So does the increase in adoption of the time-saving technology between 2000 and 2005 (shown in Fig. 3.6) explain the apparent reduction of half an hour a day spent on housework (shown in Table 3.3)? Maybe. The impact of labour-saving domestic technology, such as washing machines, on the time spent doing housework is not obvious. Indeed, it is claimed that the time spent on housework has not been reduced by new domestic technology (Bowden & Offer, 1994; Gershuny, 2000: 54). The better off work longer, and therefore have less time for other activities and can afford more domestic technology. But is there not a chicken-and-egg situation here? Is it that more technology enables them to work longer or that the longer working hours means the technology is more affordable?

The Internet at Home

The Arrival of the Internet

The internet arrived in 1992 but by 1998-9 only 10 percent of households had internet connections; by 2009, this had risen to 71 percent (as shown in Fig. 3.7).

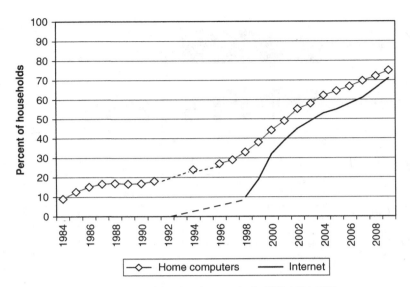

Fig. 3.7 Adoption of home computers and the internet in the UK: 1984-2009
Sources: As Table 3.5 (Data for home computers not available for all years.)

The adoption of new communication technologies differs from that of items such as washing machines because of "network externalities", that is, the value of joining the network depends on the number of people who have already joined (Varian, 2003: 631). When a network is small, there is little value to be had from joining it. But the more people who join, the more valuable it is to join. How much more valuable is debatable. Metcalfe's Law says that "the value of a communications network is proportional to the square of the number of its users" (Briscoe et al, 2006). However, Briscoe et al (2006) argued that Metcalfe's Law produced too high a value because it is based on the idea that all connections are equally valuable while it does not matter if a billion people have email; what matters is whether the people you want to contact – your friends and family – are connected.

Another way of looking at this is to argue that a "critical mass" is needed for diffusion to take-off. (See, for example, Valente, 1995: 79, 87, 130.) But how many need to adopt for a critical mass to be reached? Rogers (2003: 360) suggests that "take off" typically occurs when between 5 and 20 percent have adopted. However, Valente (1995: 83) suggested that it might be around 50 percent adoption for phones, as people will then feel that it is necessary to have one when so many others have.

When there are "network externalities", Rogers (2003: Fig. 8-5) suggested that diffusion may follow a more pronounced "S" curve for than for other types of technology: a slower start followed by a more rapid growth to saturation. Table 3.4 shows that the adoption of the internet moved quickly through the early adopters phase compared to the time taken by some other technologies: just five years compared to nine for washing machines for example. My own modeling work (Hamill, 2010: 299) suggested that without a critical mass of sufficiently digitally literate people, adoption of the internet would not have taken off. And this in part came about because by the time the internet arrived in 1992, around a fifth of households in the UK already had home computers (as shown in Fig. 3.7). The adoption of home computers and the internet then grew together. Indeed, I think it is likely that the adoption of home computers would not have risen as shown in Fig. 3.6 had they not been transformed into interactive communication devices by the internet – confirming the basic thesis of this book of course!

In 1998-9, almost no households in the bottom half of the income distribution had an internet connection; but by 2009, a third of the poorest households were connected as were almost all those in the top half of the income distribution (Fig. 3.8). But even in 2009, the majority of households with internet connections were better-off: the richest half of households accounted for about two-thirds of internet connections. Nevertheless by 2009, a third of poor, single pensioner households had an internet connection, as did 9 out of 10 two parent households with children (ONS, 2010e: Table A51).

The younger and the better educated are most likely to use the internet.

- In 2010 99 percent of people aged 16 to 24 had used the internet, only 40 percent of those aged 65 and over had done so. There is, however, a wide difference between those in their 60s and those in their 80s. Special analysis of the 2007 *Family Spending Survey* showed that only 15 percent of households headed by people aged 80 and over were connected compared to just under half of households headed by people aged 65 to 69 (Hamill, 2010: 283). Furthermore, internet non-users are not confined to older age groups: in 2008, half were under the age of 65 (Morris, 2009: 35).
- In 2005, those with degrees were four times more likely to use a computer: 1 in 6 compared to 1 in 25 of those without qualifications (ONS, 2006: online table D9505). By 2010, 97 percent of people with degrees had used the internet, but only 45 percent of those with no qualifications had done so (ONS, 2010b).

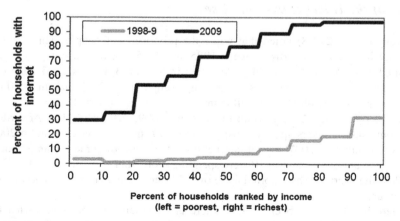

Fig. 3.8 Percentage of households with an internet connection by gross income decile: 1998-9 and 2000
Sources: ONS (1999, 2010e)

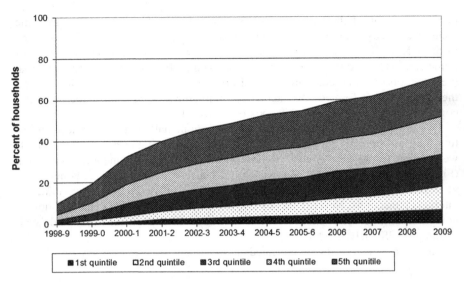

Fig. 3.9 Internet connection by gross income quintile: 1998-9 to 2009 (1st quintile is poorest.)
Sources: ONS (1999, 2000, 2002, 2003, 2004a, 2004b, 2005, 2007b, 2008a, 2008b, 2010a, 2010e)

In 2010, 9 million adults in the UK had never used the internet (ONS, 2010b). Of course, this will fall over time. Morris (2009: 35) estimated that the proportion of the adult population who are "digitally excluded" – apparently defined as those who have not used the internet in the previous three months – would, if all other factors remain constant, fall from 29 percent in 2009 to 15 percent in 2021, due to demographic change, but half of those aged 65 and over would be digitally excluded.

Effect of the Internet on Time Use

Gershuny (2007: 277-8) noted that while the proportion of people using a home computer had risen markedly between 1985 and 2005, the time spent using a PC remained at about two hours a day. As noted in Section 3, ONS's 2005 *Time Use Survey* found that more time was spent using computers in 2005 than in 2000 but we do not know how much of this time involved use of the internet.

For internet data, we need to turn to Ofcom (2009: 279; 2010: 19). According to Ofcom, internet users spent on average about 1½ hours a week online in 2004. However, by autumn 2007, half of internet users were spending more than 5 hours a week online at home; and 1 in 10 were spending more than 15 hours a week online. By 2009, the average was reported to be over 3 hours a week, more than double the 2004 figure.

Where had this time been found? There is a fundamental problem in teasing out the impact of a new technology on time use. Simply comparing the time use patterns of users and non-users at a given date does not allow for the many other differences between the two groups: I call this 'the heterogeneity problem'. For example, the ONS did just that in their 2005 *Time Use Survey* (2006a: 47, 69). Statistical techniques can be used to try to overcome this problem (as for example in Nie, Hillygus & Erbring, 2002). An alternative approach is to undertake a longitudinal study (as for example, in Anderson and Tracey, 2002); but then the problem is to adjust for the other changes that have occurred such as marriage or retirement. A variation on this is simply to ask people how, for example, the internet had affected their use of time, although this has obvious problems in that people may simply not know. Nevertheless Anderson and Tracey (2002) did just that, but with inconclusive results in part, at least, because on average use was then still very low.

Can we learn anything from past experience? When TV arrived, people found time to watch it. What was given up to accommodate this new activity? The BBC conducted time budget studies in 1939 and 1952 when there were virtually no TVs, and compared the results with a similar study conducted in 1975, when almost every household had one. The BBC concluded that time for TV was found by working fewer hours and by spending less time 'doing nothing in particular'" (BBC, 1978: 641). However, the world in 1975 was very different to that before the Second World War in 1939, and so it really is not possible to argue that TV caused these changes. (For a more detailed discussion, see Hamill, 2003).

In the 1980s, adoption of home computers was reported to result in less TV watching (Dutton et al, 1987). For instance in 2005, computer users watched TV for an average of 135 minutes while non-users watched for 160 minutes (ONS, 2006: 69). But as noted above, it is the better educated, who are known to watch less TV, who are also more likely to use computers, so we have the heterogeneity problem and although the use of computers is associated with less TV watching, it has not necessarily caused it. (See also Gershuny, 2002; Gershuny, 2003.) This heterogeneity problem also arises in relation to the impact of broadband on internet use where it was found that broadband users spent longer online than narrowband users (Ofcom, 2007: 21; Anderson & Raban, 2007: 47). It is not clear to what extent this finding was due to the fact that those who were keener users of the internet were more likely to move to broadband, rather than to changes in behavior (due, for instance, to lower marginal costs when narrowband access is charged per minute and broadband is not).

On average the number of hours spent watching TV in the UK did not change between 2004 and 2009, at about 3.7 hours a day. But once again, this average is misleading: for those under the age of 35, time watching TV fell and for those aged 45 and over, it rose (Ofcom, 2010: 160). Time may, however, have been taken from non-leisure activities. While Gershuny (2000: 5) argued that the time spent sleeping can be treated as a constant, Taheri (2006) suggested that children and adolescents found time for TV, computer games and use of the internet and mobile phones at the expense of sleep. According to Dutton et al (2009: 5), by early 2009, a third of internet users thought they spent too much time online!

As mentioned in the introduction to this chapter, one of the difficulties with time use studies is the fact that people do more than one thing at once, they multi-task. In the analysis of the *2005 Time Use Survey* (ONS, 2006: 7-8) where possible the purpose was recorded as the primary activity, with the fact of computer use as secondary, so that for online shopping the primary activity would be coded as shopping and computer use the secondary activity. In contrast, Ofcom (2010) simply double-counted so that if someone reports watching TV while sending text messages, then both activities are included. Ofcom (2010: 43) reported that "The TV set, radio set, print, music centers and portable devices (other than mobile phones) tended to be used for activities undertaken on their own." Indeed, more that 80 percent of TV watching and radio listening was undertaken as an activity on its own (Ofcom, 2010: 44). In contrast, computers and mobile phones were used at the same time as other media activity. Kenyon (2008) argued that "virtual mobility, via internet use, loosens the traditionally close links between activity, space and time" and internet increases the number of activities that that are both amenable and accessible for multi-tasking. Kenyon found that multi-tasking added 60 percent to the time reported spent on online activities and argued that undertaking more than one activity at a time is common and can in effect add some 7 hours to the day.

What did people do online? Almost all internet users – 90 percent – use email (ONS, 2010b) and there is some suggestion that email has reduced telephone and face-to-face contact (in the US, Quan-Haase & Wellman, 2002; Boneva et al, 2001; and in the UK, Stoneman, 2008). "Two-fifths of people's time spent on a computer is spent communicating with other people": more for younger people than for older people (Ofcom, 2010: 3, Fig. 3.10).

Stoneman (2008) suggested that, initially at least, internet usage simply facilitates already existing practices but that the impact of the internet will change as

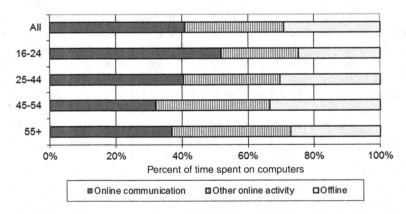

Fig. 3.10 How computers are used, by age, 2010. (Ofcom, 2010: Fig. 1.21. (Based on data from Ofcom, 2010). "Communicating" means using email, social networking, instant messaging and phone (such as Skype))

people become more proficient users, and substitution effects may take time to evolve. Brynin & Kraut (2006: 4 & 6) said that to argue that the new technology only enables people do the same things in new ways is to take a narrow view and that the internet could result in "qualitative changes in daily life" in which people accomplish new goals.

Anderson & Raban (2007: 59) argued that "there is simply not that much slack in most people's lives for major shifts in behavior in the short term". Experience with the internet shows that this is not the case. This is because people are doing things differently. The 2005 *Time Use Survey* suggested that, for example, if computer use as a secondary activity was included in social life, it would increase the average time spent socializing by computer users from 62 to 69 minutes; and for, hobbies and games from 13 minutes to 21 minutes (ONS, 2010a: 47 & 70). By 2010 (ONS, 2010b):

- instead of walking round the shops, people go online: three-quarters of those who had accessed the internet in the last three months of 2010 had looked for information about goods and services;
- instead going to the travel agent, they go online: almost two-thirds of those used travel-related services;
- instead of going to the newsagent or the library, they go online: half downloaded news or magazines;
- instead of going to the bank, they go online: half had used internet banking.

Conclusion

Measuring time use is surprisingly difficult and the data that is collected has to be presented and interpreted very carefully. The average day is very likely never to be experienced by anyone! Nevertheless, it can throw light on the way we live.

The fact that people feel pressed for time is a paradox. We enjoy longer and healthier lives than at any time in history, are spending less time in work and have homes full of time-saving domestic technology. Indeed, the survey data suggests that the spread of time-saving domestic technology might have enabled people to have more leisure in the early years of the twenty-first century (but we need to see if this is a real change or an artefact of the survey). Some people would like to work shorter hours – especially those in senior positions and women trying to combine careers and children – and their volubility may be behind the reported feelings of being 'time-poor'. Yet if Glennie and Thrift are right and people have felt time-poor down the ages, then maybe there is a more fundamental issue here. Thrift (2002) suggests that it may be due to nostalgia for a past when, it is thought, life was simpler and slower. Or maybe it is connected to our human condition, to our mortality?

Time use is not fixed: it does change, and can do so quickly. It changed when TV was introduced and it is changing now due to the internet. Although the internet arrived in the 1990s, it was very different then. Access was slow and in Britain, charged per minute. Only with the arrival of broadband for domestic users in the UK in 2000 (Connected Earth, 2010), providing much greater speeds at a flat rate price, did the internet as known today truly start. By December 2008 95 percent of households in the UK with internet connections had broadband (ONS, 2009e). Broadband enables activities that were not previously possible: Di Gennaro & Dutton (2007) argued that it enabled users to "better integrate the technology into their everyday lives". In my view, the full impact of the internet on our social and domestic life has yet to be seen.

The arrival of the internet has reinvigorated talk about the blurring of work and 'life' by enabling the spread of telework. But teleworking is an elusive concept. Nevertheless, howsoever it is measured, it has probably increased in the UK over the past decade. But if narrowly defined as someone working mainly from home and relying on phone and computer, clearly teleworking remains a minority activity. The twentieth century visions of pervasive teleworking have not materialised.

It is easy to forget that even as the second decade of the twenty-first century starts, there are still many people who are not part of the 'digital world'; in particular, there is a significant minority who have never used the internet. By 2010, while 60 percent were daily internet users, 18 percent had never used it (ONS, 2010b). So while the readers of this book are likely to live in a digital, connected world, something approaching Castell's (2000) *Network Society* or even Toffler's 1970 vision of the future, a small but significant proportion of our neighbours still live as our parents or even grandparents did.

References

Agar, J. (2003) *Constant Touch*, Cambridge: Icon

Anderson, B. & Tracey, K. (2002) 'Digital Living: The Impact (or Otherwise) of the Internet on Everyday British Life' in B Wellman and C. Haythornthwaite, *The Internet in Everyday Life*, pp. 139–63. Oxford: Blackwell.

Anderson, B. & Raban, Y. (2007) The social impact of broadband internet. In Anderson, B., Brynin, M. Gershuny, J. & Raban, Y. eds, *Information and Communication Technologies in Society: E-living in a digital Europe*. London: Routledge, pp.46-61.

BBC (1978) *The People's Activities and Use of Time*. Audience Research Department. London: BBC.

Boneva, B., Kraut, R. & Frohlich, D. (2001) Using E-mail for Personal Relationships: The Difference Gender Makes. *American Behavioral Scientist* 45, pp.530-549.

Bowden, S. & Offer, A. (1994) Household Appliances and the Use of Time: The United States and Britain Since the 1920s. *Economic History Review,* XLVLL, 4, pp.725-748.

Brand, M. (2001) *Historical Revision to Computer Produce Prices*. [Online] Available at: http://www.ons.gov.uk/ons/rel/ppi2/producer-price-index/historical-revisions-to-computer-producer-prices/historical-revisions-to-computer-producer-prices-.pdf

Briscoe, B., Odlyzko, A. & Tilly, B. (2006) Metcalfe's Law is Wrong. *IEEE Spectrum* (July), pp.26-31

Brynin, M. & Kraut, R., 2006. Social Studies of Domestic Information and Communication technologies in Kraut, R, Brynin, M. & Kiesler, S., eds, *Computer, Phones and the Internet*. Oxford: Oxford University Press, pp.3-18.

Castells, M. (2000) *The Rise of the Network Society. Vol I: The Information Age, Economy, Society and Culture*. 2nd ed. USA: Blackwell.

Connected Earth (2010) *History of the Internet: Timeline* [Online] Available at: http://www.connected-earth.com/Learningresources/HistoryoftheInternet/index.htm

Deaton, A. & Muellbauer, J., 1985. *Economics and consumer behaviour*. Cambridge: Cambridge University Press.

Douglas and Isherwood

(1979) *The World of Goods*. London: Routledge.

(1996) *The World of Goods*. London: Routledge.

Di Gennaro, C. & Dutton, W., (2007). Reconfiguring friendships: social relationships and the internet. *Information, Communication & Society*. 10(5), pp.591-618.

Dutton, W. Rogers, E M, Jun, S-H. (1987) Diffusion and Social Impacts of Personal Computers. *Communication Research* vol. 14 no. 2 pp219-250

Dutton, W., Helsper, E. &. Gerber, M. (2009) *The Internet in Britain 2009*. Oxford Internet Institute. Available at: http://www.oii.ox.ac.uk/research/oxis/OxIS2009_Report.pdf [Accessed 1 December 2010].

ECaTT (2000) *Benchmarking progress on new ways of working and new forms of business across Europe*. Available at http://www.ecatt.com/freport/ECaTT-Final-Report.pdf [Accessed 22 October 2010]

Eurofound (European Foundation for the Improvement of Living and Working Conditions) (2009) *Telework in the European Union*. Online http://www.eurofound.europa.eu/docs/eiro/tn0910050s/tn0910050s.pdf [Accessed 29 September 2010]

Felstead, A., Jewson, N. & Walters, S. (2003) *The Changing Place of Work Working* Paper No. 28 [Online] http://www.leeds.ac.uk/esrcfutureofwork/downloads/workingpaperdownloads/fow_paper_28.pdf

Feinstein, C.H. (1972) *National Income, Expenditure and Output of the United Kingdom: 1855-1965*. Cambridge: Cambridge University Press

Fine, G. (1996) *Kitchens: The Culture of Restaurant Work*. Berkeley: University of California Press.

Gallie, D. (2000) The Labour Force. In Halsey, A.H. & Webb, J. eds, *Twentieth Century British Social Trends*. London: Macmillan, pp.281-323.

Gershuny, J. (2000) *Changing Times: Work and Leisure in Postindustrial Society*. Oxford: Oxford University Press.

Gershuny, J. (2002) Mass Media, Leisure and Home IT: A Panel Time-Diary Approach. *IT and Society*. 1(1), Fall, pp.53-66. [Online] Available from: http://www.ITandSociety.org. [Accessed 24 September 2007].

Gershuny, J. (2007) Conclusion: A slow start? In Anderson, B., Brynin, M. Gershuny, J. & Raban, Y. (eds) *Information and Communication Technologies in Society: E-living in a digital Europe*. Routledge. London pp 274-280

Glennie, P. & Thrift, N. (2009) *Shaping the Day: A History of Timekeeping in England and Wales, 1300-1800*. Oxford. Oxford University Press.

Gronau, R. (1977) Leisure, Home Production, and Work - Revised Theory of the Allocation of Time Revisited. *Journal of Political Economy*, 5(6), pp.1099-1123.

Haddon, L. & Brynin M. (2005) The character of telework and the characteristics of teleworkers. *New Technology, Work and Employment* 20:1 pp34-46

Hamill, L. (2003) Time as a Rare Commodity in Home Life. In Harper, R. (ed) *Inside the smart home* pp63-78.London. Springer.

Hamill, L. (2010) *Communications, Travel and Social Networks since 1840: A Study Using Agent-based Models*. PhD thesis. Available from http://www.hamill.co.uk.

Juster, F. T. & Stafford, F. P. (1991) The Allocation of Time: Empirical Findings, Behavioral Models and Problems of Measurement. *Journal of Economic Literature*. Vol XXXIX, pp 471-522

Kaufman-Scarborough, C. (2006) Time Use and the Impact of Technology: Examining workspaces in the home *Time & Society* 15 pp57-80

Kenyon, S. (2008) Internet Use and Time Use: The importance of multitasking. *Time & Society* 17: 283-318

Keynes, J.M. (1931) Economic Possibilities for Our Grandchildren. In *Essays in Persuasion*. London: Macmillan, pp.358-373.

Matthews, R.C.O., Feinstein, C.H. & Odling-Smee, J.C. (1982) *British economic growth, 1856-1973*. Oxford: Clarendon Press.

Morris, E. (2009) *Independent Review of ICT User Skills*. Department for Business, Innovation & Skills. [Online] Available at: http://www.dius.gov.uk/~/media/ 3F79A51589404CFDB62F3DA0DEBA69A1.ashx [Accessed 20 October 2010].

Nansen, B., Arnold, M., Gibbs, M. & Davis, H. (2009) Domestic orchestration : Rhythms in the mediated home. *Time & Society*. 18. pp 181-207

Nie, N. H., Hillygus, D. S. & Erbring, L. (2002) 'Internet Use, Interpersonal Relations, and Sociability', in B Wellman and C. Haythornthwaite (eds) *The Internet in Everyday Life*, pp. 139–63. Oxford: Blackwell

Office for National Statistics (ONS)

(1997) *Living in Britain: Preliminary Results from the 1996 General Household Survey*, London: TSO

(1998) *Social Trends 28: 1998 edition*. London: TSO

(1999) *Family Spending: A Report on the 1998-1999 Family Expenditure Survey*. London: TSO

(2000) *Family Spending: A Report on the 1999-2000 Family Expenditure Survey,* London: TSO

(2002) *Family Spending: A Report on the 2000-2001 Family Expenditure Survey* London: TSO

(2003) *Family Spending: A Report on the 2001-2002 Expenditure and Food Survey* London: TSO

(2004a) *Family Spending: A Report on the 2002-2003 Expenditure and Food Survey* London: TSO

(2004b) *Family Spending: A Report on the 2003-2004 Expenditure and Food Survey* Basingstoke. Palgrave Macmillan.

(2005) *Family Spending: A Report on the 2004-2005 Expenditure and Food Survey* Basingstoke. Palgrave Macmillan.

(2006a) *Time Use Survey 2005* London. HMSO. http://www.ons.gov.uk/ons/rel/lifestyles/time-use/ 2005-edition/time-use-survey-2005--how-we-spend-our-time.pdf

(2006b) *Social Trends 2006*. Basingstoke. Palgrave Macmillan. http://www.ons.gov.uk/rel/ social-trends-rd/social-trends/no--36--2006-edition/social-trends-full-report.pdf

(2007a) *Labour Force Survey Data. Labour Market Statistics Datatset*. http://www.ons.gov.uk [Accessed 4 October 2011]

(2007b) *Family Spending: A Report on the 2005-2006 Expenditure and Food Survey* Basingstoke. Palgrave Macmillan.

(2008a) *Family Spending* Basingstoke. Palgrave Macmillan. (Reports on 2006)

(2008b) *Family Spending A report on the 2007 Expenditure and Food Survey* Basingstoke. Palgrave Macmillan.

(2009) *Internet connectivity*. December 2008. [Online] Available at: http://www.ons.gov.uk/ons/ rel/rdit2/index-of-internet-connectivity/q4-2008/internet-connectivity-q4-2008.pdf

(2010a) *Family Spending: A Report on the 2008 Living Costs and Food Survey* Basingstoke. Palgrave Macmillan.

(2010b) *Internet Access 2010*. August 2010. [Online] Available at: http://www.ons.gov.uk/ons/rel/ rdit2/internet-access---households-and-individuals/2010/stb-internet-access---households- and-individuals--2010.pdf

(2010c) Time series database. http://www.ons.gov.uk/

(2010d) *Labour Force Survey* http://www.ons.gov.uk/

(2010e) *Family Spending: A Report on the 2009 Living Costs and Food Survey* http://www.ons. gov.uk/ons/rel/family-spending/family-spending/2010-edition/family-spending-2010--living-costs-and-food-survey-2009-.pdf

Office of Communications (Ofcom)

(2009) *Report of the Digital Britain Media Literacy Working Group.* 27 March 2009. [Online] Available at: http://stakeholders.ofcom.org.uk/binaries/research/media-literacy/digitalbritain. pdf

(2010a) *The Communications Market 2010.* http://stakeholders.ofcom.org.uk/market-data-research/market-data/communications-market-reports/cmr10/ [Accessed 22 September 2010]

(2010b) *Facts and Figures.* http://media.ofcom.org.uk/facts/ [Accessed 19 October 2010]

Office for Population, Census and Surveys (OPCS) (1995) *Living in Britain: Results from the 1994 General Household Survey,* London. HMSO

Partridge, C. (2005) *Social Change, Time Use and ICTs – A Literature Review,* Chimera Working Paper, 2005-05. Ipswich: University of Essex.

Pratt, J. (1984) http://www.joannepratt.com/

Randall, C. (2010) *e-Society. Social Trends 41.* ONS [Downloaded 11 November 2010] http://www.ons.gov.uk/ons/rel/social-trends-rd/social-trends/social-trends-41/social-trends-41---e-society.pdf

Quan-Haase, A. Wellman, B. (2002) Capitalizing on the Net. In Wellman, B. & Haythornwaite, C., eds, *The Internet in Everyday Life.* Oxford: Blackwell, pp.291-324.

Rogers, E.M., (2003) *Diffusion of Innovations.* 5th ed. New York: Free Press.

Ruiz, Y. & Walling, A. (2005) Home-based working using communication technologies. Office for National Statistics: *Labour Market Trends.* October pp 417-426 Online http://www.ons.gov.uk/ons/rel/lms/labour-market-trends--discontinued-/volume-113--no--10/home-based-working-using-communication-technologies.pdf

Southerton, D. (2006) Analysing the Temporal Organization of Daily Life: Social Constraints, Practices and their Allocation. *Sociology* 40(3) pp 435-454

Stoneman, P. (2008) Exploring Time Use. *Information, Communication & Society.* 11(5), pp. 617-639

Taheri, S. (2006) The Link Between Short Sleep Duration and Obesity: We Should Recommend More Sleep to Prevent Obesity. *Archives of Disease in Childhood,* 91(11), pp.881-884

Tam, H. (2010) Characteristics of the underemployed and the overemployed in the UK. *Economic & Labour Market Review,* 4 (7) pp 8-20.

Tellis, G. J., Stremersch, S. & Yin, E. (2003) The International Takeoff of New Products: The Role of Economics, Culture, and Country Innovativeness. *Marketing Science.* 22(2), pp.188–208.

The Telephone Company (1880) *London Exchange Stations.* April. [Online] Available at: http://www.ancestry.co.uk [Accessed 9 July 2007]

Thompson, E. P. (1967) Time, Work-Discipline and Industrial Capitalism. *Past & Present* 38. pp56-97

Toffler, A. (1970/1972) *Future Shock.* New York: Bantam.

Thrift, N. (1996) *Spatial Formations.* London. Sage.

Thrift, N. (2002) A Hyperactive World. In Johnston, R J Taylor, P J & Watts, M J (eds) *Geographies of Global Change.* Oxford. Blackwell. pp 29-42 [Available on Google Books.]

Urry, J. (2000) *Sociology beyond Societies: Mobilities for the Twenty-first Century.* London: Routledge.

Valente, T. (1995) *Network Models of the Diffusion of Innovations.* Cresskill (NJ): Hampton Press.

Varian, H.R. (2003) *Intermediate Microeconomics.* 6th ed. New York: W.W. Norton & Co.

Wacjman, J. (2008) Life in the fast lane? Towards a sociology of technology and time. *British Journal of Sociology,* Vol 59(1) pp59-77.

Chapter 4
Family Life, Children and the Feminization of Computing

Alladi Venkatesh, Debora Dunkle, and Amanda Wortman

Introduction

With the entry of new technologies into the home, we are witnessing a proliferation of descriptors for the emerging home environment. These include such terms as smart homes (Harper, 2003; Chetty, Sung and Grinter 2007), home automation and devices (Hamill 2006), the networked home (Venkatesh, Kruse and Shih 2003; Little, Sillence and Briggs 2009), the home of the future (Venkatesh et al., 2001), digital living (Anderson and Tracey 2001; Bly et al., 2006), and of course the one offered in this book: the connected home. In general, they all seem to be pointing to the same story: that the modern home in this new media/internet age is undergoing a transformation. Home life as previously understood is changing. Computing and computers are of course central to this. But how and in what ways?

It is in this context that we examine the evolution of computer use at home and its impact on family life. Our focus here is based less on speculation or scenario building and more on empirical, attitudinal data that we have collected over a ten year period. During this time, beginning in 1999, we completed four waves of national surveys of U.S. households (1999, 2003, 2008 and 2010). We present the results of these surveys as a way to summarize the developments during this 10+ year period, highlighting what we think are the salient changes.[1]

The fundamental questions we address in this study are: what is the nature of computer use patterns in families over time?; who are the key players in the family who account for these developments?; and what are the attitudes of members of households to these changes?

To answer these questions we need to pause and remark on the structure of families. It is commonplace to say that this structure is based on membership: legal, biological, and affective (parents, children, companions, lovers, etc.). It is obvious

---

[1] This material is based upon work funded by the U.S. National Science foundation under Grant No. 0121232. Any opinions, findings and conclusions reflected in the material are those of the authors and do not necessarily reflect the views of the National Science Foundation.

A. Venkatesh (✉)
University of California, Irvine, CA, USA

too that the life cycle will affect a family, whether they are younger or older, for example, and all that implies about other activities – schools, work and so on. Gender too is a concern. But one should not forget either that families can be classified as single adult or multimember adult families and they can be with or without children. Granted that this is not an exhaustive list of all the ways that one might categorise families, we want to argue that these characteristics are sufficient to draw enough information from our survey results to arrive at some interesting patterns of computer use over time. More particularly, given these different configurations, our focus is on the following research questions:

- What are the longitudinal computer use patterns in families?
- What are the computer use patterns among families with and without children?
- What are the gender differences in use patterns?
- What are the age differences in use patterns?

Methodology and Research Findings

Study Sample: Data from national surveys of home computer use completed in 1999, 2003, 2008 and 2010 are used in this chapter.[2] The surveys are part of a larger study of personal computer use conducted by researchers at the Center for Research on Information Technology and Organizations (CRITO) located at the University of California, Irvine. These telephone surveys focused only on those households where there was a personal computer in use in the home. The households were selected through random digit dialing. All those within a household who were knowledgeable about the household computer use and were over the age of 18 were eligible. Respondents reported on their own behavior as well as the behavior of other members in the household. They were asked about the use of the home computer, their attitudes regarding the home computer, other electronic devices in the household as well as the contribution of the home computer to the household activities.

In 1999, according to the *US Department of Commerce* (2010), 65% of the US households owned a computer (a desktop or portable) and this increased to 78% by the year 2009. In 1999, of the households with computers, 38% had broadband connection and this increased to almost 90% by 2010.

We present some key results from our on-going study (1999 to 2010) in the following sections. First, we provide a detailed description of computer uses by families during the period of our study. Second, we examine how household computer uses vary between families with children and without children. Third, we examine

---

[2] The 1999 survey was conducted as part of Project NOAH (National Outlook for Automation in the Home); 910 households were interviewed by telephone with a response rate of 36.3%. The 2003 and 2008 surveys were conducted as part of Project POINT (People, Organizations and Information Technology); 1200 telephone interviews were completed for each survey with response rates of 44.3% (2003) and 26.2% (2008). The 2010 survey (also part of Project POINT) sampled both landline and cell phone only households with response rates of 24.1% for the cell phone only sample and 30.7% for the landline sample (landline sample also included cell phone users).

some relevant gender related issues. In the final section we draw some conclusions for future research in this area.

Our results are presented in Tables 4.1 thru 4.6. In Table 4.1 we provide a description of the different roles technology plays based on the perceptions and experiences of survey respondents. Table 4.2 is a summary of the types of uses during the periods of data collection and changing patterns of use over time. Table 4.3 provides a summary of results based on the composition of households (children vs. no children). Table 4.4, which is an elaboration of Table 4.3, provides a summary of results based on the size and composition of households. Table 4.5 presents parental views and concerns about children's use of computers. Table 4.6 is a summary of data focusing on gender based uses of the computer.

The Enabling Mediating and Transforming Nature of Technology

To capture the role of technology, we asked our respondents to indicate how computers have affected their lives. The computer has certainly played a key role as seen from the information gathered from our samples of respondents over the ten year period (Table 4.1). Its transformative role is quite evident from the responses from our subjects. While it has played a vital role in terms of its enabling and mediating functions, a larger number of its impacts are in terms of its transformation role. Our respondents have recorded progressively their agreement over the four periods of data collection on various impact statements. In this summary, for the sake of convenience, we focus primarily on the 2010 column in Table 4.1 but also use other time periods as necessary if data for 2010 is not available.

Table 4.1   The perceived roles of computer use

	Percent agreeing 1999	Percent agreeing 2003	Percent agreeing 2008	Percent agreeing 2010	Role of technology
The computer has saved us time at home	48	51	51	55	Enabling
Computers are difficult to use	16	11	13	--	Enabling
Computers have made it easier to organize family/social events	--	34	33	43	Enabling
Households with a computer are run more efficiently than those without a computer	15	22	--	---	Enabling
Computers in the home take away from family interactions	23	27	30	--	Enabling/ Disabling
The computer has increased the amount of job related work I do at home	43	37	33	--	Mediating
Computers are more useful than in the home	40	39	37	--	Mediating

Table 4.1 (continued)

	Percent agreeing 1999	Percent agreeing 2003	Percent agreeing 2008	Percent agreeing 2010	Role of technology
I have more contact with friends and relatives now that I have email	50	54	48	55	Mediating
It would be difficult to imagine life without a computer at home	44	50	58	61	Transforming
The computer has changed the way we do things at home	40	45	--	52	Transforming
The computer is as essential as any other household appliance	38	51	59	63	Transforming
Having the internet makes me much better informed about the world	47	56	61	66	Transforming
Computers give status to their owners	13	11	--	--	Transforming
Those that are not knowledgeable about computers are falling behind	68	68	68	70	Transforming
Watch less TV as a result of the internet	29	25	23	--	Transforming
The computer has become part of daily routine at home	52	62	63	72	Transforming
The internet helps me look for product information that was not possible before	58	72	72	71	Transforming
The computer has replaced telephone as major communication device	10	16	15	--	Transforming
Reduced our need of daily newspapers	--	--	40	--	Transforming
I do most of my communication with friends using social networking sites	--	--	--	21	Transforming
More productive because we have a computer	--	--	49	48	Transforming
Computer has enabled me to meet new people	--	--	--	22	Transforming

A good percentage (66%) of respondents feel that they are better informed about the world because of the internet. Computers are also seen as contributing significantly to family social life in terms of establishing contact with friends and relatives (55%) and also the use of social networking sites (21%) – which though small, is a recent phenomenon and likely to grow. Certainly there is agreement that those who are not knowledgeable about computers are falling behind (70%). Computers are seen as replacing newspapers as an information source (40% in 2008) – a sign of digital living. A large number (61%) agreed that it would be difficult to imagine life without a computer and a larger number (72%) feel that the computer has become part of the daily routine. Time saving (55%) is also reported because of the computer as well as being more productive (48%). However, very few (15% in 2008) feel that the computer has replaced the telephone which is still the most important tool for voice communication. In this context, it would be interesting to see what role smart phones would play, especially because smart phones have computer like capabilities.

In summary, the transformation is occurring in terms of technological dependence and initiatives, the indispensable nature of computers to conduct family activities and especially in the areas of communication, information, home management and social networking. While these results demonstrate people's attitudes we will now present some actual behaviors as reported by our respondents.

Computer Uses in the Home – Some Longitudinal Trends

In the 1999 survey, the number of types of computer activities queried was 9. By the time of the 2003 survey, the number of activities had jumped to 14, and by 2008 and 2010 it had increased to 16 types of computer activities (see Table 4.2). This increase reflects the advances in technology, user competencies and learning, increased application areas as well as other structural factors over the years. For example, the use of social media (e.g. Facebook, MySpace) did not show up in our 2003 survey but does appear in more recent years. Table 4.2 shows the frequency of computer use for each of the surveyed time periods along with the rate of change for those activities common across the time periods.

Clearly a significant number of activities have shown an increase between 1999 and 2003. The major increases were in the areas of email (22%), news/weather/sports (25%), online shopping (48%), travel (50%), online banking (97%) and health-related information (67%). Job related work (2%) was steady and school related work declined (-20%). (This decline is an artefact of data collection because we did not differentiate between families with children and without children. See Table 4.3.) In fact most major increases occurred during this period in both computer use activities and in usage frequency. The early 2000s were a critical period in technology development. This reflects partly the versatility of the computer, the increasing rise of the internet and the introduction of broadband (wireless) connections over this period. In other words, as the technology became more versatile, the opportunities for different uses increased.

To more fully highlight the growth and changes in use over this 11 year period, we divided the percentage of users for each activity into three categories: top quartile (75% and above), second quartile (50%-74%) and the lower half (49% and below).

In 1999 (the early internet period), only two computer activities were engaged in by a significant number of users: hobbies and entertainment (86%) and email (78%). Activities favored by the second quartile of computer users in 1999 included job related work (71%), news, weather and sports (63%), school related work (59%),

Table 4.2 Household level uses of computer over time

Percent using:	1999	2003	2008	2010	X^2 (p)	Rate of change 1999-2003 (%)	Rate of change 2003-2008 (%)	Rate of change 2008-2010 (%)
Email	77.9	95.0	96.3	98.1	0.00	21.951	1.368	1.869
Job-related work	71.0	72.2	63.4	66.0	0.00	1.690	-12.188	4.101
School-related work	59.1	47.2	45.9	62.6	0.00	-20.135	-2.754	36.383
Online shopping	51.9	76.7	79.7	84.6	0.00	47.784	3.911	6.148
Online banking	30.6	60.2	66.7	76.6	0.00	96.732	10.797	14.843
News, weather and sports	63.5	79.5	76.2	88.6	0.00	25.197	-4.151	16.273
Health-related information	45.8	76.6	82.8	82.6	0.00	67.249	8.094	-0.242
Hobbies, games and entertainment	85.8	87.9	87.4	83.8	0.01	2.448	-0.569	-4.119
Travel and vacation planning	54.8	82.0	85.2	77.6	0.00	49.635	3.902	-8.920
Calendar		38.4	38.5	45.7	0.00		0.260	18.701
Photographs and videos		54.6	75.9	84.3	0.00		39.011	11.067
Instant messaging		52.6	45.4		0.00		-13.688	
Family or personal webpage/website		15.1	24.5		0.00		62.252	
Online networking			44.4	76.1	0.00			71.396
Online phone calls			13.1	25.0	0.00			90.840
Online journals or blog			25.6	43.5	0.00			69.922
Family and household recordkeeping				59.1				

Size of sample by year: 1999=909; 2003=1200; 2008=1199; 2010=1197 and travel and vacation planning (55%). By 2003, 95% of users reported using email and 88% were engaged in hobbies, games and entertainment uses. In addition, joining the top quartile were travel and vacation planning (82%), news, weather and sports (79%), online shopping (77%) and health-related information (77%). Job related work declined, relatively speaking, in terms of its rank. As we get closer to 2008/2010, we notice some significant shifts as well as some consolidation. Email use continues to be the highest (96% and 98%) and hobbies, games and entertainment emerge as a favored use (87% and 84%). Uploading and downloading of photographs and videos increased significantly from 55% in 2003 to 76% in 2008 and 84% in 2010. Although not as meteoric, online banking continued to rise from 60% in 2003 to 67% in 2008 and 77% in 2010. Online networking, little known or used in 2003, demonstrates the speed at which new uses of the home computer have diffused. While in 2008, 44% of the households reported using an online network site such as MySpace, Facebook and LinkedIn, by 2010 a full 76% reported using these sites.

There are other significant trends of note. Job related work across the population stayed steady between 1999 (71%) and 2003 (72%), but declined in 2008 (63%) and continued steady in 2010 at 66%. Thus the prevailing view that the computer's main role is to transfer work from office to the home and is a work tool provided a limited vision of where the technology was going. It is true that school and job for many families formed the cornerstone of why the computer was initially purchased. However, other major shifts in usage reflect the changes in the use of the home computer over time. Initially, the introduction of the computer into the home was more utility driven and with progression of time, it has become an emotional as well as social technology within the family context.

Clearly, the volume of computer use has changed across the eleven year period under study. Some explanations are possible for these trends. First, as stated earlier, computers were seen less as merely work/education tools as was the case in the pre-internet or early internet period. Computers had become versatile, and also thanks to the power and potential of the internet, the usage potential offered greater depth. That is, as technology advanced and other possibilities have emerged the relative positions of work/education related uses took a back seat, as it were. In addition, computer users had become quite comfortable and familiar with computers to the point the technology was no longer alien to the family environment and was considered a necessity and an integral part of the domestic ecology. And, in the case of educational use, schools and educational institutions progressively became better equipped with computers than before and had become highly advanced presumably leading to greater and more sophisticated applications in the school environment.

Another way of looking at this is that at least in the case of educational use, there is indeed not a decline in the domestic front if we take into consideration those families with children compared to those without children. Since our sample includes both families with children and without children, our hypothesis is that educational use declines may not be recorded among families with children. To test this, we divided our sample into families with children and without children. In 1999, 83% of the households with children reported schoolwork use. In 2003, 64%

(vs. 40%) reported schoolwork use which jumped to 78% (vs. 36%) in 2008 and 80% (vs. 51%) in 2010 (see Tables 4.2 and 4.3 for 2010).

Families with Children and Without Children

Household composition is an important factor to consider when looking at the kinds of home computer uses. Table 4.3 breaks down home computer use by households with children versus households without children in 2010. It can be easily seen that for the year 2010, 80% of the families with children used computers for educational purposes compared to only 51% in those families with no children (as reported above). There are also other differences between families with children and without children. For example, differences are also observable in the use of the home computer for hobbies, games and entertainment (92% vs. 79%), for obtaining information regarding news, weather and sports (92% vs. 86%), uploading and downloading of photos and videos (91% vs. 81%), online banking (83% vs. 73%), online networking (87% vs. 70%), family and household recordkeeping (64% vs. 56%) and even online journaling and blogging (48% vs. 41%). Clearly, the presence of children makes a difference.

One other explanation for the differences between families with children and families without children may be that there may be more members per family with children compared to families without children. In other words, it may be more a question of family size than the presence of children in the household. That is, families with more members may also be using computers to a higher degree whether children are present or not.

Table 4.3 Uses of home computer by presence of children in household, 2010

	No. children (N=704)	Children (n=479)	Total (n=1183)	X^2(p)
Email	98.2	97.9	98.1	.775
Job-related work	65.1	68.1	66.3	.299
School-related work	51.0	79.7	62.7	.000
Calendar	43.9	48.6	45.8	.112
Online shopping	84.2	86.3	85.0	.334
Online banking	73.0	82.7	76.9	.000
News, weather and sports	86.3	92.3	88.7	.001
Health-related information	83.5	51.4	82.6	.360
Hobbies, games and entertainment	78.6	92.5	84.3	.000
Travel and vacation planning	79.5	75.8	78.0	.131
Photographs and videos	80.7	90.8	84.8	.000
Online networking	69.6	86.7	76.5	.000
Family and household record keeping	55.7	64.2	59.2	.004
Online phone calls	23.5	27.5	25.1	.116
Online journals or blogs	41.4	47.6	43.9	.036

To address this issue and refine our analysis further, we divided our sample into the following four categories: single adult, two adults with no children, 3 or more adults with no children and households with children (Table 4.4). The idea behind this is to see if the real differences are between small families vs. large families under the realistic assumption that families with children are generally larger than families without children. Thus the differences between households with children and households without children mentioned earlier may cancel out if we take into consideration the size of the household. As can be seen from Table 4.3, households with children still account for differences in some major categories of use - online banking, news, weather and sports, hobbies, games and entertainment, family and household recordkeeping, and, of course, school-related work. However, the 3+ adult households show greater values compared to children households on the following categories: job-related work, calendar, online journals and blogs, and travel and vacation planning. In all these cases, both categories of households (3+ adult households and households with children) score higher values than single person or and in many cases, two adults only households.

Table 4.4 Uses of home computer by size and composition of household, 2010

Percent using	Single-person household (n=149)	2-person adult household (n=337)	3+ adult only household (n=218)	Children household (n=479)	Total (n=1183)	X2(p)
Email	96.6	98.5	99.1	97.9	98.1	.348
Job-related work	57.7	61.4	75.7	68.1	66.3	.000
School-related work	33.6	40.1	79.4	79.7	62.6	.000
Calendar	39.3	38.7	54.6	48.6	45.7	.001
Online shopping	79.2	84.5	87.6	86.3	85.1	.123
Online banking	71.3	73.8	73.1	82.7	77.0	.002
News, weather and sports	84.6	85.6	88.1	92.3	88.6	.007
Health-related information	71.1	88.1	85.3	81.4	82.7	.000
Hobbies, games and entertainment	68.5	78.7	85.1	92.5	84.2	.000
Online networking	59.1	65.7	83.0	86.7	76.6	.000
Photographs and videos	72.5	78.9	89.0	90.8	84.8	.000
Travel and vacation planning	69.1	80.9	84.3	75.8	78.0	.002
Family and household record keeping	51.7	55.7	58.0	64.2	59.1	.017
Online phone calls	20.7	21.0	29.2	27.5	25.1	.047
Online journals or blogs	32.9	34.1	59.1	47.6	44.0	.000

Given the above analysis we reach two major conclusions. First, somewhat obvious, household size matters in terms of level of use. That is, the larger the household size, the greater the number of uses and levels of use. A more important result is that households with children out score any other type of household. *Thus a very important result is that one meaning of computers is that in order to call it a family computer, children's presence does matter.* This may be a typical conclusion that we may reach about some other technologies in the home. For example, one can make a reasonable hypothesis that households with children have a greater use of kitchen appliances (e.g. refrigerators, stoves, dishwasher/dryer), other appliances (e.g. clothes washer/dryer), television (entertainment), digital camera and so on. The implications for technology producers can be quite profound.

Parental Concerns and Issues Regarding Children's Use of Computers

The question of parental concerns and exercize of power and control over children through the construction and operation of rules is an important topic in the family literature (Grieshaber 1997). Such controls are instituted in everyday life settings that include mealtime rituals, educational/recreational activities and other issues concerning personal grooming, attire, language use, leisure time activities and so forth. Thus the context of home computer use may be considered another instance of parental responsibilities and supervision. On the other hand, one may ask the question, are computers qualitatively different? This is also an issue of moral ordering of the households as discussed by Strain (2003).

The context of children's use of computers is a rapidly growing area of research (Livingstone 2009, Subrahmanyam 2000). The question we pose in this section is what are the parental views and concerns regarding the use of computers by their children? (See Table 4.5 for results). Certainly, the computers are viewed as an important educational tool (75%). On a very positive note, a large percentage of parents (75%) feel that children are more knowledgeable about computers than adults. This gives credence to the fact that there has now emerged a computer generation, that is, youngsters who are growing up as users of computing technology and take to it like ducks to water. However, an equal number of our respondents (75%) also express concern about what their children are accessing on the internet. At the same time, only a small percentage (36%) feel that computers make children anti-social, while 32% disagree with this view. Roughly half of the sample (48%) think that their children are spending too much time on the computer. On the other hand, a very small percentage (27%) feel that computers discourage creativity and nearly half the sample (48%) disagree with this statement. In other words, computers are not viewed as inhibiting creative aspects of children's learning.

Parents also pursue some control measures to keep their children in check. For example, 57% of the parents checked to see which websites their children visited. Almost equal numbers of parents (58%) worked along with their children on computers. We have to presume that this is true of families with much younger children rather than teens. Half of the sample limited the amount of time children can be on the internet. Control measures were also extended to school activities. Half of the sample (51%) reported using email to communicate with teachers and half of them (53%) said they go on the school website to check for homework assignments.

Table 4.5   Parental views and controls of children's use of computers

Statements	% Agreement
Computers contribute positively to children's educational experience	75
Children are more knowledgeable about computers than adults	74
Computers make children anti-social	36 (disagree 32%)
Computers discourage creativity	27 (disagree 43%)
Our children are spending too much time on computers	48
We are really concerned about what our children are accessing on the internet	75
Checked to see what websites our children visited	57
Worked on the computer with children	58
Limited the amount of time children can be on the internet	53
(I/We) Used email to communicate with our children's teachers	51
Checked school website about children's homework	52

n=479

The tension between parental concerns and children's mildly irritable reaction to their parents' interference is humorously yet realistically captured in the following "Fox Trots" comics.

Fox Trots classics by Bill Amend. Adapted from FoxTrot © 2000 Bill Amend. Used by permission of Universal Uclick. All rights reserved

To summarize the parental concerns and views, our results show that they range from positive to cautious to negative. Reading between the figures, we might say that most parents view computers as beneficial to the educational experience of their children and their development.

Gender Related Issues – Feminization of Home Computing

Over the years, there have been active debates and issues concerning differences in technology use by females vs. males both at home and at work (Dholakia 2006, Klawe, Whitney and Simard 2009). In fact, some have argued and contested that the word "technology" itself is male oriented because of connotations associated with complex machinery, and technical-rational, non-emotional qualities – in general the meanings attached to "tool" orientation and work-related artefacts (Cockburn 1994). On the other hand, history tells us that women have engaged in industrial and farm labor as well as in operating office equipment and doing production work in factories, textile mills and the like. In addition, in the domestic sphere, there has been research showing that women, because of their domestic roles, have been the main users of many household appliances and gadgets associated with their roles and in fact are more knowledgeable than men when it comes to everyday technologies and artefacts – the implication being that there is no natural division in terms of competencies or predilections between males and females but one based on social roles men or women play. This is not the place to revisit these debates in a major way, but it is important to contextualize our present study.

To provide a deeper understanding of these issues we present some gender-based trends in our study. Our results are summarized in Table 4.6 which is reconstructed from our survey results. To keep it simple, we are presenting 2010 survey results in the table. In order to capture gender differences in usage patterns, we identify situations where differences between males and females show up in our results. We also feel that in order to refine these results, we need to take into account whether these differences show up within age categories. Thus one hypothesis is that since computers are a recent phenomenon, perhaps younger females show different patterns of use compared to older females. Consequently, their uses may be more similar to males and in some cases may even exceed male patterns based on specific contexts of use and relative familiarity. In general, as more women begin to use computers at home, this phenomenon may be described as *feminization* of computing technology at home.

As shown in Table 4.6, here are some highlights. In terms of the overall sample, there are no gender differences in the use of email, online shopping, online banking, games/entertainment, uploading photos and instant messaging. However, there is a tendency towards more male engagement in the following categories: news and sports, pursuing hobbies, job-related work at home, watching a video, calendar, online networking, online journals and blogs, and making phone calls. Conversely, in the overall sample, a higher percentage of females are involved in health-related information, and maintaining a webpage. These results show that males report higher percentage than females in their use patterns. However, if we control for age, different gender-based use patterns emerge. Here are some interesting results:

More females in the age group 18–30 use email. In the educational use of computers, there is no difference between males and females in the 18-30 age group. More females are engaged in uploading photos in the age groups 18-30, 31-45, and 46-60. As far as online journal/blogging is concerned, females and males use it in the same proportion in all age groups under 60 and there are no differences.

To sum up, in the aggregate, a higher percentage of males are involved in nine activities, more females are involved in two activities, and an equal proportion of males and females in six activities. But that is not the correct story. Once we control for age, a higher percentage of younger females are more involved than males in online networking, email, and uploading photographs. In addition, more females are involved in online banking within the 31-45 age group. In other words,

Table 4.6 Gender-age differences in home computer use

Category of use	Actual use	Total sample - all Households(%)	Age differences	Gender differences	Age/Gender differences	Summary: Female domination in general (Female, Same, Male)
Communication	Email	94	None. All ages report high level use.	None. Both genders report high level use.	More females than males in the 18-30 age group (73% to 51%) and more males in 61+ age group (70% to 50%) daily users of email	Female
Information	Health Related	80	Highest use in the 18-30 group (85%) and the lowest in 61+ group (77%)	More females (82%) than males (78%).	More females across all age categories below 60 years and more males in the older category.	Female
Learning	Educational use a) Households with children b) Households without children	a) 78 b) 30	a) 31-45 highest b) 18-30 group represents highest use	Overall more males than females	In the 18-35 group males and females are roughly the same. More males in all other groups.	Same
Household Management	Online shopping	76	The lowest is in the 61+ group (66%).	No gender differences	More males (72%) than females (60%) in the 61+ age group.	Same

Table 4.6 (continued)

Category of use	Actual use	Total sample - all Households(%)	Age differences	Gender differences	Age/Gender differences	Summary: Female domination in general (Female, Same, Male)
Information	Reading News/sports	71	The lowest is in the 61+ group (59%).	More males (77%) than females (66%).	In each age group more males than females. Males highest (82%) in the 31-45 group and next highest (80%) in the 18-30 age group.	Male
Household Management	Online banking	62	The highest (73%) in the 31-45 age group. The lowest is in the 61+ group (45%).	No gender differences	Both females (75%) and males (71%) highest in the 31-45 age group. More males (58%) than females (34%) in the 61+ age category.	Same
Entertainment/ Recreation	Hobbies	66	Highest in the 18-30 group (82%) Followed by 31-45 group (73%)	More males (79%) than females (61%)	Males (83%) and females (81%) roughly equal in 18-30 age group.	Same
Entertainment/ Recreation	Games and entertainment	67	18-30 age group the highest (88%) followed by 31-45 group (74%). Other groups much lower.	No major difference. Males slightly higher	Males generally higher across all age groups.	Male

Table 4.6 (continued)

Category of use	Actual use	Total sample - all Households(%)	Age differences	Gender differences	Age/Gender differences	Summary: Female domination in general (Female, Same, Male)
Work/Employment	Job related work	56	Higher % in age groups between 18 to 60. Fewer in 61+ group (30%)	Overall male (60%) higher than female (52%).	More males across all age groups.	Male
Learning	Educational use a) Households with children b) Households without children	a) 78 b) 30	18-30 group represents highest use	Overall more males (39%) than females (29%)	In the 18-30 group males and females are roughly the same (46%). More males in all other groups.	Same
Social	Upload photos	70	18-30 group the highest (88%)	Slightly more males (72%) than females (69%).	More females than males in all age groups under 60 except in the 61+ group.	Female
Entertainment	Watch a video	47	18-30 age group the highest users (67%) followed by 31-45 group (59%).	Slightly more males (50%) than females (44%)	Across all age groups, more males than females. Highest difference in the 46+ categories.	Male
Household Management	Calendar	34	Younger age groups more likely to use the computer for calendar.	More males (15%) than females (10%)	Highest percentage of users are males in the 31-45 age group (47%).	Male

Table 4.6 (continued)

Category of use	Actual use	Total sample - all Households(%)	Age differences	Gender differences	Age/Gender differences	Summary: Female domination in general (Female, Same, Male)
Social	Online networking	31	18-30 the highest use group (34%)	More males (34%) than females (28%)	More females (72%) than males (67%) in the 18-30 age group. In general, dominated by 18-30 group in both genders.	Female
Communication	Instant messaging	35	18-30 age group the highest users (59%)	No gender differences.	More males in the 18-30 and 31-45 age groups.	Male
Social	Online journal/blog	20	18-30 the highest use group (34%)	More males (23%) than females (18%).	Males and females roughly equal in under 60 age groups, but more males in the 61+ group.	Same
Social	Maintain webpage	20	18-30 group the highest (32%)	Males and females roughly equal (22 to 18%)	More males in the 18-30 and 31-45 age groups.	Male
Social	Phone calls online	11	18-30 group (16%) most likely to use	Males higher (15%) than females (8%)	Across all age groups more males than females.	Male

in order to study the phenomenon of feminization of computing in the home, we need to look at the data not just in the aggregate level, but across age categories. Clearly, the younger females are at the forefront of computerization as compared to older females. The really laggard group, unsurprisingly, is females in the 61+ age segment. In addition, if we examine the broad category of communication, social networking, and some aspects of home management and health related matters, females are ahead.

At the risk of generalization, one might say that there is a growing feminization of computing in the home front based on the differential roles and interests and not technical competencies.

Conclusions

The results clearly reveal the following trends during the ten year period; some to be expected, and some more surprising.

Within the home, our data shows that communication as a whole has increased, with people spending more time on email and social networking. There has been an increase in the amount of information that people seek, whether it be of a general sort related to the specifics of shopping, health or news and sports. Computer use and the internet has also increased the amount of time given to home management, with people spending more time on online banking and record keeping. Computing has also increased the amount of time given to daily leisure; to hobbies and games. Meanwhile, and external to the home, there has been an increase in the amount of community involvement family members engage in, while computing and the internet has decreased the amount of time they give to their job, to work. Perhaps equally surprising has been the slight decrease in the amount of time given to school related activities –homework and such like. More generally, and finally, our research shows that computer use is more prominent with the presence of children: having kids makes it more likely that computers will suffuse domestic life. Our research also shows that with more computing, there is a growing phenomenon of feminization of the domestic sphere. Women are using computing more and more, certainly more than males within the home – even though males are themselves using computing more. Women use computing not only to undertake the responsibilities of being in touch and being sociable, but also to undertake more of the administrative tasks of the domestic sphere. As they do so, so the home is being feminised through computing.

References

Anderson, Ben and Karina Tracey (2001), "Digital Living The Impact (or Otherwise) of the Internet on Everyday Life," *American Behavioral Scientist*, 45(3): 456-475.

Bly, Sara, Bill Schilit, David W. McDonald, Barbara Rosario, and Ylian Saint-Hilaire (2006), "Broken expectations in the digital home," in CHI '06 extended abstracts on Human factors in computing systems (CHI '06). New York, NY: ACM. 568-573.

Chetty, Marshini., Ja-Young Sung, and Rebecca E. Grinter (2007), "How smart homes learn: the evolution of the networked home and household," in *Proceedings of the 9th international conference on Ubiquitous computing (UbiComp _07)*. Berlin, Heidelberg: Springer-Verlag, 127-144.

Cockburn, Cynthia (1994), "Male Dominance and Technological Change." in Heather Clarke, John Candle and Jim Barry, *Organizations and Identities*, Thompson Publishers, 197-203.

Dholakia, Ruby (2006), "Gender and IT in the Household: Evolving Patterns of Internet Use in the United States," *The Information Society*, 22(4): 231-240.

Grieshaber, Susan (1997), "Mealtime Rituals: power and resistance in the construction of mealtime rules," *The British Journal Of Sociology*, 48(4): 649-666.

Hamill, Lynne (2006), "Controlling Smart Devices in the Home," *The Information Society*, 22(4): 241-249.

Harper, Richard (2000), Domestic Design: An Introduction to the Research Issues Surrounding the Development and Design of Interactive Technologies in the Home," *Journal of Personal Technologies, Special Issue on Domestic Computing*, 4(1): 1-6.

Harper, Richard (ed.) (2003) *Inside the Smart Home*, London: Springer-Verlag.

Hoffman, Donna, Tomas Novak and Alladi Venkatesh (2004), "Has The Internet Become Indispensable?: Empirical Findings and Model Development," *Communications of the ACM*, 47(7): 37-44.

Klawe, Maria, Telley Whitney, and Caroline Simard (2009), "Women in Computing – Take 2," *Communications of the ACM*, 52(2): 68-76.

Little, Linda., Elizabeth Sillence, and Pam Briggs (2009), "Ubiquitous systems and the family: thoughts about the networked home," in *Proceedings of the 5th Symposium on Usable Privacy and Security (SOUPS _09)*. New York, USA: ACM, 6-9.

Livingstone, Sonia (2009), *Children and the Internet*, Cambridge: Polity Press.

Nippert-Eng, Christina (1997), *Home and Work*, Chicago: University of Chicago Press.

Shklovski, Irina., Robert E. Kraut, Jonathon N. Cummings (2006), "Routine patterns of internet use & psychological well-being: coping with a residential move", in *Proceedings of CHI_2006*, 969-978.

Strain, John D. (2003), "Households as Morally Ordered Communities: Explorations in the Dynamics of Domestic Life," in Harper, Richard (ed.) (2003) *Inside the Smart Home*, London: Springer Verlag, 41-59.

Subrahmanyam, Kaveri (2000). "The Impact of Home Computer Use on Children's Activities and Development. The Future of Children." *Children and Computer Technology*. 10(2): 123-144.

US Department of Commerce (2010), *"Digital Nation: 21st Century America's Progress Toward Universal Broadband Internet Access"*.

Venkatesh, Alladi., Erik Kruse and Eric Shih, (2003) "The networked home: an analysis of current development and future trends," *Cognition, Technology & Work*, 5(1): 23-32.

Vitalari, Nicholas., Alladi Venkatesh and Kjell Gronhaug (1985), "Computing in the Home: Shifts in the Time Allocation Patterns of Household," *Communications of the ACM*, 28(5): 512-522.

Venkatesh, Alladi., Stolzoff, Norman Stolzoff, Eric Shih and Sanjoy Mazumdar, (2001) "The Home of the Future: An Ethnographic Study of New Information Technologies in the Home," *Advances in Consumer Research*, 28(1): 88-97.

Part II
Experiencing the Connected Home

Chapter 5
The Web, the Home and the Search Engine

Stephen Robertson

Introduction

When, in Eric Hobsbawm's account, the 'short 20th century' ended with the fall of the iron curtain in 1991 (Hobsbawm 1994), the revolution in information and communication technologies was just getting into its stride. On the back of such nineteenth century inventions as photography, typewriters, telephones, telegraph, radio, recorded sound, and the punched-card sorting machine, as well as popular publishing, the spread of universal education and services such as public libraries and the postal system, the first half of the twentieth century saw a huge expansion of our information horizons. Broadcast radio, film and television became sources of information available to everyone, in addition to newspapers, magazines, and cheaply produced books. For person-to-person communication, the rapidly-expanding telephone system (increasingly based on automatic exchanges) added to the postal service which had reached its apogee around the turn of the century. In business, large scale data processing based on punched cards was making inroads into previously clerical domains. And in the Second World War, the demands of the code-cracking community pushed onwards towards the computer.

At mid-century, the digital computer began its vast infiltration of our lives. At first limited to those domains where the punched card already held sway, and to a few arcane scientific endeavours (such as predicting the weather), it gradually found other niches. The symbiosis with typewriting was so complete that the electronic descendant of the old QWERTY keyboard, designed in the late nineteenth century on the basis of severe mechanical constraints, was simply absorbed to become the main method for humans to instruct machines. By 1991 the 'computer on every desk' was beginning to look plausible, and a computer in every home was not far behind; computer-like devices were being hidden away in many other gadgets. But more importantly, it had long been found useful to allow computers to talk to each other directly (rather than through the medium of human beings). The tentacles of

S. Robertson (✉)
Microsoft Research, Cambridge, UK

R. Harper (ed.), *The Connected Home: The Future of Domestic Life*,
DOI 10.1007/978-0-85729-476-0_5, © Springer-Verlag London 2011

the networks were spreading everywhere, and the reification of the global internet as the World Wide Web was just getting off the ground.

The last twenty years have seen the digital world (no longer just computers) expand to take over sound recording and many other sound processing tasks, image recording (photography) and many other image processing tasks, as well as all sorts of textual objects. Not only does a mobile phone contain a computer of sorts, the entire mobile world is inconceivable without computers and digital networks. And although many of us still buy and use paper information resources (books, newspapers, maps, invoices, receipts, scrap paper for notes to ourselves and others), all these are beginning to look increasingly archaic. A year, ten years? Yes, many of them will survive that long. A hundred? It seems unlikely.

Against this background, I would like to explore one particular aspect: the seeking and finding of information, by citizens in their everyday home lives.

Looking for Information

Every day, we look for information. The communication-rich world in which we live offers us a thousand ways of receiving information, as well as transmitting it for others to receive. To simplify to a spectrum by choosing one variable that applies to the reception stage, we might receive purely passively, or actively seek out, or function at any point in between. If I read a magazine which deals with my favorite hobby, I am opening my receptors to a variety of information within a closely-defined domain. If I listen to the conversation from the next table at a restaurant, I am not pre-defining the domain in any way (at least in the sense of subject), though I am restricted to a very specific social situation involving specific actors. If I look up someone in my contacts list, I am probably anticipating almost exactly what I will find (a telephone number or an email address – I know exactly what they look like). If I allow myself to read the advertisements opposite me on the Tube, the domain is constrained only by the fact that someone has paid to place a message in that space – I really do not know what to expect, except perhaps in a statistical sense. If I have something in mind that I wish to find, I would not in general look there. On the other hand, I might well scan my hobby magazine with the aim of picking up fairly specific ideas and information.

In this chapter, I will be focusing on the active end of this spectrum. That is, I am not concerned with the activity of looking at the advertisements on the Tube, or at a television screen, simply in the hope of being entertained. But as soon as we begin to direct our attention, to choose what to receive on the basis of some (vague or specific) idea of what we want to find, together with some (vague or specific) notion that what we want probably exists in the outside world, then we are moving into the realm of this chapter. In the world in 2012, among the many ways of seeking information, one form of device has achieved an extraordinary pride of place as a natural starting point: the *web search engine*.

This chapter is about how search engines have infiltrated our lives. It starts with some history. Search engines did not spring fully formed out of nothing with the invention of the Web; as so often with technology, they evolved from pre-existing kinds of systems. But again as so often, the course of evolution took some unexpected twists – unanticipated, that is, by the people who thought of themselves as agents of that evolution.

The Library

Let's start with a thought-experiment. Think of the last time you used Google, or whichever is your favorite search engine, and obtained some information as a result of using it. Now think what would have happened twenty, thirty, fifty years ago. How would you have gone about finding that same information then?

Of course, I don't know what particular information you had in mind, and a variety of answers might be appropriate. However, if you play this game a few times, one source of information that you are likely to think of is your local library. In Neil Stevenson's novel *Zodiac*, published in 1988, the protagonist ST (a sort of eco-Sam Spade) is a very sophisticated seeker of information. One of his best sources is a librarian called Esmerelda, whose ability to locate relevant things in the library's archive of news material and elsewhere proves crucial to many of ST's cases. ST even thinks in terms of traditional library subject headings when he is commenting on what she does for him. What's surprising about this description is that only a few years later, a similar character would surely have found similar material for a similar purpose via a search engine, using a few well-chosen words.

The library is where this history begins. Libraries have existed for several millennia; they collect information from the world, and organise it in such a way as to make it accessible to people. All sorts of organisational tools and methods have been used, some due to the librarians themselves (catalogues and classification schemes), and some coming from further back in the chain, the publishers and authors (indexes and other forms of internal organisation). A librarian might be expected to direct an information seeker to an appropriate level of tool – for example, a question about a historical event might be best answered by a general reference work or an historical treatise, depending on the level of expertise and sophistication of the seeker.

One form of tool, developed specifically for the sciences, was the abstracts journal, such as Chemical Abstracts. This was a periodical containing abstracts (summaries) of all the scientific articles published in the subject in the previous month, organised under specific headings in a specialised classification scheme, and also indexed in considerable detail. Such a tool demanded some skills, first in its preparation and construction and then in its use in information seeking. Librarians and subject-knowledgeable information specialists developed those skills.

In my youth, library catalogues were usually on cards, and indexes were usually printed in books. But in the second half of the twentieth century, both tools were obvious candidates for the gathering computer revolution. Over several decades, beginning in about 1960, paper-based operations were replaced by computer-based ones. Chemical Abstracts is now a number of different databases hosting a number of different services, all computer-based. The print version ceased production on 1st January 2010.

Online Searching

At first, the searching of a database of scientific abstracts was a tortuous process. In the late 1960s, a medical researcher could search Index Medicus (database of medical research papers) by sending off a request to the National Library of Medicine in the US, by post – that is, by what has become known as snail mail. The search would be formulated by an expert in a special query language, coded on punched cards, and run overnight, and the resulting printout returned to the user by post.

Through the seventies and eighties, it slowly became possible for a user to search such databases online, on a computer terminal of some kind. But formulating queries was still a skill, and searching was often done with the help of a librarian. Around the same time, online library catalogues began to emerge. These catalogues would support the traditional library catalogue function of identifying a particular book held by the library (so-called 'known-item' search), with only very limited support for subject or topical search (the main function of the scientific abstracts systems).

Also at the same time, networks were developing and spreading. So even if the database you wanted to search was on a computer in a library the other side of the world, it might be possible to hook up your terminal to it via the network. By the late eighties, it was possible to search a large number of library catalogues and scientific and business abstracts databases in this fashion. However, it's worth noting a number of limitations, which might not be obvious from the vantage point of today.

1. Cost: The abstracts databases (if not the library catalogues) were typically very expensive to search. It was not something you would do on a whim. Long-distance network access, too, was expensive, until the internet became accessible to everyone.
2. Separation: Each database had its own interface, maybe a little different or maybe very different from the previous one. Each one had to be searched separately, using knowledge of its idiosyncrasies.
3. Query language: Known-item searches might involve filling in a form (Author, Title, Date etc.). Subject searches would probably involve a complex query language.
4. Output: The result of a subject search would probably be an undifferentiated set of items, of arbitrary size. So if you formulated your query fairly loosely, it would result in a list of thousands of items, with no ranking or suggestion of where to start. If you formulated just slightly too tightly, the resulting set would be empty.

On this last point, while systems which ranked the most likely item first had been studied experimentally since the 1960s, the idea of ranking did not begin to penetrate real live systems until the very late eighties.

Words

The world of online searching began a trend which came as a surprise to the trained librarians. Most traditional library approaches to subject or topical searching start with a formalised scheme of classification codes, subject headings, or phrases from a codified indexing language. Each item has to be allocated by a librarian to one or more such formal descriptors. Then at search time, the searcher chooses which of these descriptors to look under. But as online searching of abstracts databases developed, it was found both feasible and moderately effective to rely on the words of the abstracts. If every word of every title and abstract is indexed, and the system provides a good way to search on combinations of words, the formal scheme and the effort of allocation are no longer strictly necessary. Already in the early 1970s, some such databases began to appear, although there was something of an ideological gulf between the proponents of word-based searching and the more traditional librarians. Word-based searching is commonly, somewhat pejoratively, referred to as the 'bag-of-words' approach.

This notion of searching on words in documents goes along with the idea of ranking the results. Different words differ in importance, both in documents and in queries, and it makes sense for the system to try to assess that importance and therefore the likelihood that a specific document is an appropriate response to a query. If many documents match the query to some degree, the system should guide the user towards the most likely items first.

A Research Field

As it happens, the notions of searching on words and ranking the results had been the subject of research since the 1960s. Search as a field of scientific research has a long history. The field was named *information storage and retrieval*, subsequently abbreviated to *information retrieval*, by one of the pioneers in the 1950s, and acquired a strong experimental tradition in the sixties. Word search and ranking continue to generate interesting theoretical and experimental work to this day. In fact a major international initiative to advance the state of the art, known as TREC, the Text Retrieval Conference (Voorhees & Harman 2005), began in 1991 with significant US government support, and continues to this day.

A basic assumption of the TREC initiative was and is that many information resources becoming available in the world would not be curated by librarians, nor prepared as coherent databases with built-in provision for searching by publishers, but would rather come in the form of chunks of free-form text. The archetypes for such material are news collections (the texts of news articles derived from newspapers or from newswire services) and legislative material; but in fact some of the interest and funding came from the intelligence-gathering community, which was and is concerned with searching every kind of formal or informal document, including private communications of all sorts. In retrospect, and in particular in the light of the anarchic nature of Web publishing today, this is a very apposite assumption.

In 1991, of course, the World Wide Web was only just beginning. The notion of a Web search engine did not yet exist, though people were beginning to address the question of how to locate sources on the (then) internet. The basic hyperlink notion with which the Web started is itself a powerful device for finding stuff, but works only if you have a good starting point for your search. The scene was set.

Early Web Search

Over the first half of the 1990s, as the Web itself began its meteoric expansion, tools to locate resources on the Web also started to appear. Not all were based on word indexing – for example Gopher (essentially a pre-Web technology) worked with filenames only. A little later Yahoo! used a more traditional librarian approach, having editors assign webpages to categories.

The idea of word indexing of the Web required another technology to be developed first: the crawler. This is a program which uses the hyperlink structure of the Web first: from a set of starting pages, each page is downloaded and analyzed, embedded hyperlinks are identified, and then followed to obtain new pages.

Given a crawler, the found pages can also be indexed, using the word-indexing methods by now well-established in the information retrieval field. From the same field, search systems can be built to search these indexes. All of these components began to be used together in about 1994, although it took a little longer for web search engines to attempt to index *every* word on *every* webpage they could find. Currently, the big search engines mostly do index every word on a page, but not every page, because they have huge lists of pages that they have not yet visited. These lists are prioritised according to some measure of how useful the page is likely to be, but many low-priority pages never do get visited.

One can argue that the more words you have to describe a page, the better (at least, this can be argued provided that you have a really good mechanism for ranking the better pages more highly). One source of words to describe the page, other than the content of the page itself, is the relevant text from other pages which link to it. Each hyperlink has a piece of text, known as anchor text, which in some way describes the page it points to, known as the landing page. Anchor text is a source of words which in some way describe the landing page – sometimes a sort of summary or heading for it – and therefore may be used to index it. It turns out to be an extremely good source for web search purposes.

By the time Google came to dominance at about the turn of the millennium, these principles were well established (Croft Metzler & Strohman 2010). Currently the big search engines all do something similar, but with many tweaks and bells and whistles. At some level, the model used by all is the old bag-of-words model, although it has now reached a level of sophistication unguessed at by the originators of word indexing. In part, this sophistication comes from a process of adaptation, to which I return below.

The Uses of Web Search

The historical origins of the web search engines, sketched above, give little indication of the explosion of uses to which they have been put, and in particular, the uses to which home users – citizens in their everyday lives – put them. Already in the late 1990s, researchers began studying search engine use, and reporting results which sometimes startled them and their colleagues. I well remember being startled myself to learn how many searches were being made for celebrities such as Britney Spears, or had an explicit or implicit sexual connotation. Although these studies start from the actual queries – *what* words people search on – they can also be quite revealing about some level of intent – the *why* of search.

The idea of search which has dominated information retrieval research for most of its life, and in particular the model which the early web search engines borrowed from the abstracts databases, is what might be described as *subject* or *topical* search. That is, there is an assumption that the user is looking for documents *about* something, or documents which contain or convey certain information, or documents which answer specific questions. This may be contrasted with the *known item* model on which much library catalogue search is based, where the user is trying to establish whether or not the library contains a specific book that she knows to exist.

What emerges very quickly from an examination of search engine use is that these two represent only a part of the wide range of uses to which search engines are commonly put. Both these purposes are well represented among search engine users; but in addition, there are both fuzzy areas between these two poles, and also other rather different kinds of purposes. There is a three-way distinction between search types which goes some way towards a more comprehensive view (Broder 2002):

1. Informational: roughly the subject or topical query described above;
2. Navigational: trying to locate a page that you know or think or expect to exist (for example, the home page of a person or company; or a tax-return form);
3. Transactional: trying to *do* something, such as order a service or product from a supplier, or download a program or a piece of music or a movie.

Within these classes, and in the spaces between them, many variations are possible.

This variety itself came as something of a surprise to many information retrieval researchers. To take the known-item extreme: if I have visited a page before, possibly many times, I *might* remember its URL, and type it directly into the address bar. Or I *might* have saved a bookmark for it, so that I can click on my Favorites list to get back to it. But URLs are hard to remember, and bookmarking requires a conscious act at a time when I am thinking about something else. It is very likely much easier to do a search on a search engine. It may indeed be much easier to remember the one- or two-word search that will get me there than to remember the URL or even to find it in my Favorites list.

So this is exactly what many people do. For many real users, the URL is gobbledegook, and Favorites are a hassle, and why bother with either when the search-engine route is so much easier. As a result, search engines see a huge number of navigational queries, often repeated many times by the same or different users.

Indeed, for many users, there is little or no distinction between the browser and the search engine. If when I open the browser it goes straight to my home page, which is one or other form of a search engine front page, then I have no need to make a distinction. For many non-technical users, such a distinction would actually get in the way of understanding. The browser+searchengine is simply the single device that allows them (with luck at least) to get where they want to go.

Web Search Engines in Context

So far, I have talked about search engines as a one-way process: they were invented, developed, produced, and offered to the users of the Web. But the interactions between the various parties involved in the Web in one way or another have been complex, and the developing notion of a Web search engine has been very much influenced by, as well as influencing, the rest of the Web world, including its users. These interactions deserve much deeper analysis.

In the rest of this chapter, I will focus on some of the interactions. These come into three categories:

1. The business model of the Web search engines: advertising.
2. Efforts on the part of website owners to get exposure: search engine optimization.
3. Direct responses of the search engine owners to users and usage.

Advertising

Web search engines are a very profitable business, and they make their profits from advertising. The model on which most engines work is as follows: given a query from a user, serve up some relevant advertisements as well as the regular results of the search. (These regular results, coming from the search engine's own crawl of the web and the resulting index, are commonly referred to as the 'organic' search results.) (Wikipedia, *Search Advertising*).

A much exercised debate in the search engine community is the relationship between organic results and ads. Generally, the big search engines try to maintain a strong distinction, to make it clear which are the paid-for ads – though depending on the search, these may be given more or less prominence. Thus if the user's intention seems to be some form of shopping, to find a supplier for some product, then ads for this product might reasonably be regarded as good candidates for the user.

In an extreme, a search engine might make no distinction, simply promoting in the ranking paid-for entries. However, this is commonly regarded as underhand, and search engines seem to lose credibility by doing this – and the business model clearly requires substantial numbers of users who trust the search engine enough to make use of it. Hence the usual distinctions (position on the page, color, style, and/or direct label such as 'sponsored site').

The detail of the business model, and the mechanisms provided by the search engines for advertisers to place ads, are increasingly complex, and not directly relevant to the present discussion. However, some aspects are worth extracting and generalising (with a complete disregard for detail!).

First, the usual trigger for payment is clickthrough. That is, the advertiser does not pay on submitting his ad; he pays when a user clicks on it. (How much he pays depends on an auction process, whose details are not needed here.) This provides a strong incentive for the search engines to serve up relevant advertisements, as well as relevant organic results. In fact, advertising through a search engine is one of the most focused forms of advertising available to many organisations today. An ad is shown only to those people who issue particular queries.

Second, many users of the Web and of search engines are in fact undertaking tasks to which ads may be relevant. A great deal of shopping, and/or preparatory work for shopping, is done via the web.

Third, despite both the above, only a small proportion of users do actually click on ads. As in so many other domains of advertising, the business model relies on having a large number of users, only a very few of whom will respond directly to any particular ad.

Fourth, in contrast again, there is evidence that the credibility of the search engine is affected by the relevance of the ads. Many users do look at the ads, and are less likely to trust the rest of the results if the ads are not relevant (Buscher, Dumais & Cutrell 2010).

Web search engines ride a somewhat tricky line. On the one hand they are completely dependent for their existence on advertisers and advertising. On the other, they have to impress users with their impartiality – they are also completely dependent on maintaining a vast number of satisfied users.

Search Engine Optimization

As the author/owner of a website, you probably would like many people to visit it. Whether it represents your CV, a hobby, a business, a charity; whether it is purely informational or can be used to order goods or services; whether it is very specialist or of interest to a wide range of people – in all these cases, it was almost certainly created with a view to people seeing it. And it is well known that the single most important route for users to reach any of the billions of pages on the web is the search engine.

It therefore follows that it matters very much to the website owner how his site is indexed by the search engines, and for what queries it is likely to get both retrieved and ranked near the top. (It is also known that most users, most of the time, look no further than the top few ranked items when they search – it matters very little what is at rank eleven, and not a jot what is at rank 101.) So savvy website owners often try quite hard to ensure that their sites are well represented by the search engines. This process requires some skills, akin to but a little different from those of the librarians or information specialists discussed earlier. This requirement has spawned an entire industry, the SEOs or search engine optimizers. Quite unlike the search engine industry itself (megalithic, with a small number of large players) SEOs form a cottage industry comprised of a large number of individuals or small organisations. The most obvious client group for this industry are businesses whose web presence may be crucial to their survival, but at least some of the SEO ideas are pervasive and even influence home users, in ways which I will explore a little further below.

The motives for web presence in general, and therefore for search engine optimization in particular, might range from the most lofty (I am trying to provide authoritative information on this medical condition) to the most base (I am trying to sell you pictures of nude underage girls). The tactics used have a similar range, from making sure the website describes itself well, containing text which is appropriate in quantity and quality, to what is commonly described as spam. In general the search engine providers encourage some level of optimization activity, because it helps them present good results, but fight against spam, which has the opposite effect.

Most people are familiar with spam email. There are all sorts of forms of spam website. Because hyperlinks are so important to search engines, one common form of spam is known as link spam. If you can arrange for many other pages on the web to link to your own page, the chances of your page being returned for a search are greatly increased. This can of course be legitimate linking from related sites, but there exist many sites whose sole purpose is to provide many links to spam pages. Another form, term spam, is to fill your page with the kinds of words or phrases people commonly search on, perhaps with no regard at all for their relevance in a content sense.

The war between the spammers and the search engines is a continuing one, a sort of guns-and-armor-plating contest. The search engines try very hard to detect and avoid spam, and the spammers discover new techniques to circumvent the defences of the search engines. Nor is the problem likely to disappear – the spammers have a lot at stake, as well as the search engines.

Usage and Response

The search engine industry inhabits a marketplace, and must of necessity pay close attention to the needs and requirements of its users. Over the period of the industry's existence, the engines have been adapted in many ways to this user context. An important feature of this adaptation relates to the mix of kinds of user, as well as of kinds of material and information available on the web. In particular, as the Web itself has expanded from serving mainly academic purposes, into a general-purpose source of all varieties of informational resource for all varieties of citizen, and as the search engines have consolidated their role as the main portal to this general-purpose source, the needs, requirements and searching habits of home users have played a huge role in this adaptation.

Search engines (that is, the organisations that run search engines) adapt to their users in all sorts of ways. One is as follows: every so often, the queries received by the engine over a period will be sampled, and the results of each search carefully examined. Individual pages will be assessed as to their relevance to the query (or to what might have been the intent of the user in issuing this query). This data will be used to evaluate possible changes to the system; a modification which generally improves the result ranking by pushing up the good stuff is likely to be accepted (modifications are being tried out all the time, possibly affecting any component of the system at any stage). So good modifications are retained, and over a period the system evolves to be more effective. The same data may be used in a more direct way, to train some part of the system in a machine learning fashion. The component which ranks the results may be trained in this way, to promote good results nearer the top or the ranking.

This method of adaptation depends to some extent on the assessors being able to guess the possible intent of a user in issuing a query – which may indeed be quite obvious, but might be more subtle. But there is another piece of evidence which helps to get around the problem of interpretation: clickthrough (that is, what the user clicks on, on each search results page) is recorded. For some users, search engines even have access to extended information, such as sequences of queries issued by the same user, or the time spent on a page (did the user return immediately to the search page?), or where she went next. Such data can be used in various ways by the search engine.

At the simplest level, if the same query is seen many times from different users, and almost all users make just one clickthrough, all on the same link, then it is very clear that this link ought to be ranked first for this query, if that is not already the case. Thus if it is apparent from the clickthrough evidence that 90% of the users who type the query 'amazon' are interested in the bookseller (as opposed, say, to the river, or the female warriors of classical mythology), then probably the link to the bookseller should come first. This may be learnt by the system in a number of ways, including purely automatic ones – which may not require any human being to notice the evidence or take action on it. In other words, some forms of adaptation are programmed into the search engines.

On another level, the same evidence also supports the observation that many queries are navigational or transactional rather than informational – these same users do not want to read *about* Amazon, but to go to the Amazon site, probably for shopping purposes. Such evidence informs the judgements of the assessors mentioned above, both in relation to the specific queries to which the evidence relates and in their interpretations of other queries for which there may be less evidence. It also informs the design of search engines in other ways: for example, knowing that many queries occur in a shopping-related context affects the ways in which advertisements may be presented, as discussed above.

In between, much may be learnt much about the kinds of things people are interested in searching on and the usage of language in searching. Many queries are or contain the names of people – often celebrities or people involved in entertainment. Many other queries are about entertainment or leisure activities of all kinds. Discovering a restaurant (or finding the phone number of a restaurant you know about), finding out what's on in any location in any one of a huge number of categories, booking tickets for the same, finding how to get somewhere, a recipe, the weather forecast, the state of the traffic, opening hours, finding and booking holidays, and so on and so forth – all these are tasks for which we expect help from a search engine. If this list is compared with the kinds of search task that were in the minds of the original search engine designers, and arose from the usage of library-type searching methods, it is very clear how far the world has moved.

How We Present Ourselves

As I have indicated, the SEO industry serves (on the whole) business users of the web. But at some level the notion of presenting ourselves as individuals has been influenced by the same ideas.

If I have a Facebook entry, I compose a profile of myself for it. It may be more or less detailed, more or less descriptive, more or less accurate; but what it consists of is words (and maybe a photograph). In the back of my mind, I am more-or-less conscious of the fact that other people may want to find me, and that in order to do that they will have to use either the links from other people's pages, or the words. (Even if they know me, and know that I have a beard, there is as yet no known way of searching for photographs of people with beards.) So I know that the words matter for this purpose.

The words do not necessarily have to be descriptive in the usual sense. The name of the school I went to might be supplemented by the name of some secret society, or some code or catchphrase, that only my immediate friends at that school would recognise. Word-based search engines are at some level purely superficial – they care not a jot for meaning or sense. And we, the citizens, have not only got used to them, we have learnt to think like them.

Googling

Many commentators have noted how search engines have infiltrated our lives, in so many ways – the coining of the verb 'to google' is just one of many examples. The concurrent adaptation of search engines to the population of users of the web, and of these users to search engines as the single most important starting point for general information seeking, over a decade and a half, has formed a positive feedback loop with extraordinarily far-reaching effects. In the process, the library and other such resources seem to have been left far behind.

To over-generalise grotesquely, we (citizens all) have come to believe not only that everything (the entire gamut of information resources in the world) is available on the web, but that we can all find it, any particular thing we need, via a two- or three-word query typed into a box. To many people born after about 1993 (sometimes known as the Google generation, CIBER 2008), this view of the information world is the only one they have ever known, and they will have been introduced to it at home before encountering it in any formal educational context. Even when, as some of them filter into higher education and academic research, they find it necessary to use more formal, librarian-curated databases of research papers and other resources, they will and do carry with them assumptions about search derived from the use of search engines in the home and elsewhere.

In James Blish's novel *A Life for the Stars*, published in 1962 but set in the far future, the protagonist Chris has occasion to interrogate the Librarian of the city of New York about some matters of history and mythology. The Librarian is one of the City Fathers, who/which are machines. Chris asks a question, the sort of question one might ask a human being, rather than choosing a subject heading in a traditional library catalogue or index, or issuing a two-word query to a web search engine. The Librarian nevertheless chooses a traditional-looking subject heading and constructs/reads an answer to the question, from its Wikipedia-like store of the sum of human knowledge. Then: '...the Librarian, which spent its entire mechanical life substituting free association for thinking, had a related subject it would talk about if he liked...' – and this turns out to be exactly the answer to the question he hadn't explicitly asked. Actually, that is a very good description of what web search engines do: give them some words and they will freely associate. Commercial pressures and adaptation have brought the art of free association with bags of words to a high point of utility, and to a central role in our lives as citizens, that are nothing short of astonishing.

References

Blish, James: *A Life for the Stars* (part of the *Cities in Flight* series). 1962.
Broder, Andrei: *A Taxonomy of Web Search*. SIGIR Forum, Fall 2002, Volume 36 Number 2 (http://www.sigir.org/forum/F2002/broder.pdf).
Buscher, Georg; Dumais, Susan; Cutrell, Edward: *The good, the bad, and the random: an eye-tracking study of ad quality in web search*, SIGIR 2010 (http://portal.acm.org/citation.cfm?doid=1835449.1835459).
CIBER: *Information behaviour of the researcher of the future*. CIBER briefing paper, University College London 2008 (http://www.ucl.ac.uk/infostudies/research/ciber/GG2.pdf).
Croft, W Bruce; Metzler, Donald; Strohman, Trevor: *Search Engines – Information Retrieval in Practice*. Addison Wesley 2010.
Hobsbawm, Eric: *The Age of Extremes: The Short Twentieth Century, 1914-1991*. Michael Joseph 1994.
Stevenson, Neil: *Zodiac*. Atlantic Monthly Press 1988.
Voorhees, Ellen; Harman, Donna: TREC: Experiment and Evaluation in Information Retrieval. MIT Press 2005.
Wikipedia: *Search Advertising*. (http://en.wikipedia.org/wiki/Search_advertising).
Wikipedia: *Search engine optimization*. (http://en.wikipedia.org/wiki/Search_engine_optimization).

Chapter 6
Changing Practices of Family Television Watching

Barry Brown and Louise Barkhuus

Introduction

There are few technologies as maligned, or as misunderstood, as the television. Television has achieved a massive prevalence in nearly every country across the world, with most households (even in developing countries) having more than one television set or display. There appears to be something uniquely compelling about watching telly, as well as in a device that works as soon as it is turned on and takes no training to use. Television is a distinctly *ubiquitous* technology and television broadcasts (such as major sporting events) act as some of the biggest simultaneous world events. Yet as a technology it is also much misunderstood – it is frequently characterized as unchanging and obsolete, anti-social and isolating (e.g. Putnam 2001). As this chapter documents, television is none of these things; throughout its history it has been in constant evolution, both technically and in terms of content. Moreover television watching is an activity that is intimately connected with the *social* life of households. Despite the growth of the internet and other competing pursuits, television remains highly relevant as the most important leisure pursuit in viewer's lives, a constant backdrop to the domestic milieu.

This chapter draws on empirical work studying existing and emerging (or new) uses of television. We draw on two studies. The first is an interview study of television and personal video recorder ('Tivo') use in 21 households conducted in the UK. The second is a study of video consumption, though enabled by the internet. This was conducted amongst American young adults. Together results from these studies give us tentative insights into both the changing nature of television as a site of action and consumption as well as a technology of content access and display. The results show how the importance of the single central household screen is being retained, despite the attraction of computer displays, laptops, tablets and the like in the contemporary context. The large screen household television set maintains its

B. Brown (✉)
Mobile Life VINN Excellence Center, Stockholm, Sweden

R. Harper (ed.), *The Connected Home: The Future of Domestic Life*,
DOI 10.1007/978-0-85729-476-0_6, © Springer-Verlag London 2011

role as the pre-eminent screen that the household orientates to together. It might be on most of the day, and although it might never actually get watched, it retains its role as the 'default nights entertainment'. In this way the television is a social technology – most of the time television watching is shared with others providing a low cost, low effort way of sharing an experience with members of the family or household. Television is also drawn on for topics of conversation, as background noise, as wallpaper, to entertain children – broadly providing a background for domestic activities. These studies also document the role of the television as a changing technology. Since its advent television has been changing – the growth of multi-channel television, the emergence of remote controllers, color, the VCR, PVR, and most recently YouTube and internet video are testament to this. Moreover there has been a gradual growth in multiple video-enabled screens, on which television can be watched, distributed throughout the house. Drawing on the results from our studies we focus on the most recent changes in television watching – in particular the use of PVRs to time shift television, and the downloading and viewing of television shows over the internet. We find interesting changes in the relationship between live television and pre-recorded, as well as the watching of television on computer screens of various types. Yet, as we will argue, the 'family set' retains its importance in domestic life.

Researching the Television

Since its invention in the 1920s television has been a technology that has undergone constant change. Indeed, in the very first months of television the fundamental technology changed from the electro-magnetic system pioneered by John Logie Baird, to the more practical electronic system pioneered by Bell Laboratories. The move to color came in the 1950s, with 'heroic' efforts by RCA to develop a television standard that was compatible with the existing deployed black and white system (Chandler 2001). Indeed, the move from black and white to color took over twenty years and it was not until 1972 that more than half of American households had a color set (ibid, p34).

Since then a series of different innovations have changed how television is supplied, how it is controlled and on what displays and devices it can be watched. While technically a small change, the remote control provided the ability to quickly change channel without actually getting up - inventing the new pastime of channel surfing. The remote control was followed by the VCR, allowing viewers to watch television programming at a different time from its broadcast, and more recently hard-disk based Personal Video Recorders that support more flexible tape-less recording of television shows. These different technological changes have influenced how television is accessed, how it is controlled, the choice of television to watch as well as how television can be collected. The most recent manifestation of change has been the growth in systems that support watching television on a plethora of mobile displays, such as mobile phones, games systems or laptop computers.

While television – and more broadly the consumption of video - has hardly escaped academic attention, there has been little attention paid to the device itself and its place in the home. Instead – and perhaps understandably – the focus has been on the content of television shows, the reaction of viewers to those shows, and the effects of television on contemporary society. One dominant theme has been the dangers of television watching - writers such as the already mentioned Putnam (2001) have blamed television for a fall in civic engagement. Indeed, television has been blamed as being behind a host of social evils – not least of all alienation, violence, and the loss of childhood (see, for example Milavsky *et al.* 1982 or the discussions in Dickinson *et al.* 1998). Yet not all accounts of television watching have been exclusively negative, authors such as Silverstone (1994) argue that TV creates an 'ontological trust' in society through the consensus view it projects. That is to say, children watching television learn a host of expected views, behaviors, responses and knowledge – the ontological "what's what" of the modern world. In part TV thus works to bind and create social order.

Within cultural studies there have also been extensive attempts to understand the role that television takes in viewers lives. Early studies in cultural studies that focused on viewer interpretations and reactions were known as 'reception studies' – in particular a set of influential studies that examined how television news was interpreted by viewers (Morley and Brunsdon 1999). The 'uses and gratifications' framework developed this further by describing a process by which viewers seek out television that gratifies their needs (such as diversion from their problems, replacing the need for personal relationships or reinforcing their values) (Rubin 1983). In more recent work, however, this focus on the consumption of television has on the whole been displaced by a focus on the content of television itself. That is to say, rather than television in the lifeworld of those who view it, those watching television have fallen to the side as the focus has moved onto the industry that produces television, and the different thematics and forms that the content itself takes. So, for example, in a recent discussion of themes in the cultural studies of television (Turner 2001) we find topics such as the nation state and television, democracy and television, performance and so on. That the television itself – as an object – might deserve some research, is not mentioned; it is not to be found in this analysis.

We do not wish to offer an at length critique of this work, but our motivations in this chapter come from a suspicion of a distance from the practices involved in 'accepting or rejecting' - the actual use of television. Television is *manifestly* enjoyed and it is these practices of enjoyment we are after. For most of television studies this enjoyment is of no interest since it is seen as epiphenomena - the sugar that makes the medicine go down – but for many viewers it is the very reason they watch television in the first place. One valuable exception to this move is Gauntlett and Hill's (Gauntlett and Hill 1999) long-term study of television watching in Britain, research that provides numerous insights into television practices in more detail, as well as people's attitudes and relationship to television. One of the first moves they make is to criticize authors such as Silverstone for presenting theories with 'little grounded analysis of neither television or everyday life as they are actually experienced in the world' (p9-10). Their study, in contrast to Silverstone's focus group based methodology, uses an audience authored diary approach. Over five years (1991 to 1996), 427 respondents reported on their television watching habits and attitudes. From this the authors explore how television is part of their life and social setting of the home. Gauntlett and Hill find that television provides their participants with great levels of enjoyment – viewers actively chose much of what they watch, and show considerable reflection on those choices. While participants report feeling guilty when watching 'too much television' they compare this guilt to the 'guilty pleasure' reported by female readers of romantic fiction (see also (Miller 1998) on the relationships between consumption, guilt and pleasure). In part, this guilt comes from some of the value attributed to work over leisure in society.

A related finding in Gauntlett and Hill's study documents how social home life was often coordinated around a television watching routine. TV brings families together in a shared experience, although not one without conflict. Disputes over what to watch, where and when, are a familiar of family life. In particular, parent's monitoring of children's viewing habits was one site of considerable conflict (results echoed by Kubery and Csikszentmihalyi (1990)). Gauntlett and Hill's study also inquired into habits in relation to VCR use. Although not all participants owned a VCR, the majority did and reported how it was used for time shifting programs, chopping too-long films into convenient chunks and entertaining children (among others). This is similar to other more recent studies (eg. Rode et al. (2005)) and corresponds to our findings in this chapter. Gauntlett and Hill describe the VCR in a positive light, as a supporting tool for watching preferred content, and the authors showed a quite radical change in how people were able to structure their daily schedules with the acquisition of a VCR. As we shall point to further down, PVRs have a similar effect in giving people 'freedom' of set schedules. Lastly, perhaps the most radical finding of Gauntlett and Hill's work is the broadly positive view towards television and expressed enjoyment of the viewers they studied. In contrast to the negative and skeptical accounts of TV and mass culture, from the Frankfurt school to Putnam's work, Gauntlett and Hill point out the emotional depth of the viewer's relationship with television. Indeed, in a strong rebuke to those who blame TV for its damage to the social fabric, Gauntlett argues that many of the criticisms of television are "part of a broader conservative project to position the more contemporary and challenging aspects of the mass media, rather than other social factors, as the major threat to social stability" (Gauntlett 1998, p122). It is not that TV is without its faults, and excessive television watching can be damaging (as with nearly any activity), but rather its demonizing effect on everyday life has been much overplayed, neglecting its pleasurable contribution to domestic life.

Our Studies

As we outlined in our introduction this chapter draws on two studies of television watching behavior. The key difference with these studies and cultural studies is, as we share with contributions to this volume, an abiding interest in design – and in particular how we can learn lessons for the design of new television technologies. For this reason we will focus not on the television content, but rather on how viewers incorporate television into their lives, how they choose what to watch when and where. These questions come into particular focus when one is interested in new television watching technologies – because although they change the types of video available (such as Youtube) on the whole the biggest impact they have is on what video is available when and where. That is, they change access to television, if not directly the production of television content. The actual object of television – the television itself is transformed if one is watching Netflix on a laptop, as compared to Coronation Street on a portable TV.

PVR Study

To get a hold on what is involved in television watching we went out and examined what was going on in front of the television. In particular we interviewed twenty-one TV watchers in the UK - we had specifically sought out those who made use of so called "personal video recorders (PVR)", such as Tivo and Sky+, and those who downloaded television to watch over the internet. These interviews were particularly powerful for giving us a viewpoint on how television was used in the homes of our viewers, but also how technology was supporting new television watching practices - particularly around the collecting and sharing of media. One absence from interviews, of course, is that it gives us very little in the way of first hand access to television watching practices. To augment these interviews we draw on some related analysis using video data of three families watching sports matches together. Again these different forms of data give us a window on the different practices involved in watching television.

Internet TV Study

Our second study focused on the television consumption behavior of a set of highly tech-savvy individuals. We interviewed college students because of their high level of technology use, their technology possession and their busy lifestyles. Another factor in our choice of this population was the fact that these participants were likely to be very social and to have greater opportunities to socialize around television and movie media than, for example, families or the elderly. We conducted hour-long, semi-structured interviews either in the participant's home or in a common area (e.g. dormitory); they were recorded and transcribed shortly after by the interviewer. In total we recruited thirteen participants who all had a young adult lifestyle; they were students, living partly with roommates and partly with parents. Only one lived with his partner 'full time'. They all resided in Southern California and were between 19 and 23 years. Six were male and seven were female and all had a personal computer with high-speed internet access at home. For comparison we interviewed two people with 'adult' lifestyles, both in their 30s, who had a similar level of access to the internet (high-speed internet access at home and at least one computer), and who had knowledge of the opportunity to watch television over the internet.

Results

Where does television come from?: A first guess at television practices might consider them somewhat bland. Don't we just sit in front of the television and watch TV? How could there be something as grand as "TV watching practices" - surely it is just a case of turning the TV on and viewing? However, in our multi-channel, technology rich world, the question of what to watch is never simple. Moreover, the provision of television now means that there is a range of different ways of collecting and recording television; there are similarly a range of ways of watching TV content.

Perhaps one of the most interesting examples of these differences is presented by households with a PVR. Eight of the nine households using PVRs we interviewed in our first study had moved almost entirely to watching pre-recorded shows from the PVR. Some interviewees even struggled to name the last show they had watched on live TV. Rather than channel surfing to find suitable TV to watch, viewers would 'queue up' recordings to be watched from the episode guide, or automatically record entire series using 'season passes'. Through maintaining a sufficient buffer of recorded shows, TV watching then took place almost entirely from the archive of shows that was collected. In this way program watching became relatively decoupled from when shows are broadcast. For those who worked or lived on different time cycles from that of 'standard' television, this was particularly valuable. For one viewer who worked shifts as a bar manager, the PVR meant he could watch 'primetime' TV early in the morning when he came in from work. For a family with children, they could watch their favorite soap operas in the late evening when they had put their kids to bed. The random access nature of PVRs, however, also supported practices that went beyond simple time shifting. For example, by allowing viewers to start and stop recordings quickly, without losing their position in a recording, multiple films or shows could also be 'grazed' with viewers moving between multiple shows, before deciding on a show to watch.

Viewers also often collected an archive of the same show that would allow multiple episodes to be collected together for viewing in one sitting. An evening's TV would then be selected from the store of a complete series. While PVR users were generally enthusiastic about this technology, its use was not without problems. In particular lost recordings caused considerable upset, since devices infrequently would fail to record shows. The PVR was also not seen as a reliable medium for long-term storage of programs. Whereas some viewers copied shows to recordable DVDs and deleted them, others waited and bought shows on DVD, expressing displeasure in having to delete shows to make space on their PVRs.

In contrast, the viewers we spoke to who downloaded television would browse through the new uploads, often downloading shows which they had not previously seen – the presence of a downloadable version of that show acting as a recommendation. Although the limited availability of content could be frustrating for downloaders (particularly as rare shows would be much slower in downloading or unavailable) it also acted as a filter on shows. Indeed, one inherent aspect of peer-to-peer file sharing is that popular shows in high demand will be shared quicker.

The downloaders belonged to two distinct groups. Four of our nine downloaders were 'supplementors' in that they still watched broadcast television and downloaded shows or movies around once a week. For these participants the internet was a way of obtaining shows that were difficult or impossible to obtain in the UK. In particular American TV shows often have a long delay before they are broadcast on TV in the UK, or released onto DVD. As one supplement downloader put it "For Six Feet Under [one popular show], the third series, I just wanted to see if the guy died or not. When I found out he was alright, I went back to the TV". These occasional downloaders were often critical of the experience of downloading – finding the process slow, full of effort as well as passing doubts about the video quality of some of their downloads. Indeed, boxed DVDs of TV shows that had been downloaded were still purchased by these users – explained by their desire to collect the high quality 'definite article'. Alternatively, 'replacers' (five of our nine downloaders) watched little or no broadcast television, downloading all their TV from the internet. These viewers would regularly check internet resources to find the 'new' TV and films available, constantly downloading a queue of video which would be watched when convenient. Unlike the supplementors, replacers were also serious about building up an archive of TV shows and films downloaded. Collecting video in this way was a source of considerable pleasure, in particular having complete TV series available. A point we return to later, the collection itself seemed important, as much as the utility of being able to watch shows from the archive, echoing results from our previous work on music listening (Brown et al. 2001).

The default night's entertainment: Particularly for the families we interviewed, TV could be considered the default evening entertainment for the family. TV, supplied from many different sources both pre-recorded and live, was a common shared activity for members of the household and it was usual for two or three hours of television to be watched most evenings. It was expected that a set number of hours of television would be watched every evening, even if not everyone in the household would actually be watching TV. Television provided a relatively enjoyable and cheap activity - something freely chosen and enthused about. TV was a reliable activity, one with its own demands, but as we will discuss also linked into household social networks.

In particular interviewees enjoyed the evening television, e.g. early evening soaps and series that are followed closely. Several participants followed the American TV drama '24' at the time of the interviews and some talked about how important it was for them to be able to watch them in the specific order. The perceived advantage with both downloading and a PVR seemed to be the selectivity that took place real-time.

One couple explain how they often made sure to stock up the PVR with television for Saturday where the broadcast television was not of their taste: "Saturday evening is usually rubbish so Isobel[1] went through and filled up the planner, so we would have something to watch. I put things in from the planner to fill the evening when it's notoriously bad for television". They enjoyed having a range of television to choose between for the weekend evening and would watch much of it together. Where Taylor and Harper talked about their participants 'viewing by appointment' which to a certain degree dictates other activities in the household such as dinner and homework (Taylor and Harper, 2003), our participants had the freedom to push this set of shows, to make a 'viewing appointment' for later, on the basis of the instant queue. The need to organize family life around the set time that a show might be broadcast, which Taylor and Harper explored, is mollified in that a missed show can be watched later. This does not mean that the broadcast time will not still act as a 'default' appointment, however. In particular, for shows where there is a communal anticipation for the show (so called 'event' television) it is likely that the time of first broadcast will still act as an appointment which the family can co-ordinate around.

In a related way, the on-going narrative of television provides considerable incentive for the regular watching of shows - that is 'following' a show. In this way shows have an inbuilt 'addictive' quality - watching television serials makes little sense as an individual single watching event, but instead as a sequence. Indeed, the end of series can be a significant event. Our informants were diverse in the amount of shows they kept up with. For the PVR users some kept up actively with up to eight series in a week; contrastingly, others held onto one soap and two weekly shows. The PVR enlarged the number of shows one could practically keep up with making one of the participants for example term his PVR an 'addictive box'. Although it should be pointed out that when we asked this participant if he wanted to change his behavior, he reformulated his TV watching as 'a hobby'. Viewing changed during the year, with many participants reporting watching significant less during the summer because they were more active outdoor (in line with general TV viewing figures), or watching more during the summer because university was in recess.

Although all participants emphasized the importance of keeping up with their favorite series, the VCR users had selected a more limited set of television series that they felt they had to keep up with. These would change their time schedule to fit the show times, similar to other research of television viewing (Gauntlett and Hill 1999), and only occasionally when, for example away for an evening, set their VCR to record. Many PVRs have what is called a series link or a season pass, which enables the user to 'subscribe' to a specific series; the show is then taped each time it is aired so the viewer can keep up. One of the complaints from the Sky+ users however, was that the series link would record every airing of the show, including repeats, which in turn complicated the management of recordings. All of the PVR

---

[1] All names have been changed for anonymity.

users still used a series link to indicate that they wanted to repeat record a specific show. One participant even set the series link on shows she watched the first time, to make sure it keeps recording, as she said, 'you can always change it later'.

There were many different strategies for keeping up with series and the informants often used a combination of tools. The PVR users, who did not supplement their television with downloading, kept large numbers of old shows and sometimes copied content to a DVD in order to keep the shows safe from accidental recording over. Alternatively, another participant supplemented his regular television watching with downloading, by having the episodes that he had missed or forgot to record ready at hand. When asked what he downloads he says:

Darren: Basically we missed two episodes [of Lost]. And 24, if you miss two episodes you can't watch it. So if I missed one or two I would watch it before the next one started. It depends on the TV show, because for example 'Still Game', if you miss one it does not refer back to any other ones so it doesn't really matter.

Interviewer: So why do you download TV series? [...]

Darren: Usually I will download a whole series. So if I miss one I always got them. So I can catch up easily.

The keeping up with episodes was in essence very important to our participants; when they watched was not as important as that they watching the shows in the correct order. With their favorite shows, the viewing was important to their everyday life in that it gave them a satisfaction to keep watching new episodes and follow the thrill of the plot. This feature of televisions shows may contribute in some ways to the results that television can have serious addictive qualities. It is an old result of the 'reception studies', for example, that viewers form emotional bonds to television characters, becoming emotionally attached to them and their experiences (Kubery and Csikszentmihalyi 1990).

Downloading and PVR use also enabled a distinctive practice with respect to multiple shows in that multiple episodes - even a complete series - could be recorded or downloaded and then watched 'back to back'. One participant described to us that she had watched three episodes of 'Lost' the night before the interview. This was particularly popular for downloaders, who described watching an individual show and becoming 'addicted', downloading further episodes and watching them in a single sitting. For the PVR users, saving up individual episodes provided a challenge in terms of being tempted to watch those shows recorded, or to prevent friends and colleagues at work from talking about broadcast shows not yet watched.

Now just watching: This 'keeping up' with shows contrasts with the activity of watching television in the background - what we would characterize as 'ambient watching'. For many, television played a role as the continual background to other activities in the home.

Bob: There's always a telly on, the little one in the kitchen if we're eating – [my wife] has pet programs that you watch foreground but if there is not a pet program on, then it goes back to the background.

When used in this way the TV acts not only as a voice in a possibly otherwise quiet house, but as a resource that can be dipped in and out of as different activities come to dominate. For television programs that are not followed by viewers, this form of watching can dip in and out of shows as they have scenes of interest. This form of watching particularly suits magazine style television shows, or single topic constantly broadcasting stations such as news channels.

Ambient watching also took place when other household members were focused on the television. The main television in the household would be watched at different times by different household members. This television was usually in the living room, and was nearly always the biggest or most advanced television. On this set one household member would watch in a focused way, with other household members watching in the background:

Bob: I think it's like anybody, you kind of watch it over the top of what you are doing.
          And there is a background awareness of what is on, but
Isobel: (interrupting) like typical men when the soaps on, they don't watch it but they
          know what's going on. [laughter]

Our interviewees described the frequent situation of their partner watching a show while they carried out household chores, such as cleaning, or used other media such as browsing the internet on a laptop. For those households with children the television would be used to entertain children in the background. For one family this was one of the main uses of their PVR - they recorded a large number of children's TV shows, and their three year old son would repeatedly watch the same recorded shows. In this situation the television is a focus for the child, with the adults having it as ambient watching.

In these ways watching television in the house was an activity integrated into the broader social behavior and arrangement of the household. When watching a show individually in the living room, one does not disappear from social contact with others, nor they from you. Watching television in the main room was thus a publicly accountable activity, watching television could be seen by others in the house and potentially be seen as a connection between that show and those watching it. The organization of the main television – a scarce resource - was also something that would be shared across the household. At times this could cause conflicts or discussion - over who watches what, with some reluctance of household members to move to another TV if there was a conflict (all the multiple occupancy households we interviewed had alternative ways of watching TV). For those households where the television was on all the time, managing what the television was doing was one of the activities of the household, but one arranged both jointly and individually.

Of course, it is possible to watch television in non-public rooms - one PVR viewer complained about her teenage sons only watching TV in their own bedrooms, and who would even record shows from the PVR to a DVD so as to watch them privately, rather than in the public room. More generally, however, most of the TV watching discussed by our participants was done on the single 'main' household TV - even for non-related student households that we interviewed.

This social nature of television is not only restricted to the home; frequently it becomes a focus for social interaction in the workplace, with friends or online. That television is a common conversation topic at work is hardly a new observation - this is behind the American idea of 'water cooler TV' - television that is so popular that it becomes a common shared television experience to be talked about over the water cooler at work. It would seem that PVRs and downloading could potentially disrupt or damage this ability of television. Certainly, multi-channel television itself has changed the extent to which television shows are shared - shows are often broadcast in advance on cable channels, and the viewership of the main free-to-air TV channels has also been reduced. However, similar to other previous research focusing on VCR use, we found that many PVR users watched recorded TV on the broadcast date so they could talk to friends and colleagues about it the next day. The only difference was a minimal time-shifting, either to avoid advertizements or to postpone to a later convenient time. One household described watching a finale to the popular 'Big Brother' reality television show. As they had a show to watch to catch up before the final, they watched this show and the final back to back. While they were watching friends and family sent text messages and phoned up so as to share and discuss the events happening 'in real time'. While this could be shared, the PVR viewers had a somewhat fragmented experience between friends discussing the show they were about to watch, but with themselves catching up as they skipped past adverts. We would also add that even having not watched the latest episode, following that show, or even just knowing the characters can be sufficient to support some talk around a new episode. We would suggest that water cooler conversation is more than robust enough to deal with missed episodes.

An interesting extension of 'water cooler' conversation occurred with three of our participants who downloaded TV. These participants spoke about keeping up-to-date with online conversations through web based forums. Since these forums frequently discussed episodes when broadcast on American TV, so as to keep up with those shows the participants had to download the shows so as to watch the shows, which were currently being discussed. One female downloader described her downloading of 'Stargate':

> But just now Stargate is getting the priority because I've got friends online, they're all in the states, and they see it anyway. So I don't like to know what's happening so I miss a lot of conversations online, skip a lot of posts because I don't want to know what's happening. So I'm desperately trying to download Stargate. I've got a livejournal account – and I do all my online stuff there now. [...] Generally online I talk about whatever you want to talk about but the people I know online are into Stargate, and the rest of them into Harry Potter. So they're all desperate for me to catch up so they can chat with me

Another downloader discussed how he shared TV shows amongst his friends at work, who were also avid television downloaders. This meant that the shows, which were discussed were those that had been most recently released - but this release was not the broadcasting on television, but rather the release on the internet by those who recorded and seeded the file. This would usually happen fairly quickly after the broadcast of a new show. This downloader also brought shows into work to share with his colleagues, usually on a laptop computer, allowing his colleagues to download the video files from his machine.

Most of the participants found great satisfaction in watching television to social-ize afterwards, some found it stressful at times. One viewer, for example, felt she had to keep up with all the series and found she had to be able to watch them all in time. This meant a great deal to the PVR users in particular, where they would spend whole weekends to catch up with episodes they had not been able to see through the week. Participants also watched older series that they had either watched when they were younger or as kids, or more special interest series that they did not share with anyone else in their circle of friends. They were often hesitant to share these titles with us and often said it was merely for nostalgic reasons that they recorded/downloaded and watched these. They were for their pleasure only, and were not talked much about, even with other members of their household.

Using a PVR: For both the PVR and internet-downloading households that we interviewed, these technologies had had a radical effect on the organization of tele-vision watching. While the technology behind PVRs and downloading share much of the same technology - file compression, hard disks and PCs, the effects they have on television viewing are quite distinct.

Although time shifting is not new (the VCR has been common in households for over 20 years), the time shifting reported by Gauntlett and Hill by VCR in the early 90s is quite different than what we experienced among our interviewees. They described the VCR as a 'Technology' that needed to be mastered in order to gain control of people's lives. Not unlike Rode et al. (2005)'s description of the house-hold Czar, the person who mastered the programming of the VCR, time shifting required significant expertize and experience to succeed. While it freed up people's schedule and was considered a great empowerment tool, they also reported difficul-ties and mishaps that occurred regularly. In contrast, our DVR and streaming users did not view the actual workings of the technology as complicated. This may in part be due to the ease of use of PVRs, or may simply be increased technological familiarity over time.

PVRs integrate a range of different functionality into one package - specifi-cally season passes which record multiple episodes of a show, the ability to record and watch at the same time as well as multiple tuners to record multiple shows simultaneously. The major feature of the PVR was not one specific feature but a combination of several types of functionality. Just as much of the impact of mobile phones comes not only from their mobility, but their integration of a host of pre-viously rare features (such as Caller ID, voicemail, SMS and so on), so do PVRs bring together a range of new features as a package. Much of the value for those we interviewed came from how they used the different features in combination. For example, shows can be queued to be recorded in advance using an onscreen program guide, with 'season passes' recording shows whenever they are on. Yet season passes for shows can often clash, particularly as TV Networks often put popular shows on in competition with each other. The ability to record two channels simultaneously (offered by Sky+ and TiVo) thus develops more value with the use of season passes. In turn this interacted with a third feature: live TV, when watched, would usually be watched on a short delay from the actual time of broadcast, as this allowed viewers to skip through advertizements. When two programs were being recorded, this required the ability to record three channels simultaneously. Thus four different features would work together in use – season passes, dual record, watch while recording and watching from a live buffer.

Downloading TV: Although downloading video from the internet (in contrast to streaming) is a different experience to using a PVRs, both involve storing video to hard disks and enable a random-access mode of viewing video. To download video files our participants used peer-to-peer software, in particular Bittorrent, as well as internet newsgroups. Most of the downloaders could stream their downloads to a TV, or burn it to a disk that they could watch using a DVD player. One participant (Martin) watched around half the television on his laptop and half on his household communal television in the kitchen/living area.

All downloaders made use of the selection of shows by 'seeders', users who make shows available for download. Encoding TV, cutting out the adverts and distributing it takes considerable effort, thus the shows that are shared are essentially a selection of what those with the technical skill and motivation consider valuable. As one would expect, availability of science fiction is high, cookery and quiz shows low. Downloaders would browse through the new uploads often downloading shows which they had not previously seen – the presence of a downloadable version of that show acting as a recommendation. Although the limited availability of content could be frustrating for downloaders (particularly as rare shows would be much slower in downloading or unavailable) it also acted as a filter on shows. Indeed, one inherent aspect of peer-to-peer file sharing is that popular shows in high demand will be shared quicker.

Watching over the Internet: Since the time of our first study, it has become easier to watch television directly over the internet – streaming from services such as Hulu and Netflix, or direct from a television network's website. This prompted our second study focusing more directly on watching television over the internet– based around interviews with thirteen University students and 'early adopters' of television. As with our downloaders, one can characterize these viewers as broadly 'supplementors' or 'replacers'. The four supplementors would watch missed episodes of a show or (in one case) catch up on a particular series that their friends had started watching regularly. The remaining nine 'replacers' watched between two thirds and all of their television as either streamed or downloaded content. In terms of specifically downloading television to watch later, five of the thirteen participants would occasionally download shows and then watch content later. One participant argued that the quality of a downloaded video is higher and others said that this was in some cases the only way they could get a hold of particular material. It was also preferred because it was easier to freely move through the media by rewinding, pausing and fast-forwarding.

Our participants did not see television as constrained to the television set, and probably due to them growing up with time shifting via VCR, it was not necessarily viewed as real-time medium. Yet, at the start of our interviews our participants would often describe watching video on their computer as something very different from 'watching TV'. For video material to 'count' as television watching it had to be watched in its entirety; they did not immediately consider clips from television viewed for example on YouTube as actual television, despite this being the original source. One male participant for example stated: "One of my favorite TV programs is 'Friends'. I do watch that on YouTube too if I just want a funny scene right there", emphasizing that as it was not necessarily television if it was just watched as a short clip. Television mainly seemed to encompass content that was watched in its full length (not necessarily in one sitting however) but it was apparent that our participants had not given much thought to the exact (new) definition of television before the interview. Their focus was on the content material, and most referred to 'shows', 'episodes' and to a certain extend 'movies' watched on computers as television. The ease of which the participants approached the concept was surprising; there was clearly nothing extraordinary about watching television through different platforms and means; instead television had seamlessly become the content, not the box.

The retained role of the family television: Even amongst those who streamed television over the internet they still had a strong orientation to the traditional television in how they defined and thought of television watching. In order to understand the root of participants' view of television we asked about their perception and use of traditional television, that is content viewed on a television set from cable, satellite or aerial antenna. With traditional television consumption there is a sense of 'watching whatever is on', with the much narrower selection of live television making the choice of what to watch much easier (although potentially less satisfying). The advantage of live television is that there is no need to search for what to watch, or to spend much time deciding what to watch - one can just turn it on and watch what is on. Indeed, the choice of what to watch was often left to another household member - one participant answered to why she was watching a specific news program: "because my brother left the TV on".

Another characteristic of traditional television was its notion of socializing; several participants described how the television in the living room was a place to socialize around with their family (this was echoed to a certain extend with common areas in the dormitories) or watching television at their friends' house. One participant explained it in terms of tradition: "Well [the living room]'s where the big screen TV is, so I get a wider view of everything, and we have surround sound so I can listen better, but that's just the way that my family is like, we always watch TV there, until we got TVs in our own room. If we want to watch our own individual shows, we're allowed to go to our room and watch it there, but when we're doing a family gathering, it would always be in the living room, we'd have dinner and then watch TV there if we wanted to watch a show, so it just always seem[ed] natural". The family dynamics here affect how this viewer sees traditional television as social, which retains Taylor and Harper's notion of television as a vehicle for 'doing family' (Taylor and Harper 2003).

Although the participants were watching a great amount of television through the internet, they were not necessarily critical towards traditional television. Surprisingly it was not commercials that deterred participants from watching real-time television but to a much higher extent the possibility for video-on-demand. One participant expressed: "...I can watch more things on the internet, I can search for more things, and TV really depends on you know what you want to watch and you have to get in front of the TV at a certain time".

New methods of television watching

It was interesting to see that our participants were frequent users of a diverse set of methods with which they watched television, often combining all four methods (streaming, downloading, DVD and classic television set). Watching television over the internet was a simple and natural habit for most of the participants, contrasting our two 'older' participants who knew about the opportunities, had the technology available, but rarely used the internet to access any television content. Our college student participants were moderating their time by picking and choosing their own 'television potpourri' through different means, regular television sets, the internet and DVDs. We found a general trend for the type of content that was watched through the different platforms.

Several participants still watched content from DVDs, however, this had taken the status mainly as 'social watching' where they would watch movies together, on a television set through the DVD player. These were most often rented or borrowed DVDs but contrasting the serendipitous nature of watching television through the television set, it was most often more planned to watch a movie through DVD with friends. Interestingly none of the students used DVD recorders. It is likely that they were in possession of one, but it was never used to record content off the television set. It seemed that the internet had taken over as the 'recording' tool.

Participants were generally not watching content over the internet together with others. Apart from one example where three roommates were watching a DVD on one of the participants' laptops, there was a clear distinction between watching from the internet, which was a solo activity, and watching on the television set, which could potentially be a social activity. The nature of socialization around the television was unsurprisingly based on serendipity. Most participants would socialize chiefly with their roommates if they happened to be around, or their family when staying home over the summer. As one participant expressed: "Well, I only really watch [traditional] TV with my roommates. [...] if they were watching [a show], maybe I would happen to be watching it too, because it happens to be on".

This is *not* to say that television watching over the internet was contrastingly asocial. If anything it was more socially oriented since the choosing of the material was often prompted by social relations, friends, acquaintances and family members, either through recommendations or social pressure. One participant for example explained how he felt the need to catch on to a specific show after his roommates had started following it: "I kind of caught on to "The Office" later [. . . after] all my roommates started watching it. [. . .] I believe my brother rented the first two seasons and then I caught up during winter break." In fact similar to how PVRs are used to compensate for missed television episodes for water-cooler talk, internet viewing and downloading was used to catch up with full seasons of shows that were suddenly popular within participants' social circles.

Generally participants were positive about television content and their selective watching. They expressed notions of 'escapism' and 'stress-freeness' alongside entertainment and general enjoyment when talking about television. As one participant expressed: "[...] my life is not really that interesting. I was telling my roommate how it's not fair that all the people on TV get to go on a bunch of adventures and we just have to go to class everyday". On the other hand eight of the participants still found television time-wasting to a certain extent or at least conditionally (television was considered a waste of time if there were more pressing things to do or if viewing exceeded a certain amount of time). They clearly recognized that for them, television viewing often indicated procrastination, but they also enjoyed the delay of doing schoolwork. Television was often used as distraction from studying, illustrated by many of the participants who often watched television during the day, for example in between classes.

Conclusions: Television and the Household

As a domestic technology the television is a familiar and almost fundamental household technology. In many parts of the world the television is definitional to the home, with televisions in offices as out of place as a filing cabinet in a home. Despite the many competing attentions to home-based leisure activities, it seems that the television still has an important role to play. Moreover, its role is shared amongst family or household members, rather than simply acting as an individual pursuit.

What this chapter has attempted to unpack is the ways in which the television is not simply wallpaper to what happens in the home, but is one of the activities that a household does together. From choosing what to watch, what to record, or what to talk about, the television provides a common space of activity and conversation. In particular, it is the 'family television' that takes pride of place. The family television does compete with other screens and ways of accessing television, yet remains important as the 'default' place where family members can come to watch television together. Moreover, as often the largest screen in the house the family television acts as the destination for event television watching. Even if only one family member is watching television, other family members can busy themselves in the same space - sharing the watching experience, even as they differ in the attention they are paying to the television set.

As we discussed in the introduction, this conflicts with the conventional rendition of the television as naturally 'anti-social'. In terms of the household the family television can actually act as a device for gathering together family members in a shared experience. Having watched television together this shared experience can act to bind together those who might spend much of their daily lives in different worlds of work or school. Despite their usual biological unity families of course frequently harbor much in the way of disagreement and misunderstanding. These can be suspended, if only for a short time, through the communal act of watching together. Indeed, this shared watching can pay further communal dividends through supporting shared conversation and discussion of what has been watched, what might happen next, and so on.

There are aspects of this watching which might seem almost nostalgic. Indeed, one contrary point might be that the advent of watching television over the internet has acted to diminish the importance of the family television. While it is true that the ability to watch television on other smaller more personal screens has acted as a centrifugal force, even the students who watched streaming television that we interviewed still retained the importance of the *household* set. Indeed, the use of the PVR helps to increase the flexibility of what can be watched on the main household television. Even the advent of downloading television from the internet still acts as a supplement rather than a replacer to broadcast or cable television.

The early attempts of television providers to prevent downloading of television have slowly changed into acceptance and support, through making content available on the internet after initial broadcast. As this is further adopted it is important that watching over the internet is seen as not only still social, but that it does not remove or prevent family watching. When designing for these new practices it is therefore relevant to think in terms of sharing. We envision sharing services where the different 'screens' in the household will for example inform people of other content being showed in the household at the same time, perhaps suggesting that they watch the same. Other interesting technologies could implement recommendations for content, based on what their friends had been watching. As a simple setup it is clear that people are still interested in the communal nature of television, yet supplemented with individual viewing.

More broadly, the household television produces a new set of design challenges that are distinct from those of individual watching. So far, these have been addressed mainly in terms of the size and distance of the television from the user. While this is important, it does not yet address the 'default' nature of the household set – that it can be left switched on, and offers a very simple and quick interface for the selection of content (switching channels). Most recent attempts at new television systems are built around allowing greater control and selection of content. While this is a suitable solution for the individual choosing and watching television, for the household set this might demand too much user interaction. An alternative design might be one that instead built sets of constantly running channels with different content selected to appeal to household members, and offering the ability to change content simply by pushing one channel switch button. This sort of interface would support both the default, and harmonious aspects of the household television set.

Whatever the success or failure of these new television technologies, it seems then that the funeral for the household television will need to be postponed yet again. The practices of television watching documented here highlight a particular contrary view of 'the family box' - as a *social, family* and *changing* technology. We argue that to understand domestic technology the family television set is perhaps the most important place to start.

References

Brown, B., E. Geelhoed and A. Sellen. 2001. Music sharing as a computer supported collaborative application. In Proceedings of ECSCW 2001, Prinz, W. et al (Eds) 179–198. Bonn, Germany: Kluwer Academic Publishers.

Chandler, A. 2001. *Inventing the electronic century: The epic story of the consumer electronics and computer science industries*: Free Press, New York.

Dickinson, R., R. Harindranath and O. Linné eds. 1998. *Approaches to audiences – a reader.* London: Arnold.

Gauntlett, D. 1998. Ten things wrong with the "Effects model". In Approaches to audiences – a reader, Dickinson, R, Harindranath, R and Linné, O, (Eds) *Op cit.* 120-30. London: Arnold.

Gauntlett, D. and A. Hill. 1999. *Tv living: Technology, culture and everyday life*: Routledge.

Hamill, L. 2003. 'Time as a rare commodity in home life', *Inside the smart home*, ed Harper, R. Springer.

Kubery, R. and M. Csikszentmihalyi. 1990. *Television and the quality of life: How viewing shapes everyday experience,* Lawrence Erlbaum: Hilsdale, NJ.

Milavsky, J.R., R.C. Kessler, H.H. Stipp and W.S. Rubens. 1982. *Television and aggression: A panel study,* New York: Academic Press.

Miller, D. 1998. *A theory of shopping,* Cambridge: Polity.

Morley, D. and C. Brunsdon. 1999. *The Nationwide Television Studies:* Routledge.

Putnam, R. 2001. *Bowling alone : The collapse and revival of American community*: Simon & Schuster.

Rode, J., E. Toye and A. Blackwell. 2005. 'The domestic economy: A broader unit of analysis for end user programming,' In *Proceedings of CHI'05,* 1757-60: ACM.

Rubin, A. 1983. 'Television uses and gratifications: The interactions of viewing patterns and motivations,' *Journal of Broadcasting & Electronic Media,* 27, no. 1: 37-51.

Silverstone, R. 1994. Televisio*n and everyday life*: Routledge.

Taylor, A. and Harper, R. 2003. 'Switching on to switch off,' *In Inside the smart home,* ed. Harper, R. Springer.

Turner, G. 2001. 'Television and cultural studies: Unfinished business', *International Journal of Cultural Studies* 4, no. 4: 371-84.

Chapter 7
All in the Game: Families, Peer Groups and Game Playing in the Home

Dave Randall

Introduction

There is, of course, nothing in the slightest bit new about game playing in and around the home. Pieter Breughel's famous painting, 'Childrens' Games', painted in the 1500s, shows how many and varied the games that were played in the home environs were, albeit with very limited resources in terms of toys or other equipment. Breughel's painting in fact shows the majority of the games in question being played outside, although whether this has to do with the available technology (mainly sticks), specific household arrangements (e.g. the domestic mode of production), architectural matters or the construction of childhood/ adulthood itself (see e.g. Aries, 1962), remains unclear. Certainly, there is a view that, for whatever reason, gaming is now something that is a more isolated and isolating experience, at least in terms of the physical locality. In this chapter, I seek to understand what both the continuities and discontinuities of game playing might be in the light of the social arrangements of domestic life. If this is true, however, it is a relatively recent development. Most of us will remember, or perhaps still experience, family games of cards, or Monopoly played at Christmas or other holiday times. Equally, such games were not limited to parents and children. It was my grandmother who taught me how to play 'Whist', a well- known card game. I can also remember quite vicious games of 'Risk'- a board game which, if memory serves, entailed world conquest, being played with friends in my early 20s (I also remember being mildly surprised that we remained friends afterwards). This is something of a preamble to questions about gaming and its role in the household, especially in the light of new technology and its affordances. If arguments about the 'connected home' are correct, and with the advent of broadband and wireless connection there is some sense in which they must be, then this has allowed for the development of new forms of game and gaming and in turn those new forms may afford new gaming relationships. Arguably, the

D. Randall (✉)
University of Siegen, Siegen, Germany

Manchester Metropolitan University, Manchester, UK

R. Harper (ed.), *The Connected Home: The Future of Domestic Life*,
DOI 10.1007/978-0-85729-476-0_7, © Springer-Verlag London 2011

fact of new technology and the way it affords 'distributed' play has produced new domestic arrangements and at the same time created new cultures and communities which have little to do with what we are used to. It may be, that is, that there are good reasons to think in terms of 'gaming communities' which flourish through the new connectedness. At the same time, however, there might be grounds for a certain amount of caution. Whether there is any particular reason to assume that the transformations that result are in any way dramatic or radical rather depends, I will argue, on the analytic focus one chooses to adopt. While new technology may create the 'connected home', the shape that home takes will undoubtedly be mediated by the fact that it is, precisely, 'home'- with concomitant patterns of relationship, bonds, emotional commitments and assumptions about the rhythm of the household and the proper use of time (see Hamill, chapter 3). If young children continue to play games with their parents, it may be because family arrangements have not altered that much over a century; if teenagers sit in bedrooms and play computer games with strangers and friends online this may have much to do with the fact that they are teenagers, constructed out of long term changes in full-time education and the resentful dependency associated with it. If students and other young people spend time with computer games, it may have to do with the somewhat unique organization of time and space associated with that population, and so on. In this chapter, then, we will examine a literature which concerns itself with the cultural aspects of gaming (and which tends to emphasize change) alongside a more orthodox sociological literature (which might point to some continuities) in order to make sense of what has changed and what has not and speculate a little on what might change in the near future. That is, there are questions to be asked and answered about new forms of gaming in relation to who plays, who with, where, when and why. I will also draw on some interview data, largely taken from university and school students aged 17 upwards. I conducted unstructured interviews with 2 adults and 8 young people (with a variety of domestic arrangements. Both adults were women, one a single parent, one with a long term partner; of the university students, there were 2 young men living in all male households; 2 young women, both gamers, living with partners, and four school kids- the latter aged 16-17 and all living at home with parent(s)). The university students were interviewed on a one-to-one basis; school kids were interviewed singly, and on one occasion in a group. This would be a very small sample if the intention were to make large scale generalizations. It is not. Hopefully, what will become evident is that, even within this small sample we can discern significant contextual variation.

Who Plays, and When?

A casual assumption is sometimes made that gaming is a solely male, teenage activity. In this respect, if it were true, it would reflect a longstanding belief in the notion that almost all aspects of computing are male-dominated. In that simplistic form, however, it is almost certainly wrong, although there are clear age and gender related influences. According to new Strategist Publications (2010), the average man aged 15 or more, plays games (*any* games, not just computer games) for .25 hours per day, and the average woman, .15. For all men aged between 15 and 19, game playing takes up an average of .76 hours per day but for those who report that they *do* play games regularly, the number of hours per day is 2.57 (2.29 when women are included). 29% of 15-19 year old men reported that they played computer or other games on an average day, whilst 12% of women did. To put this in context, for those who report that they regularly engage in specified activities, average hourly activity per day is: television 2.9; arts and entertainment 2.67; research and homework 1.94; socializing and communicating, 1.75, and reading 1.43. The editors of this survey comment,

> *Although computers and the internet are changing the way people communicate, computer use does not even begin to crack the top-ten list of time-consuming activities. Leisure computer use ranks 20th in time use (excluding sleep). The average American devotes much more time to reading for personal interest, putting reading in ninth place on the time-use list. Reading becomes an increasingly important priority with advancing age. Whether this continues to be true as younger, computer-oriented generations age remains to be seen.*

Nevertheless, there are evidently other constituencies. Quandt et al (2009) cite Business Week as suggesting that 19% of over-50s play or have played computer games. Extrapolating from a German survey, they suggest that in the youngest group (14-19) 72% are gamers, 51% of the 20- to 29-year olds, 40% of the 30- to 39-year olds, 30% of the 40- to 49-year olds, 21% of the 50- to 59–year olds, and 15% of the 60- to 64-year-olds. Similar conclusions can be reached about the UK and the USA.

Further to this, gender and age differences become apparent when we look at what *kind* of computer game. Farmville, which is apparently the most popular online game on the planet, with some 50 million players, has more female players than male. This seems as much as anything else to be to do with the fact that it is associated with Facebook. One survey

> *found that 55% of social gamers are female and 45% are male. Females are more avid gamers, too; 38% of females said they play multiple times a day, but just 29% males said the same. Women are more likely to play with people they know (68% vs. 56% for males), and men are more likely to play with strangers (41% vs. 33%) than women are. (http:// jagonews.com/2010/02/farm-ville-social-game-stats-by-gender/).*

Similar patterns have been observed with other so-called 'social games', 'The Sims' being a well-known example. Such games may allow for a 'gender-specific' policy by female gamers. (There is an extensive literature on gender and gaming. See for instance Beavis, 2005; Paulk, 2006; Flanagan, 2005; Bertozzi and Lee). Hartmann and Klimt (2006) go some way to explaining this. In an extensive review of the existing literature, they point to such matters as violence; the stereotypical characterization of females in the game itself; competitive structures and the absence of opportunities for social interaction as major elements. Nevertheless, it is clear that online games have become more sophisticated and, increasingly, pay account of these factors which might explain the increase in girl gamers. Further to this, however, we have relatively sparse data on the *contexts* in which girls do or do not play games, and for that matter on the contexts in which the subtleties of age may or may not be important. Thus and for instance, one young woman said:

I don't really play computer games at all ... apart from Solitaire ... that's just when you're bored, but you can easily watch a bit of telly or listen to your iPod ... but none of my friends do either and I think that's why. If you hang out with one group, you mainly do the same things as them and none of us play games ... they're not put off by the violence, they're put off by the, uh, pointlessness ...

On the other hand, one young man pointed to how it was quite common in his circle of 15-17 year olds for groups of boys and girls to play co-located 'tournaments':

A: *What I've found the most is that the ones with a story or adventure, they like them. But having said that, we had a tournament where there was like five girls playing ...*
H: *.. I can see why girls would be put off FPSs online just cos of the amount of crap you get ... but there's an online game called Team Fortress and the online community in Team Fortress is like really really good and there's loads and loads of girls who play cos there isn't a lot of racism or sexism ... and in a lot of these games, all of the characters are men ...*
A: *... yeah, like Call of Duty ...*
H: *...yeah ...*

Having said that, one female student commented:

you get loads of abuse ... the thing about Team Fortress is that you've got such a short lifetime before you're killed, it doesn't really matter .... But I'd never let on.

Whilst yet another opined:

I don't really get any sexism ... but that's because I'm really good at them ... I constantly finish first in Battlefield ...

Now, the main focus of this chapter is not gender and gaming, but even these brief quotes serve to illustrate some themes we will pick up elsewhere concerning the contexts in which games are played, and by whom. These include that pre-existing relationship patterns can be very influential in forming policy; that in certain types of game - the 'skill based'- being 'good at it' is a critical feature, and that the amount of time a game takes might ramify in various ways. These things, I will argue, form part of the 'moral universe' of the game player.

Of course, as Quandt et al (ibid) acknowledge, there is a methodological problem associated with the statistics they cite, and it is that no precise definition of 'gaming' was used to collect the raw data on which their figures are based, and no precise definition is entailed in any other statistical data of this kind, which leads us on to a brief consideration of exactly that problem. Thus and for instance, in some views immersive worlds should not be thought of as games at all since they may not have competitive elements or specific outcomes in respect of winning or losing. What we are talking about when we talk about 'gaming', then, is not a trivial problem.

What Games?

Obviously, any consideration of gaming, its relation to domestic life and to wider considerations of culture and community will depend on what one wants to include as 'gaming' and what one chooses to exclude. Perhaps because of the legal restrictions placed on online gambling in the US (but not in Europe), there is relatively little academic interest in such activities as playing online poker or other forms of gambling, for example. When we spend a little time looking at the more mundane forms of game-playing, it becomes apparent that some of our commonsense assumptions about who plays games, when, where and why, may be quite simply wrong. Which of us has not turned to an on-screen card game at some point in our lives, when bored at work? In Europe, at least, where online gambling is legal, millions of people engage in betting on horse races; football matches; online poker games, and so on. We have no evidence to suggest that these arenas are populated by the young and they would seem to be ludic forms, much like any other. I will argue that there is a considerable bias towards online, collaborative gaming in the academic literature such that the focus on the distributed online game leads to 'gaming cultures' becoming a predominant theme in the literature. One trend, then, is to focus almost exclusively on the internal cultural assumptions and practices of the game player without a great deal of consideration of the relationship between the game itself, the technology on which it is played, location, time, and the moral order which attends on the game player even when s/he is locked onto the screen. It is arguably the case that this produces a quite unnecessary hyperbole and we consider this below. Nevertheless I do not, of course, suggest that this trend is an exclusive one and in fact draw extensively on a literature which does consider these relational themes. These lines of argument, which pursue the complex relationships between the 'old' and the 'new' are, I argue, more useful.

Much of the current literature, as I have said, focuses on the notion of game-playing 'culture'. These 'culturalist' assumptions raise some interesting difficulties. It seems for the most part to assume that, because these games are played online, physical location and the mundane features of the social world that we are familiar with - family mealtimes, parental concerns, etc. are of no relevance here. This is an odd assumption, sociologically speaking. It is as if the simple act of sitting in front of a computer screen immediately creates a dissociation from all other forms of social life.

Reading some of the literature on online gaming is to enter into a narrative drama that is almost as exciting as playing the games must be. At least, if one believes it. This literature, which has grown quite remarkably - as fast and abruptly as the online games market itself - trades on a dominant discourse of radical difference and disconnection. Everything, it seems, has changed. As Williams puts it,

> ... a lot of people are playing together. Why? ... the social side of what happens to the players, their friends, families, and communities matters as well and matters a great deal at this particular moment. We should study games now because these networked social games are a **wholly new form of community** [MY EMPHASIS] social interaction, and social phenomenon that is becoming normative faster than we have been able to analyze it,

theorize it, or collect data on it. What do these new collections of people and interactions mean for friendships, families, and communities?

There are two ways in which this argument is sold. Firstly, and most obviously, through the purveyors of those breathless books about the Net Generation (Tapscott, 2009), the coming dominance of the 'virtual' world (Castronova, 2007) is asserted. Secondly, and in a way more interestingly, we see it in the work of sociologists and anthropologists who assert, with a little more subtlety, that significant changes in our culture are taking place. These tend to emphasize the growth of distinctive *online cultures* which are independent of (but may interact with) the mainstream. There is now a very substantial literature on game playing, remarkable itself insofar as, with a small number of exceptions (e.g. Turkle, 1997) scarcely any literature existed before 2000. Indeed, a cursory look at MIT's sourcebook on the internet and the family finds hardly any reference to online gaming as something significant in the lives of people at home. The more 'culturalist' work concerns, in large part, what are often termed MMOGs or Multi-Player Online Games. As Shaw (2010) states,

> From books that look at Gaming as Culture ... to journals such as Games and Culture ... there is a great deal of academic buzz about video game culture. There has been a great deal of "cultural" work done around video games, particularly in the past 10 years .... The great majority of recent work on video game culture centers on massively multiplayer online games (MMOGs) like Everquest, World of Warcraft, or SecondLife ... In these areas, authors look at video games with regard to knowledge acquisition, identity and performance, representation, and the relationship between media and audiences. Throughout this research, there is a pervasive sense of video game culture as separate from a constructed mainstream culture, as something new, different, and more importantly definable. (p403)

She goes on to say,

> The point of this article is not to outline the gamer stereotype yet again. Instead, it begins with the categories from which the stereotype stems. These categories include (a) who plays video games, (b) how they play, and (c) what they play. Starting with these categories and not looking for a prototypical definition of a gamer identity allows us to see that popular discourses actually offer a much more diverse view of what gaming is than they are generally given credit for. They still define "video game culture" as something very distinct and very different from mainstream U.S. culture. (p403)

There is, that is, the sense of something very new and radically disconnected from the mainstream (for a more cautious and historical view, however, see Bartle, 2010). If so, what is it? Firstly, it would seem that electronic media afford behaviors that would simply not have been possible in the past: real-time, distributed, multi-player games in which very large numbers of people who might otherwise (at least to begin with) be total strangers can participate. Secondly, it appears that particular forms of the socio-technical define behavior; games have rules, structures, procedures and so on which impact on the play and the player but – importantly – the behavior of participants is often seen to transcend them. Thirdly, they are seen as distinct in relation to the fact that players are typically involved in cooperative behavior. I might add that, fourthly (possibly) they just look more interesting to the sociologist/anthropologist than some more mundane game-playing applications (see Smith, 2006; Klastrup, 2010 for a review of the different genres). Although this latter observation may seem rather trivial, I will suggest that it ramifies in ways that we ought to take seriously.

This sense of a radical disconnectedness is, for instance, evident in Boellsdorf's (2006) observations in the first issue of 'Games and Culture', wherein he delineates three more or less distinct ways in which we can engage with game playing as anthropologists (or sociologists). The first has to do with the relationship between games and culture:

> *I continue to be surprised by the lack of scholarly interest in video games and interactive media more broadly given not only their massive and rapidly increasing impact worldwide but their usefulness for thinking through a range of key questions concerning selfhood and society. The newness of interactive media means that scholarly work in the area is marked by a refreshing intellectual openness and interest in foundational questions. (What does it mean to be a person? What does it mean to interact? What is a body? What does it mean to be equal or unequal, similar or different?) ....The moniker games and culture accurately reflects how for the emerging discipline of game studies culture acts as a secondary pivot term alongside game to define the field of inquiry. Indeed, culture is often described as encompassing the notion of game (and the notion of play, to which game is closely allied in English). Given this state of affairs, anthropology (a) can provide game studies with frameworks for theorizing culture and (b) can provide a methodology—participant observation—for investigating games and culture.*
>
> *Many games, and other forms of interactive media like metaverses or "synthetic worlds" that are less clearly game like, are taking on cultural forms in their own right ... These cultures cannot be reduced to the platform, that is, the rules and programming encoded in the game engine and the rules of the game or metaverse. One approach to studying these game cultures involves examining the relationship between the metaverse and the physical world by examining if participants play at home or at work, alone or in groups, if they play a gender different from their physical gender, and so on.*

Secondly, he suggests, we can investigate game cultures *themselves*:

> *Another approach, one that I think holds the potential to illuminate a different set of questions, takes these games or metaverses on their own terms, trying to understand their cultures as coherent systems of meaning and practice in themselves.*

He refers to this analytic choice as the investigation of 'cultures of gaming':

> *Most persons who participate in games and other interactive media like metaverses play more than one game or metaverse. We are seeing the emergence of cultures of gaming on a range of spatial scales—some local, some national or regional, some global—shaped by a range of factors from language spoken to quality of internet connection. These cultures of gaming include multiple subcultures such as youth, male versus female, cooperative versus competitive gaming, and so on. Studying these kind of cross-platform cultures of gaming poses problems not unlike those anthropologists have historically faced in terms of cross-cultural comparison and globalization.*

Thirdly, we might investigate the powerful effects these new cultural forms have on wider cultural life. Hence:

> *As it gains in significance, gaming increasingly affects the whole panoply of interactive media, from television to movies to cell phones to the internet in all its incarnations. Gaming also shapes physical-world activities in unexpected ways, including the lives of those who do not play games or participate in interactive media. Understanding the "gaming of*

cultures"— *that is, how cultures worldwide are being shaped by gaming and interactive media — represents another area of exciting new research.*

As suggested above, part of the attraction appears to be the scale of possibilities inherent in MMOGs, added to which there is the belief that 'interdependence' or cooperative behavior among groups of people who might otherwise not know each other. In sum, the resulting socio-technical constellation is viewed as somehow unique. If we take one example of this approach, Taylor's (2009a) study of Everquest, we see precisely how the logic of the 'cultures of gaming' strategy plays out. She points to the way that, although certain cooperative features are built into the game, they do not fully explain game-playing behavior. This is constructed out of player concerns for reputation, trust and responsibility. That is, and to paraphrase, the fact of a culture may be a necessary feature of the structure of the game, but the shape of the culture need not be (see also e.g. Ducheneaut and Moore, 2004).

Interestingly, however, Taylor points to the role of offline relationships in the development of interests in Everquest (see also Nardi and Harris, 2010). As she says:

> *In the course of my research it was not at all uncommon to find that people were connected to other players through a variety of pre-existing offline ties. Indeed, in the case of women and power gamers ... this is particularly noticeable. (p52)*

This turns out to be, above all, evident in family connections such that cousins, fathers and mothers, and so on can introduce or be introduced to the game. Taylor, rather hyberbolically, refers to the way in which:

> *This ability to have relationships that might not otherwise occur without the game strikes me as one of the fundamental ways spaces like MMOGs are reorganizing social life. As children and teens occupy positions of power, as intergenerational friendships develop, as partners find new friendship networks not solely reliant on a nuclear family, as people develop deep connections with those who live far from them or whom they never meet in person, these game spaces offer interesting possibilities to undo some of the constraints produced by traditional families and localized friendship pools. (p56)*

Elsewhere (2009b) she points, more promisingly, to the need for an analysis that deals in 'assemblages' which might, she argues, help us:

> *... understand the range of actors (system, technologies, player, body, community, company, legal structures, etc.), concepts, practices, and relations that make up the play moment. Games, and their play, are constituted by the interrelations between (to name just a few) technological systems and software (including the imagined player embedded in them), the material world (including our bodies at the keyboard), the online space of the game (if any), game genre, and its histories, the social worlds that infuse the game and situate us outside of it, the emergent practices of communities, our interior lives, personal histories, and aesthetic experience, institutional structures that shape the game and our activity as players, legal structures, and indeed the broader culture around us with its conceptual frames and tropes.*

We return to this later and, for now, content ourselves with the observation that, if true, this seems to point to the possibility that rather less has changed than is sometimes asserted. The posing of a relationship between, in the first instance, online behavior and family relations and, more widely, online gaming and a range of social and technological matters, offers a different, if more prosaic, way of thinking about gaming, one which emphasizes certain kinds of continuity rather than disjuncture. Sociologists interested in matters of youth culture have long since, for example, observed that for the average teenager, the peer group is of far greater importance in terms of identity than the family. Subcultural theorists of this kind have for some time now pointed, for instance, to the notion of 'bedroom culture' (McRobbie and Garber, 1976; Steele and Brown, 1995; Lincoln, 2005). According to Bovill and Livingstone (2001), in an extensive comparative study, the average European teenager spends over 50% of their waking hours in their bedrooms. Bovill and Livingstone also point to the increasing importance of the new media in this context. Although there are cultural variations, they argue that there is a real and consistent correlation between bedroom culture and the existence of screen media in the bedroom. If so, and we have no reason to doubt the accuracy of these observations, then the rise of the online game, both in single and multi-player formats, ought to be associated with this. McRobbie and Garber also pointed to the highly gendered nature of this bedroom culture. Girls, they argued, were much more likely to engage in the kinds of behavior associated with bedroom culture than boys because they lacked the extensive social networks that more masculine cultures typically had. This gender difference does not appear to have changed substantially in the last 20 years, according to McRobbie and Garber. In the context of game-playing, this might go some way towards explaining why it is that some research indicates both that girls are increasingly likely to take up online game playing, such that, as we have seen, that they might be more likely to play various computer games than boys do. The games they play, however, may be less interactive than the MMOs mentioned above. Older women, however, do seem to be increasingly engaged in interactive game-playing and, again, may now constitute a majority in their age cohort. In what follows, we will investigate this phenomenon in relation to the teenager/young person and their ambiguous relationship to family and domestic life.

The point here is to recognize that game-playing can be understood as much as an extension of existing sub-cultures as through the positing of something new. It is a tautology to say that whether something is to be regarded as 'new' or 'old' depends entirely on the analytic choices one makes when one decides on a focus. As Elizabeth Anscombe (1957) pointed out many years ago, everything is 'under a description'. Not for the first time, however, what seems to be a disciplinary need to assert the 'newness' of features of the social order such as game-playing can lead us to ignore continuities which have to do with family life and domestically- situated technology.

If so, then analysis can usefully focus on the location in which games might be played (bedrooms; living rooms) and the material factors which impinge on locational choices; the on- and offline relationships between players and others; matters such as the mediation of game playing by features of ordinary, everyday life (the demands of the family; friendship, and so on) and, as Taylor (2009b) points out, the role of technology. Nevertheless, although the idea that any study of gaming should include some analysis of the relationship between practice and the technology in which it is embedded seems self-evident, it seems to me that such analysis in large part draws on notions of media content and pays too little attention to media form. Although I wouldn't want to make too much of McLuhan's rather overblown assertions concerning 'hot' and 'cold' media (1964), they do at least serve to draw attention to the fact that 'technology' is a great deal more than its content or indeed the application which delivers it. As will be argued below, this mediation between practice and 'technology' depends as much on screen size and shape, interface and so on as it does on features of the game.

How to Study 'Gaming'

What we have suggested, then, is that one typical (though by no means the only one) and arguably dominant analytic stance to be found in the literature is radically 'culturalist', predicated on internal examinations of what game players of a quite restricted kind are engaged in when they are playing games or in activities related to playing games. This view, seductive though it is, arguably overplays - as happens so much in contemporary anthropology/ sociology - the notion of disjuncture. By emphasizing difference, it ignores similarity. Oddly (speaking as someone with extensive experience in qualitative approaches to social life), this seems closely tied to ethnographic methods. In this case (and with exceptions) however, ethnographers interested in 'gaming' appear not to have noticed how ordinary an activity it is, and how wrapped up it is in the dynamics of everyday life. It has been argued elsewhere that such stances tend to be predicated on disciplinary interests rather than a serious and principled approach to the phenomenon at hand (see e.g. Izsatt-White et al, forthcoming 2011), privileging the fashionable in respect of theory, topic, or both. The 'cultures of gaming' approach, in other words, is predisposed towards largely ignoring the various things on which gaming behavior may hinge in order to provide rich descriptions of what playing a particular game is like. There is nothing wrong with this - we get exactly what such interests suggest we will get. Studies such as that of Pearce (Pearce and Artemisia, 2009) are very effective in revealing very detailed and interesting material relating to 'communities of play' as she terms them. In much the same way, there is nothing particularly wrong with taking an interest in the way in which these new cultural forms, as Boellsdorf (ibid) terms them, may have effects on wider culture. Even so, one of the obvious initial decisions that any ethnographer has to make in order to do 'ethnography' is 'where should I go?' The fashion for 'virtual ethnography' has arguably created something of a mindset which leads us to assume that the right place to be is online. While this might serve us well as a means to uncover the communities in question, it is unlikely to be of any great use if our interest lies in the way in which game playing is a negotiated activity within the household, how it is negotiated in domestic spaces, and the role of specific material objects in those negotiations. A less dramatic attitude - one which looks at prosaic aspects of family, friendship etc., may pay off in different ways. I suggest below that, for instance, taking location, family or household dynamic and the technology seriously will reveal just as much to us.

The Moral Universe of the Household and the Use of Space

One of the strange features of the bulk of the literature on gaming cultures is the relative absence of any consideration of locality, despite the arguments produced by the likes of McRobbie and Garber rehearsed above, and by the abundant evidence that there are significant local variations in gaming practice. As Chan (2008) argues, for instance, there is a very considerable difference in the extent and form of mobile gaming in Asian countries such as Japan, and those in Western cultures. Chan examines how 'the specificities of Japanese mobile telephony are giving rise to new cultural economies of games production and engendering new paradigms of gameplay.'[1] (p13). Whatever gaming practices are or are not to be found outside the household in the UK, we should not imagine that games on mobile phones, for instance, are only ever played outside the home:

> *oh yeah, he'll sit there sometimes ... I'll be watching TV ... and he's playing 'Angry Birds' or whatever it's called on his phone ... it's alright, though, cos after all, I'm watching 'Desperate Housewives' and he's not that interested ...*

One recognition of the fact that gaming, like all online activities, actually takes place in a physical space is that of Aarsand and Aronsson (2009) who analyze and identify the ways in which game-playing spaces are negotiated by parents and children in the home. They draw explicitly on the notion of 'bedroom culture':

> *Children's use and the location of information and communication technology (ICT) have been documented in several recent studies with children and parents ... In these studies, it is argued that the location of technology has an impact on children's use, which is related to parents' ability to 'observe' their child's computer use. This implies that computer practices in the living room or other communal places may differ from practices in bedrooms or other private areas ... However, these studies also show that ICT activities at home are restricted by parents through local regulations, limiting internet access and time for gaming or the type of games allowed. Moreover, teenagers may employ various types of resistance, for instance when they disguize gaming time as 'homework' time ... Access to a computer at home does not mean that the child has exclusive access. Computers are still expensive items, and family members tend to share hardware ...*

Aarsand and Aronsson (ibid) go on to analyze what they term 'family politics' as a negotiated order, where children and parents deal with the 'territorial politics of gaming in family life'. It turns out that where the computer or gaming equipment is physically located has a significant effect on this politics. Their study of 22 children living with parents (and aged between 8 and 12) suggests that gaming practices have a great deal to do with the location of the equipment.

> *In the unique cases, where game equipment was located in the child's bedroom (as in the case of a teenager in Family 4), the parents did not join their children's gaming activities either as players or as commentators. In contrast, the parents joined or commented on children's gaming in hallways, spare rooms and living rooms. The fact that both computers*

---

[1] As an aside, according to the Independent newspaper of Jan 13, 2011, only 2% of the Japanese population are users of Facebook. If so, it demonstrates that while there are very good reasons for detailed descriptions of 'culture', comparisons can sometimes be interesting as well.

and videogame consoles were generally placed in living rooms or other public places, where people come and go during the day, still raises a question: what is the social meaning of public displays of game equipment? Many of the computers and game consoles were used by several of the family members and therefore located in places accessible to all parties. Another explanation might be that what is displayed is to be seen as an expression of what is important and central to the family members themselves.

As they point out, the location of the technology may have something to do with the age of these children. Other studies, as argued above, have suggested the bedroom is a more likely location for game-playing equipment amongst teenagers. This does, of course, not preclude the existence of a household politics, for parents will be concerned about the balance of play on computers in the bedrooms of their teenage sons and daughters as against the demands of homework and will, no doubt attempt to police such matters as best they can. In much the same way, households consisting only of adults may experience tensions and resolutions, and even young people can express some reservations about the behavior of others. As one interviewee said to me, when asked about her boyfriend's online habits:

N: *He plays rather too much, and it can sometimes get very irritating. I have to drag him out of his computer room sometimes. You know, if you've made plans with other people to go out somewhere and half an hour before you're due to meet in the pub or something, and he's still sitting there in his underpants saying, 'just a minute ... won't be long ..' ... well, it can drive you mad*

This particular respondent was very savvy about technical matters and admitted to gaming on a fairly regular basis herself. Similarly, in the following extract, we see a seventeen year old expressing quite a sophisticated awareness of the 'politics of violence' in the family:

D: *Do you know people who you think play too much?*
H: *I know people who are not even my age ... like twelve, thirteen, who get very angry if they're not allowed to go on it ... they have to go on it ... but I think it's what you're allowed to do .. like someone I know [] he's always been allowed to go on whatever games he likes ... no matter how violent it is ... like he's got the latest Call of Duty ... Black Ops .. and it's got like scenes of torture in it and actual footage ... and he plays it online with his friends and with people he's never met before ... and being only twelve, I think maybe there should be some sort of restriction ...*
C: *... I don't think it's going to influence the kids very much, but the parents ought to know about it ...*
D: *Do your parents know?*
H; *Well, Call of Duty is like my first shooting game ... I don't think I'm influenced by it ... I'm not going to go and shoot somebody ... but like my mum, she's always been like, 'I don't want you to play these violent games because they're not nice' ... but as I've got older she's given me more room ... she's never been that comfortable with me and my brother playing, like, Tekken ... and it's like such a good game ...a few people have a sort of tournament and you pick a character each and just fight ... like Kung Fu and stuff like that ... just punching each other ... until one of you is like KO-ed ... not even dead ...*

In the latter instance, my respondents drew a sharp distinction between skill-based and time-based games and, at least in part, considered their activities as a trade-off between entertainment and investment. Where parents might see a game like Tekken as 'violent', their youthful players are much more interested in the fact that they are skilful. Learning 'the moves' and getting good at them is a much more significant aspect of the game than seeing blood spurt.

Household Rhythms

Equally, of course, the dynamics of the household - the relationship between parents and their children; between partners with varying attitudes and expertise in relation to the game and so on, will be mediated through the rhythms of the day, who is doing what and when, as well as wider considerations about the moral consequences of game-playing. As Quandt et al (2009) suggest, in their study of older gamers, the dynamics in question may depend on a number of factors.

> Potential conflicts arise from computer gaming during the time that could be used productively; furthermore, life partners who do not have gaming experience cannot fully comprehend the pleasures of the gaming experience ... Similar problems were picked out as a central topic by many of the interviewed persons. Most partners seem to tolerate computer gaming as a hobby, which does not necessarily mean that they like it. There are many statements that hint at frustration or even resignation on the partner's side. They probably would like to use the "lost time" for a conversation with the partner after work or other spare-time activities in the "real life," according to the interviewees.

They also point to the way in which game players can be mindful of potential conflict and can manage their activities so as to avoid it. They give the following examples from their interview data:

> As long as it (the gaming) does not interfere with the daily routine—which means, my wife asking me to do something or expecting something from me while I am playing a computer game—it is not really a problem. I guess the acceptance of computer gaming amongst women is overall relatively small. Well, and sometimes, she says, yeah: "What a crap!" Her understanding for gaming is very small, but in the end, it doesn't matter. We don't have a row with each other because of computer gaming (Interview Thomas)
> I take care that it (the gaming) doesn't take too long. During the week, I have to get up early, half past six. And I also need some sleep! On the weekends, it depends on our (the family's) plans. If we go on a trip, then there's no gaming. Sometimes, on the afternoons or in the evenings, if there's nothing else happening, then one can sit there and keep at it. (Interview Ralph)

The rhythm of the day can, then, be consequential. This is not, however, an entirely predictable matter. As one woman in my sample said,

> E: He's actually lost interest in games now though he still watches TV series that he's downloaded rather than sit in front of the telly with me. That mainly is because we just don't like the same kind of programs. But anyway, when he used to play computer games ... I admit ... well, we didn't argue about it, but I got ... it sounds ridiculous ... I got lonely. He was up there in his bedroom playing whatever it was he was playing at three o'clock in the morning. I would wake up in the middle of the night to discover he wasn't there ...

For adults, the household has a particular moral rhythm, wherein there are expectations about shared responsibility and shared life. For parents, of course, this may mean more than simply attending to time in an immediate sense, for their concerns will be mediated by their sense of the trustworthiness of their children and their worries (or otherwise) about their progress:

> D: do your parents police it ... do they check up on you?
> H: Not so much now ... she used to ... but not so much now ... she's, like, if you want to waste your life in front of a screen ... it's your life ... I think if it had a noticeable effect on my marks and my character, she'd probably start up ... but she polices what my brother does ... cos he's, like, still little and she doesn't want him to get sucked in ... I think he plays them, not only cos he likes them but cos his friends play them ...
> C: yeah, I think it's a social thing ...
> H: I don't know if it is or not ... whether he plays them cos he wants to be in that sort of circle or if he just plays cos he's got nothing else to do ... he does like his TV ...

For young adults, living in a different kind of household, expectations may be very different:

> A: I think that ... when I got to Uni ... I found that the number of people playing MMOs was, like, well up ... and the truth is, you've got loads of time ... well, you don't have loads of free time ...
> D: Oh, you do ... (laughter)
> A: like, loads of my friends play MMOs now, but they still have a social life ... though X, one of my housemates ... he does tend to miss events ... so, Y, was in a play and he missed it cos he was playing WoW ...

We can see this as something of a continuum from disapprobation and concern to enthusiasm and commitment. Parents understandably demonstrate concerns about such things as the appropriateness of gaming content, the time their children might be spending on games, the displacement of other and more important activities such as homework. They may well see the decisions of their teenage children as carrying implications for the unity or dissolution of the family unit. Older couples may see gaming as a challenge to their relationship. On the other hand, gaming might be seen as a harmless activity in comparison to being out there 'on the street', may be viewed as actively positive (for instance in performing an educational function or as something that members of the family can all participate in together). Indeed, there is a literature about 'serious' games (see Charsky, 2010 for a discussion) which sees educational possibility in game play. A few parents subscribe to that view:

> P: It's not necessarily all bad ... don't some people think that it's good for hand-eye coordination? ... I think you can learn something from them, even if it's only about getting along with people ... or a bit of healthy competition ...

Perhaps more importantly, we should not should not assume that attitudes towards computer gaming are decontextualized views concerning whether it is a 'good' or 'bad' thing. Rather, attitudes are couched in terms of quite specific relevancies. They might be a 'bad' thing when they interfere with schoolwork, or with normal family time together. They might, equally, be a good and useful thing on occasions when getting rid of the children for a while is seen as a desired outcome. Much like alcoholism, gaming is perceived as a problem mainly when it is disruptive of other activities.

Friendship, Connectedness, Community, the Network

If games are played mainly in the household, it does not mean that wider networks or communities are not somehow implicated. It would, however, be a mistake to think that this is unidimensional:

> A: *I like genres ... adventure games ... I do play MMOs ... Guild Wars and I played that for quite an extended period of time. I like world games ... like Oblivion, it's like a fantasy world, but it's single player. When I was at school I played a lot more fighting games ... in school, we'd play tournaments against each other, but at home it would often be online ...*
>
> D: *Was this with people you knew or with strangers*
>
> A: *With people I knew ... I'm not very good ... I don't really make much of a connection with people ... like, I don't make friends online ...*
>
> D: *Cos one of the things that makes MMOs interesting, according to some, is the chat function ...*
>
> A: *Yeah ... some people do ... like my friend X., he literally has, like, loads of friends that he's made online ... but I mainly stick to people I already know.*
>
> D: *And is this sustained ... I mean, does he keep these friends ...*
>
> A: *What he tends to do is, like, play an MMO and when he gets bored with it, they'll all move to a different one ... I do the same thing with my friends when we get bored ...*
>
> D: *And how long will that be, on average...*
>
> A;   *Oh, with MMOs it can be a long time... they can last for years, it depends on how much content you have ... , when it's really grindy ...*
>
> D;   *Grindy?*
>
> A: *Grinding is when you, say ... it isn't varied game play ... it's like, say, when you're fighting and you need to get to the next level so you can move on in the game ... and so you just have the fights over and over until you actually go to the next level ... that can take hours and hours and hours and hours ... that's the boring part ... they pad them out by making you grind ... it's just something you do, even if you're not enjoying it ... it's just something you do to get to the next level ...*

In this single extract we can see a number of different possibilities. Game playing can be co-located, and often is. It can be distributed, but involve people with whom we are friends offline, or it can involve the creation of whole new groups. Sometimes, as we see above, these groups persist in such a way that we can begin to think about them as communities or networks, although it also seems that these networks can exist independently of any single game. Other times, they may not. In part, the amount of time that is taken up in learning to master a game is significant and one can well imagine that certain categories of person have significantly more available time than others:

> A: *Was that EVEOnline? ... that game is really ... I would say that's the best example of a social, creative, world game ... the whole economy's created by the gamers ... the whole game is created by the community, and selling and buying ... it's like a market inside it ... and there's a whole ecosystem of players ... the developers support it ... and it's a PVP game (player versus player) ... you make fleets and each fleet can battle with other fleets ... each person in the fleet is someone playing ... you get crazy stories of like espionage where someone will join a Corp ... they call them Corps ... and work their way up ... through the ranks ... and once the player has access to all the banks and money, they find out that this player has disbanded the whole Corp ... you have to put so many hours into it to make it work, though, I don't play it now ... I don't have the time ...*

The issue of time crops up again in this extract:

A couple of players I know ... they would play [EVEonline] for forty hours a week, but now it's more like 10 ... M., he's got two kids, so his time is restricted, but if he can he'll play with his baby in his arms ...

And,

We used to game together a lot when we didn't live together, but now we don't. I prefer Team Fortress, cos you can play it for half an hour and put it away ... I don't have much time ... but he can spend all day on EVE.

Time matters. However, we should not imagine that it does so independently of other aspects of our social lives, nor that it has significance only within the span of the day:

We don't live together, we both still live with our parents ... we mainly play FPSs we both have our Xboxes and we chat to each other online and play the same game. We actually met on the internet. I played a lot when I was a kid ... my uncle got me into it cos I used to watch him play Doom when I was 10 or 11 ... then stopped as a teenager as I got interested in other things and then it took off again ... I'm 27 now ...

The above quotes indicate that other routines, predicated on life trajectories, have an impact on behavior. Obligations of a quite mundane kind, as with everyone else, intrude on the world of the gamer. The most obsessed gamer cannot completely ignore his children (at least, not for long); the demands of essay writing and working part-time can intrude even on a relationship where both are avid gamers, and so on.

Materiality and Technology

It is easy to forget that a very ordinary and mundane usage of private space for whatever purposes will depend to a considerable degree on the material organization of available spaces. Houses have become larger and children and young people much more likely to have their own spaces than previously. Put simply, being able to play computer games in one's bedroom depends on having a bedroom. Being able to do so in isolation depends on having one's own bedroom (at least to some extent). As Williams (2006) points out,

Architecturally, families are ever more internally separated from each other. Census data show that our houses, like nearly every portion in modern society ... are ever larger and more subdivided .... Media entertainment stations can be found increasingly in the private spaces of individual family members rather than in common spaces. For example, recent data show that roughly 50% of all children now have game consoles in their own rooms, where presumably they play away from their parents

The privatized family (and how odd it is that a phrase like 'privatized family' can remain meaningful in an era when we talk, equally meaningfully here, about the 'connected family'), then, is privatized not only in relation to the wider neighborhood and community but even internally (see Putnam, 2001). Now, we need not take this too literally - even if there is evidence that children are more likely to be gaming away from family members this is probably to do with a range of other social factors rather than gaming per se (dual career families; extended working hours; working from home, and so on). Nevertheless, it remains the case that changing spaces of this kind have some impact on the moral and emotional arrangements that typify family life. ('What is he doing up there? Do you think she spends too much time in her bedroom? Is he getting on with his schoolwork?)

It is more common to discuss the impact of the gaming technology. Aarsand and Aronsson (ibid), for instance, point to the role of specific technology in the social production of gaming behavior. Hence:

> Three of the families had a videogame console (PlayStation or Xbox), game technologies that allow for multiple players. In two cases out of three, these videogame consoles were placed in the living room, where the screen was used both for gaming and for watching TV. The technological infrastructure of videogame consoles thus does not allow people to play games and watch TV at the same time. The technology as such enforces a sequential choice, where it is necessary to decide what can be done at what point in time: watching TV or gaming, i.e. decisions concerning temporal dimensions of space appropriations ('when' and 'how long').

Almost by definition, the location of gaming technologies in the home will be affected by the nature of the technology in question and in turn the placement of these machineries produces certain kinds of negotiated outcomes. Firstly, and obviously, as they point out, communal spaces will entail negotiations around timing and duration, for the use of family spaces for gaming purposes precludes (at least at present) the use of the same space for other purposes. Nevertheless, they may also afford joint household or peer group activity.

Closely related to all the above is another simple, but too little acknowledged fact, that the technology can and does impact on the use of space. In some instances, available technology has an immersive effect and can increase the sense of a 'privatized' space:

> H: I mainly play Call of Duty ... I got a Mac with a big screen and the graphics on it are really good ... it really draws you in ... and if you play it with headphones ... if you turn, the sound sort of turns with you ... it makes it really sort of addictive in a sense ... it sounds horrible to say you want to kill more people to get more points on that certain level ... you might get a better gun so you can kill even more people, quicker ... there's also, like, little challenges that you have to complete ... like twenty five headshots ... but everyone plays it in a lighthearted sort of way ...

Thus, it would seem that both the game and the technology on which it is played can have this 'immersive' effect. At the same time, other technologies seem to encourage activity and cooperation. I am far from the first to recognize that the development of the technology underpinning the Nintendo Wii and, more recently, Microsoft's Kinect affects the way games are played and the spaces in which they are played. As one respondent put it,

> A: I went to a party and they had Kinect there ... it's really active, actually ... I was really tired after playing twenty minutes or so ... you can eat pizza while you're playing which is, like, really gross (laughs) ..

And,

D: *"These different technologies, would they like make a difference in terms of where you would play games?"*

A: *"Definitely, cos like in X's room, generally it's quite empty. Kinect you can't sit down and play ... well, you might be able to but you need to stand up to calibrate it ... I know several people who've had to move, like, loads of stuff ... "*

There is evidence, for instance, about the Wii which suggests that the technology affords a more active and cooperative form of *co-located* game playing (see for instance Harley et al, 2010). Nevertheless it seems that the Wii, although designed with physical movement in mind, does not necessarily have that effect. Here, it seems to be a combination of the interface and the kind of game that is typically played that creates this:

A: *You can play almost all the games sitting down if you want ... you quickly realize that, say you're playing tennis ... you don't need to stand up and go right through the motion (swings arm), you can just stay sitting down and sort of flick and it has the same effect.*

It seems that the simplicity of the interface encourages some, at least, to get involved in co-located game playing activities:

D: *"You said tournaments ... would this be at home?"*
     "Yes, it can be single player or multi-player but everyone plays the multi-player option."

A: *"What makes it interesting is the different combos you can learn ... getting really good at it ... it's more of a skill-based one whereas the MMOs are more time-based ... you don't get better at it it's just that over time your character develops over time ... when you're really good, like I don't even look at the Pad ... but my mum ... she's hopeless ... when you've got an Xbox or a Playstation she, like, just doesn't get it? ... she just about manages the TV remote (laughter) ... she could probably learn but it would take time and with the Wii even five year olds can be good. "*

Less has been said about the potential impact of new screen technologies, perhaps because, thus far, cost and technological limitation have meant for the bedroom-based gamer, not that much has changed. It may well in the near future. Organic Light-Emitting Diode (OLED) technology in principle allows for very thin, low cost and bendable screens. Although there are no retail commercial applications as yet for this technology (as far as I know) the prospect of large scale, bendable, screens may have implications for the immersive quality of game play in ways we have yet to see. Equally speculatively, as yet we have no data concerning the way that the latest generation of mobile devices may impact on game playing behavior. Tablet computing could have a significant impact on our gaming, both outside and inside the home. We shall see.

Conclusion

The last twenty years, as this book and its precursor have shown, have seen very substantial changes in the household. Without question, the 'connected home' is, at least in terms of its potentials, the most significant of these developments. The fact of instantaneous (for all practical purposes) connection to the outside world, the proliferation of devices to support it (mobile and otherwise), the development of applications which explicitly support some kind of friendship, community, network, and the willingness of people to use these technologies and applications for some considerable proportion of their time, all attest to this. Nevertheless, we need to remember that this is not a one way street. It is hardly the case that, before the advent of the internet, people were somehow 'unconnected'. As Harper points out in his examination of *inter alia* letter writing (Harper, 2010), communications by whatever medium were expressions of various things - of friendship, of love, etc., - and expressivity remains an important feature of our daily life. While it is perfectly true that the 'connected home' entails some significant changes in our household behavior, it is equally true that firstly the 'moral universe' of the household, and secondly material matters such as location, shape connectedness as well. In this chapter we have tried to pursue an approach to gaming which recognizes that it is a geographically located activity (regardless of the rhetoric around 'distribution'), is an activity which takes place in an existing moral universe (regardless of the rhetoric of cultural discontinuity) in which the obligations of family and friendship regularly intrude and which associates with material factors (regardless of the rhetoric of 'virtuality'). In so doing, we attempt a slight rebalancing of the available literature on gaming away from a focus which insists that the online game itself, the cultural lives of the players and the consequences of these new forms for our understanding of culture and community towards one which both recognizes certain continuities in the nature of family and community life and equally recognizes that the existing moral order influences the way games are played as much as new forms of gaming are transformative. Connected households are still recognizably households. When such households consist of parents and children (in some combination), it is not entirely surprising that gaming is structured in part by the relationship between them which associate with age, with gender, with the use of time, with presumptions about 'value', and so on. Again, it is not surprising that such matters ramify in different ways in households with different sets of social relationship (like, for instance, a student household). Equally, and as we have seen, the 'connected home' does not mean that online activities necessarily replace co-located activities. The fact that some of my respondents spoke of 'tournaments' which may well involve the playing of an online game but can at exactly the same time involve friends (or family) sitting together in the home strongly suggests that we should see the connected home as sometimes adding to interactional possibilities within the home rather than subtracting from them; as creating interesting admixtures of face-to-face and online behavior rather than transforming one into the other. Further, 'connected households' are not all the same. Families with young children may see game playing in a different way to families with teenagers; young couples may (or may not) see game playing as a way of celebrating their relationship; the student may have sufficient time to spend hours on even the 'grindiest' of games or, elsewhere, the mundanities of working life intervene. Time is evidently a major feature of this. It is possible, though we should admit that this is based on cursory evidence, that the very different behaviors we see in the skilful but sometimes 'short burst' preferences of the FPS gamer are very different from the more 'social' gamer in his/her MMO or 'world' game, grinding their way through different levels, precisely because available time makes a big difference. In pursuing gaming in this way, we discover - not a culture, defined in terms of consistencies of attitude and behavior - but a set of practices, many and varied and seemingly impacted on by any number of factors. We find, in short, very considerable variation. The moral universe of the household (the practices of parents, siblings and peers); material forms (the domestic environment, the computer interface, and other technology); the nature of friendship and community networks (both real and virtual, structured by age and gender), and not least the kind of game being played, all impact on the kinds of connectedness on display.

References

Adams, T. and Smith, S. (2008) *Electronic Tribes: the virtual worlds of geeks, gamers, shamans and scammers*. Austin: University of Texas Press

Aarsand, P. and Aronsson, K. (2009) Gaming and Territorial Negotiations in Family Life *Childhood* 16: 497

Anscombe, E. (1957) *Intention*. Cambridge, Mass.: Harvard University Press

Aries, Phillipe. (1962) *Centuries of Childhood*. New York: Vintage Books

Bartle, R. (2010) *From MUDs to MMORPGs: The History of Virtual Worlds*, in J. Hunsinger, L. Klastrup and M. Allen (eds.) (2010) *International Handbook of Internet Research*. Dordrecht: Springer

Beavis, C. (2005) Pretty Good For a Girl: Gender, identity and Computer Games. *Proceedings of DiGRA 2005 Conference: Changing Views – Worlds in Play*

Bertozzi, E. and Lee, L. (2007) Not Just Fun and Games: Digital Play, Gender and Attitudes Towards Technology. *Womens Studies In Communication* 30 (2)

Boellstorff, T. (2006) A Ludicrous Discipline? Ethnography and Game Studies. *Games and Culture* 2006; 1; 29

Bovill, M. and Livingstone, S. (2001) Bedroom Culture and the Privatization of Media Use. In S. Livingstone and M. Bovill (eds) *Children and their Changing Media Environment: A European Comparative Study*. Mahjah, N.J: Lawrence Erlbaum 179-200

Castronova, E. (2007) *Exodus to the Virtual World: How Online Fun is Changing Reality*. London: Palgrave McMillan

Chan, D. (2008) Convergence, Connectivity, and the Case of Japanese Mobile Gaming. *Games and Culture* 3; 13

Charsky, D. (2010) From Edutainment to Serious Games: A Change in the Use of Game Characteristics *Games and Culture* 5

Ducheneaut, N. and Moore, R. J. (2004) The social side of gaming: a study of interaction patterns in a massively multiplayer online game. *Proceedings of CSCW '04*. Chicago. ACM Press.

Dovey, J. and Kennedy, H. (2006) *Game Cultures: Computer Games as New media*. Maidenhead: Open University Press

Flanagan, M. (2005) Troubling 'Games For Girls': Notes from the Edge of Game Design. *Proceedings of DiGRA 2005 Conference: Changing Views – Worlds in Play*

Harley, D., Fitzpatrick, G., Axelrod, L., White, G. and McAllister, G. (2010) Making the Wii at Home: Game Play by Older People in Sheltered Housing In: USAB 2010: *HCI in Work & Learning, Life & Leisure*. (In Press)

Harper, R. (2010) *Texture: Human expression in the Age of Communications Overload*. Cambridge, Mass: MIT Press

Hartmann, T., and Klimmt, C. (2006). Gender and computer games: Exploring females' dislikes. *Journal of Computer-Mediated Communication, 11*(4)

Hunsinger, J., Klastrup, L. and Allen, M. (eds.) (2010) *International Handbook of Internet Research*. Dordrecht: Springer

Izsatt-White, M., Graham, C., Kelly, S., Randall. D. and Rouncefield, M (forthcoming 2011) *Leadership in Post-Compulsory Education*. London: Continuum Books.

Klastrup, L. (2010) Understanding Online (Game) Worlds, in J. Hunsinger, L. Klastrup and M. Allen (eds.) (2010) *International Handbook of Internet Research*. Dordrecht: Springer

Lincoln, S. (2005) Feeling The Noise: Teenagers, bedrooms and Music, *Leisure Studies*, Routledge

McLuhan, M. (1964) *Understanding Media: The Extensions of Man*. Cambridge: MIT Press

McRobbie, A. (1991) *Feminism and Youth Culture: From 'Jackie' to 'Just Seventeen'*. London: Macmillan

McRobbie, A. and Garber, J. (1976) Girls and Subcultures in S. hall and T. Jefferson (eds) *Resistance Through Rituals*. London: Hutchinson.

Mitchell, C. and Reid-Walsh, J. *Girl Culture: An Encyclopedia*. Westport, Connecticut: Greenwood Press

Nardi, B. and Harris, J. (2010) Strangers and Friends: Collaborative Play in World of Warcraft, *Proceedings of CSCW '96*, Banff, Canada, Nov 4-8, ACM Press in World of Warcraft in J. Hunsinger, L. Klastrup and M. Allen (eds.) (2010) *International Handbook of Internet Research*. Dordrecht: Springer

New Strategist Publications. (2010) *American Time Use; Who spends how long doing what?* Ithaca: New York

Paulk, C. (2006) Signifying Play: The Sims and the Sociology of Interior Design. *The International Journal of Computer Game Research*. Volume 6 (1)

Putnam, R. (2001) *Bowling Alone: The Collapse and Revival of American Community*. New York: Simon and Schuster

Pearce, R. and 'Artemisia'. 2009. *Communities of Play: Emergent Cultures in MultiPlayer Games and Virtual Worlds*. Cambridge, Mass: MIT Press

Quandt, T., Grueninger, H. and Wimmer, J. (2009) The Gray Haired Gaming Generation: Findings From an Interview Study on Older Computer Gamers, Games and Culture. Games *and Culture* 4.7.

Shaw, A. (2010) What Is Video Game Culture? Cultural Studies and Game Studies. *Games and Culture* 5.

Smith, B (2006) The (Computer) games People Play: An Overview of Popular Games Content. in P. Vorderer and J. Bryant. *Playing Video Games*. London: Routledgepp43-56.

Steele, J. and Brown, J. (1995) Adolescent Room Culture: Studying media in the Context of Everyday Life. *Journal of Youth and Adolescence*. Vol 24. No 5.

Tapscott, D. (2009) *Grown Up Digital: How the Net Generation is Changing Your World*. New York: McGraw-Hill.

Taylor, T. (2009a) *Play Between Worlds: exploring Online Game Culture*. Cambridge, Mass.: MIT Press.

Taylor, T. (2009b) The Assemblage of Play. *Games and Culture*. 4; 331.

Turkle, S. (1997) *Life on the Screen: Identity in the Age of the Internet*. Touchstone Books

Turow, J. and Kavanaugh, A. (2003) *The Wired Homestead: An MIT Press Sourcebook on the Internet and the Family*. Cambridge, Mass.: MIT Press.

Vorderer, P. and Bryant, J. (2006) *Playing Video Games*. London: Routledge

Quandt, T., Grueninger, H. and Wimmer, J. (2009) The Gray Haired Gaming Generation : Findings From an Explorative Interview Study on Older Computer Gamers *Games and Culture* 4: 27.

Williams, D. 2006. Why Game Studies Now? Gamers Don't Bowl Alone. *Games and Culture* 1; 13.

Chapter 8
Digital Words: Reading and the 21st Century Home

Mark Rouncefield and Peter Tolmie

Introduction

The home is a text rich environment and people's everyday home life normally and quite unproblematically embraces many different kinds of reading associated with such things as scribbled messages, post-it notes left on fridge doors, labels, articles in newspapers, magazines, and, of course, books. Increasingly reading incorporates various electronic devices, whether it is reading text messages, reading instant message chat or reading friends' Facebook statuses on mobile phones, laptops and desktop computers. In considering reading in the 21st century home and how the process and activity of reading might change, we need to appreciate the different processes and kinds of reading (reading for pleasure, reading as work, reading as a distraction or time-filler etc.), the different circumstances in which reading is accomplished as well as the 'technologies' of reading and the interactions between them. With regard to the different technologies of reading, computer screen, e-book, magazine or book we need to bear in mind some of the very different 'affordances' of these technologies and how they therefore fit into everyday living.

As we consider the process of reading and how technology might impact on this we necessarily tend to think about what may amount to the 're-imagination' or 'remediation' (Bolter and Grusin 1999) of reading and persistent allegations, for example, that new reading technologies are 'making us stupid' (Carr 2008) or 'lazy' (Collins 2011). Importantly, we need to consider the 'situatedness' of reading, the ecological and social circumstances in which reading takes place, how it is embroiled in the rhythms and routines of everyday home life and its associated pains and pleasures, often expressed in phrases like 'curling up with a good book' and which thereby encompass a whole range of emotions and sensations including smell, and feel and sight. Above all, before jumping to any premature conclusions on the future of either the book or the e-book we need to consider the varied processes of domestication (Silverstone 1994) and innofusion (Fleck 1988), the processes of

M. Rouncefield (✉)
Lancaster University, Lancaster, UK

R. Harper (ed.), *The Connected Home: The Future of Domestic Life*,
DOI 10.1007/978-0-85729-476-0_8, © Springer-Verlag London 2011

'taming' and adaptation, faced by any technology that enters the domestic space; to reflect on the ways in which new technologies get incorporated into everyday household routines and rituals and, correspondingly, the extent to which new interactional and organizational practices emerge.

In this chapter we are talking about reading in the home, which is not just a building but also a set of activities and social relations and obligations that are played out in various ways. The shape and construction of buildings may evolve (Brand 1994) and the 'stuff' that is in them can change, but children will still need to be put to bed, people will still relax after a hard day at work, people will still choose to 'lie in' on a 'day off' and reading may well form some important part of these activities. Consequently any new device, new 'stuff' will be 'domesticated', will be accommodated to fit these routines even whilst new routines are being developed. As Sacks so cogently argues any technology is placed in an organization that 'already has whatever organization it has' - : *"...it's the source for the failures of technocratic dreams, that if only we introduced some fantastic new communication machine the world will be transformed. Where what happens is that the object is made at home in the world that has whatever organization it already has."* (Sacks (1992) - and although Sacks was talking about the telephone we believe the comment also applies to e-book readers of whatever kind and helps us to avoid some of the hype that is seemingly inevitably attached to new electronic gadgets.

There is a growing body of research on everyday domestic life (Venkatesh 2001, Crabtree 2004) its organization (O'Brien et al 1999) and the role of technology in the home (Silverstone et al 1990, Edwards and Grinter 2001). When it comes to reading in the home, and specifically reading books, the position is rather complicated. There is undoubtedly a great deal of research on reading and on the associated technologies of reading – specifically the book and various electronic devices such as the computer and the e-book. In 'Books in the Digital Age', for example, Thompson (2005) argues for the continued importance of conventional books based on the obvious failings of e-books: that they suffer from poor readability, are over-priced, have problems over copyright and format compatibility and clash with some important, long-standing and highly valued cultural practices associated with paper books. Other research has considered the legibility of text on electronic devices (Lonsdale et al 2006,) or compared reading on screen with reading on paper (O'Hara and Sellen 1997) or the academic use of e–books (Rowlands, et al, 2007) and recently a number of less formal reviews of e-readers such as the Kindle have appeared (Marr 2007, Henscher 2009) generally consisting of journalists spending a day or two playing with, and usually enjoying, the technology before pontificating usually on whether the e-reader will ever replace the book.

However, many of these studies whilst happily pronouncing on the fate of the book, reserve their interest either for specific forms of reading – such as academic reading, looking for references, comparing texts etc.; or for a general discourse on the fate of publishing in the electronic age – usually along the lines of whether we are witnessing the end of the book as we know it (Crain 2007, Chartier 1997). Our interest in this chapter is much narrower, much more particular: we are specifically interested in reading at home and reflecting on the changing role of text in the home setting and, in particular, on the evolution of reading given the emergence of E-Books, iPads and other technological competitors to more traditional technologies of reading – that is, books. As more and more of our everyday text reading involves reading from some kind of screen or device (computer, mobile phone, e-book etc.) there are a number of interesting questions concerning whether and how digital technology might change the ways in which we read and its place in the fabric of everyday life.

Our claim therefore is not that there has been no research on e-reading, or that the research on issues such as usability has not been worthwhile, since both would be silly arguments, but rather that much of the research on e-reading, e-books etc., is surprisingly un-situated, assuming that all reading is the same, and rarely being preoccupied with the kinds of reading that people indulge in within domestic spaces, within the home – specifically reading for pleasure. Many of the studies about e-reading or e-books are less concerned with reading than with publishing, with digital rights management and issues of standards (and where they are interested in reading it is often a specific form of reading i.e. academic reading). Clearly these are important issues, though for us the significance lies less in the economics of the situation than in the impact it might have on people's ideas about their possessions, about ownership and display and related matters. Furthermore, many of the studies might be regarded as premature, particularly in their technical prognostications, because their empirical work and findings are generally (and perhaps inevitably) overtaken by developments in the technology (often before publication). At the same time, many studies fail to place the activity of reading, of using an e-book in its appropriate social and domestic circumstances – that, for example, this means reading at home, at bedtime, to children and so on. As Silberman argues; *"Gadgets fail when we don't understand them, but also when they don't understand us. The measure of success for the makers of electronic books will be how much they comprehend why we pick up a book in the first place"*. (Silberman 1998:100) It is this aspect of situatedness, how books actually get used, why and how we pick up a book in the first place, and how we go about the business of reading them, the everyday, family circumstances in which we read books (or a Kindle or iPad), for which we require some empirical evidence.

A good example, both of current research on e-books and some of these kinds of problems is Hillesund's (2001) First Monday study 'Will E-books Change the World? and other similar and related papers on e-books and e-book readers (Hillesund 2007 and 2010). Written long before the introduction of the Kindle and the iPad, the major differences between the 2001 and 2010 articles is perhaps that many of the important technical issues have been resolved, though the legal, economic and social issues rather less so. Hillesund makes it clear that he is concerned with far more important issues than the replacement of one artefact – a book – with another – an e-reader. He wants to focus the debate on far deeper, more serious, questions than whether the Kindle will replace the book in our homes and affections. As he puts it`; *"the sentimentally framed questions about digital books and electronic devices replacing printed books are largely irrelevant, an artificial and distracting controversy"*. Hillesund starts from a position that suggests that the development of the e-book was 'inevitable', a further development of what Ong (1982) calls 'the technologizing of the word'- and a consequence of the rise of the network society (Castells 1996) with the associated creation of new products and marketplaces whereby e-books become the books of the network society. Hillesund perceives far more complex issues behind the emergence of e-reader devices and, to that extent at least the technology doesn't matter. Instead he hints at much wider and deep-seated issues that impact on how books are written, produced, supplied and read in a digital age. *"The real issues are more fundamental: how do we think of books in the digital world, and how will books behave? How will we be able to use them, to share them, and to refer to them? In particular, what are our expectations about the persistence and permanence of human communication as embodied in books as we enter the brave new digital world?"*

When it comes to e-readers and similar electronic devices Hillesund also wants to demolish some popular misconceptions about how they operate. In particular he argues (and casual observation would concur), that e-book readers are not just intended for reading books but for a whole range of reading activities including newspapers and magazines. Similarly it is evident that certain types of reading, certain types of 'book' have quickly developed wide public use – these are things like dictionaries, Encyclopedias, directories, product catalogues, and so on, where the digital experience has improved on, or gone beyond the paper experience because, for example, the digital format can afford rapid updating or provide hyperlinks to multimedia. Secondly, and importantly, he suggests that the e-reader is not simply a replacement for the book on your bookshelf, a slimmer, electronic version of 'War and Peace' for example, but that it effectively replaces the entire library: it's not a substitute book, or rather it's not *just* a substitute book but a substitute *book collection*: *"In a very real sense, presenting an e-book reader as a sort of substitute for a printed book underestimates and trivializes the future"*. Seeing the e-reader as simply a digital book tends to obscure much deeper issues in the evolution of technology and its use in a range of reading behaviors in a variety of contexts.

Finally, although many of the technical quality issues of e-readers appear to have been resolved Hillesund identifies a number of important questions facing e-books. Whilst many of these concern publishing and digital rights, others focus on a range of largely cultural practices that have grown up around book reading. So, for example, whilst lending books is commonplace, how can people lend digital content? How can people copy from an e-book? If people lose their e-reader do they need to repurchase the content – that is, do people own objects or access? What happens when your e-reader becomes out-dated, or the maker goes out of business? Of course none of these are actually about the experience of reading, or the actual reader experience – how reading devices might fit into a life that, as we have already suggested, already has whatever organization it has. Consequently, when we move away from the mere *technologies* of reading to consider reading as a situated *experience* our interest and focus shifts: our concern is not merely in the content of a novel for example, and whether the story moves us or angers us or inspires us, but also with the look and smell of the book, the look and feel of the pages, the evocative and sentimental descriptions of reading in the bath, making friends (see http://www.youtube.com/watch?v=mzImtwWfoMk) and so on.

We are interested, then, in what might be seen as the embodied features of reading as they occur in particular contexts. All reading is not the same. Reading is not just about content, as Mangen (2008) states; *".. the book, as a material object, consists of more than immediately meets the eye"*. Reading is not a mere cognitive or mental activity but involves bodily, physical aspects as seen in the use of hands and fingers to flick backwards and forwards through the text, or to hold the book open or mark particular pages. Reading generally involves various forms of manual dexterity and, as our empirical studies (or simple observations) show, frequently extends beyond a simple narration. It is for this reason that we need to carry out some empirical research on reading in the home, to see how people go about the everyday work of reading. This is not some simplistic comparison between books and e-readers but instead an attempt to uncover some important details of how reading is routinely accomplished and performed and how it forms part of the routine of everyday life, of the organization of the home, details that may well impact on both the possible reception of electronic readers or the continued usage of books.

Book Reading: The Data

In this part of the chapter we look at some data relating to reading practices and the ways in which they amount to a socially organized phenomenon within the home. The data has been gathered across three different households, though there was some difference in their configuration:

Household A: Two married professional parents in their 40s with three children of 11, 9 and 6 years old.
Household B: Two married professional parents, 41 and 35, with a new born baby c. 1 month old.
Household C: Two married parents, one professional, one artisan, in their 40s with four children, all living at home, of 20, 16, 14, and 7 years old.

The practices observed fell very crudely into four distinct sets of interest: 1) the individual reading of paper-based books; 2) the individual reading of books at fixed computer workstations; 3) the individual reading of books on portable computing devices (iPad, Kindle, etc.); and 4) the reading of books to others. As indicated above, these practices were not simply separable according to specific individuals in the households but were rather engaged in by the same individuals at different times according to what was evidently appropriate in a particular context. This reinforces the argument we make throughout this chapter that the situation with paper-based and electronic-based books rather reflects the situation found with regards to the use of paper in office environments (Sellen & Harper, 2002), namely that one does not simply replace the other but rather each offers up particular affordances that are turned to at particular times. As with any body of practice, there are manifest, situated logics that attach to how people reason about their reading practices and these are accountable to the moment, to the social organization in play, not the technology in and as of itself.

The actual approach to gathering data was a mixture of direct observation and non-structured interviews. The analytic approach throughout has been ethnomethodological and the focus is upon manifest, accountable reasoning and practice. Of course reading is not just a matter of consuming words off the page but rather about accomplishing a range of possible activities within the home environment such as: 'relaxing', 'killing time', 'informing', 'having a break', 'putting to bed', and so on. Here we hinge our discussion of the data around our observations of bedtime reading because these most clearly demonstrate the placement of a particular household activity within a routine whilst at the same time bringing into view a wide variety of the organizational characteristics of reading from matters of embodiment to spatiotemporal placement, from affordances to visibility and coordination.

Findings

Reading is embodied: The first thing we want to emphasize about reading is its embodied character, for upon this many other aspects of reading as a social phenomenon can be seen to turn. In the following observations the mother in household C (M) is reading a bedtime story to her 7 year old daughter (S):

(M picking up the book to sit down as S reaches out to her)		(M gets ready to open the book)	
(M flicks through the pages)		(M opens the book)	
(M holding the book in place as asking S to recall the last part)		(M starting to read) M: Chapter twelve. Cold air burned in Torak's throat as he tore through a willow thicket...	

M: ...big and dark (opening at a new page [note it's visibly the last couple of pages of the chapter]) ...		S: More story M: (flicking forward page by page - note the finger still held in place at the beginning of the chapter)	
S: Up to (.) there M: Up to that one? (pointing)		S: Yes (.) There (pointing) ...	
M: ... Right. That's where I'm stopping. (M reaches over and gets the bookmark from the arm of the chair)		(M puts the bookmark in the book, shuts it, and puts it over to her right)	

The above data illustrates many of the ways in which the embodied character of reading is visible: the manner of sitting; of holding one's arms; of holding one's hands; the angle of the head; the direction of the gaze; the actual relation and orientation to the object held; and how each of these proceeds dynamically in order to accomplish something that looks like, in this case, 'reading to your daughter' and 'being read to by your mother'.

If we look at how the mother holds her arms as she is reading to her daughter we can see how they are positioned so as to support being able to hold one side of the open book with her right hand, the other with her left, whilst also encompassing her daughter with her left arm and holding the book open in such a way that both parties can see the open pages. As we discuss later, these embodied practices of reading are one of the ways in which the relationships between different members of a family can come to be articulated and made manifest. Even the position of their heads is a feature of the embodied practices of reading. The direction of the gaze itself is also important. It must accommodate the actual work of reading, the eyes tracking along lines in an appropriate fashion to preserve fluidity without losing one's place. As with the head the gaze is visible and diverting the gaze to some other object is accountable.

All of these embodied matters together make up both an appropriate positioning of the object for the on-going work of reading aloud and being read to and make visible the orientation of the participants to just that, with any variation in their accomplishment being commonsensically readable as 'inattention', 'getting distracted', 'falling asleep', 'pausing for comment', 'about to ask a question', or whatever.

Clearly an important part of the above data is the way the reading is accomplished as a shared activity between parent and child. However, very many aspects of the parental accomplishment, setting aside matters of orientation to the child and actual vocalizing of the words, are extremely similar to how the reading of a book is embodied when reading alone. Matters of posture, direction of gaze, angle of head, grosser orders of keeping place and turning pages, the handling of bookmarks, and so on, are apparent whether reading to someone else or to yourself and many of these things are important for the economical and effective realization of seeing the words on the page and engaging with them in an appropriate order.

The latter point emphasizes how much of reading on other devices such as Kindles and PCs must also be reasonably accomplished. Kindles, it turns out, get engaged with in similar places to books and with wholly similar bodily orientations:

> So I've got quite a few books now which are down the side of my bed and in my hand at the same time in the Kindle and I will sometimes be reading it in bed - the Kindle - and then put that down and pick up the book.
> So where, when you are at home, do you use the Kindle?
> ... So most places I would - including the loo - I would use the Kindle ... if you went to my bedroom now you'd see a pile of books and the Kindle on top of it. And I just pick that up as I would pick up another book perhaps by chance, and then, moving into the other bedroom, there's a pile of books in that room too and I would take the Kindle with me
> So where do you read the physical books in that case?
> In all the same places.

Evidently there are certain kinds of manipulation for beginning to read in terms of positioning the device and locating the thing to be read, and for the turning of pages in the course of reading and shutting the thing down at the end, which involve physically distinct movements by hand and arm. But having said this, Kindles are of reasonably similar size and weight and shape to a book (if somewhat flatter) and this enables many of the same kinds of postures and orientations one encounters with physical books. Indeed, taking something of a similar shape and size where the point is to 'consume words' so to speak, and where one already has the competence to do that job of consuming words, it's hard to imagine how the engagement with the device would be radically distinct in these respects.

Reading is manifest: One of the most important corollaries of the embodiment of reading is that, by virtue of its embodied character, it is also manifest to other people in a variety of ways. This makes it open to ordinary recognition and reasoning as a feature of the environment it inhabits. Thus reading comes to have as much of a place within the social organization of a setting as anything else. The fact that someone is reading, just what they are reading, just where they are within the thing they are reading, where they themselves are reading, how other things are organized around them, and so on, is all available to others in the setting and carries a number of important implications for how others orient to the reader and what is being read.

In the bedtime reading example, any competent member of the setting can see that 'Mum is reading to Sarah' (or the mother is reading to the daughter in other words). This turns upon at a glance recognition of many of the embodied features mentioned above which are available to just anyone who might be looking. This has implications for matters such as: can I interrupt?; can I listen in as well?; can I put the TV on (or some music or whatever)?; and so on. The very way in which the mother is reading the story, out loud, with appropriate voices, nuances of vocal timbre and attention to cadences at the close of paragraphs, etc. all make the reading of a story by Mum to Sarah a very evident matter, such that all of the preceding considerations can be brought to bear. Another thing that is pretty readily available is just where they are in the book (beginning, end, in the middle, etc.) and, with only a little more inspection, perhaps even just where they are in a chapter in terms of 'just started', 'somewhere in the middle', or 'near the end', or even 'approaching the end of a section' and this can provide affordances such as the ability to ask things like, is it worth me hanging around to talk to Mum or is she going to be reading to Sarah for a while? Nor does it end there. The fact the 'reading to' is happening at this time of day, in this place, and that Sarah is in her pyjamas, all contribute to a ready recognition of this as quite specifically 'reading to at bedtime'. That in turn makes available a body of other reasoning to those who know the household for they can presume that after this Sarah will be going to bed, she'll be in the bathroom for a while, mum will shortly be available or else mum will shortly be doing the washing up, and so on.

Now, when we turn to other kinds of reading we can make the following observations. For the reading of books alone rather than out loud to others, many of the same features are once again available: who is reading; what they are reading; just where they are in the book; just how they are taking pause or stopping; the where's, when's and what else's of the matter, and so on. The implications of these things are much the same in many ways as they are with bedtime reading.

However, there are other noteworthy matters that play an important part in how reading is a part of the broader social organization of the home. Just who is reading what and when can have implications. For instance, if the person doing the reading is your teenage daughter who is known to have a mountain of homework but who is sat there reading a novel instead, they will in all likelihood be called to account for the very practice of reading. Notice here also that it is the very recognizability of a novel *as* a novel that carries implications. In turn the offending teenager could claim that this was set reading for English or whatever, but if it's about teenage vampires this might itself be open to contestation, making even the very kind of novel an accountable affair, not in terms of this being inappropriate reading per se (though some parents might also want to argue this) but rather accountable in terms of how other matters are also attended to and organized within the home, such as the doing of homework.

Beyond all of this, as the following quotation taken from a conversation between a husband and his wife makes visible, other broader considerations can be seen to ride upon what is manifest about people and their reading:

... when I've got a book for you, for instance, when I've been travelling and it's looked like it might be quite a good book but I don't know, and you're reading it, I quite like to ascertain your opinion of the book, but it would be a meaningless question to ask before you were at least half way through the book. You see what I mean? Because you wouldn't have read enough of the book to have an opinion probably at that point in time. So I actually use your bookmark, and how far I can see through the book you are with your bookmark, as part of what enables me to ask a question like that or not.

And when matters of enquiry can turn upon how these kinds of things are made manifest, there are clearly questions to pose about what kinds of affordances Kindles or iPads may offer for similar kinds of reasoning.

All of this makes clear the extent to which how reading gets organized as a social matter turns heavily upon the nuanced character of how the different aspects of it are embodied in various ways in the larger context of the home setting and its routines.

All of this social organization and the accountability to others of one's available practices does not just disappear simply because the reading of something happens via some other medium than the physical printed page. The accountable character of reading a Kindle, for instance, is made quite apparent in the following observation:

With the family I have never used the Kindle at breakfast, whereas I would once I've got up and gone out and got the Guardian and come back and the newspaper's on the table and the kids are running around and having breakfast and stuff. Newspapers are passed around and with a newspaper then you have multiple parts and other people can take them, and you know, you think about when you have friends round for the weekends. As soon as you bring the newspapers back, people take different bits. If you've just got your Kindle with all the sections of the Sunday Times on, it's not so social. In fact, it's anti-social to dip into your own machine.

What falls out of the considerations we have been making so far is that the manifest character of reading in the home has significant implications for how it is accommodated within the home and organized in relation to other domestic activities. Where such manifestness is less available, the ways in which the practice is reasoned about may themselves be open to challenge and this can have consequences for how the technology is 'made at home'.

The work of reading has a visible order: Another important aspect that contributes to the manifest characteristics of reading is its very visible order. This is alluded to in a number of ways above. It has a beginning: books are located, picked up and brought to readiness for reading (which, as we have already noted can involve positioning the book in just the right way, locating one's place, perhaps removing a bookmark, and opening the book out in such a way that it can be appropriately engaged with (right way up, where the head can be comfortably tilted, not too far away, not too close, etc.)). There is a middle: books are on-goingly engaged with, with visible attention to the printed page, with the positioning of fingers just so for the fluid turning of the page, with attention to the ordering devices of the book itself (not just pages, but sections where one may take pause, chapters, etc.), perhaps with back reference or forward reference in the book using the artful placing of fingers to look elsewhere yet keep one's place, perhaps with momentary attention to the cover of the book, with the competence of taking breaks (laying a book aside for a moment as opposed to definitively putting it aside until the next time), and so on. These things are only intelligible for what they are because of how they are ordered in relation to what has gone before. To see books being engaged with in this fashion is to be able to impute, as a member, the original opening out of the book in readiness. Each turn of a page is implicated by, and can be retrospectively and prospectively reasoned about in terms of, both the prior page and the page to come. This visibly systematic turning of pages, within visibly ordered sections, with a clearly imputable proper settling to and opening out in readiness of the book, is what makes reading of this order intelligible for what it is rather than, say, flicking through, or browsing. Then there is an end: books are closed, perhaps bookmarks inserted or pages turned down, they are put to one side just so, so that their very placement speaks to how they are done with for the present rather than being just left for a moment but still ready to be returned to[1].

There are similar presumptive orders to be grasped about other kinds of reading as well, for these too are situatedly ordinary occurrences in homes, otherwise people would be forever asking what they each were up to every time a book was produced. Nor should it be presumed that the activity of reading on Kindles or iPads, is any less ordinary and *orderly* from the point of view of those who encounter such happenings in their homes. This is not to say there is not some period of account where what is going on is not just visible in the way reading physical books might be. But part of the making of such technologies 'at home' is that the retrospective-prospective organization of engaging with them becomes a matter of presumption and just what is seen when such an activity is happened across. Of course, as a matter of visible work there are some important distinctions here. The finding of the book on a Kindle or an iPad is subsumed within the process of switching it on and making ready. The book is not located within the broader topology of the home and this makes certain aspects of the order somehow less visible. Some of the consequences of the distinctive character of engagement with other devices are made apparent in the earlier quotation regarding how that particular Kindle user would not use his Kindle at breakfast. However, the capacity of others in a household to just be able to see that someone is reading a book on their Kindle testifies to there being some evident set of ordered practices that are available and that do therefore allow for reading on the Kindle to be deemed appropriate on other occasions.

Reading has spatiotemporal characteristics: Something important that has begun to feature in the above discussion is the extent to which, as a reasoned activity within a household, reading has spatiotemporal characteristics. It can't just happen wherever and whenever without account.

In the case of the bedtime reading example this spatiotemporal order has a number of characteristics. Notionally, of course, bedtime reading could happen any-where. However, notice that it doesn't tend to happen at the kitchen table, in the bathroom, on the stairs, or whatever. Each household may reason about these things

---

[1] Indeed, this has its own subtleties. An opened out book left face down in one place, say on the seat of a chair, may be imputable as ready for return in ways that a book left opened out on, say the arm of a chair or a table doesn't. To someone competent in the ordering of the setting one may say that the reader will return imminently, whilst the other may say they intend to carry on reading sometime soon, but not straight away.

differently but an important part of what is going on is the bodily contact, the 'snuggling up' so to speak, visible at the outset of the original example. Thus sofas, beds, large comfy armchairs, etc. afford for this kind of activity much better than say wooden chairs at kitchen tables, or stools. And these kinds of things are most often found in living rooms and bedrooms. Indeed, they are one of the things that provide for the recognition of certain places as living rooms and bedrooms. This is testified to in the following comment:

> *I usually read to her down here just because it's not very comfortable for me to read upstairs and we can snuggle up together on the settee.*

Temporally, this is a thing that happens at bedtime: that's why we're calling it bedtime reading because that's the local locution for this thing. Bedtime, of course, has some degree of flexibility. Move it elsewhere or elsewhen and it will probably be reasoned about as something else. A caveat to add here is that what is being spoken of as a phenomenon is really 'reading stories to children'. This is not necessarily understood to be a thing that happens at bedtime in all households. Hence the following:

> *The boys have taken off and read every night themselves, you know, before they go to bed for an hour ... but Jill still reads in the morning to all of them in bed, which is still nice.*

What is clear, though, is that this kind of reading has a particular time and place where members of the household will unproblematically see it for what it is in ways that would not work and would be called to account if it was shifted to a different location or a different time of day.

The spatiotemporal order of reading is just as pertinent to how other kinds of physical reading practices may get accomplished. Once again the just where's and just when's of the matter are an integral part of local reasoning by competent members and can't be divorced from what happens in this household. What is clear is that the places and times people choose to do their reading are understood to be somehow accountable and they will account for them if asked. Thus, if there are times and places where it is presumed to be reasonable to read a book, there are other times and places where it isn't. The range of potential breaches is enormous but what is clear is that at least one feature of how people will reason about their reading as somehow appropriate is in terms of the specific places and times where it happens. The following comments attest to this in a variety of ways:

> *I read if I've got nothing else to do. And then I read at bedtime to make me feel sleepy. If the sun's shining and I'm sunbathing and it's too awkward to do crosswords or something so I take my book out and read then. I like reading if I want to escape from things ...*
>
> *If it's a really good book then I come straight down and I sit in my little corner and read a book rather than do the crosswords.*
>
> *At the moment I pretty much only read at night, when I'm going to bed before I go to sleep. It used to be I would read anything I had at every opportunity I had. That was before the computer.*
>
> *If I'm reading a book sitting on a chair downstairs and I want a drink or something then I'll leave the book open, put it resting on the arm of the chair. If I'm up here reading in bed then before I go to sleep I always put a bookmark in and put it to one side.*

Nor does this concrete spatiotemporal reasoning disappear just because the reading is being done on a Kindle:

> *So, on weekends, often I wake up long before anyone else and I get out of my bed ... and go into another bedroom at the back of the house, and then the Kindle comes on and it downloads the newspaper... And I get a cup of coffee and sit in my bed and read the newspaper that way. What I used to do was get up and wander down the shop and buy a Guardian, which I do later in the day. So it hasn't displaced that activity in any way ... So I sit there and read the newspaper in bed and it feels much the same as it used to feel sitting there, Sunday morning newspapers, you know that sort of classic British routine.*
>
> *... primarily I've either bought a physical copy and then bought a digital copy in order to take it away with me. Or I've bought a digital copy and then thought 'I quite like having my reading in places' so I put the physical copy by my bed and sometimes that physical copy reminds me to look at the Kindle ...*
>
> *Now the difference with the Kindle is it does - you know, it can accurately remember where you were and it doesn't promote - it doesn't promote that random picking up. So for the random, I just want to read something to - coz there's this ritual at bedtime, or I'm jet-lagged, or something - the physical copy's better. You just pick it up and open it and you know. Whereas the Kindle, you'll open it and you're exactly where you were, and it hasn't got a button as far as I can see that says 'pick me some random page'.*
>
> *... the fire might be on, the television might be on in the background, and some people might be playing on their CDs, I might - Classic, certainly when I'm sitting in the sitting room, or whatever's happening, music or television or just kids in there, I will have a pile of books and the Kindle and a laptop and lots of newspapers and lots of magazines and I just, sort of like a washing machine, shuffle around them.*

Matters such as light, specificity, and tractability are all articulated as points of contrast across the use of different kinds of device here. What is important, however, is the extent to which even the contrasts and complaints make visible the use of particular positioning and particular times of day as objects of concern.

Reading has a place within the household routine: Something that has been a vein running through all of the discussion so far, is the degree to which reading has a place within the household routine.

'Bedtime' has certain, very definite characteristics: particular times of day, in particular places, in particular clothing, perhaps with particular accompaniments such as drinks, and with particular understandings that what will follow is the actual act of going to bed and that what should precede is whatever it takes for that to happen, e.g. getting in pyjamas, pouring out a glass of milk, mum having finished the washing up, dad being done with work for the day, the homework being finished, and so on. This is not invented on the spur of the moment to be figured out on just this occasion but rather is something that is done recurrently in similar ways such that no-one might think to comment upon its regular, its ordinary character. In other words it is a routine and it has its place within other routines, and everyone understands that, once it is undertaken, there are other routines that will quite reasonably and ordinarily follow, like actually going to bed, for instance. This gives the enactment of bedtime reading as a routine a certain power for other things are expected to reasonably come next, as the following quote makes visible:

> *It's usually last thing before she goes to bed. It's usually the enticement for her to hurry up and get changed ready for bed and there's the threat that if she doesn't get changed quickly*

then she won't get read to tonight. Normally it's enough of a bribe for her to want to get ready for bed quickly.

Furthermore, as this thing is a routine, a recurrent matter, it can be easily recognized for what it is and oriented to by others as well. This can be to do with what you might accountably undertake while it is going on, but it also provides for others to have a more positive engagement with it as well:

If you're reading to Sarah and I'm washing up then I prefer the music off so I can hear too. And often, the other children, if they're doing crosswords or whatever, if they're down here, or even playing on the machine, they tend to lend an ear. So it isn't necessarily just Sarah being read to. But it is focused on Sarah so if none of the others are here she'd still get read to.

Clearly bedtime reading is centrally articulated around the routines of younger children and the work they and their parents do together to move towards a point where they are in bed and sleeping. However, other kinds of reading testify just as strongly in their accomplishment to various elements of how a household organizes its day and who is accountable to whom and for what.

This situation of reading practices within the broader context of household routines does not become irrelevant just because the reading is being done on a digital device. Indeed, a number of the previous examples regarding how people use a Kindle, express quite clearly the ways in which that use gets articulated around its placement within other recurrent patterns of everyday life in a house.

Members of a household are eternally accountable in some way to the routines and rhythms of that household and it is hard to imagine how anyone, however easy it may be to make the claim, really reads 'whenever they feel like'. This goes straight back to the preceding discussion regarding embodiment, order and the placement of different kinds of reading activities at different times and places within the home. If you're doing the drying up and you take pause whilst some of the stuff is draining to flick through a book at the kitchen table that may well attract no kind of comment. But try walking off and settling on the sofa and picking up the book you are currently reading to continue and see how long it takes for the person doing the washing to ask you just what it is you think you're doing. Even for adolescents, who may eschew all kinds of household chores and who may have developed rhythms that are semi-nocturnal, to be found downstairs on the sofa at three o'clock in the morning, reading, would not be passed by without comment in a large number of different households. Even the rhythms of conversation are consequential. When people arrive home from school or work it is a common practice to enquire after details of their day and, to come straight in and open a book, is to invite recurrent interruption that, by order of the placement of their return within the pattern of their day, is given a certain licence that might not be presumed on other occasions.

The affordances for reading and the topology of the home: Something that is massively visible in the data we collected regarding people's reading practices is the extent to which aspects of the topology of the home are organized with the clear purpose of supporting various reading activities. This has a number of elements:

One of the things that one finds has a quite definite place within the spatial organization of a home is just where people put the books they are currently reading. This is sufficiently fine-tuned that one will find that, by very virtue of the placement of a particular book, competent members of the household will be able to tell you just who is probably reading that book. And members can be seen to actively use these understandings for things such as 'Oh, I see you're reading the next Iain Banks. What are you making of it?'

Another topological resource is the 'general store'. In other words there are places in houses where larger numbers of books are recurrently situated together, typically on bookcases. These are usually places where people put books that are *not* being currently read and these are understood to be available for reading.

Many people have some small subset of books set aside quite specifically as books to be read. They may even be arranged in piles that imply a definite order of reading. These books are not 'available' for anyone to read. The placement of books here amounts to a claim upon priority for their reading by the person who is understood to maintain this particular book pile.

There is a counterpart to the pile of books for reading: a pile of books that are now finished. The placement of this pile within the topology of the home provides a resource for reasoning about it and what rights one have. This can inform a range of potential interests from discussion about what you have been reading to judgments of preference. It also has different accountabilities, a book be taken without undue consequences, though requests and verifications may still be forthcoming.

A much more fluid and transitory grouping of books are the books that are specifically positioned for putting away. In one of the households studied there was a small pile of books that gathered recurrently about three stops up from the bottom of the stairs. Everyone understood these to be books that were now waiting for someone to return them to the bookshelves.

Books newly arrived in a house can also have specific places within its topology which make available that very fact that have only just been bought or borrowed and are thus not firmly allocated to anyone to read. In one of the households books just purchased were recurrently placed upon the kitchen table. Those with an interest then routinely took note of the presence of the book, its status as currently unallocated, and would enter into negotiation as to whose book it should be first.

Another resource the topology of the home can provide for is an indication of for whom a book might be intended. In one household the eldest son had a specific practice of announcing 'you're next' to his mother by placing the book on the banister outside her bedroom door.

Even the book for reading at bedtime will have some specific placement within the home's topology that allows for its recognizability as just that, with a whole set of potential consequences should someone else claim it and wander off with it.

A fascinating demonstration of how easily certain kinds of reading on the Kindle can be subsumed within this order is the way in which it can become just another part of a person's book-pile:

So if you went to my bedroom now you'd see a pile of books and the Kindle on top of it. And I just pick that up as I would pick up another book perhaps by chance, and then, moving into the other bedroom, there's a pile of books in that room too and I would take the Kindle with me.

Yet the very retention of physical books may also be a part of how these different topological arrangements are accomplished:

I've given most of my books to charity and only kept those I don't have e-books of - I don't want to spend money on things I've already bought - which are stored upstairs in our top room. I've also kept cookbooks which live in the living room and are used prior to shopping or cooking, though I periodically sift through and discard what I don't use, cutting out useful recipes and putting them in a folder in the kitchen. And I've bought some physical books recently - a small collection of philosophy, science, and natural history books for reference - I don't plan to buy more though - which also live in the living room where they're ready to hand. We also have a couple of bookends in the living room where we put books to be read or being read. This we'll probably maintain as people buy us both books as presents.

Once again, something that is highly indicative of the ways in which physical books will continue to associate with certain kinds of activity, is the extent to which physical books can be easily parleyed into the existing topological arrangements of a home. A Kindle or an iPad is manifestly just that when shut and placed upon a table or wherever. Its placement, as with books, is readily reasoned about. However, it is resistant to much further enquiry. To look at a person's physical book pile and to know that it is arranged in an order of reading and to see just where a book is placed within that pile, permits for other kinds of discussions such as, if the book is next perhaps not asking to borrow that one, whereas if it's way down the pile and you're looking for something to read, asking for it would seem entirely reasonable.

In a world where everyone has their own iPad or Kindle and everyone has their own 'pile' of books ordered within it, and where duplication across devices is no kind of an issue these kinds of negotiations might seem to lose their purpose. However, we patently do not inhabit such a world and, for many of the reasons we have been discussing about embodied practices, manifestness and accountability it seems that physical books are likely to continue to cohabit with their electronic counterparts and serve different purposes. In that case the inspectability of a book within the topology of a home will continue to be an affordance for how people reason about one another's activities and how their reading gets situated within the broader social organization of the home.

Reading and the manifestation of rights and responsibilities: In this section we take a close look once more at just some of the aspects of the bedtime reading example in order to delineate another important aspect of how reading in domestic settings is itself organized in relation to the broader social organization of the home. In this case we want to explore some of the ways in which reading makes manifest the rights and responsibilities of different members of the household.

So, at the outset, just prior to the data provided in section 1, the daughter is sat on the sofa, fidgeting around, waiting for someone to come and read her story. She asks her father to do it but he tells her it's going to be mum tonight so she continues to sit there, fidgeting. Her mother comes out of the garage where she has been getting the rubbish ready for taking out and the daughter calls out to her to remind her she's waiting:

S:	/My story? Wolf Brother. A good story. Mummy? Ready?
M:	Just get my hands washed
S:	Okay

The daughter continues to sit for a while, then goes and gets the book from the cabinet where it is kept and puts it behind a cushion on the sofa. When the mother comes into view the daughter becomes more insistent:

S:	Ahhem Ahem
M:	(to son) Are you going to /go-
S:	/Mum/mummumma
M:	/Are you going to come back through the garage?
T:	Hmm?
S:	Allez au part=
M:	=shut the garage up afterwards
S:	Zitdownpa
M:	Where's your book?
T:	I usually /don't
S:	/Sit! ((producing book))
T:	come back through the garage
M:	Well come back through the garage coz/I've
S:	/((putting book on chair)) SIT!
M:	left the door open for you
T:	Why leave it open? I don't come through that way
M:	The light! I thought you needed the light
S:	hwer
M:	Yup, yup
((M picking up book to sit down as S reaches out to her))	

Once the mother is sat down and they've snuggled up together and the book is opened out, the mother asks her daughter what's been happening:

M:	What happened in the last chapter d'you remember?

Once the daughter has recounted what happened, the mother begins to read.

Notice here how a bunch of things are unremarkably (that is, they are not commented upon) presumed about what each of the parties to the reading should do and what each of them *can* do. The daughter can visibly wait for and expect to be read a story. She can remind her mother about the fact she is waiting for it, even nag, even order her mother to sit, because it is understood to be the responsibility of the mother to deliver just such a story and the mother is accountable for its delayed production, e.g. 'just get my hands washed'. Whilst they are reading it can be seen that the mother continues to keep hold of the book in various ways and do the reading out loud, although the daughter does occasionally touch the book tentatively. At the same time, the mother also occasionally rests her hand on her daughter's head or strokes her hair, and the daughter responds with occasional touchings. This continues to demonstrate the mother's differential rights to control and management of the book itself and the daughter's deference to this, though it is important that this does not deny the daughter the right to touch the book at all.

Where things get more interesting is when the mother arrives at the finish of the chapter where there is a negotiation as to whether more reading should happen. The daughter has some claim for more because she suggests the chapter was 'a short one'. The mother resists reading the next chapter because 'it's long'. But she has a responsibility to read 'for a reasonable period of time' and, clearly, what counts as reasonable is open to contestation. Once the end of the chapter is reached, the mother is able to assert that she is stopping. The daughter checks this is where they agreed she'd be stopping and actively wants to see proof of the matter:

> M: *She'd been useful for helping him evade the ravens but that didn't change the fact that she'd taken his weapons and called him a coward and she still had her knife pointed straight at him. (M raises hand) Right. That's where I'm stopping. (M reaches over and gets bookmark from arm of the chair)*
> S: *Is that the second /(...)?*
> M: */That's the second one. That's the one we agreed on. Okay?*
>   *(M puts bookmark in book and goes to close it)*
> S: *Is it? (Pulling book back open)*
> M: *It is*
> S: *Let's see. (S flicks back through the pages of the book - pauses at a section mark, then flicks back to beginning of chapter - then flicks back to where she's kept the place with her other hand as M gets ready to put in bookmark)*
> *(M puts bookmark in book, shuts it, and puts it over to her right)*

In this final part of the interaction the mother's right to terminate the reading is exercized, though it should be noted that the mother accepts the daughter's right to demand an account for this and to verify the accuracy of the account when it is given. This speaks volumes about how absolute her exercize of control might be. There are reasonable places where parents might effectively 'lay down the law', but this is not such an appropriate place and the very insistence upon it might itself be deemed accountable, e.g. they're touchy because they've had a bad day, or there's somewhere they urgently need to get to.

The point to emphasize about the above analysis is the way in which, at the point of reading a bedtime story, the playing out of these rights and responsibilities does not get worked up anew. Instead, the ordering of these concerns is accountable to the on-going ordering of their relative rights and responsibilities within the household. Both mother and daughter have a common sense understanding of what their rights and responsibilities are to each other and how these might play out in the case of reading a story at bedtime. This is not to say what they each should do and what they each have the right to do is not occasionally open to challenge, but the challenge itself then demands some kind of an account. In the above case, for instance, the daughter's account for challenging the mother's decision to stop is based upon a doubt she is honoring their agreement. Once it is clear the agreement *has* been honored there is little else she has to say.

These rights and responsibilities being articulated here are powerfully omnipresent concerns in any household and they do not get massively re-written according to each new activity. Thus reading of any kind, together or solo, on a Kindle or on a PC, is still ultimately testifying in how it is organized and how it is called to account to these broader sets of assumptions regarding who has the *right* to do what, at what time and where, and who *should* be doing what, at what time and where. In this vein, once again consider the following:

> With the family I have never used the Kindle at breakfast, whereas I would once I've got up and gone out and got the Guardian and come back and the newspaper's on the table and the kids are running around and having breakfast and stuff.

In this example the respondent is articulating quite clearly what rights and responsibilities hold in his household and it is quite clear that, just because he has decided to do the bulk of his reading on a Kindle, not just anything goes. And around that there hinges a consideration of not just what he might do with the Kindle but whether he should be using the Kindle at all.

Reading and household relations: A somewhat specialized aspect of the preceding discussion regarding how people's rights and responsibilities get made manifest through their reading practices is how those reading practices can make quite tightly visible the actual relations between the different members of the household. Indeed, ways of reading are an aspect of how those relations are on-goingly accomplished.

The example of bedtime reading brings this home especially forcefully. In fact, it is an important aspect of how parent-child intimacy gets accomplished. The example we have presented is replete with these kinds of details, e.g.:

> (M picking up book to sit down as S reaches out to he))...
> (M puts arm round S)...
> (M Straightening out book and resting hand on top of S's head)...
> M: 'Don't move' breathed a voice in Torak's ear ((stroking S's head)...
> M: Pardon me. (Laughingly as continuing to stroke S's head) He couldn't see anything. He was huddled in a rotten smelling blackness with a knife pressed at his throat. He gritted his teeth to stop them chattering. (Shifting arm to put round S)
> (S puts her hand on M's)...
> (M strokes S's head and rests her hand on her head, holding the book with one hand, as she continues)
> (S raises her arms to take hold of M's hand)...(M moves her hand down and puts it on S's knee))
> (S lifts her hand to hold M's hand on her knee and M glances down and strokes her knee)...
> (Kisses her on top of her head)

Something to consider here is that pretty well everyone, including the children who are parties to it, understand that this kind of reading is about something quite particular. And that particularity is not about the consumption of stories per se. The child in these examples is a highly accomplished reader and could, without any difficulty, be reading this story for herself. Why then should this reading matter so much to her? And it clearly does. The above observations of embodied and accomplished intimacy are core to the response to this. What the child and the parent, both, get out of this is a degree of physical contact that can only be accountably demanded and provided in so many ways. Children can ask cuddles of their parents pretty well any time within reason (e.g. not if the parent is visibly occupied or the child should be getting on with their homework). And those cuddles will usually be provided. However, to keep on asking for those things is to quickly start to become accountable for the recurrent request, e.g. they're obviously worrying about something, they're being clingy, or whatever (see Tolmie, 2010 regarding this). What things like bedtime reading do is they quite neatly provide licence for those kinds of contact to happen without fuss or account and on a regular basis. Thus bedtime reading is not just an opportunity for intimacy to occur or a place where, amongst other things, intimacy happens to be present. It is a *mechanism* for intimacy and, as concrete part of a day's routine, there aren't so many of those.

It is not that the content of the book doesn't matter and the claim here is not that bedtime reading is all about intimacy. What is being proposed is that at least one extremely important aspect of bedtime reading is the fact that it quite systematically provides a mechanism for intimacy to occur and that this is something that matters to young children. All of the presumptions of touching rights and stroking rights and cuddling rights and kissing rights made visible above are things that make accountably visible very specific relations between these particular individuals such that, were the person being read to very much older, or patently of a similar age to the person doing the reading, different understandings of who they are and what they are up to would apply. It also provides for the subtle recognition of potential troubles. If one or other of the parties resists the intimacy or is patently unresponsive to it people may well figure there's some kind of trouble between them. And that could even be the source of being called to account, e.g. 'What's the matter with Sarah tonight? She seems to be cross with you.'

Whilst this discussion may seem to be an appendix to the broader matter of rights and responsibilities, take note of the following:

> *We do a lot of reading to children and when they were very small that was the classic routine. Now we do for Sally- She reads to us because she's still sixish ... And would I use the Kindle? No::: Beco:::z Its- You know, often with reading it's the- you know it's the cuddles that are the king, not content, or the close proximity, so that technology- And I'm pretty sceptical too about, you know, say on the iPad, kind of interactive kid's books.*

This both testifies to the above explication of how intimacy might get accomplished and alludes to something of key relevance to this chapter: different kinds of reading implicate different kinds of modes for its accomplishment. In the case of bedtime reading there are enormous subtleties regarding all of the topics we have already been discussing: embodiment, manifestness, visible order, spatiotemporal matters and the organization of the household routine, the placement of reading and its accomplishment within the topology of the home, rights and responsibilities, familial relations, and so on. The fact of the matter is that it is not just one of these but rather all of them together, as a background to the ways in which people reason about activities such as reading in general or quite specifically reading to children, that inform the sense of it being inappropriate to do something like bedtime reading on a Kindle. This is not really an in principal consideration but rather one that hinges upon not quite being able to see how something like a Kindle could be parleyed into all of these concerns when something like a physical book has already been made a part of them without any need to ever make its affordances for that explicit. Quite simply the question is, why change when it would make some of these things unnecessarily visible and potentially harder work?

Reading and accountability: Something that sits in the background of the bedtime story example – and all of the other data for that matter - is how the book to be read was arrived at in the first place.

The shared work of finding specific books to read next has some distinct characteristics according to the different kinds of books being chosen. In the case of bedtime reading the situation is notably complex. Here there are effectively two readers, each with their own particular concerns and interests: the person doing the reading out loud (a parent); and the person listening to the reading (a child). What makes something a children's book and a book to read out loud is not a straightforward matter and is not simply understood as being about a proposed age group on the cover (though this can provide for some crude decision making). Some of these concerns are articulated in the following:

> *She's at the age now where she can cope with something a bit more involved. It's got to be exciting enough to hold her attention, not too wordy that it bores her silly. She doesn't really need pictures either any more. And we tend to go for the classics as well, that we loved when we were little.*

We can see in this at least two other grounds of reasoning that parents may apply: does it have pictures (and if so, are they any good?)?; is it something I already know works because it was read to me when I was a child? In addition parents may exercize moral concerns regarding content. An issue, however, with all of these concerns is that, outside of books that were read to them previously or they have read themselves, parents may be no wiser than the child they are reading to about the contents of a book at first sight. This makes book selection for reading out loud an eminently negotiable activity.

For any kind of reading it should be noted that members of a household can't just read anything. There are a wide range of concerns regarding what might or might not be appropriately read by any member at any particular time. These are organized around matters such as the following:

> *Who has the right to read a book?* E.g. is it a book that belongs to someone else? Have you asked if you can read it? Do certain constraints apply (for instance fragility) that might make the reading of it by certain people questionable?
> *Who should read a book?* E.g. 'Haven't you read that one yet? It's a classic.' Has it been lent to you or given to you with the implicit assumption that you will therefore read it?

Who should be reading a book next? E.g. (and as an extension to the matter of rights) are there several people in the household who want to read the same book? Who has priority in that case? Is there an agreed order making it your turn next? Is there an implicit order because your bigger brother always has first claim? Has the book just come into the house and, if so, who gets to read it first? Is it yours to read first because you are the one who bought it?

Who is the right age to read a book? E.g. is it full of words you won't understand? Does it have content you are too young to understand or that would be too embarrassing to recommend to you? Will the content offend you in some way? Is it a book for babies?

Who will appreciate a book? E.g. is it well-written? Is it the kind of genre you like? Is it a moving story? Is it something everyone should read?

In short, reading is just another activity within the household that testifies to the moral order of that household. However, it is more than this. What gets read, how it is selected, and how it gets into the hands of particular people is itself a communal matter. In fact, the reading of 'what is appropriate' is on-goingly accomplished by members across a household in terms of how they are each implicated in selecting what one another may read. Consider the following:

I: *Do you share books with [your sister] and [your brother] much?*

T: *Yeah, if it's a series they're interested in or author, then they can just come and take books.*

I: *Is that how you handle it? Do you say come and take a book if you want it or do you actually give it to them?*

T: *If there's a specific book they can't find, like say the Hogfather, then I'll search it out from my bookcase and give it to them, but if they know it's on my bookcase then they'll just come and take it if they want it.*

I: *That's what you say to them? You don't do the same, for instance, as you do with regard to mum and passing the book on and everything?*

T: *Sometimes but again, there isn't so much of an overlap because of their different ages. I read different things to them. So I don't pass books on to them like that often.*

M: *... with Chris it's fairly easy because he's less interested in relationship books as well. I think with Chris science fiction, that sort of stuff is more Chris's style. Family stories less so as well, even with historical sagas, unless it's blood and gut ones as it were, he doesn't think much of.*

Nor does it end there. These considerations are also formulated around peer groups and specific cohorts:

I do an exchange with Alan's[2] mum as well. She gives me books which she thinks I might enjoy that she's read, and I swap them with books I've read and enjoyed that I think she might enjoy.

I read pretty much anything that people recommend to me first. I suppose that's when I get introduced to new styles from around things like that. Just new series of books.

---

[2] *Alan is a friend of her son.*

In the latter example the people doing the recommending include, notably, correspondents he interacts with online in a site dedicated to the display and exchange of original artwork.

We are a long way here from matters of medium. The accountabilities people share across households and across their groups of friends and associates are largely agnostic as to whether your preferred mode of consumption is physical or digital.

Reading and other household activities: Thus far in the chapter we have taken the reader on a journey through some of the various ways in which reading, as an activity, is not something set apart from but rather constituted by, and constitutive *of* the social organization of the home. In taking this journey we have gone ever further it would seem from the simple 'turning of a page' yet we would hope that the reader can see that all of the different things we have been discussing are intertwined with and premized upon one another. It is worth briefly concluding by noting that these observations exist within the larger canvas of familial concerns and predicates. The fact that reading is not outside of but rather an integral part of the social organization of the home makes it yet one more place where a whole range of considered activities may get accomplished that are understood to be something other than about reading for the pleasure of reading alone.

One such concern might be matters of recollection. Often stories may serve as prompts for particular kinds of recollections. Another concern might be something like pedagogy. Thus, specific books may get chosen because they are seen to be somehow educational. It could also be about things like aesthetic reflections. People may pick up on a particular phrase, the construction of certain passages, even read them out to one another when they happen across them. The list of possibilities here is endless but what we want to point to is that reading can be about many things and this too has implications for how people make choices about things like the medium. Something about a Kindle or an iPad, for instance, is the fact that it can take active inspection rather than just a glance to find out what someone is reading. And to do that is to become accountable for the interest in the first place rather than it just being to hand and visible. This means that the incidental arising of talk about what one is reading is more difficult. Consider again the following extract:

> ... when I've got a book for you, for instance, when I've been travelling and it's looked like it might be quite a good book but I don't know, and you're reading it, I quite like to ascertain your opinion of the book, but it would be a meaningless question to ask before you were at least half way through the book. You see what I mean? Because you wouldn't have read enough of the book to have an opinion probably at that point in time. So I actually use your bookmark and how far I can see through the book you are with your bookmark as part of what enables me to ask a question like that or not.

One of the important things that reading does is it makes available talk about what one is reading. And it is through talk about what one is reading that many of these other activities like recollection, pedagogy, aesthetics, etc., get done. This is one way in which the medium may continue to matter. In many other cases it may not. So here again we arrive at the point where we can say that the choice of physical and digital books is something utterly embedded within, not just the nature of physical and digital per se, but rather the social organization of the environment within which a book is being consumed and what particular activity is understood to be being accomplished at that moment in time.

Conclusion: Reading in the 21st Century Home

"A scene from Christmas 2020: At home, a wife is reading from an oblong screen, grey-backed. Her husband doesn't know what she is reading without asking her. Still, he knows that at breakfast time on Christmas Day she will wake up to find that the text of the Man Booker prize winner this year, Dame Katie Price's Emerald, has been downloaded on to her reading device with a cute reindeer logo attached.... Bedtime comes, and our hero goes upstairs with his reading engine to give the kids a bedtime story. Unfortunately, the story of Please Don't Eat the Chairs, Mr Crocodile is over in 49 words, and the pictures, though carefully designed for the reading engine, are small and difficult to see. He gets through 17 electronic stories before little Ethel hits the engine with her fist, breaking the screen. Father is downcast: he won't be able to read anything until a replacement comes, which could mean three weeks." (Henscher 2009)

Our own research has highlighted the particular ways in which reading is accomplished as an everyday activity in the 21st century home. We have indicated the manifest embodied visible order of reading and how it accountably fits within and supports the organized routine of the household and associated rights and responsibilities. But, as the quote above illustrates, much of the debate about 'the future of reading in the 21st century' is less about reading as an activity, situated within a household or daily routine, than it is about the technologies of reading – about books and e-readers. In this it mirrors other, similar, debates about the impact of technology on the household, where the emphasis has been on the technology rather than the way in which it is embedded in various domestic routines and rhythms:; the relevance of the technology to people's everyday lives (see Harper 2003). Making firm predictions about the future of books or e-readers and of our patterns and modes of recreational reading in an age of technological change is a risky business. It's easy to give way to false sentiment or nostalgia, and as Mandel suggests; *"Ultimately, reading isn't about feel and smell and the sound of pages turning. Reading is about the words, the content. While I'm in my living room, it's nice to read a book. But otherwise it's not always the most convenient way".* (Mandel 1998) Nevertheless, the book has been pronounced dead several times, as new gadgets, new reading devices, have been developed and marketed. In 'Technology Matters: questions to live with' David E. Nye (2006), argues that technology is part of our 'creative relationship with the world' in which questions such as whether we shape them or they shape us resist any easy or final answers. New technologies often take considerable time to develop, are not always readily or willingly adopted, and are shaped by social context. Nevertheless, most researchers studying the influence of technology apply some kind of contextual point of view in which economical, social and technological conditions are said to work together to produce a kind of soft technological determinism.

   Those who anticipate a bright future for e-readers of various kinds do so not merely on the basis of shiny novelty but on claims of a perceived shift in reading behavior brought about by digital text. A number of researchers claim to have noticed some important changes in reading behavior as a consequence of the movement to reading on screen – computer, mobile phone, e-reader etc and the availability and proliferation of digital documents. At its simplest this is seen in Carr's question; 'Is Google Making Us Stupid' (Carr 2008). "Over the past few years I've had an uncomfortable sense that someone, or something, has been tinkering with my brain, remapping the neural circuitry, reprogramming the memory. My mind isn't going—so far as I can tell—but it's changing. I'm not thinking the way I used to think. I can feel it most strongly when I'm reading. Immersing myself in a book or a lengthy article used to be easy. My mind would get caught up in the narrative or the turns of the argument, and I'd spend hours strolling through long stretches of prose. That's rarely the case anymore. Now my concentration often starts to drift after two or three pages. I get fidgety, lose the thread, begin looking for something else to do. I feel as if I'm always dragging my wayward brain back to the text. The deep reading that used to come naturally has become a struggle". (Carr 2008)

In Carr's analysis and interpretation of current reading behavior, our thought processes are being moulded by our experience of digital text in such a fashion and to such an extent that our ability to concentrate, to perform 'deep reading', is gradually diminished to be replaced by shallower forms of thought. More academic studies (Lui 2005, Hillesund 2010, Wolf 2007, Kress 2003) though often focused on academic reading have hinted at similar issues (though in a less spectacular, headline grabbing fashion). For example, Ziming Liu's (2005) analysis of changes in reading behavior identifies a screen-based reading behavior characterized by more time spent on browsing and scanning, and keyword spotting, with less time being spent on in-depth reading. Hillesund (2010) provides an essentially similar analysis. His interview study of the reading habits of expert readers highlights their facility at using the Web for browsing and skimming.

In a number of papers Mangen (2006, 2008) adopts a soft technical determinist view to suggest ways in which we have been and are being moulded by technological innovations such as the e-reader and that as more and more of our everyday reading is from screens of various kinds, computers, mobile phones, e-books and so on, so such digital technologies may actually change some characteristics of the way we go about the business of reading. She suggests that we read differently when reading digital texts, compared with when reading print. Mangen is intrigued by two particular aspects of reading books; firstly, the 'materiality,' that is the way in which the book is held and pages handled'. Reading books, compared with reading digital texts requires particular and different forms of manual dexterity, different control over our fingers and hands as we turn pages and follow the text. Mangen's interest lies in particular in whether and how the materiality of the experience – specifically the use of the hands – impacts on the immersive experience of the reader, thereby referring to common, if sentimental, complaints, in the comparison of the book and various e-readers about the physical features of the book, its weight, the turning and marking of the pages, its smell, its mustiness etc. "The tactility of a mouse click, of touch screen page turning or of a click with the e-book page turner bar is very different from that of flicking through the print pages of a book. The feeling of literally being in touch with the text is lost when your actions – clicking with the mouse, pointing on touch screens or scrolling with keys or on touch pads – take place at a distance from the digital text, which is, somehow, somewhere inside the computer, the e-book or the mobile phone. Because of this ontological intangibility of the digital text, our phenomenological experience – reading – of the digital text will differ profoundly from that of a print text."

A second area of interest is concerned with the 'immersive' aspect of book reading, how readers can become lost in a story that is, Mangen claims, partly a by-product of materiality of the printed page. Mangen outlines the different forms of immersion offered by books and, for instance, electronic games – whereas books offer a form of 'phenomenological immersion' where the experience of being lost in the story is the product of the reader's own imagination. In contrast, digital games provide a different form of 'technological' immersion, where immersion is a product of the interest and plausibility of the world created by the technology. E-readers or e-books seemingly provide for a very different form of immersion.

Kress (2003) similarly identifies a 'new agenda' for reading indicated by particular technical and cognitive features of the differences in reading online and reading books and what he sees as the impact of the growing dominance of the screen as opposed to the page: specifically the difference between the world told and the world shown: "'the world narrated' is a different world to 'the world depicted and displayed'" (Kress 2003: 2). In the new media age the screen has replaced the book as the dominant medium of communication. Kress argues that a reader learns about the world and imagines it differently from the way a screen viewer does and may even think differently. One important difference between text and image is that with text, with the book, meaning awaits and is provided by the reader (we are left to imagine what Harry Potter or Hagrid, for example, are like) but with the screen and its emphasis on the image, meaning is effectively provided (Harry Potter will always be Daniel Radcliffe, Hagrid will always be Robbie Coltrane):"in the new landscapes of communication, with the dominance of the new media, and with the 'old' media (the book for instance) being reshaped by the forms of new media, the demands on readers, and the demands of reading, will if anything be greater, and they will certainly be different. That constitutes the new agenda for thinking about reading." (Kress 2003: 167)

But whilst there are those who envisage massive social, cultural and psychological changes attendant on the development of digital reading technologies, others are far more sanguine and point to the historical experience of other technologies. In some cases and for some groups of people that experience is one of adoption followed by rapid disappointment and rejection – or as Wyatt et al put it, 'they came, they surfed, they went back to the beach' (Wyatt et al 2002). For others, complex processes of 'domestication' (Silverstone 1994, Berker et al 2006, Haddon 2007) and 'innofusion' (Fleck 1988) impact on the usability and acceptance of the new device. Domestication refers to the 'taming' or 'house-training' of a technology once it has been introduced into a home. Like the family dog, any new technology needs to be house trained to make it acceptable. In contrast, 'innofusion' points to the ways in which new social or family practices are developed as a technology comes to play some important part in people's lives – we make the technology and then the technology makes us. Just as the 'book at bedtime', the idea of 'bedtime stories', has developed over time into acceptable and expected social reading practices in some sections of our society, so too might a whole series of essentially similar or subtly different social practices evolve with the adoption of the iPad or Kindle (see for example Schraefel 2010, Clark et al 2008, Coker 2009).

Historical studies of technology, perhaps especially domestic technologies, (see, for example Wajcman, J and Mackenzie, D. (1985) 'How the refrigerator got its hum') seem to suggest that simple attempts to predict the future are generally ill-advized and occasionally rather foolish. When Jeff Bezos claims that; "Amazon.com customers now purchase more Kindle books than hardcover books—astonishing when you consider that we've been selling hardcover books for 15 years, and Kindle books for 33 months." (Roychoudhuri quoting Jeff Bezos in The Boston Review) - we are obviously impressed but not entirely sure what to make of it. While some confidently predict a future where e-readers replace books and imagine a world in which reading books is the preserve of an effete, aesthetic elite, others point to the continued existence and even growth of other 'obsolescent' paper technologies (Sellen and Harper 2002, Lui and Stork 2000). As Darnton writes in 'The New Age of the Book': "Ever since the invention of the codex in the third or fourth century AD, it has proven to be a marvellous machine — great for packaging information, convenient to thumb through, comfortable to curl up with, superb for storage, and remarkably resistant to damage. It does not need to be upgraded or downloaded, accessed or booted, plugged into circuits or extracted from webs. Its design makes it a delight to the eye. Its shape makes it a pleasure to hold in the hand. And its handiness has made it the basic tool of learning for thousands of years ..."

Navigating between the enlightened optimism of the technophiles and the ancient skepticism of older, if not exactly wiser, heads, many end up attempting some kind of balance, what Mitcham (2003) terms 'romantic uneasiness'. Such uneasiness is reflected in Lynch's (2001) comment: ".. presenting an e-book reader as a sort of substitute for a printed book underestimates and trivializes the future. ... These are very large, complex, and serious questions that go far beyond asking whether a plastic-encased machine can satisfactorily substitute for paper pages bound in leather or cardboard." Whilst new technologies such as the e-book or reader are commonly misperceived and misunderstood as simple and total replacements for older technologies, the evidence (and perhaps common sense) suggests something far less radical. This is not a particularly novel resolution of the debate. Nor will it be the first time supposedly competing technologies happily coexist serving differing functions or different audiences at different times (Harper 2010). There is little evidence to indicate that the printed book, with its extraordinary resilience and staying power will completely disappear. Accordingly, the 21st century Smart Home is likely to see the happy coexistence of paper and electronic documents, of books and newspapers alongside e-readers. The reason for such continued coexistence, as our research suggests, rests on how the choice and use of physical or digital books is embedded within the social organization of the environment within which a book is being used, and what particular activity is being accomplished at that time. In documenting some persistent, longstanding features of *reading* in everyday family life we are pointing to aspects of the moral order of the family that, in the face of changing technologies, appear to remain relatively persistent, a feature of the world in which technology is 'made at home'.

References

Berker, T., Hartmann, M., Punie, Y and Ward, K. (eds) (2006) *Domestication of Media and Technology*. Open University Press.
Bolter, J. (2001) *Writing space: The computer, hypertext, and the remediation of print*. Lawrence Erlbaum. Mahwah, N.J.
Brand, S. (1994) *How Buildings Learn*, New York, Viking,
Carden, M. (2008) E-books Are Not Books. *Proceeding of the 2008 ACM workshop on Research advances in large digital book repositori*es.
Carr, N. (2008) Is Google Making Us Stupid? *What the Internet is doing to our brains* Atlantic Magazine July/August 2008 http://www.theatlantic.com/magazine/archive/2008/07/is-google-making-us-stupid/6868/
Castells, M. (1996). *The Rise of the Network Society*. Oxford: Blackwell.
Chartier, R. (1997) "The end of the reign of the book" translated by Eric D. Friedman, *SubStance*, volume 26, number 82 pp. 9–11.
Clark, D., Goodwin, S., Samuelson, T., and Coker, C. (2008) "A qualitative assessment of the Kindle e–book reader: Results from initial focus groups," *Performance Measurement and Metrics*, volume 9, number 2, pp. 118–129.
Coker, C. (2009) 42 Kindles: A Discussion on the Evolution of Text. *Journal of e-Media Studies* Volume 2, Issue 1, 2009 Dartmouth College
Collins, N. (2011) E-readers 'too easy' to read *Daily Telegraph* 13 Jan 2011
Crabtree, A. and Rodden, T. 2004. Domestic Routines and Design for the Home. *Computer Supported Cooperative Work*, 13(2), 191-220.
Crain, C. (2007) Twilight of the books: *What will life be like if people stop reading? The New Yorker* December 24, 2007
Darnton, R. (1990). *The kiss of Lamourette: Reflections in cultural history*. New York: Norton.
Darnton, R. (2009) The Case for Books: past, present and future. *Public Affairs*. New York.
Dillon, A. (1992) "Reading from paper versus screens: A critical review of the empirical literature," *Ergonomics*, volume 35, number 10, pp. 1,297–1,326.
Edwards, K. & Grinter, R. (2001) At home with ubiquitous computing: seven challenges, *Proc. 3rd International Conference on Ubiquitous Computing*, Springer, (2001), 256-272.
Fleck, J. (1988). Innofusion or Diffusation? The Nature of Technological Development in Robotics, *ESRC Programme on Information and Communication Technologies. Working Paper Series*, University of Edinburgh.
Gomez, J. (2008) *Print is Dead: Books in Our Digital Age*. Macmillan, 2008
Haddon, L. (2007) Roger Silverstone's legacies: domestication. *New Media Society* 9: 25.
Henscher, P. (2009) Curling up with a good e-book? *Daily Telegraph* 17 Dec 2009
Harper, R. (2010) *Texture: Human Expression in the Age of Communications Overload*. MIT Press. Boston
Hillesund, T. (2001) "Will e–books change the world?" *First Monday*, volume 6, number 10, at http://firstmonday.org/htbin/cgiwrap/bin/ojs/index.php/fm/article/view/891/800,
Hillesund, T. (2007) "Reading *Books* in the Digital Age subsequent to Amazon, Google and the long tail," *First Monday*, volume 12, number 9, http://firstmonday.org/htbin/cgiwrap/bin/ojs/index.php/fm/article/view/2012/1887
Hillesund, T. (2010) Digital reading spaces: how expert readers handle books, the Web and electronic paper. *First Monday*, Volume 15, Number 4 - 5 April 2010 http://firstmonday.org/htbin/cgiwrap/bin/ojs/index.php/fm/article/viewArticle/2762/2504

Kress, G. (2003) *Literacy in the New Media Age*. Routledge. London.

Liu, Z and Stork, D. (2000) Is paperless really more? Rethinking the role of paper in the digital age. *Communications of the ACM* Vol. 43 No. 11, Pages 94-97

Liu, Z. (2005) "Reading behavior in the digital environment: Changes in reading behavior over the past ten years", *Journal of Documentation*, Vol. 61 Iss: 6, pp.700 – 712

Lonsdale, M., Dyson, M., and Reynolds, L. (2006). "Reading in examination–type situations: The effects of text layout on performance," *Journal of Research in Reading*, volume 29, number 4, pp. 433–453.

Lynch, C. (2001) The Battle to Define the Future of the Book in the Digital World *First Monday*, Volume 6, Number 6 - 4 June 2001 http://firstmonday.org/htbin/cgiwrap/bin/ojs/index.php/fm/article/viewArticle/864/773

Mangen, A. (2006). *New narrative pleasures?: A cognitive-phenomenological study of the experience of reading digital narrative fictions*. Trondheim: Faculty of Arts, Department of Art and Media Studies Norwegian University of Science and Technology.

Mangen, A. (2008) "Hypertext fiction reading: Haptics and immersion," *Journal of Research in Reading*, volume 31, number 4, pp. 404–419.

Manguel, A. (1996) *A history of reading*. Harper Collins. London

Marr, A. (2007) Curling up with a good ebook. *The Guardian*, 11 May, 2007. http://books.guardian.co.uk/ebooks/story/0,,2077277,00.html

McHoul, A. (1978) Ethnomethodology and literature: Preliminaries to a sociology of reading. *Poetics* Volume 7, Issue 1, March 1978, Pages 113-120

Miall, D and Dobson, T. (2001) "Reading hypertext and the experience of literature," *Journal of Digital Information*, volume 2, number 1

Mitcham, C. (1990) Three Ways of Being with Technology. In Scharf, R and Dusek, V (eds) (2003) *Philosophy of Technology: the Technological Condition: An Anthology*, Blackwell. Oxford. Pp490-506.

Nye, David E., (2006) *Technology and the Production of Difference* American Quarterly - Volume 58, Number 3, September 2006, pp. 597-618

O'Brien, J. et al. (1999) "At home with the technology", *ACM Transactions on Computer-Human Interaction*, Vol. 6 (3), pp. 282-308.

O'Hara, K, and Sellen, A. (1997) "A comparison of reading paper and on–line documents," in Proceedings of *CHI 97* Proce*edings of the SIGCHI conference on Human factors in computing systems*. http://www.sigchi.org/chi97/proceedings/paper/koh.htm

Ong, W. (1982). *Orality & Literacy: The Technologizing of the Word*. London: Methuen.

Rowlands, I., Nicholas, D., Jamali, H., and Huntington, P. (2007) "What do faculty and students really think about e–books?" *Aslib Proceedings*, volume 59, number 6, pp. 489–511.

Roychoudhuri, O. (2010) Books After Amazon. *Boston Review* November/December 2010

Sacks, H. (1992). *Lectures on conversation*. 2 vols. Edited by Gail Jefferson with introductions by Emanuel A. Schegloff. Oxford: Basil Blackwell

Schraefel, M.C. (2010) Apple iPad review - finding a health niche: bathtub reading http://www.begin2dig.com/2010/11/apple-ipad-review-finding-health-niche.html

Sellen, A., and Harper, R. (2002). *The myth of the paperless office*. Cambridge, Mass.: MIT Press.

Silberman, S. (1998) Ex Libris: The joys of curling up with a good digital reading device. *Wired*, 7/98, 98-104.

Silverstone, R. (1994) *Television and Everyday Life*. Routledge. London.

Silverstone, R., Hirsch, E and Morley, D. (1990) 'Information and communication technologies and the moral economy of the household' in Berg, A. (ed) *Technology and Everyday Life: Trajectories and Transformations*. University of Trondheim Press. Trondheim. Pp13-46.

Taylor, A. and Harper, R. (2003) Switching On to Switch Off. *Inside the Smart Home*, R. Harper (ed.). London:Springer-Verlag, 2003, 115-126.

Thompson, J.B. (2005) *Books in the Digital Age*. Polity Press. Cambridge.

Tolmie, P. (2010) *Everyday Intimacy: Recognizing Intimacy in Everyday Life*, Saarbrücken: LAP Lambert

Venkatesh, A., Stolzoff, N., Shih, E. and Mazumdar, S. (2001) "The home of the future", *Advances in Consumer Research*, Vol. 28, pp. 88-96.

Wajcman, J and Mackenzie, D. (1985) *The Social Shaping of Technology: How The Refrigerator Got its Hum,* Open University Press. Milton Keynes.

Wolf, M. (2007). *Proust and the squid: The story and science of the reading brain*. HarperCollins. New York

Wyatt, S., G. Thomas and T.Terranova (2002) `"They Came, They Surfed and Then Went Back to the Beach": Conceptualizing Use and Non-use of the Internet', in S.Woolgar (ed.) *Virtual Society? Technology, Cyberbole, Reality*, pp. 23—40. Oxford: Oxford University Press.

Chapter 9
Nearness: Family Life and Digital Neighborhood

Siân Lindley

Introduction

When asked to consider what a 'smart home' is, one might imagine a house containing a plethora of devices, seamlessly responding to one's needs and doing so without supervision. Definitions from scholars are similar, albeit more nuanced; for example Aldrich (2003) suggests that different degrees of 'smartness' can be assigned according to the presence of appliances that are automatic, autonomous, or interconnected. Such definitions tend to focus on the home itself, but interconnections underpinned by technology increasingly need to be understood as extending outwards, beyond those four walls. Householders might receive text messages to remind them of the lack of milk in the fridge as they pass the local supermarket, for example, and technologies that connect the home office to the workplace, or that enable family members to look into the living rooms of their far-flung relatives, are increasingly well-established. Despite this focus on interaction and connectedness, however, current depictions of smart homes seem to lack any real sense of geographical location or community. The focus is on the home rather than the street or town, on the family rather than the neighborhood, with technology being used almost as a means by which distance is dissolved. Yet, it is evident that distance cannot, in reality, be so easily collapsed. Our relationships with our neighbors are profoundly different to those who live far away; the same is true for family who live down the road as opposed to in distant locations. We implicitly understand that nearness, as a property of relationships, influences why we communicate with others, what our obligations to them are, and what might emerge from these interactions. How then, can we think about nearness in the context of designing future technologies?

Research and innovation often focuses on one extreme or the other when it comes to addressing this question. Considering people whose lives are inherently entwined, researchers have explored family members' practices surrounding the leaving of notes (Perry & Rachovides, 2007), creation of lists (Taylor & Swan, 2004), use of

S. Lindley (✉)
Microsoft Research, Cambridge, UK

R. Harper (ed.), *The Connected Home: The Future of Domestic Life*,
DOI 10.1007/978-0-85729-476-0_9, © Springer-Verlag London 2011

calendars (Neustaedter & Bernheim Brush, 2006), and even how people position letters within the home so that others will encounter them (Crabtree & Rodden, 2004, Harper & Shatwell, 2003). Other studies have explored how routine is an intrinsic characteristic of daily life and how householders and neighbors draw on their knowledge of one another's habits in organizing their own schedules (e.g. Tolmie et al., 2003). Such research has prompted the design of electronic notice-boards that householders can post content to (O'Hara et al., 2005, Sellen et al., 2006, Romero et al., 2007), visual answer machines for families (Lindley et al., 2009), and kitchen displays that show the whereabouts of the home's occupants (Brown et al., 2007). At the other extreme, a body of work has explored the problem of connecting remote friends (Dey & de Guzman, 2006), family (e.g. Hindus et al., 2001, Saslis-Lagoudakis et al., 2006, Langdale et al., 2006, Bernheim Brush et al., 2008, Tee et al., 2009) and lovers (e.g., Kaye et al., 2005). Technological innovation within this space often uses what we know of people who live in close proximity as inspiration, attempting to recreate the sense of intimacy that comes when someone is a familiar feature of one's life (see e.g. Vetere et al., 2005). Designers have attempted to merge physical spaces (Grivas, 2006), they have aimed to give a sense of when a remote partner is lying in bed (Dodge, 1997) or drinking tea (Chung et al., 2006), and they have drawn upon the empty moments in one's day, such as when washing the dishes, as a way of connecting couples (Lottridge et al., 2009). Where families are concerned, notice boards and planners continue to predominate, with researchers aiming to make information that is manifest in the 'near field' accessible over a distance, for example through creating shared calendars, or supporting the remote sharing of notes and photos in order to support a sense of connection (Romero et al., 2007, Neustaedter et al., 2006, Tee et al., 2009).

This overview points to the ways in which nearness has been used as a source of inspiration in research and design, the view being that technologies might be designed to provide those who are far apart a sense of closeness. However, in practice, the majority of available communication technologies are used to sustain widely dispersed networks of people as well as those that are proximal. In other words, people frequently and artfully use an ecology of technologies that span distances both short and vast, with phone calls, text messages, emails, instant messages and status updates being used in the context of long-distance relationships as well as to connect people who live in the same street. Even video-chat, mainly thought of as a resource for people who rarely spend time together, is also known to be used by teenage friends who see each other every day (Kirk et al., 2010). Of interest here are the choices that underlie whether and when to use particular technologies, for what purposes, and how these actions are bound up with the relationships that they underpin. Why, for example, do teenage friends feel the need to connect through video? Researchers have shown that video links to their best friends are used in conjunction with instant messaging windows connecting them with others, allowing those linked by video to talk whilst typing to other contacts (Kirk et al., ibid). The use of video, of course, makes such behavior transparent; it is difficult to talk behind someone's back whilst on camera. So although video is generally seen as a way of providing a special connection over long distances (see, for example, Kaye's chapter in this collection), the choice to use it in other contexts is, in itself, a marker of a noteworthy relationship. What this underlines is that use of the same technologies, in ways that appear superficially similar, imply different meanings in different contexts.

In this chapter I will present findings from a study of a prototype communication device, Wayve, which was used by networks of family and friends over distances near and far. As hinted at above, nearness, as a property of relationships, inevitably affected the communication mediated by the device, from what was talked about, to the opportunities for interaction that arose, to how meanings were realized through it. In what follows, I hope to illustrate how, instead of viewing technology as a means of emulating neighborliness for those who are far apart, we might instead position it as a means of supporting these different types of relationship in different ways. In other words, homes that are truly 'smart' might be equipped with technologies that allow us to be neighborly with our neighbors, while supporting an alternative type of intimacy with remote family members. As previously argued by Taylor et al. (2007), smart technologies serve as a resource with which people themselves imbue their homes with intelligence. Before exploring this in more depth however, some background research that motivated this work will be presented.

Background

As already noted, researchers have considered how technology can be used to support communication over distances both large and small, considering couples in long-distance relationships, families that communicate across different time-zones (e.g. Cao et al., 2010), friends who wish to maintain an awareness of one another after relocating, and remote colleagues (e.g. Olson & Olson, 2000). On the other hand, within families and also local communities (e.g. Taylor & Cheverst, 2009), researchers have primarily focused on the use of situated displays as communication and organization tools. The technology that I will discuss here, Wayve, is an example of a situated display. Such devices tend to be designed to support the leaving of messages at home for family members to encounter, or to provide a sense of community within certain groups, although they have also been used as a way of connecting remote households (Saslis-Lagoudakis et al., 2006, Langdale et al., 2006). Wayve itself was largely inspired by findings from fieldwork with two situated displays, which had been designed to explore the possibilities offered by person-to-place messaging. TxtBoard (O'Hara et al., 2005) and HomeNote (Sellen et al., 2006), and their deployments in the kitchens of family homes, illustrated the potential for 'messaging to place' to support families in managing the practical aspects of organising home life, as well as to provide an outlet for playfulness and displays of affection. To give more specific examples, family members used the screens to reassure one another of their whereabouts, to place calls for action such as requesting lifts, and to scribble reminders, as well as to broadcast themselves through the drawing of self-portraits or scrawling of their names (this was especially common for children). Finally, and most frequently, family members posted 'social touch' messages, written simply as a way of demonstrating care and affection. Practices similar to these have also been reported when situated displays are used to connect remote couples, with messages being written to express affection, keep in touch and provide a sense of presence (Saslis-Lagoudakis et al., ibid).

Wayve was built primarily using lessons learned from HomeNote and TxtBoard. Like its predecessors, it was designed with the intention that it be located in a communal space in the home (such as in the kitchen), and to be left always on, so that the scrolling display of notes and pictures might be seen at a glance. Notes can be created by either scribbling on the touch screen or by capturing images using the built-in camera. These can either be displayed locally, in the same way that one might write a note for someone and place it where they will encounter it, or they can be sent outwards, either as text messages, picture messages or emails. The easy sending of messages is supported through an address book with six 'favorite' slots. Messages from mobile phones and email accounts can also be sent to the device, with each Wayve having a unique phone number and an email address. The form factor, which was designed to be informal in look and feel, and a close-up of the display, can be seen in Fig. 9.1.

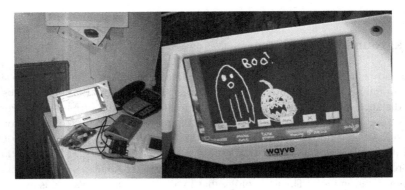

Fig. 9.1 Wayve in situ and a close up of the interface

The emphasis on content creation and the easy sending of messages in the design of Wayve meant that, unlike HomeNote and TxtBoard (which were only able to receive content, and so might be considered notice boards), Wayve could be interpreted as a communication device, where communication is bi-directional. Generally speaking, the field trial demonstrated that the device was perceived as being a very simple way of sending messages. However, its communication functionality was not interpreted as broadly as might have been the case. In particular, Wayve was not seen as a means of communicating with just anyone, despite the large number of potential recipients that participants could send content to (this being anyone with a mobile phone or email address). Rather, the device was perceived as a means of sending content to other Wayves. Consequently, Wayve became a way of primarily supporting contact within existing networks of friends and family, who were participating in the field trial as extended networks.

To be more specific, a total of 24 households were involved in the field trial. Sixteen of these formed small networks of family and friends, while eight were 'lone' families, who knew none of the other participants and therefore used Wayve in relative isolation. In the analysis presented here, the focus is on the networks, which were distributed across England as shown in Fig. 9.2. Some of these comprized people who lived very near to one another and had daily contact. For example, two households in which the mothers were friends were within easy walking distance of one another, and an additional two houses featured an older couple and their son, who lived around the corner from each other. For other households, participants lived in neighboring towns and villages, and in one case, a family of four lived approximately 100 miles from their relatives. In total, the networks encompassed a quartet of friends, two trios of extended family members including grandparents, and two pairs of siblings and one pair of friends.

Fig. 9.2 Networks of families and friends that participated in the field trial, and their distribution across England

These 16 households were loaned a Wayve for an average period of 85.3 days; the maximum being 99 days and the minimum 56. Each household was visited at the beginning of the field trial in order for the researchers to set up and demonstrate the device. The households were then interviewed three times: by telephone after two weeks, face-to-face after six weeks and then again at the end of the trial. These interviews were recorded and messages sent to and from the Wayves throughout the field trial were logged; a selection of messages were used to prompt discussion in the final interview. Messages sent from the device were free for the duration of the trial, whether sent to other Wayves, mobile phones or email addresses.

The findings presented below are derived from message logs, interview transcripts, and observations of what was displayed on the Wayves when participants were interviewed. Inspection of the message logs reveals that a total of 3744 messages were sent from the 16 networked Wayves during the field trial, while 2918 messages were sent to them. Both figures exclude messaging on each household's first day to control for initial testing and demonstrations. Novelty effects were apparent but usage was sustained throughout the field trial: in week 1, an average of 39.94 messages was sent per household; in week 4 this figure was 15.13 and in week 8 it had risen to 28.25. Even in week 12, when the sample was depleted (and there were fewer other Wayves within the networks to send messages to), an average of 13.64 messages was sent per remaining household. A graph of the average number of messages sent and received per day across the whole trial period is given in Fig. 9.3.

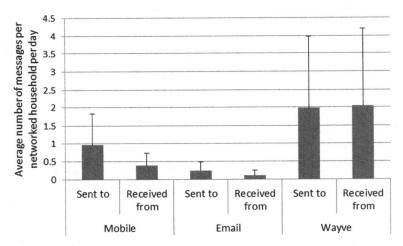

Fig. 9.3 Graph to show the average number of messages sent/received per household per day, to and from different media (standard deviations are shown by the error bars)

Figure 9.3 demonstrates that, although usage varied considerably across households, Wayve messages were most commonly sent to and received from other Wayves as opposed to mobile phones or email accounts. In other words, communication was primarily within the networks that were recruited. Through the analysis that follows it will be demonstrated that when the households in these networks were physically near to one another, the motivations for sending messages and the resources drawn upon in interpreting their meaning were quite different to those for messages that had to breach longer distances. However, it will also become evident that geography alone is not sufficient to explain the different messaging practices that were observed. Nearness needs to be understood in social and emotional terms as well, and understanding this is just as important to informing design.

Home, Family and Neighborhood

Nevertheless, physical distance will form the starting point in this investigation: we will begin by focusing on how the messaging practices of networks that were confined to neighborhoods differed from those that connected remotely-located homes. As already mentioned, Wayve was designed following studies of situated displays, somewhat akin to electronic notice boards, that were deployed with what we have called 'lone' families. As an initial question then, we might consider whether the types of usage reported in these previous studies, including broadcasts of identity, calls to action and social touch messages (O'Hara et al., 2005; Sellen et al., 2006), would extend outwards, beyond the boundaries of the home and into those of others. After all, what does it mean to push content of this kind to a display in someone else's home, and who has the rights to do this?

As might be predicted, participants who lived in the same neighborhoods used Wayve in a way that was in many ways similar to how families living together have been reported to use situated displays. The sharing of spaces, responsibilities and routines meant that reminders could be jotted, requests for favors posted, and passing questions asked (see Fig. 9.4). For example, notes drew attention to upcoming 'bin days', the need to return borrowed items, and were posted to find out where one's children were, or to provide reassurance whilst looking after someone else's. The speed, ease, and immediacy of sending messages, coupled with their glanceability on arrival, made Wayve an ideal device for these types of communication. The device was also used as a way of coordinating visits and broadcasting one's availability within local networks. For example, one man, who lived around the corner from his parents, described his use of Wayve as a means "to sort of let my folks know when I'm sort of conscious and receptive to visitors if you like, whereas before they'd sort of knock on the door and if they didn't get any answer they didn't get any answer, we've been sort of coordinating things and using it that way". This was particularly important in this case, as the son worked night shifts and his father tended to visit him on a daily basis, timing this so as to arrive neither when he was asleep during the day nor once he had left for work in the evening. The fact that Wayve messages were persistent but non-intrusive suited the often asynchronous communication pattern across these two households, with the father noting, "Because of the nightshift pattern he's on, he tends to send me messages at 6 o' clock in the morning, I pick them up at 10 o' clock, or 11 o' clock [in the morning]". While this need for asynchronous messaging is bound up with the somewhat atypical working patterns of this particular son, these participants were not alone in using Wayve to signal awareness regarding their availability. People in local networks often used the device to let one another know of their whereabouts, or if they were likely to be difficult to contact for a while (such as when taking a child to hospital, for example).

Fig. 9.4 Notes sent to post reminders and alert others to one's current whereabouts

Such findings echo Ito and Okabe's (2005) description of a persistent social space that is maintained by teenagers in Japan, who are close friends or in a relationship with each another. Drawing on their fieldwork, Ito and Okabe suggest that text messaging and emailing are used to create a sense of ambient availability, with the sending of a message not so much marking the opening of a communication channel as being predicated on the expectation that the recipient is within "earshot". The pervasive nature of this techno-social setting is such that youths mark boundaries regarding their (un)availability through the sending of 'goodnight' emails, or messages to say that they are taking a bath. Although Wayve differs from mobile phones in that it is not a personal, portable device, it too was used as a way of managing expectations regarding one's availability. The fact that neighboring participants had routines that were grounded in one another, and further, on a notion of shared physical spaces, meant that the device could be used to signal one's presence within certain locales. So in this case, place was assumed, with messaging indicating one's availability in terms of time.

These examples are obviously driven by a practical need to coordinate, but they also reflect the etiquette of managing one's affairs when those affairs involve others. Both of these are important in the smooth running of the home, and have been previously highlighted in the ways in which families use situated displays. With Wayve too, occasions arose in which messages, which ostensibly served a practical purpose, could not really be explained by our participants in these terms. For example, the pair of messages presented in Fig. 9.5 represent an exchange that, while on the face of it is about coordination, in reality had little to do with scheduling. This same message ("Normal time tomorrow?") was sent in some form on the evening before each workday, seemingly to arrange the subsequent day's car-sharing. However, in reality, these arrangements never changed. Further, when pressed, neither sender nor recipient could really explain 'why' the messages were sent. It seems that, although messages such as these are bound up with the decorum of coordinating activities with others, they are also (as is evident by the playful nature of the scribbled notes) simply an expression of friendship.

On other occasions, messages that signaled availability also offered up opportunities for action. These were fairly typical in our field trial, and can be distinguished from the explicit 'calls for action', reported by O'Hara et al. (2005) and Sellen et al. (2006). Sellen et al. describe how their participants posted content to HomeNote's shared display, rather than to a family member's mobile phone, because this was seen as a less demanding way to request that something be done. This subtlety

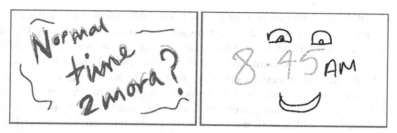

Fig. 9.5 An exchange sent to support coordination across homes

seemed even more exaggerated amongst our local networks, with messages being sent to highlight opportunities for action but without expectation or obligation. For example, participants would let one another know when they were going to the shops in case a neighbor wanted to join them, but the offer would be given in such a way that no response would be needed. This can be seen in Fig. 9.6; a timely response is required if the offer of a walk to the shops is to be accepted, but no action is necessary at all if the recipient isn't interested.

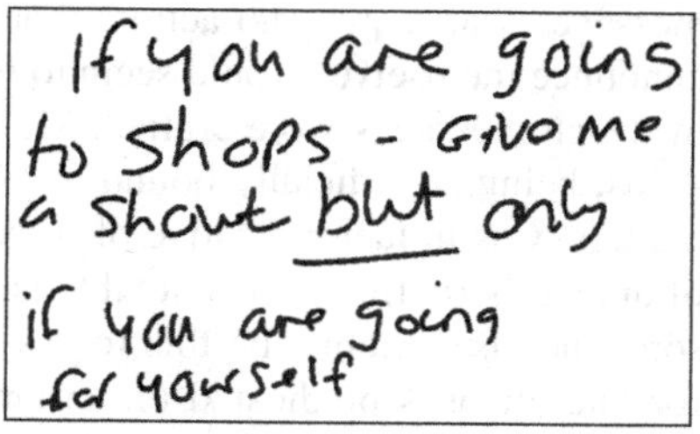

Fig. 9.6 A message highlighting an opportunity for action

Perhaps the most extreme example of messaging that was predicated on physical proximity can be seen in a practice that developed across the two households comprising a couple and their night-shift working son. For this extended family, phone calls and visits needed to be carefully managed if the son was to be caught at home without being disturbed whilst sleeping, and consequently daily visits tended to be quite short. In order to make the most of them, the father started sending Wayve messages to his son's device, designed to serve as prompts for conversation, or reminders of things that he wanted to talk about. As he explained, this practice of posting notes-to-himself in his son's home developed to allow him to make the most of the limited time that he had to spend with his son when "popping round" before the night shift:

> Each day, [my wife] puts his [food] up for him for overnight and I take it round at a pre-described time, which is normally about four o'clock or six o'clock if he's on late shift, I get five minutes with him then, then I'll come to the door [at home] and say, 'Oh I forgot to mention so and so', and by that time he's away to work, so that's when that machine comes into its element.

We might think of Wayve as offering a window into someone else's life in some of the examples given above. Information easily acquired when sharing the same house, such as whether one is awake or asleep, in or out, or whether the children are about, was specifically communicated via Wayve. Indeed, the son who worked night-shifts described the messages between himself and his parents as "what you'd have within a household, just round the corner". More than this though, these practices suggest a degree of thoughtfulness that has as much to do with the manner in which things are said as with what is actually communicated. Harper (2010) has argued that one's choice of communication technology, and the way in which it is used, is as important (if not more so) than the content of a message; communication channels have as much to do with social grace as they do with the simple transmission of information. Further, O'Hara et al. (2005) and Sellen et al. (2006) have described how messaging to a situated display demonstrates a subtlety and courtesy that messaging to specific individuals sometimes lacks. By sending to a place rather than a person, messaging is less intrusive and does not seem to demand a response in quite the same way. Messaging practices underpinned by Wayve show how this is even more evident when messaging to place extends beyond the home. This is perhaps unsurprising: the nagging of one's immediate family might be more socially acceptable than the pestering of people in other homes, and so the placement of messages that require no action, that are not distracting, and that do not strongly announce themselves would seem to be preferable. This is reflected too in the ways in which messages were crafted. Much of the communication that crossed households, being superficially bound up with routine and the management of practical matters, was in fact indicative of social etiquette or the thoughtful accommodation of another's routines. Also notable is that the acceptability of pushing content into someone else's home, be this to ask favors, place reminders, or even write notes for oneself, was predicated on an entwining of the daily lives of those involved. There is obviously much more than simple geography to this; the practices made evident through Wayve were built upon a foundation of shared routines and mutual responsibilities.

Demonstrating Closeness

As alluded to above, in addition to contemplating nearness as a property of geography, we might also deliberate on its other forms, such as in closeness of daily routines and the common responsibilities that this engenders. In this section, forms of nearness that might be considered 'social' will be considered in more detail, following prior work that has highlighted how use of communication technologies is bound up with different types of social relationship. As an example, Rivière and Licoppe (2005) show how relationships that differ in closeness (in terms of how often one sees someone, shares common activities with them, and is emotionally close to them) are associated with different expressions of etiquette. They report how in Japan, the need to provide visible markers of respect is made manifest in choice of communication technology. For example, text messages are used to mediate interactions when one does not want to intrude with a phone call. However, such conventions are relaxed when contacting the closest members of one's inner circle; for people who are very close, such as husbands and wives, shows of restraint are not needed. This sentiment seems to be echoed in the conventions that developed around Wayve; posting notes-to-self in someone else's home suggests the lack of a need for restraint in just the way that Rivière and Licoppe describe. Indeed, such behaviors can be seen not only as an expression of a particularly close relationship, but also as a way of underpinning it; that those who are close allow others to intrude in this way is a marker of their regard for one another. Rivière and Licoppe go on to detail how communication practices differ with weaker relationships. For example, in what is termed the 'second circle' of contacts, described as friendships that are 'elective', communications are used primarily to maintain bonds in the absence of much face-to-face contact. In our study of Wayve, it also became apparent that messaging served a different purpose when breaching longer distances. In what follows, it will be shown that keeping others up to date of one's current activities, through messages ostensibly similar to those already described in the context of neighboring households, served a different purpose when communicated over longer distances.

Interviews with members of extended families distributed across larger distances revealed that there were a different set of commitments underpinning their communication practices, both via Wayve and through more established media. Messages that entailed the broadcasting of awareness information were fairly common across these networks, but these could not be described as being bound by or underpinning routines; they did not highlight opportunities for a trip to the shops or provide updates about the whereabouts of children, for example. Instead, remote family members upheld their sense of closeness by messaging as an activity undertaken for its own ends. The notion that this was an obligation, and one that was at times difficult to uphold, was evident in our participants' descriptions of their communication practices. For example, the father of our most remotely-located household told us how, despite his wish to keep in touch with his parents, other demands associated with daily life, such as organising his two teenage children and balancing his and his wife's careers, often got in the way. Whilst he had initially had a routine with his parents whereby they phoned each other once a week, this habit had slipped; in fact interviews with both parties indicated that they felt that they were slightly losing touch. This slippage was not really seen as problematic; both sides commented that they were available if needed, and the grandfather commented that the family was fairly independent in general. However, there was an underlying sense that they felt that they should keep in touch more, and that a means to enable this to happen would be beneficial.

Fig. 9.7 Messages relating to on-going activities or recent special events

For this family, messages that disclosed information about unfolding activities were appreciated as a means of "dipping in and dipping out of someone's life", as the father put it. They included notes sent to share special events such as holidays or days out, as shown in Fig. 9.7, but also those pertaining to everyday events, such as the weather, the making of a sandwich, or what was currently being watched on television, as shown in Fig. 9.8. Unlike the messages described in the previous section, these tended to function as updates about one's life (in the same way that people post generic status updates to social network sites) rather than as a means of providing opportunities for action, and they provided a sense of being in touch with others that was difficult to achieve using other communication technologies. For example, the father of the remotely-located family described the types of contact that Wayve afforded:

> It's kind of less consequential stuff, it's more, it's more chatty stuff, I guess rather than, rather than a month's catch-up, so you think yes this happened that happened, we went out to that thing, we'll come home and we'll say, 'Oh, it's chucking it down here', [..] then he'll say yes it is and then we'll take pictures of the weather and that sort of thing, where if we're communicating, if we're telephoning once a week or that sort of thing then we probably wouldn't talk about the weather, but it's nice cos I imagine if the family were in the village it might be the sort of thing you'd sort of bump into each other every other day and then talk about, but it's kind of brought us closer together not geographically but virtually together, really.

The sharing of mundane content in particular allowed for a different sense of feeling in touch, with family members feeling a stronger part of one another's lives as a consequence of this.

Fig. 9.8 Messages that give an insight into more mundane aspects of daily life

It is also worth emphasizing that, although this particular family was separated by approximately 100 miles, the sharing of this type of awareness message was not limited to participants communicating over such long distances. Similar descriptions of Wayve were offered up by families who lived in neighboring towns and villages. For example, a pair of family homes, headed by a brother and sister, reported that Wayve allowed them to learn a bit more about what was going on in each other's lives, with the sister commenting, "He's busy with his life and we're busy with ours, and that's the way it is, but it gave you a, you know a door into their lives and the girls, and vice versa". It seems then that an appreciation of some insight into the smaller details of everyday life was evident wherever family members were not heavily involved in one another's lives, even if this was simply because they lived a short car journey away.

Another notable feature of the interactions of these families was the sending of, sometimes routine, social touch messages (cf. O'Hara et al., 2005; Sellen et al., 2006, and see also Taylor & Harper's (2003) and Ito & Okabe's (2005) descriptions of text messaging practices amongst teenagers). These encompassed birthday greetings, good luck messages and other general expressions of affection. It was common across the whole field trial for such messages to be sent via Wayve on special occasions (birthday greetings are a good example of this), but remote family networks also started to build routines around these, for example by sending goodnight messages, as shown in Fig. 9.9. These might be thought of as a way of trying to stay a part of someone's life, being described by the grandfather as a way of saying "don't forget that we're here", and by his son as opening up a line of communication between his own family and his parents:

> I've really enjoyed having it [Wayve] really, it's opened up a lot of communication between sort of, myself and my parents [..] my dad sort of signs off on an evening, he'll say oh goodnight all, and [my son] or someone will say oh goodnight grandpa and that sort of thing.

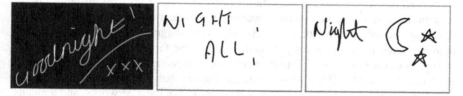

Fig. 9.9 Social touch messages sent as a way of staying in one another's lives

In contrast, within near networks messages about on-going activities or special occasions could usually be interpreted as a way of demonstrating closeness rather than as a means of upholding it. Far from being couched as obligatory, or even special, such interactions tended to be viewed as silly, drawing on common ground to tease, crack in-jokes, and highlight recent shared experiences. For example, the leftmost message in Fig. 9.10 (captioned 'Chillies coming on well') was sent from a son to his father, as a way of mocking him about his own rather less healthy plants:

> Oh yes, the chillies that are on my bedroom window at the moment, yeah now I think this went to my old man, [..] there's an on-going, I don't know if he's mentioned this, he's actually kidnapped one of my tomato plants [..] yes so there was this on-going thing that erm his plants were doing better than mine, so this was a ner-ner-ne-ner-ner message, saying you're not growing chillies I know, but these are coming on really well, a lot better than your weak and feeble specimens are.

Similarly, the central message shows an illustration of a house that two women had visited together as part of a school trip, and the note on the right was sent in reaction to a flood that was occurring near the homes of four of our households. Unlike the messages in Fig. 9.8, these were not sent so as to offer a window into one's life. Rather they are posted to amuse, to express oneself or to connect with someone; the central image in Fig. 9.10 sent simply because "I just thought what a nice picture, I'll send it to her". We might think of this as a different type of social art. Goodnight messages were not seen in these geographically near networks, and there is a sense that for participants who were already an intrinsic part of one another's lives, making such contact was somewhat superfluous. Instead, they used the device to underscore their friendships in different ways.

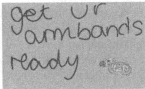

Fig. 9.10 Messages that build on shared events

These differences highlight two aspects of nearness. The first relates to geography. People who live near to one another and whose lives are closely entwined inevitably have different things to talk about to those who are at a distance. The second relates to kin and the expectations that are bound up with different family relationships. It is notable that there were no remote networks of friends within our field trial, despite the fact that the networks were suggested by participants rather than being recruited specifically. This may reflect the fact that people note a 'need' to stay in touch with remote family that is more pressing than that to stay in touch with remote friends. The findings indicate further that whilst Wayve was understood primarily as a way of easing coordination within local networks, and a means of sending messages that were often perceived as being silly, entertaining and fun, it took on a different, more explicitly valued, role when networks were located more remotely. The need for communication to broach these further distances raises its own difficulties, ones which are not solved by the addition of a new messaging device, but that can be addressed differently through it. We might consider the sharing of the mundane across these networks as offering a different type of opportunity for action. So instead of broadcasting one's on-going activities so that others can join in with them, the sharing of the making of a sandwich, for example, was found to open up opportunities for conversation. Harper (2010) describes communication as a kind of moral order, composed of expressive acts and judgements about the values of those acts, made in relation to time, place and the skills that they embody. Here we can see how messages were skilfully positioned so as to augment relationships predicated on proximity, or to underpin those being maintained across distances. In these ways, even apparently dumb activities, in this case mediated by technology, can be seen to enable smart acts of friendship.

Creating a Closed Network

In our analysis so far, we have focused on how Wayve was used to support Wayve-to-Wayve messaging. However, a feature of the device that differentiates it from other situated displays is the fact that our participants could have used it to communicate to a wider circle of friends and family, by sending messages more broadly to mobile phones and email addresses. It is interesting to note that our participants chose largely not to do this. Instead Wayve was felt to provide a means of communicating within a closed network of other Wayve users. Furthermore, because of the small numbers that were recruited (the largest cluster comprized only four households), their delimited nature underpinned a further sense of nearness:

> It's a more personal thing, I think, than the internet, and I think from the point of view, I don't know how to put it, I think from the point of view you knew the net you were in, you knew the net you were in that could receive stuff and see what you were trying to put over.

This is an artefact of the field trial rather than a consequence of design, yet it does raise other questions for the notion of the connected home. Connections that are all-encompassing are interpreted differently to those that link specific households. While in our field study, Wayve represented "a line of communication which pipes straight through to them", in another situation it might be understood as a scribble-based instant messaging tool, capable of supporting connections to an unlimited set of recipients. The importance of Wayve messages being displayed to an audience but within a closed circle has been discussed in previous papers (see Lindley et al., 2010; Lindley, in press); therefore we will limit the discussion here to highlighting the balance that is struck between the fact that content is openly displayed, and the notion that the locale of display as well as the audience to whom it is being displayed is understood to be, in a sense, restricted. Participants described how they were more motivated to be creative in the sending of playful and inventive messages to Wayve than would be the case if they were sending content to a mobile phone, where their efforts would be glanced at before being placed in a pocket. So the simple fact that content would be displayed was important to them. Yet their knowledge of the context in which this would occur, i.e. the home, to an audience of family and friends, was also crucial: they felt free to express themselves given this knowledge of the setting in which their messages would be encountered.

The emphasis on creativity and play that emerged around Wayve, and the notion of place to place rather than person to person messaging, were two factors that also seemed to draw children to the device. Children could be 'seen' through actions such as doodling on photos, engaging in scribbled exchanges across households, and playing games such as noughts and crosses with extended family members. Even teenagers were noted as partaking in something akin to conversation, as one uncle described:

> I mean I said to you last time about connecting with the kids a lot more as well, and that's really sort of bridged a big gap, and again they can come in from school or whatever and scribble something down and quickly send it off [..] it certainly seems as though there's been a lot more communication with that than email or messenger or anything, and to me that's absolutely brilliant because I'm finding all sorts of stuff I just would never have known about, [..] that's really bridged a gap, and of all of the things to do with the trial that's been the most pleasing.

The fact that Wayve was a less direct or demanding mode of communication also seemed to increase children's willingness to interact with their relatives through it, who were pleasantly surprized when children responded to messages not necessarily intended for them. As the grandfather commented:

One of the times I sent, oh I forget how I worded it, to the effect of I wouldn't be around tomorrow cos [my wife] was going for a check-up, [my granddaughter] came back and said, 'I hope everything goes well', which was a bit unusual for [her . . .] I thought it was lovely, getting it from her, without prompting [laughs].

Again, children were drawn into communications that unfolded via the device by responding to messages that were intended for no one in particular. This allowed them to be included in interactions in a way that can be difficult with more direct modes of communication:

I think the conversation tends to build up because the children will see the same conversation, it's more, it's a more inclusive thing whereas a mobile's a very sort of point-to-point thing, you know the children wouldn't see what I'm saying to my parents or my brother and I wouldn't see what they were saying, but it was, if it's like a to and fro thing then, then it gives a chance for all of us to chip in, so it's not the sort of thing I would do with a mobile.

The above illustrates how use of Wayve became intrinsically linked with notions of family and home-life, serving a means of placing interaction specifically in this context and opening it up to children. This was a point of departure from the norm: aunts, uncles and grandparents all commented on the general difficulty of communicating with the children in their families, a problem that was said to be due to a number of reasons, including that children would rarely be willing to speak on the phone and were in some cases also unable to type. As one aunt commented, "I also think the little ones, because they're shy, like [my niece], she wouldn't pick up the phone and say hello to me, but she sends a [scribbled] message going 'hello'; I've seen her so much more through the Wayve than I've ever heard before". Evident in the above is the fact that this contact was desired and appreciated, even when it was fleeting or took the form of game play and doodles. Indeed, family members (and adults more generally) often scaffold interactions with children in this way, by creating puzzles or simple activities for them to participate in (see for example, Davis et al.'s (2008) discussion of this in the context of grandparenting). Wayve allowed our participants to engender such interactions without them seeming overly-engineered or arduous, and further, aspects of the design encouraged the application of creative efforts.

Concluding Discussion

When connecting remote parties, be these family members, friends, lovers or work colleagues, distance is frequently treated as a factor that needs to be overcome. Design efforts have been inspired by the experiences of collocated people or are undertaken with the aim of replicating these, with efforts focusing on the merging or otherwise linking of spaces, support for peripheral awareness, and the provision of resources to underpin remote communication, such as the use of video to support common ground. The extent of this effort suggests that researchers and designers are very much aware of the difficulties that distance can throw up in communication. In this chapter, I have tried to unpack more carefully what distance means when supporting interaction mediated by technology. What is evident, however, is the fact that physical distance in itself is insufficient as an analytical lens when trying to unpack the various practices that have emerged. Instead, a number of factors, including physical proximity, kinship, and social and emotional closeness, have surfaced in our analysis. In this final section, I will consider how these various elements underpin a general sense of propinquity in relationships, and consider in more depth how this concept might be used as a driver for design.

One point that is immediately apparent when examining our results is that participants whose lives were closely entwined, be these neighbors or close family members, used Wayve in fairly similar ways, developing practices that might be contrasted with those undertaken by extended families who felt that their lives were somehow separate. The cause of this separation, whether it was due to a large geographical distance, or simply the existence of different routines played out in neighboring villages, did not matter so much as the fact of separation in itself. People who have daily routines that are closely linked, geographically and socially, need to communicate in order to sustain these ties. In contrast, those whose relationships are not framed in this way may nevertheless feel compelled to keep in touch, and this can be especially so for family. Our findings suggest that Wayve was utilized in the context of these relationships in different ways.

For families who were not a part of one another's daily lives, there is a sense that they were using Wayve literally as a resource for making conversation: the device became part of the work that they undertook to sustain their relationships. Indeed, it is precisely because their lives showed little overlap that they had neither particular cause to interact nor obvious common ground to build upon in their conversations. Consequently, Wayve was used as a means for playing games or engaging in small talk, allowing families to meet their felt responsibilities to stay in touch with one another, even where the practical, geographic and moral circumstances did not serve to tie them together. It is important to note that such contact was viewed as a form of obligation; in fact, grandparents, aunts, uncles and sons all reported that they would like to communicate with their relatives more, but found this difficult in the context of their busy lives. Furthermore, while we make no claims that our sample is representative, these scenarios are certainly not atypical. Kin are less likely to live near to one another than friends (Coulthard et al., 2002), but nevertheless tend to be amongst one's 'core ties', whom people feel obliged to contact when they are not able to see them in person (Boase et al., 2006). Yet maintaining contact, especially with children, can be difficult. The uncle and grandparents of the remotely-located teenagers both joked that the major occasion at which they spoke to these children was around Christmas, as a way of meeting expectations surrounding gift-giving. That it is easy to lose touch with family outside such seasonal rituals is highlighted by the fact that even families who lived in neighboring villages found it difficult to stay in one another's lives, especially when also faced with the need to breach the generation gap. For these families, their sense of union was made manifest through communication, with the idea of 'family' enduring principally because its members worked to sustain it. Such remarks echo arguments made by Ames et al. (2010) and Kaye in this collection, who have suggested that connecting through video calls is one way in which people sustain their sense of being a family.

In contrast, relationships between neighboring family and friends were not underpinned in this way. Here, obligations were bound up with each specific relationship and its geographic and social auspices. Neighbors looked out for one another's children, shared car journeys and shopped together or for one another, and often these activities were undertaken routinely. Harper (2010) highlights shared routines and the mutual dependence, but more importantly, the trust that these entail, as representing a means through which relationships are played out, or 'done'. So while these routines are to some extent a necessary part of one's day, it is also apparent that they are accomplished mindfully. The etiquette bound up with communications between neighbors via Wayve can be seen as an illustration of the moral order of communication that Harper describes, with activities as repetitive as car-sharing being supplemented with playful exchanges of picture messages. In the event of less habitual goings-on, such as spontaneous shopping trips, *opportunities*, rather than *calls*, for action predominated. Furthermore, common knowledge and in-jokes became the basis for an additional layer of messaging, which seemed geared towards cementing communities of practice.

Of course, this discussion resonates with prior analyzes, in which the home has not been the focus. For example, Brown and Duguid (2000) highlight the importance of various contextual factors in encountering and making sense of information, presenting the view that neither geographical nor social distance can easily be overcome. More specifically, a body of research has explored topics such as awareness and common ground, aspects of interaction that are frequently considered when designing technologies to support remote communication (especially when set in the workplace). There is a good deal of previous work that has explored how awareness might be supported across dispersed collaborators (see e.g. Schmidt, 2002) and that explores the process of grounding (cf. Clark & Brennan, 1991) in remote conversation. The analysis presented here highlights how the reasons for making someone aware of what is going on in one's life is predicated on having a world in common: being continually aware of what is going on in someone's home is only useful if you can act on that information. Manifest in our analysis is the fact that propinquity, be this geographical, social or emotional, is important in determining how this will be so; remote family members communicated information pertaining to their current activities as a way of creating opportunities for interaction, whereas those whose lives were closely entwined did so as a way of highlighting opportunities for action. Indeed, we can interpret these remote conversations as attempts to establish common ground, in contrast to those communications by near networks, where messaging was a demonstration of this.

We might finish by considering what the implications of design choices like these are for smart home technologies more broadly. Although Wayve was not part of a broader network of embedded and interconnected devices in the home, as is typically the vision for smart homes, it does provide an example of firstly, what it means to situate a display in the home and secondly, the ways in which new devices fit into a broader ecology of existing technologies. Considering the notion of situated displays first, Wayve provides an interesting example of a technology that allows others to broadcast into the home. It is notable that while participants had the option to make their Wayve contact details available to whoever they pleased (in fact, contact cards detailing the phone number and email address for each household were created especially to make this process easier), very few of them did so. That the device was essentially understood as one for linking family and neighbors within the Wayve network was striking. This sense of a restricted circle, no doubt partly reinforced by the design of the field study, raises a further question, that of scalability. Let us imagine for a moment what it would be like if all homes were equipped with a Wayve. What would this mean for such a device? While it is perfectly possible that the device would be used as some kind of broad instant messenger in this instance, our analysis also suggests a move away from such limitless connectivity. The right to push content into the home of another is suggestive of a degree of intimacy in itself, one that seems to be taken to its extreme by the father who posted notes-to-himself in the home of his son. A move against open connectivity is also suggested by the ways in which other technologies, which on the face of it support forms of very public broadcasting, are appropriated. Harper (2010) points to the use of Facebook by teenagers as a mode of communication that limits contact to a circle of peers, at the exclusion of parents; he suggests that such sites are used as a way of keeping the world small. In our field study, the restricted circle that Wayve implied meant that for some participants, the device became all about family, supporting a sense of connectedness with them simply by dint of being used. This sense of closeness with some only makes sense when it is juxtaposed with the exclusion of others.

Also worth noting here is the distinction between broadcasting everything that is unfolding within one's own home, and choosing to highlight certain events. Much of the work surrounding linking of spaces to support awareness utilizes always-on connections. However, the sense of deliberately making one aware of what is happening in one's life was found to be important in this field trial. Unlike systems where peripheral awareness is supported through open video links, for example, the choice to send a message via a device like Wayve gives a sense that those involved are deliberately engaging in a discussion, even if it is only about the weather. The value of having children unexpectedly participate in such conversations was particularly notable. Interestingly, we saw some of our participants using Wayve to signal their unavailability, in practices that resonate with those described by Ito and Okabe (2005). Those who shared routines and responsibilities highlighted unexpected disruptions to those routines, whilst those separated by further distances used the device to send simple goodnight messages. Ito and Okabe have described how youths signal breaks to the ambient availability that they experience through their mobile phones. It seems that our participants experienced something similar, despite the lack of an always-open channel such as a video link. This sense of connection could then be escalated to a conversation where appropriate.

As a final point for discussion, this field study of Wayve provides some insight into how new devices are understood by their users in relation to the milieu of technologies already available to them. Despite what we have noted regarding the ways in which Wayve was used within local networks, it was often interpreted by our participants as being best suited for long-distance relationships. This seemed partly bound up with its support for rich yet simple picture messaging, a feature that evokes remote communication, and partly with the fact that its value seemed more evident in the context of such relationships. For remote families, the device supported a bond that allowed them to share parts of life that would otherwise be missed. Such values are easily articulated. In contrast, the sending of messages, which are often perceived as being fun but inconsequential on the one hand, and apparently practical but minute on the other, are more difficult to justify (especially if one would have to pay for them). Interestingly then, the recognition of distance as a factor that is difficult to breach was intrinsic to the way that Wayve was understood and appreciated by our participants. Those who noted the device was successful in helping to overcome large distances felt it important, while those for whom it provided a rich layer of communication on top of their everyday interactions considered it less so. This way of thinking raises questions for designers wishing to innovate in this space, regarding how they might market technologies that relate to the micro-management of daily life. While relationships are underpinned by apparently small, prosaic routines and minute social graces, the subtlety of these acts, and the fact that they are often taken for granted (except for, perhaps, when they are absent), can make them difficult to recognize. Yet, it is through such acts that people nurture their relationships. 'Smartness' in this context has less to do with novel forms of technology that enable interaction, and more to do with small, careful gestures, which are mediated through it.

In summary, the purpose of this chapter has been to present findings from a study of how Wayve was used across networks that differed both in terms of geography and kinship. This is not a comparative study, but our analysis suggests some of the ways in which these factors were important in shaping how the device was used. For remote families, the device was a way of enacting family relationships, allowing members to meet their felt obligations to stay in touch by creating common ground and highlighting opportunities for conversation. For those people who were already within one another's lives, the device was used to subtly highlight opportunities for action and to cement existing relationships. In both cases, the flexibility of the medium meant that participants could appropriate it to suit their needs. Further though, I have emphasized the fact that 'remote' need not be interpreted in terms of mileage; the idea of family is interwoven with propinquity, but not in a way that precisely mirrors geography. Propinquity is about a mingling of lives, a knowledge of routine, or a need to co-exist.

References

Aldrich, F K (2003) Smart homes: past, present and future, in R Harper (ed.) *Inside the Smart Home*, pp. 17-40. London: Springer.

Ames, M G, Go, J, Kaye, J and Spasojevic, M (2010) Making love in the network closet: the benefits and work of family videochat, *Proc CSCW 2010*, pp. 145-154. New York: ACM Press.

Bernheim Brush, A J, Inkpen, K M, Tee, K (2008) SPARCS: exploring sharing suggestions to enhance family connectedness, *Proc CSCW 2008*, pp. 629-638. New York: ACM Press.

Boase, J, Horrigan, J B, Wellman, B and Rainie, L (2006) The strength of internet ties. *Pew Internet and American Life project report*. Available at: http://www.pewinternet.org/~/media//Files/Reports/2006/PIP_Internet_ties.pdf.pdf (accessed 31st May 2011).

Brown, B, Taylor, A, Izadi, S, Sellen, A and Kaye, J (2007) Locating family values: a field trial of the Whereabouts Clock, *Proc UbiComp*, pp. 354-371. Berlin: Springer-Verlag.

Brown, J S and Duguid, P (2000) *The Social Life of Information*, Boston: Harvard Business School Press.

Clark, H H and Brennan, S E (1991) Grounding in communication, in L Resnick, J M Levine, and S D Teasley (eds.) *Perspectives on socially shared cognition*, pp. 127-149, Washington DC: APA.

Cao, X, Sellen, A, Bernheim Brush, A J, Kirk, D, Edge, D and Ding, X (2010) Understanding family communication across time zones, *Proc CSCW 2010*, pp. 155-158, New York: ACM Press.

Chung, H, Lee, C J and Selker, T (2006) Lover's cups: drinking interfaces as new communication channels, *Ext Abstracts CHI 2006*, pp. 375-380. New York: ACM Press.

Coulthard, M, Walker, A and Morgan, A (2002) *People's perceptions of their neighbourhood and community involvement: results from the social capital module of the General Household Survey 2000. National Statistics*. London: The Stationery Office.

Crabtree, A and Rodden, T (2004) Domestic routines and design for the home, *Computer Supported Cooperative Work*, Vol. 13, pp. 191-220.

Davis, H, Vetere, F, Francis, P, Gibbs, M and Howard, S (2008) "I wish we could get together": Exploring intergenerational play across a distance via a 'Magic Box', *Journal of International Relationships*, Vol. 6, pp. 191-210.

Dey, A K and de Guzman, E S (2006) From awareness to connectedness: the design and deployment of presence displays, *Proc CHI 2006*, pp. 899-908. New York: ACM Press.

Dodge, C (1997) The Bed: a medium for intimate communication, *Ext Abstracts CHI 1997*, pp. 371-372. New York: ACM Press.

Grivas, K (2006) Digital selves: devices for intimate communications between homes, *Personal and Ubiquitous Computing*, Vol. 10, pp. 66-76.

Harper, R H R (2010) *Texture: Human Expression in the Age of Communications Overload*, London: MIT Press.

Harper, R and Shatwell, B (2003) Paper-mail in the home of the 21st century, in R Harper (ed.) *Inside the Smart Home*, pp. 101-114. London: Springer.

Hindus, D, Mainwaring, S D, Leduc, N, Hagström, A E and Bayley, O (2001) Casablanca: designing social communication devices for the home, *Proc CHI 2001*, pp. 325-332. New York: ACM Press.

Ito, M and Okabe, D (2005) Intimate connections: contextualising Japanese youth and mobile messaging, in R Harper, L Palen and A Taylor (eds.) *The Inside Text: Social Cultural and Design Perspectives on SMS,* Dordrecht: Springer.

Kaye, J 'J' (this collection) Love, ritual and videochat, in R Harper (ed.) *The connected home: the future of domestic life*, London: Springer-Verlag.

Kaye, J 'J', Levitt, M K, Nevins, J, Golden, J and Schmidt, V (2005) Communicating intimacy one bit at a time, *Ext Abstracts CHI 2005*, pp. 1529-1532. New York: ACM Press.

Kirk, D S, Sellen, A and Cao, X (2010) Home video communication: mediating 'closeness', *Proc CSCW 2010*, pp. 135-144. New York: ACM Press.

Langdale, G, Kay, J and Kummerfield, B (2006) Using an intergenerational communications system as a 'light-weight' technology probe, *Ext Abstracts CHI 2006*, pp. 1001-1006. New York: ACM Press.

Lindley, S E (in press) Shades of lightweight: supporting cross-generational communication through home messaging, *Universal Access in the Information Society*, doi: 10.1007/s10209-011-0231-2.

Lindley, S E, Banks, R, Harper, R, Jain, A, Regan, T, Sellen, A and Taylor A S (2009) Resilience in the face of innovation: household trials with BubbleBoard, *International Journal of Human-Computer Studies*, Vol. 67, pp. 154-164.

Lindley, S E, Harper, R and Sellen, A (2010) Designing a technological playground: a field study of the emergence of play in household messaging, *Proc CHI 2010*, pp. 2351-2360. New York: ACM Press.

Lottridge, D, Masson, N and Mackay, W (2009) Sharing empty moments: design for remote couples, *Proc CHI 2009*, pp. 2329-2338, New York: ACM Press.

Neustaedter, C and Bernheim Brush, A J (2006) "LINC-ing" the family: the participatory design of an inkable family calendar, *Proc CHI 2006*, pp. 141-150. New York: ACM Press.

O'Hara, K, Harper, R, Unger, A, Wilkes, J, Sharpe, B and Jansen, M (2005) TxtBoard: from text-to-person to text-to-home, *Ext Abstracts CHI 2005*, pp. 1705-1708. New York: ACM Press.

Olson, G M and Olson, J S (2000) Distance matters, *Human-Computer Interaction*, Vol. 15, pp. 139-178.

Perry, M and Rachovides, D (2007) Entertaining situated messaging at home, *Computer Supported Cooperative Work*, Vol. 16, pp. 99-128.

Rivière, C A and Licoppe, C (2005) From voice to text: continuity and change in the use of mobile phones in France and Japan, in R Harper, L Palen and A Taylor (eds.) The *Inside Text: Social Cultural and Design Perspectives on SMS*, Dordrecht: Springer.

Romero, N, Markopoulos, P, van Baren, J, de Ruyter, B, Ijsselsteij, W and Farshchian, B (2007) Connecting the family with awareness systems, *Personal and Ubiquitous Computing*, Vol. 11, pp. 299-312.

Saslis-Lagoudakis, G, Cheverst, K, Dix, A, Fitton, D and Rouncefield, M (2006) Hermes@Home: supporting awareness and intimacy between distant family members, *Proc OzCHI 2006*, pp. 23-30. New York: ACM Press.

Schmidt, K (2002) The problem with awareness. *Computer Supported Cooperative Work*, Vol. 11, 285-298.

Sellen, A, Harper, R, Eardley, R, Izadi, S, Regan, T, Taylor, A S and Wood, K R (2006) HomeNote: supporting situated messaging in the home, *Proc CSCW 2006*, pp. 383-392. New York: ACM Press.

Taylor, A S and Harper, R (2003) The gift of the gab? A design oriented sociology of young people's use of mobiles, *Computer Supported Cooperative Work*, Vol. 12, pp. 267-296.

Taylor, A S, Harper, R, Swan, L, Izadi, S, Sellen, A and Perry, M (2007) Homes that make us smart, *Personal and Ubiquitous Computing*, Vol. 11, pp. 383-393.

Taylor, A S and Swan, L (2004) List making in the home, *Proc CSCW 2004*, pp. 542-545. New York: ACM Press.

Taylor, N and Cheverst, K (2009) Social interaction around a rural community photo display, *International Journal of Human-Computer Studies*, Vol. 67, pp. 1037-1047.

Tee, K, Bernheim Brush, A J and Inkpen, K M (2009) Exploring communication and sharing between extended families, *International Journal of Human-Computer Studies*, Vol. 67, pp. 128-138.

Tolmie, P, Pycock, J, Diggins, T, MacLean, A and Karsenty, A (2003) Towards the unremarkable computer: making technology at home in domestic routines, in R Harper (ed.) *Inside the Smart Home*, pp. 183-206. London: Springer.

Vetere, F, Gibbs, M R, Kjeldskov, J, Howard, S, Mueller, F, Pedell, S, Mecoles, K and Bunyan, M (2005) Mediating intimacy; designing technologies to support strong-tie relationships, *Proc CHI 2005*, pp. 471-480, New York: ACM Press.

Chapter 10
Love, Ritual and Videochat

Joseph "Jofish" Kaye

Introduction

Technologies such as Skype and iChat have become increasingly commonplace in the home, and are being used more and more often by families to communicate at a distance. In a recent study, we found one family with French-speaking grandparents living in France using a combination of text chat and video chat to communicate with their nine-year-old, non-French-speaking granddaughter living in California. We saw another pair of grandparents using iChat to watch their grandson play the trumpet from hundreds of miles away, and watched a two-year-old who had convinced herself that she didn't need a nap start crying and fall asleep on her father's lap while her grandparents watched over Skype. While not yet statistically common, such interactions are mundane and everyday for thousands of families across the world. There is clearly significant potential for videochat between homes.

In this chapter, I look at the ways that we have addressed the topics of videochat and intimacy in the twin fields of human computer interaction (HCI) and computer-supported cooperative work (CSCW), and propose one approach to taking such interactions seriously. I use a system called the Five Love Languages, drawn from a series of couples-counseling books by Gary Chapman, as a framework to unpack and explore an existing corpus of interview transcripts of families in the San Francisco Bay Area, and use this to try and make sense of the way that videochat is becoming increasingly important in a wide variety of extended families who live apart.

The fact that videochat is becoming increasingly common at home is itself an interesting phenomenon, as videochat presents certain difficulties. Some of these are technical challenges: videochat requires reliable networking and relatively high-bandwidth internet connections, with potential cost constraints. As my colleagues and I have discussed elsewhere (Ames et al. 2010), there are also a series of non-technical challenges that videochat poses to the user: the difficulties of staying in

J."J". Kaye (✉)
Nokia Research, Palo Alto, CA, USA

R. Harper (ed.), *The Connected Home: The Future of Domestic Life*,
DOI 10.1007/978-0-85729-476-0_10, © Springer-Verlag London 2011

frame so that one can be seen by the person on the other end of the connection, or the difficulty of coordinating schedules so that both parties are available at the same time. Both of these can be made easier by the constrained nature of office interactions: desks and conference room tables are commonplace and assumed places for placing computers for videochat. Similarly, the relatively constrained nature of business hours, as well as corporate-wide openly accessible calendars provided by systems such as Microsoft Exchange and Lotus Notes, provide opportunities for scheduling that are rarely matched by home users: I can put a videochat meeting request on any of my 100,000+ colleagues' calendars, but I can't do the same with my mother.

Despite these advantages available to the work user of videochat, my colleagues and I have been struck by the frequency by which we see families engaging in videochat. In previous work, we have discussed how families use technologies, including videochat, to articulate and express their family's values: encouraging the use of the Nintendo Wii while constraining the use of other gaming systems because the Wii is 'about exercise' (*ibid*). In a similar way, we saw that taking the time to converse with remote grandparents, particularly over videochat, was a way for families to articulate and substantiate their values.

Videochat for families has distinct value for all parties involved: for grandparents building a bond with their grandchildren, for parents able to satisfy both grandparents and children with their desires for attention simultaneously, and for children able to play with a grandparent from afar. In this chapter, I want to take a closer look at the nature of those relationships and make an attempt to look seriously at the role of love in the family. My aim is to find a way to articulate the aspects of relationships that families find important, and then to discuss the implications for videochat of those factors. Importantly, the aim here is to start not with the technology of videochat itself, but with the families and their practices.

Prior Work: Videochat

Videoconferencing in the home and office has been studied for nearly half a century (Bell Labs 1968). In particular, videoconferencing in the workplace has been extensively studied in ubiquitous computing and its sister fields of CSCW and HCI. A lot of early work studied individual and group videophone systems in the workplace, notably at EuroPARC, PARC, and Bellcore (i.e. (Fish, Kraut, and Chalfonte 1990); (Gaver et al. 1992; Dourish and Bly 1992; Bly, Harrison, and Irwin 1993). Much of the emphasis in this work explored the possibilities of always-on video systems for promoting presence and activity awareness in the workplace through media spaces and the like.

Studies of videoconferencing in the home are more limited. One reason for this is that it is only in the last few years that software packages such as Skype and iChat and hardware configurations such as built-in cameras or cheap external webcams have made videoconferencing feasible for families and other casual users. Perhaps the most well-known study of family videoconference use is the

VideoProbe deployed as part of the Technology Probes project to investigate family practices, which was presented as an experimental rather than established technology (Hutchinson, Mackay, and Westerlund 2003). O'Hara et al. explored more day-to-day use, and found that their 21 UK-based early adopters of mobile videochat on 3G mobile phones successfully used video calling on average once every two weeks (O'Hara, Black, and Lipson 2006). The most common setting for making a call was the home (30%), and the primary reason for making calls was "small talk" (50%), followed by show-and-tell and achieving a specific goal. Other studies are more anecdotal: Gregg found that dedicated-use videoconferencing units helped four elderly users feel more connected to their community (Gregg 2001), and Yarosh mentioned that a third of the divorced families she studied occasionally used videoconferencing (Yarosh 2008).

I am part of a research group at Nokia Research in Palo Alto called the IDEA Team. One of the topics we have been studying for the last several years revolves around the theme of family communication. Much of this work has been in collaboration with Sesame Workshop, a non-profit organization that has focused for over forty years on the importance of teaching kids through television and, more recently, other forms of new media. They are most well-known for Sesame Street, the children's television program, and in 2007 founded the Joan Gantz Cooney Center, for the study of digital technologies for children's literacy. This collaboration has been a rich source of inspiration for my group, and has led to successful designs such as StoryPlay (Fig. 10.1) and Story Visit (Fig. 10.2) (Ballagas et al. 2009; Raffle et al. 2010; Ballagas et al. 2010; Raffle et al. 2011), both of which use videochat to provide opportunities for grandparents to engage with their grandchildren by reading to them at a distance.

Our first design, Story Play (Fig. 10.1), was a tangible interface involving a wood framework, which held an augmented book and two small tablet computers with embedded cameras, enabling both videochat with a remote partner and the incorporation of video content featuring custom content from Elmo, a Sesame Street character (Raffle et al. 2010).

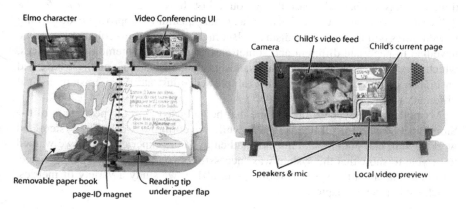

Elmo character   Video Conferencing UI

Camera   Child's video feed   Child's current page

Removable paper book   Reading tip   Speakers & mic   Local video preview
page-ID magnet   under paper flap

Fig. 10.1   Story play

Our second design, Story Visit, iterated on this design with the intent of enabling a much larger user base, by building the videochats and video content into existing browser technology (Raffle et al. 2011) (Fig. 10.2). In one study of the system, Story Visit was used by 61 families, and incorporated several design features drawn from the results of our Story Play study and the initial research. For example, after the initial setup, each side would automatically connect to the remote family member when the page was opened: a simple feature, but something that avoided many of the difficulties we had seen with existing videochat systems.

Fig. 10.2 Story visit

This collaboration has produced some excellent work, and, I believe, has been very productive for both Nokia and Sesame. The collaboration with our colleagues at Sesame Workshop has meant that much of the work is grounded in an educational perspective, which brings with it a set of epistemological assumptions, such as determining the success or failure of the system in terms of learning and education. That has not been the case throughout all of these studies; *Story Time for the 21st Century* (Ballagas et al. 2010) takes a notably qualitative approach to describing how families communicate at a distance. But in the course of our collaborations, we have had to negotiate different and sometimes competing epistemological stances, which have impacted the projects' aims, designs and evaluation, and these have had an impact on the work. Perhaps an example will illustrate these epistemological differences best.

My colleague Hayes Raffle told me that he had used a prototype version of the Story Visit system to call his daughters while travelling for work. The system had worked well, and both he and his kids had enjoyed the experience. But we wanted to be able to show that the system was successful beyond such anecdotal evidence. So in our paper on the system (Raffle et al. 2011), we study a variety of metrics, which we list in the chapter:

- Number of Reading Sessions
- Average Reading Time per Session
- Total Reading Time Across all Reading Sessions
- Total Number of Pages Read Across all Reading Sessions
- Average Reading Time per Page
- Average Amount of Pointing per Page
- Average Number of Elmo Activations per Page (for Elmo and Elmo+Tips Conditions)
- Average Number of Reading Tip Activations per Page (for Tips and Elmo+Tips Conditions)

As we show in the paper, we were able to show that we were successful in increasing metrics such as "total reading time" under conditions such as the presence of Elmo on the page, and we considered the system to be a success.

But when a father calls his daughter when he is travelling for work, is he doing that because he wishes her to read better, or because he wants to express his love and attempt to mitigate the difficulties of maintaining a sense of intimacy at a distance? My sense is that the latter desire predominates. Such an experience does indeed confirm and draw from some of our other conclusions on that paper, such as the significant value from having a shared topic of conversation, or a shared medium of play. But that further suggests that a focus on an education-based evaluation may not fully represent the experience. I believe this example suggests that taking love and intimacy in families as seriously in HCI and CSCW as we currently take education could provide an opportunity for thinking about and designing technology in a significantly different way. With this in mind, I will now discuss the existing work in HCI and CSCW on intimacy and love in family life, before suggesting a different but potentially valuable approach.

Prior Work: Intimacy

This is far from the first work that asks questions about the role of love and intimacy in technology. There is a long history in the fields of computer supported cooperative work (CSCW) and human computer interaction (HCI) of systems to support intimacy for romantically engaged couples who are geographically separated, whether temporarily or on a more long-term basis.

Many of these can be read as deliberate alternatives to the high-bandwidth connection of videochat, exploiting the pre-existing nature of the relationship to provide a sense of intimacy despite the ethereal, transitory and ambient nature of the communication. One of the earliest examples in the HCI literature is Gaver & Strong's paper *Feather, Scent and Shaker*, which proposes three designs for providing ambient representations of distant partners: a feather, which wafts in a column of air under the remote partner's control; a bronze dish containing aromatic oils, with a heater that can be turned on by the remote partner, making smells drift across the room; and a small rattle kept in a pocket which shakes when its pair is shaken by the remote partner (Strong and Gaver 1996). Each project provides a sense of the remote partner's presence and desire to communicate, but in a gentle and ambient manner. Heather Martin's *Kiss Communicator* has a similarly focused design. It is a handheld device, controlled by gently blowing into it (Buchenau 2000). When one person picks up the device and blows into it, it creates a message "in the form of an animated light sequence as the device responds to your breath". If you are satisfied with the sequence then you relax your grip and the message is sent to your partner. A third early and oft-cited work is Chris Dodge's *The Bed*, which uses microphones and projectors to provide a sense of connection between two beds, converting sounds produced in one bed into an abstract video representation at the second bed (Dodge 1997).

My own work has explored the use of smell (Kaye 2004) to let one member of a couple know that their partner is thinking of them, as well as exploring the design space of systems for couples in long-distance relationships by using interviews and sketches (Kaye and Goulding 2004). The most detailed result of this research involves the Virtual Intimate Object (VIO), a small circle that would appear in each partner's taskbar. When one partner clicked their circle, their partner's circle would turn bright red and then fade over time, and vice versa (Kaye et al. 2005).

This theme of shared objects and experiences for couples has been an on-going topic in HCI: lovers cups (Chung and Lee 2006), decor (Tsujita, Siio, and Tsukada 2007), shared music (Lottridge, Masson, and Mackay 2009), armbands (Wang et al. 2010), hugs (Tsetserukou 2010), holding hands (O'Brien and Mueller 2006), shared coincidences (Tsujita, Siio, and Tsukada 2007), slippers (Chen, Forlizzi, and Jennings 2006), private screens (Gibbs et al. 2005), a shared video message box (Thieme et al. 2011) and no doubt many more. These explorations have many factors that make them attractive as short research topics: they are often relatively simple to build, they have a compelling story of intimacy and communication, and evaluation – in those rare cases where there is an evaluation - to a sufficient level to show functionality is relatively simple. At the same time, these works have a familiarity and sameness, which I believe we as a field could now move beyond. Nearly all the work discussed in this section embraces unquestioningly what would be seen by some in fields outside of HCI, such as relationship counseling, human relations, and parts of psychology, as being a remarkably naïve attitude to love and relationships.

In this chapter, I propose a different approach to dealing with love and intimacy. Rather than joining a chorus thousands of years old bemoaning the difficulties of *defining* love (Moss and Schwebel 1993), I propose engaging with an existing framework that focuses how people *express* their love for each other, and using that as a lens to try and unpack and understand the value of videochat within the home. What we will find, I will argue, is that this framework looks remarkably like the frameworks that people themselves use as practical schemas and maxims of conduct that guide their efforts to show love, judge the love of others, and choose to adopt new technologies to let them enact their own performances of family love. Thus I will come to the position of saying that many of the debates about defining love miss the point, which is that such definition can be seen to be the concern of those who are doing the lovemaking. In families this means parents and grandparents wanting to show love to their offspring; it means children figuring out ways of letting themselves be loved in turn; and between partners and parents it entails figuring out when a touch of hands is a gentle gesture of love as against an embodied rebuke. Finally, it entails understanding how codes of conduct and maxims of appropriate and inappropriate use guide the use of technological means of communication such as videochat. To videochat, I will show, is not, let us say, a means of information exchange, a mechanism to let practical family affairs be managed, but has a special emotional valence; it deepens family relations. In these ways I will suggest that for some of the families we have studied, videochat is the multi-visual sonnet of the twenty first century. It is making love.

The Five Love Languages

The Five Love Languages (henceforth 5LL) is a book by Gary Chapman, written as a result of his experience counseling couples about their relationships (Chapman 2010). It details five different ways that people in romantic relationships express love and feel loved. 5LL is a self-help book, not a scholarly work. It is focused on providing a way for couples having difficulties in their relationships to articulate those difficulties, and therefore move towards improving those relationships. It is not designed for engaging with the kinds of non-romantic relationships that we find in, for example, intra-generational family relationships. As a self-help book, the epistemological approach – the way in which Chapman provides evidence for the knowledge he imparts – is different from much of the existing work in human-computer interaction. In large part, it relies on casual description, anecdote and personal experience. In contrast to more scholarly works, there are no *p*-values and no *n* subjects, no references (other than to bible verses) and it is not necessarily representative of the field of human relationship research[1]. As such, I am sure there are readers from both the fields of HCI and from human relationship research who will question this decision.

However, the great advantage of the 5LL categorization system is that it provides one solid, simple framework for understanding love; a framework that I argue is sorely missing from much of the previous work on love in families in CSCW and HCI. The framework has itself been popular, with Chapman's website claiming that over five million copies of 5LL have been sold in over 36 languages (http://www.fivelovelanguages.com). I also admit that this framework may well *not* be the right framework for much of the studies of intimacy and love in CSCW and HCI. Indeed, one of my hopes for this chapter is that other researchers will respond by proposing other frameworks for talking about love and intimacy. There are multitudes of

---

[1] In particular, Chapman, a pastor in a Baptist church, brings with him a set of values, particularly around homosexuality, that I do not endorse.

such frameworks: in their literature review attempting to find a canonical definition of intimacy, one study identifies 62 separate definitions of intimacy (Moss and
Schwebel 1993), and a second documents a similar level of confusion about definitions of love (Brander 2004). But in view of such a profusion of opportunity, 5LL
provides a simple place to start.

5LL takes as its foundation that *people have different ways in which they feel
loved*. That is to say, some people feel loved when they are given gifts; others only
feel loved when people do things for them. The same applies to the different ways
that people express love: some people find it important to give physical gifts whenever possible, while some show their love by doing things for others. I make explicit
the distinction between giving and receiving love, as there is no particular reason
why one person must necessarily both express and receive love in the same language. Chapman refers to these ways of being loved and expressing love as "love
languages". The metaphor of language shows up repeatedly: spouses are described
as speaking different love languages, and he describes dialects of particular love
languages. Chapman enumerates five different kinds of love languages.

The first is *words of affirmation*: expressing feelings of love in words. These may
take the form of verbal compliments ("You look great in that hat") or encouraging words ("This is great work! Those reviewers don't know what they're talking
about.").

The second is *quality time*: giving focused, undivided attention to the other partner. As Turkle has observed, undivided attention is an increasingly rare commodity
(Turkle 2011), and for some, this is the primary way by which they feel loved,
or express love. For example, many of the families we studied always had family
dinner on Friday nights: time deliberately set aside for family.

Chapman's third language is *receiving gifts*. The giving of gifts is a particularly
nice example of a love language, as customs of gift-giving are common throughout
many cultures. Everyone gives and receives gifts at some point, but attitudes to the
importance and role of these gifts differ. The economic value of gifts is not necessarily important, but rather the gift itself. For example, for my grandmother-in-law, an
intelligent and generous woman in her eighties, greeting cards are an important part
of how she expresses love. She remembers the birthdays and anniversaries of every
person in her extended family, including all thirty-two grandchildren, their partners,
and their children, and sends each a birthday card. Wedding and baby showers,
births, deaths and marriages are all marked with cards. Sicknesses are marked with
get-well cards; my father-in-law, her son, received at least one a day following a
skiing injury, and sometimes more. It is clear that for my grandmother-in-law, these
greeting cards serve a purpose of expressing her love, and one feels loved when one
receives one of these cards.

The fourth love language is *acts of service*. Acts of service means, simply, doing
things for people you love. For some parents this means making particularly special
lunches for their children to take to school each day; for others it may mean waking
up early on weekends to take their children to swim meets and soccer matches. In
my studies of couples in long distance relationships, I found that some couples in

long distance relationships would frequently engage in this particular love language before they would reunite. They would not just clean the house, but clean the house *for* the other person; not just take out the recycling but – at least on some level – take out the recycling *for* the other person.

The fifth and final love language is *physical touch*; not necessarily sexual touch, or even explicit hugging or touching, but the gamut of physical contact. For some people, there is an emotional connection that comes from touch, even if it is casual and fleeting: a pat on the head in passing, having a foot touching one's partner while in bed. For others, these expressions of intimacy can seem suffocating and frustrating, reinforcing the point that not everyone speaks the same love language.

My aim in this chapter is not to prove in a robust and scientifically reliable way that videochat provides a certain set of affordances for love languages above and beyond the affordances provided by, say, text messaging or telephony, thereby to prove its superiority. Nor is my aim to compare the expression of love in the home with the absence of love in the workplace, and conclude that perhaps the home is better suited for the love-transmitting abilities of videochat. Rather, my intent is to demonstrate how we can use a framework for love as a lens to unpack the experiences and rituals that people have with their family, and use that lens to try and understand the appeal of videochat within the home.

Field Study of Existing Family Love Practices

Having established this framework of the five love languages, I will now use that framework to look at an existing dataset: a series of field observations and interviews with a total of 23 families in the San Francisco Bay Area, including seven who reported themselves as using videoconferencing. My group and I have previously worked extensively with these interviews and observations, resulting in a series of papers. Our paper *Making Love in the Network Closet* was based on a study of the advantages and disadvantages of videoconferencing (Ames et al. 2010). For example, we noted that videochat has many difficulties that make it hard to use: the connection is unreliable, both video and audio sometimes drop out with no apparent reason, and it can even be difficult to ensure both sides can find each other to make a video call. On the other hand, there are significant advantages over perhaps more reliable technology, notably telephony: grandparents feel a sense of connection to their grandchildren, parents are able to articulate the importance of family through taking the time to videochat, and grandchildren can have fun and engaging experiences.

We also continued this analysis recently with an exploration into the role that socioeconomic class plays in technology choices (Ames et al. 2011). In this paper, we showed that social class, while rarely if ever discussed in HCI and CSCW, is highly correlated with various behavior patterns around technology use. For example, we noticed that working class families had more technology in their lives, and particularly in their children's lives than middle class families, and that technology was often seen as a tool for improvement. By contrast, the middle class families saw technology as something to be controlled and limited in their children's lives.

Each family in this study included at least one child aged two to ten and their geographically-distant grandparents, for a total of approximately 116 participants. Families were recruited using a range of techniques, including snowball techniques, ads placed on Facebook, and to try and ensure some level of diversity in our sample, a recruitment agency. For each interview, two researchers visited the family in their home. In the initial eighteen studies, researchers would interview parents and children, and children would give the researchers tours of their rooms. We would also observe a "typical" call to remote family. In the remainder of the interviews, among families recruited explicitly because of their use of videochat, the interviews were shorter and more focused on the use of communication technologies, and include an observation of a video call to distant family. In five of these seven interviews, the two researchers then split up to separately interview the local parents and the remote grandparents. In two of the family interviews, we were not able to interview the remote grandparents. In these interviews, we asked how the family started using videochat, what they think of it now, and how it fit into their broader communication patterns and the work they do to create a sense of "family." We video- and audio-recorded all interactions, and the interviews were later carefully transcribed by my colleagues Morgan Ames and Janet Go. Of the videochat-using families, four of the seven used Skype (two on PCs, two on Macs), and three used iChat on Macs. Five of the seven used (often multiple) laptops, and all but one had built-in webcams. The remote grandparents used a similar mix of technologies. All families had been using videoconferencing for a few months to several years (one early-adopter family had been using various technologies on and off for 14 years).

I will now look at the records of these interviews and transcripts through the 5LL lens in an attempt to tell a story about what I saw there. My hope is in this piece to persuade the reader that the rituals and acts that families describe here are, at their core, acts of love by which families express their affection for each other, and that, furthermore, there is value in taking such expressions of love seriously.

We can see these interactions between family members as a sort of moral code, related to the expression and substantiation and making of family love. This code consists of a heterogeneous set of practices that are mutually understood and orientated to by all members of a family – even though these understandings will vary in depth and comprehensiveness. So, for example, children will understand that mum is showing them love with a kiss, but may not recognize that grandparents are trying to show similar acts of love merely by talking to them, for example. Nevertheless, with this code, members of families can see whether others are trying to make love and are doing so successfully, just as they can see when these efforts are failing or ill-conceived.

Words of Affirmation: Words of affirmation are perhaps the easiest part of love to recognize. I found examples of such practices throughout the transcripts. For example, in Family 9, Chanel described her relationship with her daughter Indria, aged 7.

> *Interviewer:*   Does she also send emails and text messages?
> *Chanel:*   Yes, but that's not when she's at school. She does that when she's here, and I'll probably get the email the next morning when I'm at work. If she's over at my cousin's house, or my mother's, she will email or text me: "Mom, what are you doing?", or "When are you coming?", things like that, "I love you".

Later, Chanel described how she encouraged Indria to interact with their extended family:

> *She looks at examples. She sees how her mom is with her family. You always tell your family you love them because you never know if this is going to be the last time you see them. You can always let them know that you love them. Even if it's just a call to say hi, how you doin', alright, bye. Just something.*

Chanel and Indria are typical in many ways in their use of words of affirmation. These are not words of affirmation of physical qualities – although those are present as well; rather, they affirm love.

Quality Time: Quality Time is often a feature of family relationships. It's particularly striking how often families had explicit policies of family quality time around meals. For example, in Family 9 we saw the mother describe the importance of spending time with her mother:

> *Every weekend, we have to see her, or we'll cook Sunday dinner together.*

Similarly, Family 18:

> *We go to Mother Dear's house every Friday for fish dinner.*
> *We eat dinner with the family every night.*

Family 4 also tried to make Friday nights special, although it was sometimes difficult:

> *And then Friday nights we try to have family night, where we all go do something together, like go take a train and eat somewhere. Or just go out to a restaurant. So we try to do that every Friday. We haven't done it as much recently. I don't know why – I guess just parties and stuff going on.*

This notion of quality time and the importance of that time to the family was articulated in family rituals. For example, the mother of Family 7 said:

> *My number one priority is for a strong family. That is my only goal in life, is strong family and we know we love each other. When we have dinner together we're not religious, we don't pray, but we say we love our family before we eat.*

Family 18 also talked about the things they did to create a sense of family with their son, who lived with his father half the time:

> *When we have him on the weekends we try to plan family outings – a museum, getting together with friends...*

Family quality time rituals focused on topics other than eating, however

> Interviewer: What do you do to feel like a family?
> Chanel: Just being together, even, and enjoying each other's company. Playing domi-
>   noes, watching old recorded videos [of the family]. And we laugh, have
>   birthday parties...

Quality Time obviously manifests in different ways. These examples clearly focus on pre-planned and ritualistic Quality Time: opportunities to codify and articulate the importance of that aspect of love in the family.

Gifts: One aspect of many of our interviews was a tour of the child's bedroom. This gave us opportunities to start to understand some of the material characteristics of these families' lives. As mentioned, my colleagues and I have discussed some of the differences between different families' technologies choices as a function of social class in an earlier publication (Ames et al. 2011). One particular characteristic of several of the working class families in comparison to the middle class families was an increase in the amount of technology in children's bedrooms, such as TVs, DVD players and game consoles – something we never saw in the middle class homes. We did not attempt to fully explain *why* such technology was more prevalent in these households, but one hypothesis is that it is related to the increased frequency of absent fathers. A PlayStation, Xbox or similar is a significant gift from an absent parent: it is desired by the child, and likely may not be at the top of a to-buy list generated by the parent with whom the child lives most of the time. For example, in Family 18, a mother noted that the father of her child, who did not live with them, often gave him gifts:

> I don't really buy him that much, and as you can see he has plenty... His dad probably buys him a lot more things than I do, and he brings stuff over from his dad's house... We don't have a lot of space in this house, and to me it's just... the clutter drives me crazy. And he has so many toys he doesn't play with, too.

One single mother put a great deal of effort into giving her child the things she wanted (Family 9):

> If her homework is done, if her room is cleaned up, she can play... She has a lot of choices about what she can do. I just try to give her everything that I wish I had when I was younger... Shoot, I wish I had a scooter like this. You know, I always wanted to drive when I was little. If I had something like this, if my mom would have bought that for me, I'd have thought I was the stuff. I wish I'd had the million video games, I wish I'd had my own room.

Other parents expressed concern with the quantity of gifts that were given – again, in this case, by a parent who lived apart from the child:

> I think it's just cultural. His dad grew up poor and didn't have a lot of toys, and I think that it's his way of showing him that he loves him. My parents are kind of the same. They slowed down a lot because we asked them to. I... asked them not to send so many – they send a lot of cheap toys, the ones that end up in the garbage can a week after, and I'm also a pretty green person and I hate waste and I see all this junk and I think ugh, more to go in the landfill.

We saw similar resistance to gift giving in Family 7:

My family in Texas, we made a rule that we don't send gifts. When we get together we have an unbirthday party for [the kids] – it takes the pressure off getting gifts. I actually suggested it because I could feel my sister feeling the pressure.

These kinds of tensions suggest a particular value to the 5LL system. It is clear that within the (extended) Family 7 there are multiple love languages, and that there are tensions resulting from different expressions of love in different ways. Indeed, one of the striking things about Gifts as a love language is that it's amenable to execution from a distance, in a way that can be difficult for other love languages.

Acts of Service: For some of the parents we talked with, there was a sense that parenting was an on-going act of service. This is a common theme in studies of love within families. For example, Danny Miller, in an influential essay in *A Theory of Shopping*, describes housewives engaging in 'making love in supermarkets': articulating and expressing their love through the food purchasing decisions they make for their families (Miller 1998). Shopping for food for the family is an act of service by which parents engage with their love for their families. We saw many acts of service by parents for their kids, on a wide variety of topics. A common one was reading to kids at bedtime, an act appreciated by both parents and kids. We also saw families with school-age children often provide an on-going framework for kids to get their homework done:

We have a pretty consistent routine here on the weekdays. He usually sits at that table and does his homework, and we have to support him a lot because he gets distracted so much. He's good with doing his homework if he has that support. It's not like he needs us to help him with the answers, he just needs us to support him with staying on track. And while he's doing homework we're often cooking and we'll have dinner together usually. (Family 13)

In addition, we often saw actions that could fit into multiple 5LL categories. For example, one family (4) described what happened when a grandparent came to visit:

... They come out periodically, my family. Like, my mom came out and visited and she went through 20 pounds of flour, baking. We still have bread in the freezer. In one week, she probably baked 30 loaves of bread.

This is an interesting question. Is this a gift or an act of service? There is clearly a gift here, in that the family has 30 loaves of bread that they didn't have before. On the other hand, the important thing about this bread, the thing that distinguishes this bread from other bread, is that the grandmother made it, and the grandmother made it for the family. This is not bread as a commodity; this is family bread, made by family, of family, and for making family. Clearly, the grandmother could have purchased 30 loaves of bread, probably for less than the raw ingredients would cost – and yet there is an intrinsic value to the family, and to the grandmother, in the act of bread making. Similarly, we saw one family put significant time and effort into making videos to send to distant relatives:

The first France movie, we made DVDs and sent them. And they loved it. At least they said they did; I don't know if they watched the whole thing.

The family also described how these videos were created for particular family members, showing us a video they had made for their Uncle Robin, including a tour around the house, family members saying hi, answering questions from the father behind the camera. Specific items in the house were tied back to the remote relative:

Recognize this tree over here? This is your... We call it Uncle Robin tree. And it came back to life! Isn't that amazing...

The father described how they expected Uncle Robin to react:

He'll love it. It's personal, it's timely, it captures everything.

Once again, there is a gift here – the DVD, or, later, the digital video on YouTube. But what characterizes *this* digital video on YouTube is the content, and the creation and selection and editing of that content is an act of service.

Physical Touch: What is perhaps most interesting about the discussion of physical touch in our transcripts is how rarely it is discussed. The transcripts do contain the odd mention of physical touch and the ritualistic nature of touch – a mother working at her kids' school hugging one of her daughters when she saw her, another parent discussing the difficulties her autistic child had learning appropriate touching behaviors – but such mentions are rare and brief by comparison to the other expressions of love as detailed above. However, one place where we saw deliberate engagement with the role of physical touch at a distance was in Family 1, who had a tradition they called Skype Kisses. At the end of a Skype call, the whole family would take it in turns to kiss goodbye to the remote grandparents – including the family cat. While clearly not the idea solution, the Skype Kisses ritual suggests that there can be a role for physical intimacy, even when mediated through the non-physical interface of the webcam.

The Role of Ritual in Expressing Love: Many of these examples are expressed in a particular ritualistic way. In each love language we can point to the ways in which that love is expressed in a repeated and ritual manner. In this chapter, I do not want to go into detail and address the ritual nature of these acts of love; that is a separate argument for some future chapter. But I want to emphasize that I am not referring these rituals in the sense of empty rituals; the way that anthropologist Mary Douglas describes Mertonian sociologists' conceptions of 'ritualists':

...one who performs external gestures without inner commitment to the ideas and values being expressed (Douglas 2003)

Rather, these are rituals in Douglas's sense; ways of affirmation of self and familial identity. For example, for Words of Affirmation, we noticed that phone calls were often completed with a ritualized "I love you" – and in the case of one family, Skype calls were completed with a ritualized exchange of 'Skype kisses', in which all members of the family would air-kiss close to the camera – including the cat. Quality Time, too, often had a ritualized nature to it: "We go to Mother Dear's house every Friday for fish dinner" [Family 18], "We eat dinner with the family every night." [Family 1]. Gifts are given to mark occasions, birthdays, Thanksgiving, Christmas, explicitly family rituals of gathering and eating. Acts of Service were also often ritualized, such as the daily making of packed lunches by the mother in Family 14. Greetings, leavings and goodnights were marked by physical touch: hugs, pats, kisses.

What is important to recognize is that the expression of love is not itself diminished by the ritualized nature of these expressions of love. There is an argument that can be made that there is a comfort expressed in this very ritualization. Saying "I love you" to a potential partner for the first time can be a terrifying leap; there is a comfort in the ritualistic nature of its use to end a telephone call after the thousandth time. In previous work I have explored how technologies allow the enactment of novel rituals: a projected called the VIO used a small circle in the computer's Task Bar for both partners in a couple (Kaye et al. 2005; Kaye, 2006). When clicked on one computer, the circle on the other computer would turn bright red, and then fade over time. Couples in long distance relationships quickly developed rituals around the VIO: the last click of the night to say good night before going to sleep, the first click of the morning upon waking, games like 'clickwars', trying to respond as quickly as possible to your partner's click. The ritualized nature – and technological nature – of these interactions does not make them any less important, and does not diminish their ability to express love.

Thus, in a roundabout way, I am back to videochat as a kind of act in itself. Videochat's meaning is not in and of itself; videochat, like any mode of communication, can enable almost anything to be done. Rather, through the way that act is manufactured and controlled, love comes to be an important value or property; a desired consequence of its use. Through ritual, for example, the act of using videochat becomes a routine part of the family; through emphasis and articulation in the conversations that videochat enables, the emotional valence of the acts are sedimented; through participation, family identity is validated; through videochat, families express love.

Understanding the Role of Videochat in the Home

The suggestion I am making here is that videochat facilitates these expressions of love. It is, of course, particularly amenable to certain *kinds* of love languages: Words of Affirmation, Quality Time. Some remain beyond the province of current technology, Physical Touch, for example, although such absence clearly provides an interesting research direction - (Brave, Ishii, and Dahley 1998) comes to mind as one response. Others, too, provide some interesting insights into ways to build upon and understand videochat in the future. For example, my group's research has explored ways that grandparents can read to their grandchildren at a distance: an Act of Service, perhaps, and perhaps even more so an opportunity for Quality Time. Farmville, Facebook, Second Life and other online environments, notably those in South Korea, have shown the very real way in which digital gifts can be given and exhibited to express affection and love.

At the same time, I recognize that the description of love that I engage with here is a distinctly impoverished account. It is simplistic, which is not surprising from a system that has five categories. In particular, it fails to address the complex and sometimes negative ways for which love can be expressed: as manipulation, as cajoling, or as outright abuse. We are guilty as a field of seeing love solely through rose-tinted spectacles, without recognizing and addressing any negative aspects, and the treatment in this chapter is as guilty as any other. Perhaps this, too, can be something addressed appropriately in future work.

These observations are inherently based on a set of work around families that, predominantly, do not currently use videochat on a regular basis. This is perhaps not surprising: despite the increasingly common nature of Skype, iChat and Google Video, such interactions are still the exception rather than the rule, particularly in the cross-generational context that we were exploring. My hope is that the examples discussed in this brief chapter, and the 5LL-based approach to understanding them, provide a sketch of a way to understand how videochat will continue to become a technology of particular value in the home – despite, as mentioned, the plethora of supporting technologies and infrastructure available in the office environment. In short, videochat is particularly good at affording ways to say 'I love you' – something more important at home than at work.

References

Ames, M., Go, J., Kaye, J. and Spasojevic, M (2010). Making love in the network closet: The benefits and work of home videochat. In *Proceedings of CHI 2010*, Atlanta, GA, USA: ACM.

Ames, M., Go, J. Kaye, J. and Spasojevic, M. (2011). Understanding technology choices and values through social class. In *Proceedings of the ACM 2011 conference on Computer supported cooperative work - CSCW '11*, 55. New York, New York, USA: ACM Press.

Ballagas, R., Kaye, J. Ames, M. Go, J. and Raffle, H. (2009). Family communication. In *Proceedings of the 8th International Conference on Interaction Design and Children - IDC '09*, 321. New York, New York, USA: ACM Press. doi:10.1145/1551788.1551874.

Ballagas, R., Raffle, H. Go, J. Revelle, G., Kaye, J., Ames, M., Horii, H. Koichi, M and Spasojevic, M (2010). Story Time for the 21st Century. *IEEE Pervasive Computing* 9, no. 3 (July): 28-36.

Bell Labs. (1968). The Picture of the Future. Special Issue on the Picturephone. *Bell Laboratories Record* 47(5), May/June.

Bly, S., Harrison, S. and Irwin, S. (1993). Media spaces: bringing people together in a video, audio, and computing environment. *CACM 36*, no. 1: 28-46.

Brander, B. (2004) *Love that works: the art and science of giving*. Templeton Foundation Press.

Scott, B., Ishii, H., and Dahley, A. (1998). Tangible interfaces for remote collaboration and communication. In *Proceedings of the 1998 ACM conference on Computer supported cooperative work - CSCW '98*, 169-178. New York, New York, USA: ACM Press, November 1.

Buchenau, M. and Suri, J. (2000). Experience prototyping. In *Proceedings of the 3rd conference on Designing interactive systems: processes, practices, methods, and techniques (DIS '00)*, Boyarski & Kellogg (Eds.). ACM, New York, NY, USA, 424-433.

Chapman, G., (2010). *The 5 Love Languages: The Secret to Love That Lasts*. Northfield Publishing.

Chen, C., Forlizzi, J., and Jennings, P. (2006). ComSlipper. *CHI '06 extended abstracts on Human factors in computing systems*. New York, New York, USA: ACM Press.

Chung, Hyemin, and Chj Lee. 2006. Lover's cups: drinking interfaces as new communication channels. *CHI '06 extended abstracts*: 375-380.

Dodge, Chris. 1997. The bed: a medium for intimate communication. In *Extended Abstracts of CHI '97*. ACM, New York, NY, USA.

Douglas, Mary. 2003. *Natural Symbols: Explorations in Cosmology*. Routledge.

Dourish, Paul, and S Bly. 1992. Portholes: supporting awareness in a distributed work group. In *Proceedings of the SIGCHI conference on Human factors in computing systems*, 541–547. Monterey, California, United States: ACM.

Fish, R.S., R.E. Kraut, and B.L. Chalfonte. 1990. The VideoWindow system in informal communication. In *Proceedings of the 1990 ACM conference on Computer-supported cooperative work*, 1–11. Los Angeles, California, United States: ACM.

Gaver, W, Thomas Moran, Allan MacLean, Lennart Lövstrand, Paul Dourish, Kathleen Carter, and William Buxton. 1992. Realizing a video environment: EuroPARC's RAVE system. In *Proceedings of the SIGCHI conference on Human factors in computing systems*, 27–35. Monterey, California, United States: ACM.

Gibbs, Martin R., Frank Vetere, Marcus Bunyan, and Steve Howard. 2005. SynchroMate: a phatic technology for mediating intimacy. In *Proceedings of the 2005 conference on Designing for User eXperience*. New York: AIGA: American Institute of Graphic Arts.

Gregg, J.L. 2001. Tearing down walls for the homebound elderly. In *CHI '01 extended abstracts on Human factors in computing systems*, 469–470. Seattle, Washington: ACM.

Hutchinson, Hilary, Wendy Mackay, and Bo Westerlund. 2003. Technology probes: inspiring design for and with families. *Proc. CHI 2003*. Ft. Lauderdale, Florida, USA: ACM.

Kaye, J "J." 2004. Making Scents. *Interactions* 11, no. 1 (January 1): 48-61.

Kaye, J. "J." 2006. I just clicked to say I love you: rich evaluations of minimal communication. In *CHI '06 extended abstracts on Human factors in computing systems*, 363–368. Montréal, Québec, Canada: ACM.

Kaye, J. "J.," and Liz Goulding. 2004. Intimate objects. In *Proc. Designing Interactive Systems 2004*, 341-344. Cambridge, MA, USA: ACM.

Kaye, J. "J.," Mariah K. Levitt, Jeffrey Nevins, Jessica Golden, and Vanessa Schmidt. 2005. Communicating intimacy one bit at a time. In *CHI 05 extended abstracts on Human factors in computing systems*, 1529-1532. Portland, OR, USA: ACM.

Lottridge, D., Masson, N. and Mackay, W. (2009). Sharing empty moments. In *Proceedings of the 27th international conference on Human factors in computing systems - CHI '09*, 2329. New York, New York, USA: ACM Press.

Miller, D. (1998). *A Theory of Shopping*. Cornell University Press, March.

Moss, B., and Schwebel, A. (1993). Defining Intimacy in Romantic Relationships. *Family Relations* 42, no. 1 (October 19).

O'Brien, S., and Mueller, F. (2006). Holding hands over a distance. In *Proceedings of the 20th conference of the computer-human interaction special interest group (CHISIG) of Australia on Computer-human interaction: design: activities, artefacts and environments - OZCHI '06*, 293. New York, New York, USA: ACM Press.

O'Hara, K., Black, A., and Lipson, M. (2006). Everyday practices with mobile video telephony. In *Proceedings of the SIGCHI conference on Human Factors in computing systems*, 871–880. Montréal, Québec, Canada: ACM.

Raffle, H., Revelle, G., Mori, K. Ballagas, R. Buza, K. Horii, H. Kaye, J. (2011). Hello, Is Grandma There? StoryVisit: Family Video Chat and Connected E-Books. In *Proceedings of the 2011 annual conference on Human factors in computing systems* (CHI '11). ACM, New York, NY, USA, 1195-1204.

Hayes Raffle, Glenda Revelle, Koichi Mori, Rafael Ballagas, Kyle Buza, Hiroshi Horii, Joseph Kaye, Kristin Cook, Natalie Freed, Janet Go, and Mirjana Spasojevic. 2011. Hello, is grandma there? let's read! StoryVisit: family video chat and connected e-books. In *Proceedings of the 2011 annual conference on Human factors in computing systems* (CHI '11). ACM, New York, NY, USA, 1195-1204.

Raffle, H., Spasojevic, M., Ballagas, R., Revelle, G. Horii, H., Follmer, S., Go, J., Reardon, E. , Mori, K. and Kaye, J. (2010). Family story play. In *Proceedings of the 28th international conference on Human factors in computing systems - CHI '10*, 1583. New York, New York, USA: ACM Press.

Strong, R., and Gaver, B. (1996). Feather, scent and shaker: supporting simple intimacy. In *Proceedings of CSCW '96*, 96:29–30.

Thieme, A., Wallace, J., Thomas, J. Chen, K. Krämer, N. and Olivier, P. (2011). Lovers' box: Designing for reflection within romantic relationships. *International Journal of Human-Computer Studies* 69, no. 5 (May): 283-297.

Tsetserukou, D. (2010). HaptiHug: a novel haptic display for communication of hug over a distance. In *Proceedings of the 2010 international conference on Haptics: generating and perceiving tangible sensations*, Part I, 340–347. Berlin: Springer-Verlag.

Tsujita, H., Siio, I. and Tsukada, K. (2007). SyncDecor: appliances for sharing mutual awareness between lovers separated by distance. In *CHI '07 extended abstracts on Human factors in computing systems*, 2699–2704. San Jose, CA, USA: ACM.

Sherry, T. (2011). *Alone Together: Why We Expect More from Technology and Less from Each Other*. Basic Books.

Wang, R., Quek, F., Teh, J., Cheok, A. and Lai, S. (2010). Design and evaluation of a wearable remote social touch device. In *International Conference on Multimodal Interfaces and the Workshop on Machine Learning for Multimodal Interaction on - ICMI-MLMI '10*, 1. New York, New York, USA: ACM Press.

Yarosh, S. (2008). Supporting long-distance parent-child interaction in divorced families. In *CHI '08 extended abstracts on Human factors in computing systems*, 3795–3800. Florence, Italy: ACM.

Chapter 11
Family Archiving in the Digital Age

Abigail Sellen

Introduction

Look around any family home and what you will see is "stuff". Whether it is displayed with care, organized in neat containers, or heaped up in piles of clutter, this is one of the ways that homes acquire their own unique character. It reflects the people that live within, and instantly gives some indication as to who makes up the household, whether they are chaotic or tidy, what their interests and hobbies might be, what country they come from, who their relatives are, and many other things besides. In other words, the things that occupy a household, and how they are arranged, stored and displayed, are important clues as to the identity of that household—who are the people that live there and what they are about.

If we consider this collection of stuff not from the point of view of an observer or visitor but as an inhabitant, we may have different, somewhat more emotional views on this. It may be frustration at the constant battle to manage the growing collection of things our household accumulates, guilt that we haven't yet dealt with the clutter or put the photos into albums for many years, pride in the way we have expressed ourselves through some of our most precious things, or deep sentimental attachment to special objects that may spark memories for us. Whatever the case, there can be no question that objects have many different meanings for a household.

While many things in our homes are just so much detritus, it is also clear that some kinds of objects are cherished. Anecdotally, fire fighters and insurance adjusters confirm that family photos and home movies are the first artefacts people attempt to save in a fire (second of course to the living members of the household). A few years ago, whilst working at Hewlett Packard, I conducted a study of the everyday problems of working parents. In a survey of 715 of them, the number one problem parents cited was the guilt they felt at not organising their "family memories" properly (Sellen et al., 2004). So, while we all have objects we care deeply about—things that belong "to the family"—at the same time, especially those of us with extremely busy lives, can feel at a loss as to how to manage them. One can

A. Sellen (✉)
Microsoft Research, Cambridge, UK

R. Harper (ed.), *The Connected Home: The Future of Domestic Life*,
DOI 10.1007/978-0-85729-476-0_11, © Springer-Verlag London 2011

surmize that it is only because we care about them so much, and feel a sense of duty towards these objects, that we feel such guilt.

The Digital Age has exacerbated these issues. The explosion of digital photos and videos is an obvious challenge which comes to mind. Now in addition to the shoeboxes of "to be sorted" printed photos, many of us have hundreds if not thousands of images and home videos sitting on our computer hard drives too. But, in fact, as this chapter will show, the digital objects we care about are much richer than just photos and videos, and can encompass anything from text messages and emails to other kinds of documents we keep in digital form. And, increasingly, the glut of digital data will confront us anew when those we care about pass away and we are left with not just the PCs and mobile phones from our loved ones, but their social networking data, online bank accounts and memberships, and many other aspects of their "digital footprints" too.

This is not to say that the only *physical* objects that families care about keeping are printed photos and videotapes. As in the digital realm, a growing body of research confirms that there is a diverse range of physical "things" which households cherish, and which are collected, managed, displayed and protected (e.g., Csikszentmihalyi & Rochberg-Halton, 1981; Hendon, 2000; Miller, 2008; Petrelli et al., 2008; Van den Hoven & Eggen 2008). In fieldwork which this chapter will describe in more detail (Kirk & Sellen, 2010), these objects can range from stones found on a beach to children's artwork, to clothing and mechanical parts from a motorbike. The things we keep are part of the work of making a home, and they are as varied and as idiosyncratic as the households they represent.

Understanding the role that technology might take in the home of the future, then, must take into account our relationship to these things that make up the "family archive". Further, this is not just a question of understanding the value we place on physical objects or digital ones, but it is about the *reasons* why we value them. Accordingly, this chapter brings together a body of research we have been carrying out in our research group examining the value that people and that households place on objects, both physical and virtual. This began with examining practices around the use of photos and videos by householders (Kirk et al., 2006; Kirk et al., 2007), extended to studies of physical objects in homes (Kirk & Sellen, 2010), and more recently has focused on issues to do with death and bereavement and how the bequeathing and inheriting of home possessions has changed in the Digital Age (Massimi et al., 2011; Odom et al. 2010a; Odom et al. 2010b). Drawing on this work and the work of others, it considers the role that technology has played in our home possessions, and tries to trace a future trajectory in which we participate as designers and developers of future concepts. The work is on-going, both in terms of underlying research and the building of new prototype technologies.

A Broader Perspective

In what follows, we examine the range of reasons why we value objects in the home, both physical and digital, why we choose to keep particular things, and how we manage and even "curate" those things for the sake of the household. Much has been written about how objects are important for our personal memories, and that such objects help to trigger recollections of our past (Csikszentmihalyi & Rochberg-Halton, 1981; Gonzalez, 1995; Middleton & Brown 2005; Petrelli et al., 2008; Petrelli et al., 2009; Van den Hoven & Eggen 2008). But our own research has shown that the value of objects in the home setting is about much more than memory. Importantly, these objects are often about personal and family identity, connecting with the past more broadly, honoring those we care about, fulfilling duty for the family and even forgetting. Added to this, many of the reasons why we keep objects are related to the household rather than any individual person, and to our aspirations for creating a collective space we call home. Thus, rather than limiting our vision to thinking about memory and how objects trigger an individual's memory, to deeply understand the issues of archiving for a household, we have to broaden the range of human values under consideration. Further, it is not until we unpack these values and understand the range of reasons why we cherish certain objects that we can begin to think about how new technologies will play a role in the home of the future.

This chapter also focuses on the differences between the digital and physical objects that we cherish and keep. In considering both virtual and tangible objects, it becomes clear that they have very different kinds of affordances. Digital systems facilitate such activities as the accurate indexing, cataloguing and retrieval of information, combined with the ability to edit content, append meta-data and to otherwise manipulate and often almost effortlessly share these objects. The other obvious aspect of digital data is the almost negligible amount of physical space required for storage compared to physical objects. But it is pointless to view any of these characteristics as either positive or negative in a general sense.

For example, we have noted in our fieldwork (Kirk & Sellen, 2010), as have others (Petrelli & Whittaker, 2010), that the lack of physicality of digital objects means that they are often hidden away, either buried within the household PC, or living on the internet. Such objects thus, while easily amassed, are often also forgotten about and therefore have no real presence in the household. On the flipside, while we can bemoan the fact that physical objects cause clutter, their careful placement and arrangement draws attention within the interior of the home, helping to create the visual landscape.

As another example, a digital object can be easily reproduced. This has important advantages for protecting and sharing a digital photo or video, but at the same time it is sometimes the very quintessence of a physical object that can make it special. One man in our research carefully kept the cog from his motorcycle that caused him to have an accident many years before. It was important that this object was *the* object—the one that caused him so much grief. Another participant, a mother, felt sad that her child's first drawing of the family had faded, yet she was reluctant to copy or in any way modify the original. Finally, after some time had passed, she carefully traced over her daughter's original lines in what she hoped were the same materials and in the same way. To her, however, this altered drawing was never really "the same".

The issues, then, are many and complex: they force us to consider the meaning of objects not just for any person, but for a household. The meaning of an object, in turn, is bound up with its material properties (or lack of them). As we shall see, these are the issues that become important when we design new technological systems.

The Future of Family Archiving

Taken together, we are arguing then for both a broad perspective on the range of reasons why households keep objects, as well as a deep understanding of how the characteristics of objects (both physical and digital) help to realize the value that people—households—get from them. This, we would argue, enables us to cast our minds forward to where the future might lead us. For example, when we unpack the affordances of various digital and physical objects, it is interesting to specu-late on how new technologies in future might confer some aspects of one to the other, how they might merge, or how they might augment one another. As a simple example, digital objects tend to be buried deep within computers, or live on some server, somewhere. What are ways we can embody these virtual artefacts and give them more of a presence within the home? Likewise, physical objects are not easily shared remotely, but advancements in technology might well provide new ways of transmitting not just images or objects but 3D representations of them across time and space.

Such technological interventions may well change the meaning of the objects we keep and our practices around them. Furthermore, looking into the future, it is unclear whether digital technologies will help or hinder us in our aspirations to keep and manage the things that matter to us and our families. On the one hand, it is easy to imagine how the proliferation of digital objects, applications and tools, not to mention the increasing existence of data "in the cloud", might only serve to exacerbate our problems in managing our "stuff". On the other, new technologies might offer up new ways to deal more efficiently with it all, as well as enriching our ability to do the things that matter to us, such as capturing, creating, protecting and sharing the objects we cherish. Ultimately, what happens will sometimes be a matter of the confluence of emerging trends, sometimes it will be about people taking up and adapting technology in new ways, but also, we hope, sometimes it will be driven by thoughtful design based on an understanding of human values. With regard to this latter goal, the assumption is that if we can understand some of the important reasons why households keep and treasure certain objects, then we can project into the future and speculate in a more informed way on how new technologies might enrich or otherwise alter the ways in which we engage in these practices.

The section that follows describes some of the studies that seek to deepen our understanding of the values and practices in archiving different kinds of objects. This section begins with research on the archiving of photos and videos, examines the plethora of other kinds of digital content that might be meaningful to us, and then turns to studies of physical objects in the home. A goal here is to sketch out what some of the key values of archiving are for households, a central one being that of identity, and more specifically "family identity". It also aims to outline some of the challenges that people have, either with digital systems or physical objects, in realizing those values.

Following on from this, the second section will examine some of the attempts that have been made to produce new kinds of digital technologies to enable family archiving. These have sometimes been confined to the digital world, but, perhaps more ambitiously, others have attempted to connect the physical with the digital world. These range from centralized archiving systems to appliance-like objects. This section includes some of our own prototype technologies, some of which have been deployed in real homes. The findings here will be critically reflected upon, pointing to areas and concepts that hold out promise. Finally, the chapter concludes with speculation on archiving in the home of the future, and comments on where technology might take us.

Home Life, Archiving Practices and Values

Research is increasingly drawing attention to the fact that designing technologies for the home is and should be a very different kind of undertaking from designing for the workplace. Work within the field of Human-Computer Interaction (HCI) shows how the relationships, roles and activities of people within the home differ strongly from those in the workplace (e.g. O'Brien & Rodden, 1997; Plaisant et al., 2006; Taylor & Swan, 2005). Other studies highlight the fact that the value of information technology in the home must be thought of more broadly and quite differently from technology in the workplace, such as in a more open-ended, less task-focused way (e.g. Sengers & Gaver, 2006; Sellen et al. 2006). As one example, privacy and the right to know where others are and what they are doing, is vastly different in a family home than it is in a workplace (Brown et al. 2007). Here awareness of the activities of others is as much about showing affection for the family, expressing "social touch" and broadcasting the identity of the family as it is about the sharing of information for getting things done. Archiving too, is one such area in which there are important distinctions across the home/work divide. There is, of course, a vast literature and vibrant research community directed at professional archiving and new technologies, the "Digital Libraries" community being one example. For years, too, both the Human-Computer Interaction community, and related work in Computer-Supported Cooperative Work has, as a cornerstone of its research agenda, looked at archiving and document practices in workplaces. Yet archiving in the home brings out a set of values that are special to families and households.

For one thing, archiving in the workplace has, as a central issue, created tools to effectively help individuals share and preserve knowledge with their workgroups and the organization at large. In the home, however, families have different roles and concerns when it comes to archiving, and different motivations for keeping objects and data. With regard to archiving, just as in most kinds of domestic work, there are often well understood roles within the family as to who curates the objects in the family home, though this depends on whether we are talking about digital or physical objects. Roles are also changing with the advent of digital photography, with increasingly more men becoming involved in what was traditionally more under the control of the women (or more specifically mothers) within the family unit in the era of snapshot (film) photography (Sarvas & Frohlich, 2011). Who has access to family memorabilia, and tensions over what gets displayed within households are also important issues which are special to home settings, and are inextricably tied to issues of family identity. For example, Durrant's work (2009, 2010) has underscored how family identity can sometimes be at odds with personal identity in a home—while the curator in a home (for example, the mother) may work to display an idea of "family" in the home setting through the careful arrangement of photos, this may jar with, say, a teenage daughter's wish to say something different about herself. These and other issues are simply not ones that would come to the fore in a workplace setting.

As another point of distinction between work and home when we consider archiving, it is interesting to consider the longevity of the value of objects for work and home. Whilst in the workplace organizations may worry about the preservation of knowledge for the wider organization, with individuals coming and going, in the home our concern may extend much further back into the past, and be concerned with the preservation of archives far into the future. Thus we may treasure heirlooms that we inherit from our dead relatives, but equally desire to create new objects not just that our children will treasure, but that generations to come will inherit and value. This wider envelope of time also has implications for how we think about possessions and how we might create new ones to be passed on (Odom et al., 2010b).

Finally, we need to consider the nature of the home more broadly. It is of course true that the home is a place where work takes place and running the home must be accomplished. Indeed, the home shares many features of organizational work such as the need for complex coordination and communication amongst its inhabitants (Crabtree & Rodden, 2004; Taylor and Swan, 2005). But as the first "Smart Home" book has highlighted (Harper, 2003), to focus on this aspect of home life when we develop technologies (including archiving technologies) would be to misconstrue much of what the home is about. Crucially, while there is no doubt that running a home involves the execution of tasks, homes are also aspirational places. In other words, they are places where the *idea* of home and family is continuously worked upon, and where the identity of the family is bolstered and expressed (see also Miller, 2008). In fact, focusing on the home as an archive highlights these issues. Central to the process of constructing a home are the objects that we use to decorate our homes, and the things we collect and keep. In other words, the home is different from work, not just because it is a place to switch off from our "paid" work and do domestic work instead, but rather because it entails a different kind of work—the work of making home a place that reflects the household that lives in it.

Home archiving thus presents a set of unique requirements for the development of new technologies, and here it seems that starting with office technologies, or even some of the underlying assumptions on which office archiving systems are built, may be the wrong approach. At this point, it is helpful to examine what previous research has had to say in more detail about different aspects of home archiving and how new technologies have changed those practices, starting with studies of photos and videos, moving on to consider digital content more generally, and then considering heterogeneous physical objects.

Photos and Videos

When we think of family archiving, often our minds naturally turn to thoughts of family albums and home movies. To date, there has been a substantial literature on photography and the family album, coming from fields as diverse as cultural theory, literary theory and anthropology (e.g. Barthes, 2009; Sontag, 1979; and Chalfen, 1987). Home movies have received less attention, but nonetheless parallels have been drawn with family snapshots in the way both photos and videos are used to create a representation of the family (Buckingham et al, 2011; Moran, 2002). Here, the use of the term "home mode", first coined by Chalfen (1987) is used to describe a set of practices in which the capture of images (or indeed moving images) is used to create an idea of family, and to preserve a connection to the past for the family. Both photos and videos are in fact not just ways of documenting family life, but to tell stories about it. As Chalfen has pointed out (1987), this starts early on in the process in the selection of shots in the first place and in decisions about what events are important to document. Later, the construction of albums and the careful editing of videotapes help to express those stories more carefully. Ultimately, photos, albums and videos are used in different ways for different audiences, but often to convey a narrative about family life for some kind of audience whether this be through the use of framed photos (Durrant, 2010; Taylor et al, 2007), or storytelling in the moment around photos (Frohlich et al., 2002) or videos (Chalfen, 1987). This can be for reminiscing and connection to the past, or about sharing family life in the present (Sarvas & Frohlich, 2011). In addition to the value of sharing images with others, other work (Frohlich 2004, and Kindberg et al., 2005) has pointed out the value of photos for private reflection and reminiscing, a sometimes overlooked but nonetheless important aspect of image capture.

While the fundamental value of photos and videos for us may not have changed, new technological shifts in recent years have had a huge impact on both home photography and home video practices (see Sarvas & Frohlich, 2011, for an excellent review). For one thing, since the advent of photography in the mid-19th century, where photographic practices were firmly in the hands of professional portrait photographers, digital photography has helped us all to be skilled at capturing, editing, printing, and sharing images. Such practices have made use of, and also sometimes driven the acquisition of many new digital devices in the household alongside digital cameras including PCs, printers, scanners, digital photo frames and tablets. The impact of digital photography has been substantial too, in terms of the collection of images we own. Most obvious is the increase in size of people's collections as the costs of film and printing no longer apply and the costs of digital storage decrease. But there are other changes too. Not only are more pictures being taken, but people are taking more pictures of highly similar things such as the same object or scene from a variety of subtly different views. Other changes include the ability to "tinker" with individual images, and to be more creative with their images, such as stitching together multiple images (to create panoramas, or montages). Added to this is easy duplication which means the same image can exist in many different locations.

Taken together, these changes mean more flexibility in our photo practices, but they also mean more complexity in the kinds of things users can do and the collections that result. It is no longer a question of simply having your photos printed at a photo lab, and choosing a few to put in an album, or some favorites to have framed. Such changes have brought about substantial problems of browsing through, triaging, and managing these burgeoning archives. Other issues for households include considerable challenges in backing up and storing photo collections when there are often multiple cameras and multiple computers in a single home (Kirk et al., 2006). And while we have many more choices now as to how to display or curate our image collections, the resulting diverse artefacts we can now create (including printed albums produced through Web-based services, on-line albums, posting or publishing on photo sites or social networking sites, and displays on digital photo frames) further complicate the situation. Photos can exist in many different forms, as part of many different collections, and we may well struggle to completely understand what our complete "photo archive" is and where it actually resides.

It is no wonder then that the changes brought about by digital photography have also resulted in increased enthusiasm for technologists to build new tools to help us capture, visualize, and search through large digital image archives. A preponderance of such tools have looked for faster and richer ways of searching large collections, often relying on machine-learning techniques to do such things as content-based retrieval or automatic detection of duplicates (see, for example, Datta et al. 2005, for a review).

But the switch to digital photography has also meant that disciplines other than the social sciences and cultural theorists have begun to contribute to the research. For example, the HCI community has recently become interested in understanding people's practices with image collections. Studies have explored how photos are stored (Rodden & Wood, 2003), managed (Kirk et al., 2006) and displayed in the home (Durrant, 2010; Taylor et al, 2007), as well as how they are oriented to and talked around (Balabanović et al., 2000; Crabtree et al., 2004; Frohlich, 2004). A particular emphasis has been on sharing photos, resulting in various recommendations for "photoware" that better supports sharing both co-present and remotely (Frohlich et al., 2002) both for reminiscing and storytelling with others. However, as has been pointed out (Kirk et al, 2006; Sarvas & Frohlich, 2011, p. 111) there is perhaps a more pressing need for technologists to address some of the main issues that remain for families, such as more flexible ways of browsing through digital photos, managing these collections, and maintaining an integrated, protected database for the household.

Home video, too, has undergone massive change in recent years. One only has to look at online repositories of video such as YouTube to begin to understand how growing access to digital video is widening participation in a new culture of video production, exchange and viewing that was hitherto left to professionals. As the capacity to capture video is being incorporated into increasingly diverse artefacts (such as mobile phones), the opportunities for home video-makers to make, watch and exchange video have equally increased.

Having said that, users' practices with home video as a research topic has received far less attention in the literature than photography. Within the HCI literature, there is scant research: one study proposed a system for the storage and annotation of home video (Abowd et al., 2003) with reference to prior work from a project called the "Living Memory Box" (Stevens et al., 2003) and based on focus groups. However, the development of the Living Memory Box concept focused exclusively on the use of media to record memories, not addressing the creative aspects of using video such as video editing, and considering mainly the browsing, annotating and retrieving of centrally stored home video snippets.

More recent work of our own has sought to more fully describe home video use (Kirk et al., 2007). In this work we found evidence for two distinct types of practice: a *lightweight* type of video work in which video is captured spontaneously in an ad hoc way often through mobile devices such as phones, and a more *heavyweight* set of practices in which video is captured in a more planful, intentional way to document important occasions often using more high-end camcorders. Of course, since publication of that work, new kinds of devices such as the "Flip Video" have entered the market, which undoubtedly are beginning to blur the boundaries between lightweight and heavyweight video use. Flip Video and devices like it offer high quality video capture capabilities combined with a range of editing and sharing tools, in a physically lightweight, robust and inexpensive form.

In considering the work on both photo and video practices in domestic use, there are some obvious gaps as we think about the home of the future and the place of photo and video technologies. One concerns how we deal with the legacy of printed photos, and the outdated video cassettes, tapes and so on that most households possess. While we may choose to keep our printed photos separate from our digital collections, or hang on to now obsolete technologies in order to play back our old tapes and cassettes, the issue of integration and preservation of our image and video archives over the longer term will continue to challenge us until we arrive at better solutions for managing and protecting these heterogeneous collections. In addition, as will be discussed later, there may be new value in aggregating not just across our photo and video collections, but in creating more coherent archives by linking photos and videos with other kinds of sentimental objects too.

Further, when considering where photos and videos now reside, and the many different ways in which they are captured, it is obvious that new technology trends make the situation even more complicated. With regard to capture of images or video, cameras are now not only embedded in mobile phones but increasingly in laptops. The pictures and video themselves may end up not just on our hard drives, but shared through on-line tools, posted on social networking sites, or published more broadly through on-line sites. These places, all, in some ways, become archives of their own. Yet at the same time, they are distinct, rather fragmented ways to store the things that matter to us, making management across these tools and applications time-consuming and effortful. Added to this, increasingly, images and videos are posted by others, which raises all kinds of questions around ownership. For example, we may be tagged in a photo, but not own the photo. It may be meaningful and important to us, but it is not really ours.

Our Digital Footprints

This leads on to broader consideration of the kinds of digital content that we might, in the home of the future, consider to be of importance for the family archive. Up to this point, we have mainly considered cameras and camcorders as the main instruments by which sentimental digital material gets captured for the home archive. Of course, we are talking here about the deliberate capture of material, and the process of decision, selection, uploading and management that this entails. However, increasingly, as already alluded to above, we must also consider other kinds of digital materials that may become important parts of the archive even if they are captured for other reasons. In other words, we are increasingly beginning to talk of our "digital footprints" as important records of our personal lives, leaving data behind about us that we might become quite sentimental about in future.

The kinds of digital data we might be talking about here include all traces of our communications with others, including email, voicemail, text messages, and of course all of our social networking archives. Sound recordings are especially interesting here, as the tragic events of 9/11 have taught us. The archives of the final messages left by those that died have subsequently taken on treasured status. It is interesting that though sound and voice messages from the past can be so imbued with sentiment, often evoking a deeply emotional response, they are hardly ever deliberately captured, as recent work has confirmed (Oleksik et al., 2008). Text messages too are known to take on "gift-like" qualities when exchanged, and often are cherished (Taylor and Harper, 2003). And evidence from recent fieldwork also suggests that email archives can also be held to be special, especially if they contain the record of the unfolding of a relationship between people (Kirk and Sellen, 2010), or correspondence with someone who has recently passed away (Odom et al., 2010b).

Taking this to an extreme, there are those who would seek to capture as complete a record as possible of their everyday lives. This would include not just complete records of communication, but all documents and Web pages one encounters, and in fact any activity in the digital world. The vision does not stop at the digital desktop, however. Devices, such as Sensecam (Hodges et al., 2006), have also been devised that allow the continuous capture of people's activities in the course of everyday life. Sensecam, worn around the neck of a user, not only takes hundreds of still images triggered by movement and changes in light (amongst other things), but also captures data such as ambient temperature. It is only a matter of time before such technologies include audio, and full motion video, as well as other kinds of data such as location and perhaps even biosensor data. Thus the result is a vast archive of data relevant to the course of someone's personal activities. Some, such as Gordon Bell (Bell and Gemmell, 2009), paint a utopian picture in which the human fallibilities of memory can be circumvented with this kind of effortless digital capture of an entire life. Thus, the motivation for these kinds of "lifelogging" endeavors is often primarily functional rather than sentimental. Having said that, the argument is also made that we may not know in advance what we are likely to treasure in the future, so logging as much as we can will ensure that we never miss those special moments. A similar kind of argument has been made by Kientz and Abowd (2009) in their development of a specialized recording device that attempts to capture the lives of young children in as automatic a manner as possible.

One might well ask, then, what role aspects of our digital footprints will play in the family archive in future? One of the most obvious problems will be mining and managing all of this. In a recent study of people recently bereaved, participants complained of inheriting hard disks and other digital devices from their loved ones, and not knowing how to cope with large unfiltered collections of data (Odom et al, 2010b). Yet these same people expressed a strong desire to be able to bequeath or pass on many different kinds of digital objects to those they care about including personal narratives or diaries written on-line, blogs and Twitter feeds, social networking content, digital photo or music collections and digital artwork. This points to some important problems in passing digital data from generation to generation. But even dealing with our own digital footprints will be daunting. While we might be in a much better position to determine what matters, and what is meaningful, we do not yet have a coherent set of tools to let us cope with what will become an increasingly vast and diverse archive of personally relevant data.

When one puts these issues in the context of a household, the picture becomes even more complex. In a recent study of teenagers and their possessions, it is clear that both physical and digital objects are used to manage and experiment with different ways of projecting one's identity (Odom et al., 2011). An important part of this is determining who the audience is, and who has access to what materials. In the physical world, teenagers' personal things may be managed by careful curation within the private space of the bedroom, whilst more public spaces within the home are typically under control of parents. Digital possessions are also carefully controlled for different audiences. For example, whether or not parents have access to postings on Facebook is an issue of concern, some teens opting to post only for friends and peers, whilst others carefully filtering materials when they know parents or a wider audience have access. Teens practice many ways of managing their identity then, adjusting and crafting it accordingly using a whole range of objects and possessions. This raises an interesting question of how tools that somehow amass an archive for the whole family will deal with issues of identity, ownership and privacy, teenagers perhaps being the most extreme case within the household.

In considering how digital objects and data will matter in the home of the future then, we have seen that those features that make digital data so powerful - easy and ubiquitous capture, reproducibility, modifiability, instant sharing, widespread access, and almost invisible storage - are, at the same time, the aspects which present the greatest challenges for realizing value from digital content in the future. Capturing ever more data and creating more diverse ways to share and express ourselves through that data has generated problems of its own, and it appears that we now need to perhaps step back and reflect on how we rein in, re-possess, protect and preserve the explosion of personal data we are creating.

Archiving Physical Objects

After spending some time discussing the value and practices surrounding the archiving of digital content, let us now consider the physical objects that families keep and treasure. Throughout our own work, we have repeatedly observed an attraction towards the physical amongst technology users. For example, try as we might to understand practices of digital storage of photos and videos in isolation, tangible objects kept cropping up. Archiving practices often bore witness to transformations from the digital to the physical: select digital pictures were still printed and framed, and videos were often turned into nicely edited and packaged DVDs (Kirk et al. 2006, 2007). And as our own studies and those of others confirm, when asking householders to show us objects that they care about the most, it is physical objects rather than digital ones that figure most prominently in those discussions (Kirk & Sellen, 2010; Petrelli & Whittaker, 2010). Further, while some of those objects seem in some sense obvious (a baby's first pair of shoes, a special framed photograph, a collection of souvenirs from a holiday), we have found many others to be strange and idiosyncratic indeed - a broken mug, an old t-shirt, and even a frozen apple tart. If nothing else, these observations should tell us that if we want to design better technologies for family archiving, we should be "taking things seriously" (Glenn and Hayes, 2007).

When we do so, it becomes evident that objects can be seen from a variety of perspectives. The kinds of sentimental artefacts found in homes have variously been described as evocative objects (Turkle, 2007), biographical objects (Hoskins, 1998), and sacred objects (Belk et al., 1989). The importance of physical things for people has been well documented by anthropologists, sociologists, cultural theorists and psychology. For instance, if we consider existing anthropological studies, we find a long tradition of studying material cultures and the processes of exchange economies, an understanding of which essentially sensitizes the reader to the importance of structured practices of gift giving (Appadurai, 1986; Douglas and Isherwood, 1979; Mauss, 1954). In many respects this forms the precursor for our understanding of the importance of objects and why we might accumulate them. This work, often culturally bound, tends to speak to broader issues than we are concerned with here.

However, there are studies of more direct relevance. For example, anthropologist Daniel Miller (2001, 2008) has written extensively about why things matter to people. In a recent study of 30 households on a street in South London, he describes in rich detail how the things in a household help us "read" its occupants: understand what they are about, what they care about, and what their life stories are.

There has also been a preponderance of literature mainly from psychology and more recently, HCI, which has focused on the role of objects for the individual within the home setting. Central themes here concern the role of objects in supporting both individual memory and individual identity in domestic settings. For example, Csikszentmihalyi & Rochberg-Halton (1981) use psychological notions of selfhood to explain the role and importance of objects throughout a person's lifetime. In a more recent study of the role of mundane objects in home archiving practices, Petrelli et al. (2008) maintained a strong focus on archiving as a way of supporting an individual's memory, specifically through the keeping of physical objects to remind people of past events, people and places.

It is clear from studies of cherished objects in people's homes that many ordinary and idiosyncratic objects can act as triggers for memories of the past: found objects such as collections of shells or feathers can remind people of family holidays, photos of loved ones who have died bring back memories of times gone by, books and artwork can have important connections to our childhood, but even mundane artefacts such as receipts, train tickets, furniture and clothing can spark emotional memories for the people who own them.

What these and other studies draw attention to therefore, are the relationships between a person and the objects that matter to them. However, as part of this it must also be remembered that the domestic environment is a negotiated space. In other words, there is a social construction to the fabrication of the ecology of the home (Hendon, 2000). This means that decisions about which and whose artefacts are stored, displayed, and otherwise accessed is a negotiated activity within the context of the household.

Our own work examining the things that matter to households also takes this broader perspective. This work, by contrast, has shown that what family archiving practices really reveal is the social structure of the home. And what is important in family archiving practices are the ways in which these practices shape, and are in turn shaped by, the relationships among the family members. This approach also helps reveal that the values people get from the objects that they care about in their homes are not necessarily just about their personal relationships to these artefacts, but that these values can sometimes only be understood within the context of the whole household, or indeed the family unit.

Six Values of Archiving Objects

To focus in on just what these values are for households – why families keep certain objects — we conducted a field study of both the physical and digital objects that households cherish (Kirk & Sellen, 2010). As discussed, this study was different from previous work in that this research aimed to uncover the reasons behind archiving not just from the angle of any one individual in a household, but also for the household *as a whole*. In doing so, we also discovered that in contrast to other work, the value of archiving objects was perhaps not so much about memory and the triggering of memories of the past for any individual, as it was about other things.

In this study, eleven diverse households were recruited including families with children, couples with no children, and older couples whose children had left home. In each household, we asked for a guided tour of the home focusing on objects — either physical or digital — that were in some way special, or cherished by them. These tours and the spontaneous stories that they generated about objects were recorded and analyzed. In addition, these were followed up by in-depth interviews seeking to clarify why these objects had been selected, and what practices surrounded them. Most objects were in fact physical, ranging from furniture, toys and books through to found objects and things that had once been functional (such as engine parts). Paper-based artefacts were also found to be important such as certificates, letters, photos, newspaper clippings and children's artwork. Some digital artefacts were found to have sentimental value too. Unsurprisingly, these were mainly digital photos and videos, but also included emails, work documents, and digital artwork. The participants also made mention of text messages and blog content that was felt to be important, but these were not shown or discussed in any depth. A final class of artefacts we called "hybrid" being as they were physical instantiations of digital content such as old cassette tapes and videotapes.

From these *in situ* interviews and observations, we derived six main reasons why these various and diverse objects were held to be special: some of which pertained more to individuals within the household, and some which were distinctly about the household or, more particularly, the family unit. In doing so, we found that these objects served as much more than mementos or triggers for past events or memories, though this could be important. While they are sometimes about connecting with the past, we also find that they do important work in the present, and thus span a larger range of value than has been previously explicated. This includes for example, how objects can draw attention to people of special status, how they play a role in personal and family identity, how they help people fulfil a sense of duty, and how they can even help people forget the past (see Fig. 11.1).

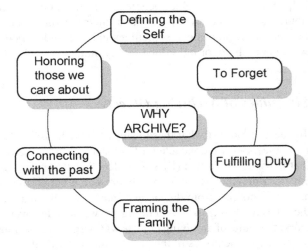

Fig. 11.1 Six values of home archiving

Defining the Self

The first of these reasons was for the purpose of self-identity, and is one of the most frequently cited reasons for archiving in the literature. In this way, as has been noted, individuals express something about themselves, surround themselves with objects which embody aspects of their past, and thereby trigger memories of personal events and relationships. We too found many examples of objects of a personal nature, which represented some aspect of self, being archived for the purpose of *defining* the self. Sometimes this was done in private ways, such as the mother of one household who had an old Bay City Rollers annual stored up in her loft reminding her of her teenage years. Other objects were kept so as to make a more public presentation of self, such one participant who framed and hung on the wall the last circuit board he ever designed and made. The construction of self-identity through the archiving of *digital* items was also evident although it often manifested itself in different ways. Largely, it was more personal and less publicly displayed. The presence on hard drives of old bits of work, photos of a personal nature, music collections, or even just the particular arrangements of the digital desktop environment were seen to be a reflection of a person's identity and which are all candidates for things to which people talked about becoming sentimentally attached.

Honoring Those We Care About

While many objects were displayed by those who wanted to say something about themselves, we also found artefacts being displayed so as to draw attention to and honor *others* in the household or those of important friends and family. Framed photos featured strongly here, as did the framing or display of children's artwork. Often care was taken here not just to elevate the status of different people in the household in this way, but also to make sure that there was equitable representation of, say, all of the children within a household. Objects were also displayed for the purpose of honoring social relationships that extended beyond the home. For example, we were told that strange or disliked gifts were often given pride of place when the people who gave them visited, and in other work we have seen that framed pictures of relatives have to be given equal spatial billing (Drazin and Frohlich, 2007; Taylor et al. 2007) lest distant family members become offended. While this was a clearly defined set of practices in the physical world, it was difficult to find examples of this occurring with digital artefacts in the households we studied. It appeared that honoring someone is tied to public display, and hence our participants said that important digital photos or art produced digitally by a child would most likely be printed out and made physical. This might be done with a digital photo frame, but none of our participants had these or showed particular interest in acquiring them.

Connecting with the Past

Beyond keeping objects to define oneself, or honoring close friends and family, another reason for keeping sentimental objects was to form connections with the

past. By connections with the past, this was not necessarily in the sense of recol-
lecting it or reliving some past experience. Rather we saw that, in the act of using,
displaying, or keeping objects, different members of the family are drawn closer to
important people, places, times and events in the past. For instance, we saw many
examples where parents kept objects in order to make a connection with the past for
children, giving them a sense of heritage or kinship. This could be made manifest
in the passing on a recipe book of jams passed on from a grandmother (complete
with her annotations), to displaying photos of deceased relatives so that children
grow up somehow "knowing" relatives that they had never actually met. Forming
connections with the past was also seen with digital artefacts. This was perhaps
most evident in the way in which households scanned versions of older print photos
to include in their family collections. But here we also saw some households collect and create genealogical information either by gathering census record copies to
provide missing information on ancestors, by storing information in "family tree"
programs on the family computer or by collecting audio records of grandparents'
stories. Here the value of the digital was in the way in which it might be able to
preserve and share important data in ways not considered possible with physical
objects.

Framing the Family

In line with Hendon's (2000) view of the spatial relations of objects in the home
being indicative of the social structures within it, we found many instances of
artefact storage which spoke more to the social organization of the home and
the framing of the family, than the individuation of the self. In particular, in our
study, mothers were often observed to be making active decisions about which
objects should be kept in the home, which things were to be displayed, and how
they were to be displayed. This is not to say that these homes were not also
negotiated spaces, with participation from all members. There were many examples of spaces within these homes being appropriated by others, bedrooms being
a common example. But particularly in shared family spaces, the mother of the
family had most control over how the "public face" of the family was config-
ured, as if in essence to say, "This is the type of family we are." In addition to
the display of family photos, this included the careful positioning of ancestral artworks, objects collected from foreign lands, and religious artefacts. The ability to
present a family face was less evident in the digital realm. We found no examples of these practices of framing the family so evidently exploited in the physical
world. Digital data, largely locked away inside a physical object (the PC), could
of course be displayed in many ways. Screensavers and digital photo frames can
cycle through family photo collections; family websites are also ways of constructing digital representations of the family which can be publicly shared. However,
for whatever reasons, we saw little evidence of such practices in the households we
studied.

Fulfilling Duty

Another reason for archiving that emerged in the course of our fieldwork had to do with the drive to fulfil a sense of duty. We found that the motivation to archive can often be suffused with a sense of duty towards preserving artefacts for the sake of the household, for those whom one cares about, and sometimes even for no one in particular. An interesting example was provided by one of the families in our study who had adopted children at an early age. The children had arrived with a box of items such as various toys, which the mother of the family had diligently stored away. She felt strongly that these items held a special status and were not hers to do with as she wished. She felt that these objects represented a tangible link for the children between themselves and their former lives (despite the fact they had no memory of them), and knew that one day this link might have a renewed significance for the children. With digital artefacts, we found no instances in this study where these were archived out of a sense of duty. However, in other more recent work (Odom et al., 2010b) the preservation of blogs, social networking data, email and voicemail conversations from people who have recently died can be seen to take on a treasured status. It may follow that preserving and protecting these digital artefacts for the future will emerge as more important as time goes on.

Forgetting

A final aspect of archiving practice, and another underlying motivation that is rarely considered, is the extent to which we archive items to forget them. In one conversation we had with a young couple, one woman mentioned letters she had received from her mother, which she still kept, but which were painful to her. In another example, one participant told us about an apple tart that her mother had made just before going into a home, which she had kept frozen in her house. After the mother had died, the apple tart lived on frozen, but she could neither eat her dead mother's apple tart or get rid of it. In the end she had to get her husband to dispose of it without telling her whilst she was out of the house. In this way she could avoid confronting these conflicting feelings. Analogous practices were evident with digital artefacts too. We found evidence of emails kept and pictures stored that had upsetting or embarrassing connotations. These items were too important in a sense to discard, but at the same time they were stored in the deeper recesses of hierarchical file structures where they would be less frequently accessed, a practice we also observed in later work talking to people who had been recently bereaved (Odom et al., 2010b). Evidently, a purpose of an archive in the home can be not just to protect objects but to protect the owner *from* objects as well. It raises the question as to why objects such as these are not simply thrown away or gotten rid of. It would appear that in some instances, such as the letters we have discussed, there is a palpable sense in which the objects are constitutive of the person. While their contents might be embarrassing or painful, to destroy the objects would be to dishonor the memory, the experience or the sender that they signify.

Challenges for Designing New Technologies

We have seen that there are many reasons why sentimental artefacts (whether they be physical, digital or hybrid objects) are kept in the home. Through these archived objects, which often form an integral part of the very fabric of our homes, we can celebrate our identities and achievements, show and honor our connections with significant others, connect with our past, help us construct an idea of the family, fulfil a sense of duty, and even forget the past. In achieving these goals, the placement of objects, how they are stumbled across or rummaged through, how they are shared or kept private, and how they are collected or singled out are all aspects which we have seen to be important.

This raises some real challenges in designing new technologies for archiving in the home of the future. These can be summarized as follows.

Managing Heterogeneous Collections

On the one hand, we can now capture more about our lives than ever before, and more kinds of data than ever before. This raises the challenge of managing the growing collection of objects or data both deliberately kept and inadvertently created. Further, these are heterogeneous collections of legacy media and new content, physical objects and digital ones. Collections of such objects can be organized around us, or hidden and distributed across many containers and devices, each acting as smaller archives unto themselves. Managing and integrating across these collections, should we want to do so, is no small task.

Being Creative

Another challenge we face is in relation to creativity. With the explosion of new digital tools, such as on-line photo albums, video editing tools, and ways to collectively share and create artefacts together in the digital world, we have more ways than ever to be creative with the things that we treasure. Indeed, the very act of constructing narratives with these tools allows us to produce entirely new objects that become sentimental and cherished in turn. This will depend, however, on being able to access and find the materials we wish to work with within the vast archives we are accumulating. Added to this, there are few tools that allow us to be creative with different kinds of objects. It is difficult enough to combine things in the digital world, such as photos and videos, let alone create amalgams of objects across the physical/digital divide.

Managing Presence and Absence

Managing the presence or absence of objects is one aspect of archiving practice that we are used to coping with in the physical world. We find ways to hide those things we deem to be personal, painful or private, and display those things we want to share. In the digital world, ways of hiding things is not so straightforward or flexible. Likewise, there are limited means to give digital data a presence in the family home beyond screensavers and digital photo frames. This issue then presents a design challenge for digital tools.

Private Versus Shared Archives

We have seen that the family home contains some objects for private reminiscence and self-identity, and others that frame the family, or are kept for the family. This suggests that sometimes it makes sense for the family to create a collective archive, but other times, there is a need to keep some materials separate for different members of the household. A challenge here, then, is to create systems or artefacts that are either specifically designed for the household or for individuals within the household, or which allow the flexible partitioning of parts of an archive for private control and use.

Constructing Narratives

Another set of issues surround how we share our archived objects with others, whether this is in the present or in the longer term. Part of the challenge here is how to give meaning to objects, and to make it clear why things matter. As discussed, making traditional photo albums or home movies is a way of doing this, but most physical objects are made meaningful through the telling of stories. The digital world may be able to offer some support here. But what of the vast array of digital materials we own? Sorting through these and creating narratives is no easy task, and when we consider the fact that more and more of us will either inherit or leave behind hard drives and other devices full of digital data, it is clear that most of us would be hard pressed to know what is meaningful and what is not.

Keeping Archives Safe and Accessible

Finally, there are many issues to be considered when it comes to keeping the things in our family archives safe and protected, especially in the longer term. In some sense, we can feel reassured when we have back up our most important photos and videos to the cloud. But in the longer term, how can we be guaranteed to have access to them? We may not really "own" them anymore, nor have access to the applications that are needed to "read" the data. These are technical as well as social challenges. And when it comes to physical objects, there may be ways we can capture facsimiles of physical objects, or even create copies of them via digital means. This may undermine the quintessence of an object, however, which may matter some of the time and not others.

All of these features of objects, and the systems and practices we have in place to deal with them, impose constraints on the new technologies we develop at the same time as they open up the design space. In the next section, we examine some of the concepts which researchers and designers have generated that point toward future directions.

Designing for the Future of Home Archiving

Consideration of the various underlying values of home archiving for households can inspire new ideas for systems not only designed to cope with changes in technology (and the potential problems that this raises) but which in fact might enrich those values. These values might be better understood as aspirations that we might have in relation to objects we treasure, such as helping us to frame the family in new ways, helping to make stronger connections to the past, giving us a richer sense of our own identities, or helping us fulfil our duty to the family by offering up easier ways to manage the materials that matter to us. In the face of this, there are various and important challenges, both in terms of the specifics of the interaction design, and in the underlying technology. In looking for these opportunities, however, it makes sense to think about how we can exploit the natural affordances of the physical and digital world to create these new systems. More specifically, as we move into the future, primarily this will hinge on how we design the role of new digital technologies in relation to the physical world. There are two ways of thinking about how we can approach these design opportunities:

Affordances of the Digital

It is worth initially considering what we see the benefits of digital archiving to be. Digital systems facilitate such activities as accurate indexing, fast retrieval of information, the ability to edit content, copy it, append meta-data, and remotely share data. Alongside all of these affordances, there is a significant reduction in the amount of physical space that is necessarily required for the storage of sentimental artefacts. Consequently, it is worth asking if a system designed to help capture, manage, share and keep safe digital materials could be expanded upon and enriched to incorporate aspects of the vast array of physical things that we may also keep and care about. In other words, when we look at our computers and think about existing tools for helping to manage and archive digital photographs and videos, we can begin to ask ourselves what a digital archiving system would look like if it took the diversity of other kinds of objects into account and tried to apply the strengths of digital archiving to a broader set of artefacts. How might this change the nature of physical artefacts such that they can be incorporated with the digital artefacts or be connected to them in richer ways?

Affordances of the Physical

A second approach is to consider the affordances of the physical and to understand the properties that this engenders and to explore how this might shape our experiences with digital objects. Amongst other things, such an approach would prompt us to consider the ways in which digital objects might be displayed like the plethora of display practices observed with physical objects. Equally, the repurposing of physical objects over time might suggest designs for the repurposing of digital data, much in the way that antiques often move from a life of use to a life of decoration after significant time. Additionally, as physical objects age they degrade, but this fragility is often cherished, and the development of patina through use or neglect can add value to an object. Such affordances of the physical are not normally applied to our digital artefacts (after all — digital is supposed to be forever) but evidently such aspects of physicality might lead to intriguing redesigns of digital objects giving them new values.

In either case, we propose that the design process needs to take into account a deep understanding of the values that physical and digital objects deliver, and how the affordances of the objects themselves as well as the *ways* they are archived help to achieve these values. At the same time, as has been pointed out, there are significant design challenges to be dealt with which help guide us in *how* these higher level values might be achieved. Building on the two potential approaches outlined above, let us then examine what this might mean in more concrete terms for new kinds of family archiving systems.

An Integrated Digital Archive

One way of thinking about new kinds of archiving technologies is to explore what it might be like to use technology to create a single, integrated digital database for the home. There are many obvious advantages to this approach. As pointed out earlier, changes in technology have led to more disjunct and disparate archives of different kinds of digital content such as photos and videos, and as has become clear, there are many other kinds of digital objects too that we might cherish, even if they are initially captured or created for some other purpose. An integrated archiving system might then allow us to flexibly organize all of the materials that are important to us, to create new digital collections and associations within those materials, to search and browse through our digital objects in powerful ways, to share these objects through networked connections and to back-up and keep safe these important materials — addressing many of the requirements we have already highlighted. Indeed the rising popularity of Web-based tools for managing, sharing, and storing photos and videos attest to people's desire for such centralized systems (often perhaps because of the inherent ease with which digital materials can be curated). At the same time, the quest for systems which allow for increasing capture of more personally relevant materials through automatic recording devices (such as Sensecam, Hodges et al., 2006) along with attendant software for storing and managing these vast personal archives (such as MyLifeBits, Gemmell et al., 2006) are in some ways an attempt to construct an integrated digital archive.

But what we might design with human values in mind, and bearing in mind too some of the design challenges we face in family archiving, is not something which aims to encompass and capture more and more of our digital footprint within some monolithic, personal digital database. Rather, it has as its focus a place where we store, manage, create and share the things we care about within the context of the family home. If nothing else, the empirical work we have presented suggests that a fundamental aspect of the archiving of cherished objects is the way in which they are enmeshed within, and constitutive of, the material fabric of the home. This itself suggests a heterogeneous distributed collection. But this is only when one is thinking from within the perspective of the home. The home taken as a whole can be conceptualized as a dynamic and socially shaped collection of artefacts (cherished or otherwise). Thinking at this broader level we can see advantages to enriching connections, between objects (physical and digital) within this space as a curated collection. Having some sense of integration, connection, and collection between heterogeneous elements of the home, such as disparate display devices or disparate distillations, collections and gatherings of artefacts and the content itself would allow greater flexibility in how artefacts can be meaningfully handled. An integrated approach is thus like thinking about the connective (technological) tissue between objects and one layer of the socio-material fabric of the home.

Thinking further on what things constitute the meaningful, cherished, artefacts of the home, we suggest that an integrated archive would not just be a place where digital photos and videos are kept, but would also be a place where legacy materials might be amassed and integrated. For example various kinds of digital materials, such as those stored in what we have called "hybrid" objects might also be valuably integrated with (as in given some connection to) existing material collections. For example, it suggests that people would value easy ways to capture and incorporate into this database the media stored on cassette tapes, CDs, and video tapes.

More interesting and challenging questions arise when we also consider how we might integrate physical objects into such an archive. Obviously, we can think here about quick scanning of printed photos, but also other paper documents such as certificates, children's artwork, tickets, notes and other paper objects might be valuable even when digitized. When it comes to physical objects, however, the findings of our research raise many different kinds of questions about how such objects could ever be represented in a digital world. We have seen that even paper-based objects can have important tangible qualities, hence our use of the term "2 1/2 D." Under what circumstances, then would a digital copy of that object be valued? Likewise, we have seen that other objects are made special by their very quintessence — by the fact that they are unique. Copying that object in any sense, even if that copy were high fidelity, then undermines the very value of the object. The issue of authenticity is well illustrated by the example of the mother who was torn by the need to draw over the lines on her daughter's artwork to preserve it, and the desire to retain its authenticity.

Physicality too has other important implications, as we have seen. For example, some of the objects in our study were valued because of their functional use. For example, a ladle handed down from a grandmother was valued not just for the memory it sparked, but because it sparked that memory through use — something a digital copy could never achieve. Likewise, we saw that physical objects afforded display in public regions of the house, and a way to draw attention, invite conversation and to become a part of the physical fabric of the house in ways that digital objects did not. Physical objects naturally afford the kind of persistent but peripheral display that allows us to surround ourselves with the things that are meaningful to us.

There are many reasons, therefore, that we can never equate a digital copy of a physical object, no matter how veridical, with its original. This is not to say, however, that there is no potential value in digital copies of physical objects. The question is whether such digital copies could achieve some of the range of values we have seen in other ways, or even achieve *new* kinds of values by considering their incorporation into an integrated database. The digital copy may never replace a sacred object, but it may provide a resource to a digital system that allows new kinds of creativity with a wider range of materials. In this way a digital database which incorporates such objects allows us new ways to honor others, connect to a shared past, frame the family, and so on.

More than this, copies of physical objects may take on new value through being part of a larger collection enabled by the digital system. We have seen, for example, that children's artwork was sometimes framed and treasured, but other times was seen as a problem and conundrum because of the sheer amount that children produce. Scanned collections of artwork over time might become valued objects in themselves not because of their authenticity, but because the collection and the way the artwork can be seen to evolve over time becomes a new and compelling arte-fact in itself. The values expressed through physical objects, such as ways to fulfil one's duty as a parent, can be achieved in new ways with new objects through such a digital system.

Relatedly, for those objects which one wants to "deal with," a digital system may provide easier, clutter-free ways of doing this. Certainly in the case of wanting to keep things but to hide them, or for examples where we saw expressions of guilt or tension about ridding oneself of physical objects, a digital system might provide a middle ground for ways of keeping objects in new ways.

Finally, an obvious benefit of digital systems is that they provide other ways to back up and safeguard materials, even if those materials can never be as good as the originals. We may not choose to rid ourselves of cherished objects, but there may be times when they are lost or damaged beyond our control. Of course the digital is not infallible, and while it might be easy to imply that digital records last forever, we already know that this is not the case. As technology standards develop, file formats become obsolete, and this has already had significant impact in people's lives. However, the ability to design digital records to last, by considering the longevity and the design of digital file formats, is still present and obviously needs to be an issue of urgent consideration.

Considered broadly, all of this suggests that there may be a much richer landscape for digital systems if they begin to incorporate more diverse kinds of materials, whether these originate from other digital sources (such as email, documents, and ambient sound) or whether we begin to incorporate new ways of capturing aspects of physical objects to create amalgams and collections of materials. By attending to the various kinds of value that these materials deliver for people, we might begin to open up the design space for integrated digital archiving systems. Doubtless, this will, at the same time, alter our relationship with things in the home as such technology plays with the form of objects, connects them together in new ways, and perhaps provokes us to think about or put away objects in new ways too.

The "Family Archive"

Moving forward on this agenda, we have attempted to design prototype systems that would allow us to explore the potential of such an archive within a family setting. Our first attempt, Family Archive (Kirk et al., 2010) focused on providing one place in the home where families could not only upload all of their digital photos, but where physical objects could be captured too using an overhead camera. This bespoke device was designed to fit within the family home, being large enough for more than one person to use, and incorporating an FTIR multi-touch surface on which digital objects could be displayed and manipulated (see Fig. 11.2). A simple dock allowed pictures to be easily uploaded from a camera, and a physical button next to the surface allowed any object placed on the surface of the Archive to be scanned.

Fig. 11.2 The design of the family archive

Once scanned into the Archive, images of physical objects could be manipulated like any other digital objects. In fact all of the objects in the Archive were manipulated in a world which used virtual physics, so objects could be moved, rotated, flipped over, and piled on top of each other. They could also be shrunk or expanded, annotated, and put into virtual boxes using multi-touch input (see Fig. 11.3). Thus, scanned physical objects could be stored with photos in boxes which contain these loose collections of objects.

Fig. 11.3 The interface of family archive

Family Archive, being a first prototype, only attended to some of the features we wanted in a full system. It focused on widening the envelope of things that could be digitized and captured in a family home. Primarily, we were interested to see whether this device would be used collaboratively by a household, whether physical objects would be scanned in as part of the archive (and for what reasons), and whether this sort of loose storage and interaction model would find a useful place within family archiving practices.

In fact, when deployed in three family homes for a month long trial, the field study highlighted some interesting issues to do with family archiving practices, some of the values that were realized through this device, as well as some of its shortcomings (Kirk et al., 2010). One unexpected finding was that in providing a single, integrated archive for the family, existing roles in the family concerning who usually did what (who uploaded things, who managed and triaged them, and who curated them, for example) were undermined. This was particularly the case in one family where the 6 year old son, normally kept well away from the family's digital collection of photos on their PC, began to rearrange the boxes of photos his parents had so carefully sorted. Added to this, he had scanned in his entire collection of plastic dinosaurs, scans of which would randomly appear in boxes of family holiday snapshots and the like. So creating a place where the family could all access and play with the contents of the archive created new tensions, and disrupted roles in the family that up to that point, had been well understood.

At the same time, there were other aspects of the Archive which created value for some members of the household, but undermined it for others. For one thing, the use of physics made it a playful device, inviting young children and older more "tech-shy" members of the family to participate and interact with its contents. However, this was also indicative of the fact that it was difficult to get any real "work" done with the contents of the archive, in terms of triaging, managing and storing them. Thus, while fun, it was an inefficient system getting in the way of parents wanting to fulfil their duty with regard to managing their collections. Parents did not want to be playful here, doing such things as emptying out boxes, filling them, and moving them around the Archive; they wanted quick ways to sort the contents out, tag them, and tidy them away. In addition, it was clear that they system needed to attend more to efficiency in helping people to scan in physical objects. While we began to see families think more creatively about what could be in a digital archive (they scanned such things as toys, printed photos, CD covers, and notes of best wishes written at a wedding) the whole process took too much effort. All of this underscores the fact that, while archiving systems for home life might be quite different from those that we would design for office life, the ability to do things quickly and efficiently can be as important for sorting out stuff in the home as it is in the workplace.

Another issue for this prototype was that while people clearly wanted to be creative with the system, there were no real tools to do this beyond displaying the contents using a slide show feature. Here, the issues highlight that much of the work of archiving in families is really about showing affection for others by creating new and special objects that honor others, frame the family and so on. In this system, the ability even to create a simple album of photos was not supported, and thus the chance to both curate and create materials from the materials in the Archive was clearly a crucial aspect missing from the system.

Finally, the families wanted to be able to connect and share the images in the Archive not just with others remotely, but through the local display of materials within the house. None of these things was possible with this first prototype. This aspect of the prototype emphasizes the fact that a system such as this ought not to be viewed as a kind of storage box or container for objects, but rather as a dynamic collection of materials that can be brought into the landscape of the home, and shared beyond its confines too.

All of the findings outlined above eventually led us to develop a second prototype in which we tried to improve aspects of the efficiency of interaction, provide more tools for creativity, and better connections to other devices and systems for sharing. The important lesson here, however, is that as much as these systems can be improved through this kind of iterative testing in the field, they also give us a lens through which we can view family archiving practices. In this one study, we began to understand more deeply the importance of roles and routines around archiving in the home, and the importance of being able to efficiently carry out the work of archiving. But perhaps most significant is the understanding that this work not just about family management and a sense of duty, but it is love's work — the work of creating a sense of the family within the home. And, accordingly, the archiving tools that these families wanted would give them the scope, flexibility and power to create and express that sense of family.

Physical Augmentation

Rather than considering how we might digitize new kinds of materials, an alternative approach is to consider how to make the most of physical affordances by augmenting physical objects with digital data, or enhancing digital objects through physical embodiment.

For example, the importance of storytelling when it comes to cherished artefacts suggests that ways of capturing or playing back stories associated with particular objects might be a way of preserving or passing on the meaning or importance of those objects. As our fieldwork has shown, picking up a physical thing which we hold to be special can spark impromptu stories about the past, or even about the present. Further, the stories associated with different objects can become part of a shared family history. Some years ago now, the "Memory Box" concept (Frohlich and Murphy 2000) attempted to illustrate how this might be done. Memory Box was a physical box containing a number of objects (such as a necklace, a printed photograph and a pebble) which, when lifted out, played associated stories from an audio speaker embedded in the lid. While built more as a probe for discussion rather than a full working prototype, Frohlich and Murphy found that users wanted very simple ways of both recording and playing back these sound snippets. In addition, they wanted the box to be totally self-contained so that it could be given as a gift to loved ones. Building on this soon after, and based on some ethnographic work with families with young children, Stevens et al. (2001, 2003) conceived of their "Living Memory Box." Again, mainly a concept rather than a working prototype, this device sought to archive and annotate a more diverse range of objects than Memory Box, but focused on parents with young children. Frohlich et al (2003), around that same time, suggested various ways in which the stories and ambient sounds associated with printed photographs might be captured and played back, such as through a specialized desk around which people can gather.

One can also imagine other ways in which objects in the home might be annotated with digital data in order to create narratives for others. Imagine for example, stumbling across your grandmother's voice as you open her jam book, or having it occasionally play back a story your mother told about your grandmother, or causing pictures of your grandmother to be displayed on your digital picture frame. Making such an explicit connection between objects and their associations might be either disturbing or delightful. Perhaps a more compelling possibility is thinking about other ways to share or pass down stories across generations. Here, one could imagine recording stories about objects that could be stored or accessed through paper or RFID tags attached to the objects in question. These could be played back using various different kinds of readers, as others have suggested in the past (Frohlich, 2004), or by using special places in the home such as shelves where objects trigger associated text messages, or sounds or images. Photos too can be associated with physical objects. More recent work by van den Hoven & Eggen (2008) proposed a system which uses souvenirs and mementos from holidays to bring up associated digital photos on a tablet. Clearly there is an interest in developing technologies in this space but efforts thus far have been somewhat limited to concepts or research probes.

Associating digital data with existing physical objects is one approach to designing new ways of archiving, but we can also consider new ways of giving digital objects physical form. For example, throughout our fieldwork and that of others (Petrelli & Whittaker, 2010), we have found that digital objects tend to be hidden away, with the consequence that it was usually physical objects that were displayed in order to draw attention to oneself, honor others, frame the family, and so on. Although digital picture frames go some way toward giving digital data a presence in the home in the way that physical pictures, photos, and artwork do, it seems plausible that in future, more diverse forms of digital display might find their way into people's homes. These might give us more choice about how digital objects can be given a different status in the home: to draw attention to them, to elevate them, and to make them points of discussion. One can imagine different kinds of situated displays that might for example, provide a dedicated space for materials relating to certain events, specific people, or specific times and places. These objects would then take on a new kind of persistence and establish a physical and social space within the household.

We have developed some concepts such as this in our own research group. For example, Shoebox is a concept which allows at once the digital storage of photos in a tangible box, which incorporates a display (Banks and Sellen, 2009, see Fig. 11.4). Different Shoeboxes might correspond to different events, like a wedding or a birthday, or belong to different people. Opening the top of the Shoebox and running one's finger along the top navigates through the collection, displaying those pictures on the embedded display. Shoebox thus provides a place where those pictures "live" but also allows users to browse through the collection in an easy, ad hoc way. Because they are tangible, self-contained objects (which could also be backed up to "the cloud") they can be grabbed in case of fire, arranged decoratively, or given as gifts.

Fig. 11.4 "Shoebox" by Richard Banks

TimeCard by Richard Banks and colleagues (see Odom et al., 2010a) is another physical display for the home, this time focused on honoring others. Timecard is a service coupled with an appliance (Fig. 11.5). The service component allows the user to create timelines around the life of someone they care about. They might, for example, create a timeline of their baby's development, or their grandfather's life. Once the timeline is created, the content is displayed in a dynamic digital photo frame kept in the home. Touching the Timecard zooms in on different images, scanned objects and so on that appear along the timeline. This kind of device allows households to reflect on someone's life, and create experiences that have sentimental value for a family, connecting to a shared past.

Fig. 11.5 "TimeCard" by Richard Banks

In addition to giving presence and drawing attention to objects, we also remarked on the various ways in which physical objects can be hidden or stored away out of sight. Some objects were kept in deep storage because they are highly personal; others because they are painful; and yet others because they are simply forgotten. It is interesting to speculate on how the design space for digital objects might be opened up by considering these aspects of the physical. First, it suggests that looser metaphors for storage, such as boxes as containers, might be more suitable for storing digital objects in the home than highly structured filing systems, such as is the norm in digital systems. Second, it was clear that people took often great delight in coming across collections of objects, or as one woman in our fieldwork put it — time capsules — that they might stumble across accidentally. This suggests that exploring ways of enabling new kinds of serendipitous display for digital objects, otherwise buried deep in collections, would be compelling (Petrelli et al. 2009). Of course, screen savers in a sense do this, but they tend not to be very rich, simply cycling through objects. It might be more interesting to be able to rummage through your heterogeneous digital collections in a more hands-on way. Equally, we can begin to think about ways in which digital materials might be compartmentalized in new ways, not simply in the sense of restricting access, but in ways that they can be bundled perhaps physically.

Fig. 11.6 "Back-Up Box" by Richard Banks

An obvious possibility here is the bundling of digital objects in a physical object that can be passed on almost like an heirloom, something we have written about elsewhere (Odom et al., 2010a; Kirk and Banks, 2008). With this in mind, we have built a number of more prototype concepts such as "Back-up Box" (Fig. 11.6). Back-Up Box is a way of storing Twitter feeds over the years, storing them as they are created in a separate, personal archive. By removing the lid of the box, users can browse through years of data, going back in time and touching on different items for reminiscing and reflection. Similar kinds of "technology heirlooms" might also archive social networking data, email, voicemails, blogs and the like. Overall, as we amass more and more personal digital information, we will have to look for new technological solutions to deal with the inheritance of not only physical but also digital materials and have a concern for how these artefacts of sentimentality, these cherished objects, should be treated to give them the significance and respect they deserve.

Conclusion

To conclude, this chapter has shown the archiving of digital and physical objects by families offers up a lens through which family life can be understood. People in families keep, hide, display, create and protect objects that spark special memories, or that say something about themselves as individuals. But, perhaps more significant, objects within homes say something profound about families: about the identity of a family, its connection to the past, the importance of different people within the sphere of the family, and how a family wants to be remembered in the future. All of this takes work, in the present, to realize these aspirations. But this is a special kind of work, not like office work, where, though efficiency matters, so too does the ability to capture new materials, to be creative with them, to manage presence and absence, to tell stories and to keep things safe. Further, we have seen that this kind of work underpins and helps construct the essence of what a home is. This is set about as an on-going concern, with different people in a household taking on different roles and responsibilities in that endeavor.

In the midst of all of this are the transformations brought about by new technologies, which act to shift and further disrupt an already ever-changing, dynamic set of practices. These new digital technologies are giving us the opportunity to capture more and more kinds of heterogeneous objects, existing in more places (or indeed in no one "place" at all), being reproduced, shared, and modified in ways we can no longer hope to control, or have complete awareness of. This chapter has tried to make the case that it is time to reflect on both the problems this may increasingly entail as well as the opportunities for design that these changes offer up. The point is that though many new technologies realize their value through both chance and co-evolution with users, when it comes to developing technologies for home archiving, we have an opportunity to make a difference through design which is sensitive to human values, and to the problems that we all currently face in dealing with our digital legacies. In other words, rather than to simply speculate on a future trajectory, we have an opportunity to steer that path. In some sense, then, the choice is ours as to whether archiving in the home of the future is a more complicated, burdensome and anxiety-ridden undertaking, or whether it sees us harnessing digital tools for greater creativity, flexibility and efficiency in connecting to our past and protecting the things that we care about.

References

Abowd, G. D., Gauger, M., & Lachenmann, A. (2003). The family video archive: An annotation and browsing environment for home movies. In *Proceedings of the 5th ACM SIGMM International Workshop on Multimedia Information Retrieval (MIR'03)*. ACM, New York, 1–8.

Appadurai, A. (Ed.) 1986. *The Social Life of Things*. Cambridge University Press.

Balabanovic, M., Chu, L. L., & Wolff, G. J. (2000). Storytelling with digital photographs. In *Proceedings of the SIGCHI Conference on Human Factors in Computing Systems (CHI'00)*. ACM, New York, 564–571.

Banks, R. & Sellen, A. (2009). Shoebox: Mixing storage and display of digital images in the home. In *Proceedings of the 3rd International Conference on Tangible and Embedded Interaction. (TEI'09)*. ACM, New York, 35–40.

Barthes, R. (2009). *Camera lucida: Reflections on photography*. Vintage Classics.

Bell, G. & Gemmell, J. (2009). *Total Recall: How the E-Memory Revolution Will Change Everything*. Dutton Books.

Belk, R. W., Wallendorf, M., & Sherry, J. F. (1989). The sacred and the profane in consumer behavior: Theodicy on the Odyssey. *J. Consumer Research*, *16*, 1, 1–38.

Brown, B.,A. Taylor, S. Izadi, A. Sellen, J. 'J.' Kaye and R. Eardley (2007). Locating Family Values: A Field Trial of the Whereabouts Clock. *Proc. Ubicomp 2007*.

Buckingham, D., Willett, R., & Pini, M. (2011). *Home Truths? Video production and domestic life*. The University of Michigan Press.

Chalfen, R. (1987). *Snapshot Versions of Life*. Bowling Green State University Popular Press.

Crabtree, A. & Rodden, T. (2004). Domestic routines and design for the home. *Journal of CSCW*, 13(2), 191-220.

Crabtree, A., Rodden, T., & Mariani, J. (2004). Collaborating around collections: Informing the continued development of photoware. In *Proceedings of the ACM Conference on Computer Supported Cooperative Work (CSCW'04)*. ACM, New York, 396–405.

Csikzentmilhalyi, M. & Rochberg-Halton, E. (1981). *The Meaning of Things: Domestic Symbols and the Self*. Cambridge University Press.

Datta, R., Li, J. & Wang, J. (2005). Content-based image retrieval: Approaches and trends of the new age. In *Proceedings of 7th ACM SIGMM (Multimedia Information Retrieval)*.

Douglas, M. & Isherwood, B. (1979). *The world of goods: Towards an anthropology of consumption*. Routledge.

Drazin, A. & Frohlich, D. (2007). Good intentions: Remembering through framing photographs in English homes. *Ethnos. 72*, 1, 51–76.

Durrant, A. (2010). *Family Portrayal: Photo displays and intergenerational relationships at home*. PhD Thesis. University of Surrey.

Durrant, A., Frohlich, D., Sellen, A. & Lyons, E. (2009). Home curation versus teenage photography: Photo displays in the family home. IJCHS, Special Issue on Collocated Social Practices Surrounding Photos (Lindley, S., Taylor, A., Kirk, A. & Durrant, A., Eds.). *Vol., 67, Issue 12*, 995-1112.

Frohlich, D.M. (2004). *Audiophotography: Bringing photos to life with sounds*. Kluwer Academic Publishers.

Frohlich D. & Murphy, R. (2000). The memory box. *Pers. Technol. 4*, 238–240.

Frohlich, D., Clancy, T., Robinson J., Costanza, E. (2003). The audiophoto desk. In *Proceedings of 2AD, Second International Conference on Appliance Design*, 11–13th May 2004, Bristol

Frohlich, D. M., Kuchinsky, A., Pering, C., Don, A., & Ariss, S. (2002). Requirements for photoware. In *Proceedings of the ACM Conference on Computer Supported Cooperative Work. (CSCW'02)*. ACM, New York, 166–175.

Gemmell, J., Bell, G., & Lueder, R. (2006). MyLifeBits: A personal database for everything. *Comm. ACM 49*, 88–95.

Glenn, J. r& Hayes, C. (2007). *Taking Things Seriously*. Princeton Architectural Press.

Harper, R. (Ed) (2003). *Inside the Smart Home: Interdisciplinary perspectives on the design and shaping of domestic computing*. Springer Verlag, London and Heidleberg.

Hendon, J. A. (2000). Having and holding: Storage, memory, knowledge, and social relations. *Amer. Anthrop. 102*, 1, 42–53.

Hodges, S., Williams, L., Berry, E., Izadi, S., Srinivasan, J., Butler, A., Smyth, G., Kapur, N., & Wood, K. (2006). SenseCam: A retrospective memory aid. In *Proceedings of Ubicomp*. Lecture Notes in Computer Science, Springer 177–193.

Hoskins, J. (1998). *Biographical Objects: How Things Tell the Stories of People's Lives*. Routledge.

Kientz, J. & Abowd, G. (2009). KidCAm: Toward and effective technology for hte capture of children's moments of interest. *Proceedings of Pervasive '09*.

Kindberg, T., Spasojevic, M., Fleck, R. & Sellen, A. (2005). The ubiquitous camera: An in-depth study of camera phone use. *IEEE Pervasive Computing, Vol. 4(2)*, pp. 42-50.

Kirk, D. S. & Banks, R. (2008). On the design of technology heirlooms. In *Proceedings of the International Workshop on Social Interaction and Mundane Technologies (SIMTech'08)*.

Kirk, D. & Sellen, A. (2010). On human remains: Value and practice in the home archiving of cherished objects. *ACM Transactions on Computer-Human Interaction, Vol. 17(3), July. 2010*.

Kirk, D. S., Sellen, A.,Harper, R., & Wood, K. (2007). Understanding videowork. In *Proceedings of the SIGCHI Conference on Human Factors in Computing Systems (CHI'07)*. ACM, New York, 61–70.

Kirk, D. S., Sellen, A.,Rother, C., & Wood, K. (2006). Understanding photowork. In *Proceedings of the SIGCHI Conference on Human Factors in Computing Systems (CHI'06)*. ACM, New York, 761–770.

Kirk, D., Izadi, S., Sellen, A., Taylor, S., & Banks, R. (2010). Opening up the family archive. *Proceedings of CSCW 2010*.

Massimi, M., William Odom, Richard Banks, and David Kirk (2011). Matters of life and death: locating the end of life in lifespan-oriented HCI research, In *Proceedings of the 2011 annual conference on Human factors in computing systems* Association for Computing Machinery, Inc.

Mauss, M. (1954). *The Gift*. Routledge Classics.

Middleton, D. & Brown, S. D. (2005). *The Social Psychology of Experience: Studies in Remembering and Forgetting*. Sage Publications.

Miller, D. (Ed.) (2001). *Home Possessions. Material Culture Behind Closed Doors*. Berg.

Miller, D. (Ed.) (2008). *The Comfort of Things*. Polity Press.

Moran, J. (2002). *There's no place like home video*. University of Minnesota Press.

O'Brien, J. & Rodden, T. (1997). Interactive systems in domestic environments. *Proc. DIS '97*, ACM, New York, NY, 247-259.

Odom, W., Richard Banks, and David Kirk (2010a). Reciprocity, deep storage and letting go: Opportunities for designing interactions with inherited digital materials. In *Interactions, Volume 17, Issue 5*, Association for Computing Machinery, Inc.

Odom, W., Harper, R., Sellen, A., Kirk, D. S., & Banks, R. (2010b). Passing on & putting to rest: Understanding bereavement in the context of interactive technologies. In *Proceedings of SIGCHI Conference on Human Factors in Computing Systems (CHI'10)*. ACM, New York, 1831–1840.

Odom, W., Zimmerman, J., & Forlizzi, J. (2011). Teenagers and their virtual possessions: Design opportunities and issues. *Proceedings of CHI '11*.

Oleksik, G., Frohlich, D., Brown, L. M., & Sellen, A. (2008). Sonic interventions: understanding and extending the domestic soundscape. In *Proceedings of the SIGCHI Conference on Human Factors in Computing Systems (CHI'08)*. ACM, New York, 1419–1428

Petrelli, D., Whittaker, S., & Brockmeier, J. (2008). Autotopography: What can physical mementos tell us about digital memories. In *Proceedings of the SIGCHI Conference on Human Factors in Computing Systems. (CHI'08)*. ACM, New York, 53–62.

Petrelli, D., Van den Hoven, E., & Whittaker, S. (2009). Making history: Intentional capture of future memories. In *Proceedings of the 27th International Conference on Human Factors in Computing Systems (CHI'09)*. ACM, New York. 1723–1732.

Petrelli, D. & Whittaker, S. (2010). Family memories in the home: Contrasting physical and digital mementos. In *Personal and Ubiquitous Computing, Vol. 14(2)*.

Plaisant, C., Clamage, A., Hutchinson, H. B., Bederson, B. B., and Druin, A. (2006). Shared family calendars: Promoting symmetry and accessibility. *ACM Trans. Comput.-Hum. Interact. 13, 3* (Sep. 2006), 313-346.

Rodden, K. & Wood, K. R. (2003). How do people manage their digital photographs? In *Proceedings of the SIGCHI Conference on Human Factors in Computing Systems (CHI'03)*. ACM, New York. 409–416.

Sarvas, R. & Frohlich, D. (2011). *From snapshots to social media: The changing picture of domestic photography*. London: Springer.

Sellen, A., Harper, R., Eardley, R., Izadi, S., Regan, T., Taylor, A., & Wood, K. (2006). HomeNote: Supporting situated messaging in the home. In *Proceedings of the 20th Anniversary Conference on Computer Supported Cooperative Work (CSCW'06)*. ACM, New York, 383–392.

Sellen, A. A. J. Hyams, J., & Eardley, R. (2004). *The everyday problems of working parents: Implications for new technologies*. Hewlett-Packard Labs Technical Report HPL-2004-37.

Sengers, P. and Gaver, W. (2006). Staying open to interpretation: Engaging multiple meanings in design and evaluation. *Proc. DIS 2006*.

Sontag, S. (1979). *On photography*. Penguin Press.

Stevens, M.M., Abowd, G. D.,Truong, K. N. & Vollmer, F. (2003). Getting into the Living Memory Box: Family archives and holistic design. *Pers. Ubiq. Comput. 7*, 210–216.

Stevens, M. M., Roberts, J., Bandlow, A. & Newstetter, W. (2001). *Capturing memories: An investigation of how parents record and archive items about their child*. GVU Center Tech. rep. GIT-GVU-01-18.

Taylor, A. & Swan, L. 2005. Artful systems in the home. In *Proceedings of the SIGCHI Conference on Human Factors in Computing Systems (CHI'05)*. ACM, New York. 641–650.

Taylor, A. S., Swan, L., & Durrant, A. (2007). Designing family photo displays. In *Proceedings of ECSCW'07*. Springer-Verlag. 179–198.

Taylor, A. S., & Harper, R. (2003). The gift of the gab: a design oriented sociology of young people's use of mobiles. *Journal of Computer Supported Cooperative Work (JCSCW)*, 12(3), 267-296.

Turkle, S. (Ed.) (2007). *Evocative Objects: Things We Think With*. MIT Press, Cambridge, MA.

Van Dijck, J. (2007). *Mediated Memories in the Digital Age*. Stanford University Press.

Van den Hoven, E. & Eggen, B. (2008). Informing Augmented Memory System design through Autobiographical Memory theory. *Personal and Ubiquitous Computing journal, Vol. 12*, No. 6, pp. 433-443.

Chapter 12
Absence and Family Life: Understanding and Supporting Adaption to Change

William Odom, Richard Harper, Abigail Sellen, Jodi Forlizzi, John Zimmerman, Richard Banks, and Dave Kirk

Introduction

What and who a family is, is continually changing. Family is a place, an ever changing set of social relationships, an evolving archive of precious artefacts and the actions collectively unfolding that bring all of these elements into meaningful cohesion. Over space and time familial structure shifts; it expands, contracts, solidifies and dissolves. As people grow older, family members may grow apart, move away, craft a new family with another spouse, or experience the loss of those that once were core to the family's foundation. In any circumstances, and perhaps especially these, characterizing and understanding family life is complex. What is certain is significant and diverse work is done by a family to adapt to unfolding changes, and the practices and processes though which this work is achieved is partly constitutive of the evolving idea of family itself. While the ways members of a family personally and collectively work to adapt to unfolding changes are heterogeneous, it is clear that interactive technology is becoming a common part of the fabric of this kind of work.

Not surprisingly, there has been a growing interest in the human-computer interaction (HCI) community over how technology can improve the lives of families. Researchers have explored a range of issues such as the coordination and scheduling of domestic activities (e.g. Neustaedter et al., 2009), the work of families to creatively design their own routines and support tools (e.g. Taylor and Swan, 2005), how core familial relationships are supported across distances (e.g. Williams et al. 2008, and in this collection, Lindley et al.), and the ways in which technology could be better designed to support the values of families (see for example, Strain, in Harper Ed, 2003; also Brown et al. 2007). This body of work has nearly all focused on understanding and designing for intact families. Little work has embraced the very real and evolving problems that many families must face and work through when being in touch is a difficulty: when families break up or threaten to do so, for

W. Odom (✉)
Carnegie Mellon University, Pittsburgh, PA, USA

R. Harper (ed.), *The Connected Home: The Future of Domestic Life*,
DOI 10.1007/978-0-85729-476-0_12, © Springer-Verlag London 2011

whatever reason. In these instances, 'family' is indeed an idea that turns around the concept of togetherness, but on occasion this very idea slips out of the hands of those involved even as they try and make it real. Divorce, trial separations, break-up and of course bereavement are as much constituents of the family as their converse – binding, solidarity, continuity. Broadening our understanding of what it means to design for 'family' as its structures and relationships shift in these respects over time remains relatively unaddressed.

Aims

In this chapter, we present two cases of field research related to the work families do to adapt to experiences and circumstances following a divorce or bereavement. As we will discuss, taking a closer look at how families adapt to circumstances following these events provides salient insights and foundational points from which a more holistic understanding of the work families undertake can be developed. In both cases, families must work to adapt to the changes that come with these events and it is the very nature of how this work unfolds that shapes the patterning and texture of family identity, structure and organization. Drawing on rich descriptions from our fieldwork, we describe how the design space might be better sensitized to support the social processes that unfold after a divorce or the loss of a loved one with a critical eye towards future technologies in and around the home. A particular goal is to explore how technologies might be designed to support the shifting social organization, practices and needs of families as they adapt to experiences of absence.

In what follows, we first present research we conducted with divorced families. This is then followed by a description of fieldwork conducted with participants who have lost close family members (and in a few cases close friends). In each section, we present related literature, draw on select rich cases of field evidence to illustrate our findings, and then interpret these findings in the context of research and design opportunities and issues. These sections draw on prior work that the first author conducted at separate times, in different places. The research on divorced families was conducted in the United States. The research on bereavement was conducted in the United Kingdom. In both cases, this research is reworked and described within the broader framing of the chapter. This chapter concludes with some remarks on the broader design opportunity and issue areas collectively emerging across these cases as we consider the role of smart technology in (and across) domestic sites of family life now and into the future.

The Case of Divorce: Motivation and Framing

One can start making the case that fragmentation is an important feature by high-lighting the fact that millions of families are affected by divorce. In the US Census report of 2005, for example, 40% of all marriages end in divorce, over half of which have children (US Census report, 2005). At that time 32% of children in the United States live away from one of their parents due to divorce or spousal separation). It is likely that these figures will have worsened since then and even if they have not they remain very striking. Even before that time, the evidence showed that children growing up in a home in which their father is absent are significantly more likely to experience teen pregnancy, commit suicide, drop out of school, abuse drugs or go to jail (US Dept of Health, 1999). In divorced families, parents face a range of functional and social challenges associated with adapting to a new life without their ex-spouse. However, their children are most at risk for critical problems associated with adjusting to a post-divorce reality (Amanto, 2001).

When a family divorces, they often suffer an economic downturn as they begin to adapt to maintaining the cost of two homes. However, a breakdown in parent-child relationships appears to have the most negative affect on children (Amanto, 2004). Prior research has shown that *co-parenting*, where parents seek consensus on child raising issues and appear as a united front to their children can mitigate some negative outcomes associated with divorce (Cowan et al., 1996; Kelly, 1997; McCale 1997). Researchers have noted that actions reinforcing family integrity and the appearance of parents as a united front on "corrective action", despite the absence of a central home or familial unit, are particularly beneficial for children (McHale, 1997). Nonetheless, co-parenting remains difficult to sustain because the divorce process often exacerbates the underlying hostility that lead to the divorce in the first place (Amanto 2004). This same research indicated that it was common for parents to undermine one another's authority in reaction to hostility and underlying moral conflicts, providing further barriers to co-parenting.

Coordination and Scheduling

Divorce and the breaking up of parental relationships are not the only concern, however. When people separate, the logistics of family life become even more complex. Unfortunately, these logistics are typically already very complicated in family life. Recent research in the HCI community has indicated that mobile phones and computers emerge as primary mediums of communication for parents in divorced families (Yarosh et al., 2009) and one very likely reason for this is that these technologies are necessary tools for practical affairs of 'doing family', irrespective of the legal or emotional standing of the adults involved.

The lives of busy families have been characterized as a state of constant "rush hour" (Frissen, 1999). As they balance diverse daily responsibilities, families can experience feelings of being controlled by their schedules and of being out of control when breakdowns occur (Beech et al., 2003; Darrah et al., 2001; Davidoff et al., 2006). These busy families tend to be aggressive adopters of 'smart' technologies that can aid them in managing their daily logistical challenges (Darrah et al. 2001; Frissen 1999). More recently, research has explored how new technologies can help these kinds of families feel more in control of their lives (Davidoff et al., 2010).

The HCI community has had a focus on how technology can help busy families manage their responsibilities and gain more flexibility. Researchers have looked at reminder systems at key locations in the home (Kim et al. 2004) as well as smart devices, such as a child's activity bag that can sense its contents and communicate when something is missing (Park et al. 2010). As mentioned above, digital calendaring systems and other technologies have been another large area of inquiry, particularly in terms of how they might better enable family members to access family information at various locations in and outside of the home (e.g. Neustaedter et al. 2009, Brown et al., 2007). Recent work has also speculated on how smart systems can learn the routines of busy families in order to provide more support for planning and improvization around deviations in routines (Davidoff et al., 2010).

The absence of parents living together, and the necessity to transport children and their things across two houses, clearly creates additional difficult challenges for divorced families. First, more detailed planning needs to take place to ensure children fluidly move from house to house along with the possessions needed for their daily activities. Second, the ability to react to unexpected situations as they unfold has typically been addressed through improved communication. In divorced families, parents often attempt to limit direct communication as it can lead to hostility (Amanto, 2004). There appears to be an opportunity to support key work commonly undertaken by divorced families through new kinds of domestic and mobile technologies that are sensitive to their conflicts, and that connect scheduling with parental responsibility, with transportation of children and equipment as they move in, between and around multiple domestic environments.

Identity and Place

If logistics are one concern, muddled by the wilfulness of individuals trying to undermine the practical arrangements of others (namely, their former spouses), these same logistics are made all the more tender by the fact that the physical circumstances of family life are endowed with emotion. It is a commonplace to say that people develop attachments to the places they inhabit but the power and vitality of this emotional connection can be great and this is often highlighted when families strain. Prior research has speculated that people tend to perceive the home as the most significant place where family life unfolds, grows and is nurtured (Proshansky, 1983; Csikszenthmihalyi et al. 1981; Fitzpatrick et al. 1995). For children and teenagers, the place with the strongest attachment is most often their bedroom (Chawla 1992). In their bedrooms, children tend to surround themselves with their most precious possessions, representing a material infrastructure where they can experiment with their identity through their display of self to their parents and friends (and self also) (Steele & Brown, 1995). Accessing and displaying media such as music, movies and celebrities, etc. has been documented as a central practice children and teenagers draw on to take ownership of their bedroom space and communicate their values and desires (Bovil & Livingstone 2001).

Interestingly, virtually no research exists on bedroom culture for children in divorced homes, and little is known about how they make sense of and exert control over the different domestic environments they inhabit. What is clear is they cannot easily move all of their possessions between two homes each time they move. At the same time, interactions with digital media and technology have become a key part of young people's lives around the world and well-established fixtures of their culture (Ito et al., 2010). This begins to raise several interesting questions for HCI researchers: In what ways do children in joint custody situations perceive differences between their personal places across two domestic environments? How do children reconcile the absence of a single, central domestic location? What resources do they draw on to support these practices? What roles could smart technologies play in potentially better enabling children to construct a sense of place across two houses?

Method

It was with these questions in mind that we recruited 13 divorced families from a mid-sized city in the United States. Our goal was to see what we could learn from an in-depth investigation of the strained life of these families. Participants included one parent and one or more children from each family. We interviewed a total of 13 parents and a total of 46 children whose ages ranged from 10-17. The occupations of parents ranged from secretary to school teacher to IT project manager to hotel manager. All families had joint custody arrangements. In 11 families the children typically spent equal time at each parent's home. Interviews were conducted in participants' homes and lasted between 1.5 to 2.5 hours. They began with parents and children together to collect basic information such as the ages of the children, the number of years since the divorce, and the general visitation models. We then split up and interviewed the parent and participating child (or children) separately. We chose to separate the parent and children so they would feel free to share details and raise issues and concerns they may have been uncomfortable speaking about in front of each other.

We used a semi-structured interview approach. Questions for parents were designed to elicit reflections about how their lives had changed since the divorce, the routines that now characterize their everyday lives, how they communicate with their children (when together and separated), how parents coordinate with each other and with children, how children's living conditions were perceived to be different in each home (e.g. bedroom and rules), and the key things children typically took when they moved between homes. Interviews with children usually took place in their bedrooms with the aim of developing a better understanding of their everyday lives, experiences of transitioning between homes, common activities, cherished physical and digital possessions, technology usage trends, and key differences between the social and material arrangements of both homes.

We videotaped the interviews and took field notes, capturing reflections of the individual interviewers. Interviews were transcribed and thematically organized. We coded the textual documents and field notes using methods modeled after Strauss and Corbin (1990). These methods involve identifying key themes in the data and creating conceptual models to illustrate relationships among emergent themes in the data. In addition, we created affinity diagrams using sticky notes to find unexpected connections across participants.

When describing data collected from field observations with families, we refer to participants by their role—Mom, Dad, S (Son), D (Daughter)—followed by a number indicating the family. In the case of children, the reference includes a second number indicating the child's age. For example D2-10 would stand for a 10-year-old daughter from family 2.

Select Findings

The Communication and Coordination of Post-divorce Family Life

In nearly all the families we interviewed, parents had moved on to a life in which their ex-spouse was largely absent. But this word hardly conveys the moral complexity of what is involved. Though divorced parents might be physically separate from each other for most of the time, they do meet, occasionally; they have to drop off and pick up children for example. By absence is meant moral absence – a systematic and purposeful way of demonstrating and achieving a symbolic distance. Separation, even after the courts have adjudicated, needs to be worked at, day in day out. Most of our subjects avoided verbal communication with prior spouses, for example. All too often it would result in conflicts and uncomfortable social exchanges. As a case in point, Mom2 proudly proclaimed that after 15 years of being divorced, she still was unaware of her ex-spouse's phone number. In some cases, parents attempted to fill communicative gaps by sending messages related to co-parenting issues through children. This child-as-mediator approach was reported to be largely unsuccessful. In 2 of the families (F2 and F4) the paternal grandmother played the role as mediator, nearly always stepping in as a proxy for the Dad in communications with the Mom.

Nonetheless, parents still had to maintain some form of communication in order to manage their joint custody arrangement. Parents in our study most often relied on text messaging and emails. The asynchronous nature of these technologically mediated exchanges appeared to mitigate some of the problems associated with verbal and physical interaction to varying extents. We found that most parents used text messaging for improvizational purposes to handle unanticipated events that could manifest on any given day. Emails emerged as the main form of textual communication. It had two main purposes: (i) planning the logistics of children's everyday lives, and (ii) discussing broader issues, such as longer allocations of time a parent wanted to schedule with children (e.g. vacations) and decisions affecting a child's future requiring consensus from both parents. Importantly, our interviews with parents all either explicitly or implicitly suggested the coordinated work of successfully completing mundane logistical tasks was essential in constructing scaffolding to support parents' higher-level work of developing consensus related to the long term goals they held for their children.

Benefits and Complications of Shared Digital Calendaring

In addition to emails and text message, all families used some form of calendar to structure and schedule their lives. Parents' lack of frequent (if ever) collocation, shifting familial, personal, and professional schedules, and strained social interactions collectively complicated the use of paper calendars, however; all but one family (F1) in our sample reported relying on shared digital calendar systems. Whereas electronic messaging had the advantage of keeping spouses apart, digital calendars had the curious effect of helping bring them together, at least in terms of orientations around the kids. For example, several parents reported how collaboratively coordinating weekly events opened a space to build consensus on deeper issues. Consider Dad11's reflection:

> *Recently we had to figure out the dates of a music camp my son wants to go to this summer and once we did, we started thinking together about whether he's spending too much time playing the drums and not enough time on school, because he hasn't been doing great. ...We decided to let him go to the camp over the summer if he pulls his grades up.*

We also encountered several instances in which parents' observations of their ex-spouse's individual work to plan new events on the calendar played a subtle yet important role in shaping perceptions of collective investment in the co-parenting relationship. Mom10 provides an exemplary reflection exemplifying this emergent unobtrusive value:

> *...I feel like in some ways it helped build trust between us ...because I can see when he also updates it ...and it doesn't usually mean I have to do anything but I like knowing about it because it makes me recognize we're both doing things to make it work*

This sample of instances highlights some of the often subtle ways in which the work of using a shared digital space shaped parents' perception of each other and in part helped to fortify an often shaky foundation from which consensus could be built on parenting issues.

Digital calendars could undermine any move towards a renewed solidarity, though. Parents reported instances in which shared calendars complicated the goal of co-parenting, particularly when private information was accidentally shared. A classic example of this came in Mom9's description of her ex-spouse's Alcoholics Anonymous meetings and dates with this new partner mistakenly appeared on the digital calendar displayed in, among other places, Mom9's home. This mismanagement of information eventually led to her ex-spouse permanently refusing to use the shared calendar, which resulted in, "the kids missing things they didn't before because it's easy to get everything confused again." Several other parents, both Moms and Dads, reported the accidental appearance of dates scheduled with new partners in their shared family calendars led to a range of undesirable outcomes with their respective ex-spouse. Collectively, these instances illustrate how problematic situations can arise when information about a parent's post-divorce identity collides with a shared space in which they are continuing to enact their on-going role as parent. They additionally begin to make clear that an important aspect of the work of post-divorce family life may very well have to do with better supporting ex-spouses' balancing of their role as parent to their children, while they continue to develop their own personal identities in a new or altered setting.

Breakdowns in Transitioning: Avoiding the Routine Absence of Children's Things

Despite many planning and coordinative efforts (or perhaps in part due to interpersonal tensions that emerged around them), we observed it was occasionally hard for divorced parents to know who was responsible at any given time. The absence of a single unified domestic space required children and parents to move an ongoing diverse and evolving assortment of artefacts between homes. Not surprisingly, the most common breakdown all families reported owed to key artefacts being left behind. For example children commonly forgot to take long-term homework projects, which typically started in one home, but needed to be finished or turned in from the other. Other forgotten items included children's personal possessions used on a daily basis (e.g. iPod, backpack), activity specific clothing (e.g. swimsuits) and activity specific equipment (e.g. golf clubs).

Making sure this changing assortment of artefacts routinely moved between homes appeared to serve important functions for both parents and children. In particular, several parents reported that children having shared activities across both homes (e.g. biking in the neighborhood, camping in the backyard) provided parents with a shared set of experiences, which could serve as productive framing mechanisms for social exchanges and further fortify a foundation to support co-parenting activities. For example, Dad13 reflects on how his kids' practice of occasionally biking at both homes helps facilitate social exchanges with his ex-wife:

> *Having something the kids do at both of our homes is good. It makes it easier to start out [talking]. ...Sometimes we do end up talking for a little while. It's good for us to start to get back on the same page.*

However, these kinds of artefacts appeared particularly prone to being forgotten as they were uncomfortably situated outside of the core set of everyday equipment transitioning with children across homes, while at the same time often used in impromptu ways that did not necessitate the scheduling of a 'formal' event. In general, the breakdown in transitioning any artefact caused problems for parents, requiring them to make repeated trips between homes, if the artefact could be located at all. Many parents reported breakdowns leading to on-going conflicts with their ex-spouse, while feeling powerless to keep track of the presence and absence of every artefact in, or revolving around, their home. Breakdowns also further magnified the differences between parents' homes, which in some cases caused children to call the other parent, pleading to return back to her or his home.

We observed families adopting several different strategies to avoid routine absences of key artefacts. One coping approach was to purchase multiple versions of the same item. For example, in F5 and F11 the children had almost all the same toys and books at both homes, including expensive toys such as bicycles. F2 represented an extreme case where D2-17 was not allowed to move her clothing between the two homes. When she arrived at her paternal grandmother's home (the home where her father resides), she was expected to immediately change into clothes for that home.

Another strategy we observed was parents staging key objects needed to support children's inevitable transition. While they varied in content and location, the organizing spaces were areas in which artefacts that transitioned with children were informally stored and cataloged. Oftentimes these areas had lists posted that were used in part to help make kids responsible for keeping track of their own personal possessions, which also served as rough checklists for parents as kids entered and exited the home. In addition to their utility, these spaces also supported social rituals for parents as they prepared to part with their children for the next few days before they returned. Typically parents used this time to discuss key activities associated with children's assorted packed possessions and assured children of their imminent return back to the parent's domestic space. When these staging interactions proceeded smoothly, they provided parents with positive reinforcement related to their domestic parenting practices and children with a better understanding of transitions in their upcoming schedule. However, parents reported these staging rituals were often disrupted as they rushed to find objects absent from the final checklist.

Making Home(s) Following a Divorce

A core tension that emerged between parents had to do with how shared domestic possessions were divided between the two households. Sentimental artefacts owning to children's lives were often the most contentious point of argument. In some cases parents had come to consensus over who would receive which artefacts. However, in most families, one parent typically retained the vast majority of these kinds of possessions, which were often prominently present around their home. These imbalances in presence and absence of pre-divorce family heirlooms often magnified children's perceived differences between parents' homes, which could fuel further conflict between parents. S10–13, who splits time equally between households, describes this distinction in relation to his Dad's home:

> "There's nothing that makes me think of home there. ...like there's nothing of us ...around or on the walls."

Mom10 has no intention of giving up these things in spite of the emergent tensions with her ex-husband:

> "He doesn't like it now but he didn't want anything when we got divorced and now they're part of my home ...I can't just split them up now."

In an extreme case, parents in F11 had been unable to come to an agreement and resigned to rotate precious artefacts, such as the children's artwork, on a bi-monthly basis. Parents would often archive new objects made by their children by taking digital photos, and in some cases, they reported emailing copies to the corresponding parent.

When describing other ways in which domestic artefacts and spaces differed in parents' homes, shifts in content of domestic photo displays emerged as a key theme.

Nearly all parents reported that photos exclusively featuring their ex-spouse were intentionally absent from view (although most reported they still retained possession and had buried them away in boxes and closets). In general, photo displays had nearly exclusively migrated to focus on children, and to a lesser extent friends and relatives of the parent. Interestingly, many parents did display photos of their kids engaged in activities that their ex-spouse had organized; some of which even contained the ex-spouse. These included images of vacations, baseball games, and even backyard events. Displaying these types of photos in parents' households was generally viewed as a productive, unobtrusive way of projecting support for children across homes. Mom7 reflects on her photo display that prominently features her kids in a range of activities:

My ex is in some of them, he even took some of these [photos]. ...He has some of me too. ...Our connection is the kids, so it's ok to see him like this. ...[The kids'] lives are different enough between our places, and we want to support them, so this is some way of trying to do that.

When parents were probed about how they obtained these photos, oftentimes they reported a similar type of photo exchange through email. Dad13 describes the value of these exchanges:

Every once in a while I would send a photo of the kids as a gesture, and get one back here and there. ...It ended up being something we could do that didn't have all the stress of getting through the next week associated with it. ...it was something positive we had to relate to.

This kind of photo exchange emerged as a subtle practice that offered potential to help facilitate productive interactions between parents not explicitly focused on the logistics of coordination and scheduling. This practice had the advantage of not requiring actual articulation; written or spoken words were not always required, for example (though they were sometimes sent, depending on the state of relations for those involved). Importantly, these digital-mediated interactions, as well as the resulting photo archives, worked to provide parents with a broader perspective on the outcomes of their on-going co-parenting efforts; on their former spouse. This perspective could be cultivated in morally neutral ground, where images taken and shared could provide resources for informed guesses about a previous partner's intentions and ability.

The Work of Children to Construct Identity and Cohesion Across 'Homes'

A key problem children in joint custody families commonly face is a lack of the same resources and spaces in both homes. This can include differing technological setups, the absence of cherished possessions, and, in some cases, even the absence of a bedroom. In the bedrooms we did encounter, children revealed a range of material possessions valued as deeply significant. These things included photographs of family and friends, artefacts created by other friends (e.g. pillowcase signed by friends), self-made artefacts (e.g. pottery), mementos owing to various trips, and objects symbolic of personal achievement (e.g. trophies, scout badges). Children expressed strong conflicts over only having access to these possessions when in one location; the unavailability of these key things worked to amplify differences between their parents' homes. D11–14 describes a bulletin board of memorabilia owing to her friends in her bedroom at Dad's place:

> It's something I love. It reminds me of all my friends and I look at it and add things to it. It's a relaxing thing I do. ...At Mom's I can't. My room there isn't so comfortable, no one else stays there but it doesn't feel like mine. ...I want to see [Mom] but I'm also usually wanting to get back [to Dads]. ...I wish I could bring it over to my room there but there's no way.

This quote helps illustrate some of the complexities of children's desire to construct some sense of material and social cohesion across two houses. Similar to D11-14, most children expressed a desire to carry these material possessions across both domestic settings, but obvious physical constraints made this largely impossible.

Digital technologies of various kinds offered workarounds of various kinds, as well as new opportunities for constructing place. Our interviews made it clear that children perceived their personal digital devices to be significant possessions. The majority of children in our sample owned personal camera phones, media/music players and thumb drives. Several also owned digital cameras and some had access to personal laptops. These devices typically traveled with them everywhere they went, and they were always kept close.

We found children appropriated their various personal devices to mobilize extensive archives of digital photos, which included images of friends and family, vacations, popular culture, and, interestingly, digital copies of cherished physical possessions. In some cases, archives of photos had been curated in their mobile form in and across several devices as participants had been transitioning between homes. One participant reported possessing over 400 images of school friends on her phone. Many had over 100 digital photos in archives that moved with them between homes. In general our participants appeared to deeply value having their mobile archives near them, even when not in direct use.

We encountered several instances in which participants leveraged the immediacy of these archives to cope with differences between homes. For example, Dad9's home had very few family photos, which his children brought up as a key distinction between homes. S9-12 and S9-14 described several instances in which they used their iPods to make digital photos present at Dad9's:

> S9-14:   [Dad's] house doesn't have any of the old photos of us. ...Mom has them all. In books and in our home. ...I took some [pictures] of them on my phone.
> S9-12:   And I have some [photos] from our trips [with Dad] on my iPod.

These acts compensated for the lack of key familial artefacts and, in doing so, opened a space for collective reflection on different pre and, importantly, post-divorce trips the family had taken, an outcome that appeared productive, if not critical, to moving on with life after a divorce.

We observed that children also relied on their devices to make digital copies of precious physical objects, which were often constrained to their bedroom in one parent's home. Several participants described making these copies present at the parents' home in which they were unavailable. For example, S9-14 describes a virtual proxy of his latest lacrosse award:

> I've been playing lacrosse for a long time and I've won some trophies. Like I got best defenseman. ...[Dad] doesn't go to many games and you know doesn't come over here. I didn't know if he knew I won. ...I took [a picture] on my phone to show him.

Uploading virtual proxies of precious physical objects to social networking sites also emerged as a key practice employed by children; in several instances it appeared to result in new values being attributed to these things. In what represents a classic example of this phenomenon, D10-15 describes the impetus for uploading an image of her prized pillowcase:

> All my friends signed it, it reminds me of them. It's a big part of my room [at Mom's house]. ...I don't have anything like it in my room [at Dad's house] and it's too fragile to take. ...I took a picture of it and put it up on Facebook and my friends that signed it commented on it. It's pretty special. ...When I'm [at Dad's] at least I can go there and look at it [online] and see what they wrote.

Similarly, 3 children had digitized objects of personal achievement (e.g. trophies, framed certificate, Boy Scout badges) and uploaded these photos to Facebook. A particularly compelling instance of this centered on S11-15's practice of meticulously updating his online photo archive of Boy Scout badges in order to present them to both parents across both homes. Dad11 reflects on an emergent benefit of his son's digital archive:

> The kids don't see much of [my ex-wife and I] together. ...even though we're not friends [on Facebook] we could both see his badge photos and congratulate him on the new ones together ...because we're both friends with him [on Facebook]. I think it was good for him, that we could both support him. ...the kids don't get enough of that.

These instances collectively illustrate how children leveraged their social networking sites to make virtual proxies of key material possessions accessible across domestic spheres and, in F11's case, work to open a space where parents could engage in the practice of collectively congratulating their son on achievements despite rarely speaking to each other.

Online Places and the Work to Construct Cohesion in Transition

Nearly all of the children were frequent users of social networking sites, such as Facebook and MySpace. This in itself is perhaps not surprising; there is an abundance of emerging research documenting pervasiveness of social media and technology use among youth across demographic boundaries (e.g. Ito et al. 2009). What we want to highlight is the ways these children, in their particular circumstances, tended to describe their relationships with online places. This may be contrasted with research on the use of social network sites by children in stable families – discussed for example by Boyd, (2011) and Harper, (2010). In those circumstances social networks were used as a means to keep Mum and Dad out (of the social network world such as the child's own Facebook account); in our corpus, the reverse was the case.

More specifically, a key emergent theme in their reflections owed to comfort that appeared to be provided by having some sense of a consistent place in which they could reach family and friends despite their perpetual state of transitioning between and around two homes. D11-14 provides an exemplary comparison of the reliability of her Facebook page in relation to a life sometimes fraught with unpredictable transitions:

In a way it's like somewhere that's always the same...it's kind of always there and doesn't change and I can go there when I need it no matter where I'm at, because sometimes our schedule changes and I don't even know where I'm going to be.

The reliability of these online places coupled with the ability to augment them to reflect changes in personal identity appeared to play a significant role in the work of many of our participants as they reconciled how to construct a sense of home and personal place across two houses. For example, consider S10-13's reflection on managing his MySpace page:

I have to take my clothes and things between [Mom and Dad's] a few times a week so I never put stuff away. ...[the rooms] don't really feel like mine because I'm not there long enough to make it feel like my own. ...I like my [MySpace] page because I can control the way it looks and change it. If I feel in a different mood ...I can change the music and the colors. I spend a lot of time on it, so what I have on it is important to me and I like I can always find it.

Collectively, these instances are exemplary of how several children drew on technology as a resource to engage with both parents on their own terms, which worked to bridge communicative gaps between households often characterized by strained post-divorce social relations.

Adaptation in the Face of Absence: From Divorce to Loss

We can see then what are some of the complex needs and requirements imposed on members of divorced families as each person - not just the disputing spouses - have to work through the challenges of adapting to a new social organization. All of the participants, in one way or another, have to construct a productive post-divorce future. Adults work to maintain their social role as a parent, while they have to reconcile a newfound identity in the absence of their former spouse. Children develop strategies and coping mechanisms to construct some sense of cohesions as they move between two often socially and materially unsettled environments. The work we observed by all members is both supported and complicated by technology; and indeed these findings suggest several implications for better supporting the diverse social processes and needs that unfold after a divorce. A clear lesson from the case of divorce is how essential it is for families to adapt when their structures shift and evolve.

We now turn to the case of bereavement to better understand the delicate social processes that unfold after a family *permanently* loses one of its members. Here our concern, as it is with divorced and broken families, is to better understand the social organization of families as they go through the process of dealing with bereavement and also, how digital technologies might aid or constrain in this. Ultimately our aim is to offer direction for design – and we shall see, we then conclude by remarking on how the HCI design space might be better sensitized to support family members' personal and collective work to adapt to the occasioned or the permanent absence of a loved one.

The Case of Bereavement: Motivation and Framing

Just as arguments (and hence separation and divorce) are a natural part of family life so death is a natural part of living. Whether through dealing with the loss of a family member and their continued absence or considering one's own mortality and who will be left behind, experiences of death in all its forms shape people in profound ways in family life as it does elsewhere. Death can disrupt the social cohesiveness of everyday life, unsettling people's most familiar routines and practices.

Whereas various digital technologies allow people to ameliorate some of the difficulties of separation, new technological trends compel people to confront a range of issues having to do with death and bereavement that are not so helpful. For example, deceased family members' social networking web pages often persist after their passing, typically without measures in place to appropriately handle this content. There are few mechanisms to enable family members to pass information to loved ones or, importantly, withhold information from them. That this is so, only serves to deepen the sense of loss that bereavement induces. Many of these concerns point to the fact that there is a proliferation of digital data produced by individuals, but little is being done to consider the means by which the digital remains will be treated after the individuals who have produced it are gone, how they will be managed and made sense of, and the various roles they may play in the lives of the surviving family members. Issues such as the sensitive treatment of inherited or bequeathed virtual content and archives appear to be a largely unaddressed, but increasingly relevant issue to the HCI community.

Researching issues related to bereavement presents complex practical, theoretical and ethical challenges deserving careful framing. Death is experienced in many ways; there are many artefacts associated with death as well as many rituals. The processes through which families develop their own support structures to deal with absence are heterogeneous and unpredictable. What we are primarily interested in is how families adapt to the loss of a member, the work that goes on to continue with family life, and how the digital may be affecting these processes.

Method

A total of 11 participants (6 men and 5 women) were recruited through advertizements in online bereavement forums, bereavement community email lists, and through a bereavement counselor. All participants came from the South Eastern region of the United Kingdom. The resulting pool of participants had all experienced bereavement of a close friend, spouse and/or family member at some point within the past 1-6 years. However, all participants had also experienced some form of bereavement that dated earlier than this timeframe. In some cases, participants had experienced multiple losses of loved ones in the past 6 year period. The breakdown was as follows.

Fig. 12.1 Participants' relationship(s) to the departed

Relationship to departed	Participant
spouse	P3, P8, P9, P10
family member	P1, P2, P5, P6, P7, P10
friend	P2, P4, P6, P7, P11

While experiences of grief are complex and can be unpredictable, it is accepted that under normal circumstances, after 6-12 months the average person is able to re-establish a sense of physical and emotional equilibrium (Kubler-Ross 2005). Our timeframe was selected to allow participants enough time to re-establish everyday routines and behaviors, while at the same time the experience of death was likely not a distant memory.

Our sample also represented people at many different life stages (noted in Fig. 12.2).

Age	Participant
mid-20s	P4, P11
mid-30s	P1, P7, P9
mid-40s	P5, P6
mid-50s	P2, P10
mid-60s	P3, P8

Fig. 12.2 Participant ages

Occupations included a historian, a teacher, a computer security professional, a graphic designer, a civil servant, and a homemaker. No participants reported strong religious or spiritual affiliations. All interviews were conducted in participants' homes. A semi-structured interview approach was used, in which the researcher posed questions designed to prompt discussion rather than obtain specific answers. Some questions were designed to elicit a range of *retrospective* reflections on their experiences of bereavement and the many issues that came along with it. For example: *How long has it been since you have lost your loved one? How often do you think about him or her?* Additionally, interview questions aimed to elicit *prospective* speculations on participants' own mortality and how they envisioned that their legacy would live on, which included: *Do you think about how your own legacy will live on? What digital or physical things do you think will come to represent you?*

We also conducted a tour of the home, in which in situ discussions emerged about domestic objects and spaces that emerged during the interview. All interviews were audio taped. Photographs were additionally taken to document objects and spaces discussed during the interview. We listened to recordings and transcribed relevant segments, which were organized into themes. Weekly meetings were held with the research team to discuss and corroborate emergent themes. We coded the textual documents using these themes.

Select Findings

A consistent theme across our interviews suggested that for participants, despite the occurrence of death, relationships appeared to continue on. Consider the following from P9:

> *I put his mobile phone in his coffin with him, right next to his ear. He got commiserated with his mobile. I would text 'miss you' or the score when Arsenal won [football] matches or ...something about the happy times we had together. Things like that.*

This example reflects the way in which many of our participants talked about the departed in relatively mundane ways and how they also evoked a sense that the death itself was not entirely what experiencing bereavement entails. Quotes such as this illustrate how death is as much a social act (as it were) as it is a biological one (a distinction described by Sudnow, 1967 as *social death*). Even from this small sample it becomes evident that, while these kinds of relationships might unfold gradually and in peculiar ways, they nonetheless seem to persist despite the physical absence of a loved one.

This raises a number of interesting questions. For example, how is it these relationships continue – relationships between the dead and the living? How do exchanges occur and how do they unfold over time? In what ways do they affect the work of family members to deal with, and inevitably adapt, their familial structure to compensate for the permanent absence of a loved one? Presumably the fact that there is a difference between the actual biological fact of death and the continuing presence of the dead individual as some kind of social actor allows for that person's death to be gradually accommodated to. And, if so, in what ways does the process in question affect how personal and familial identity is thought about by members?

In the following sections, we first describe a sample of field evidence illustrating key ways in which social relationships with the departed linger on after their death. We then describe the work of family members to invoke, manage, and, in some cases, ultimately put to rest relationships with the departed.

Practices of Bequeathing and Inheritance

A central way in which relationships manifest themselves is through the presence and use of things. We know a commonplace issue of normal social relationships is that when things are exchanged between people, the receiver is implicitly obligated to take care of them. Over time these things come to signify our relationships with each other and, indeed, can mediate the ways in which we remember and relate to our loved ones (Csikszentmihalyi & Rochberg-Halton, 1981; Hallam & Hockey, 2001). There is a growing literature exploring the process of *passing down* objects as not merely reflecting our relationships with loved ones, but in essence *constituting* them (Finch & Mason, 2000).

Consistent with this, our field evidence suggested a primary way the departed communicate to the bereaved is through the bequeathing of things, the act of bequeathing having certain sorts of properties. It also became clear that understanding the ways in which these properties manifest is essential as the process of passing things down invokes the social relationship. A key quality of this relationship is that it is asymmetric — in the absence of a loved one, the bereaved must nonetheless come to terms with what was passed to them; at times requiring them to grapple with why they were chosen to be the bearer of particular things.

Artefacts bequeathed to our participants came in diverse forms; several different qualities could be used to categorize these digital and material possessions. We observed many instances of *objects of personal significance* that emphasized idiosyncratic aspects of personal relationships with the departed. A sample of these objects included: an old pipe, collections of figurines, a sword, musical instruments, a pocket watch. In contrast, *objects of historical legacy* were regarded as heirlooms in the classic sense and ownership had been retained within the family for many decades (in some cases over a century). These objects owed to the broader family line, rather than the life of the loved one that had recently bequeathed them. A brief sample includes: early photos of long deceased family members, paintings illustrating family crests and genealogical tree, marriage certificates, and family bibles.

We also encountered objects bequeathed to participants that *did* owe explicitly to the lives of the departed and were anticipated to achieve historical legacy. A brief sample of these kinds of things included a toolset, several artworks and photographs produced by family members, a World War II era rucksack and various types of furniture crafted by the departed. A particularly compelling and unusual example emerged in P2's discussion of her extensive collection of journals composed by her late grandmother and late mother, which housed entries for nearly every day over the past 3 decades. The scope and content of these entries varied. For example, P2 reflects on how the systematic recordings of mundane information now richly evoke the past:

> So many of the diaries just say things like 'Cleaned kitchen. Joy went to rehearsal all day. I did some gardening. Took a nap. ' ... just really dull, ordinary, everyday things [that] seem so boring, but now they're really important ...there's a whole of social history of our lives in there.

Important and tragic events are interwoven with the mundane:

> [Later] diaries have the weights of my daughters when they were born ...and then there's my Grandmother's experience of her daughter dying. ...I sometimes feel emotional and sometimes amused and sometimes heartbroken when looking through them, but that's life isn't it.

P2 further reflects on being bequeathed this collection and its potential legacy within her family:

> It hasn't been easy having them ...but I think they felt like it was necessary so they can remind us of the dull stuff and the good times and the hard times. ...it's their lives and in a way my life and I think they will become part of my daughters' lives.

This statement in part conveys P2's perception of the instructive properties latent in her grandmother's act of bequeathing these collections to her, which when paired with the broader historical factors of the documents, shaped her own interest in passing on these objects to her daughters. While only time will tell whether objects like the diary archives will continue to be passed down, what we want to highlight is the nature of exchange. One might say the act of her mother bequeathing these specific objects of historical legacy worked to communicate a "changing of the guard" and, with that change, came the obligation to preserve these objects as a matter of preserving her broader familial heritage. The objects, like the diaries, do appear to have historical qualities, while also being imbued with deep personal meaning. The bereaved came to understand this exchange as one with didactic properties: like in the case of P2's diaries, through the act of bequeathing these things, elder family members communicate lessons about life even after their own death. Importantly, these acts create an impetus for the bereaved to work to preserve these artefacts potentially for generations to come as a matter of honoring departed members and passing on knowledge of familial heritage.

Bequeathing and Complications of Social Relationships

The experience of being bequeathed objects was not always described as positive. In many cases participants conveyed uncomfortable feelings about objects they had been bequeathed, but nonetheless felt obligated to maintain possession over. These instances represented strange paradoxes in which the bereaved could neither come to terms with objects nor get rid of them. As a result they were often troublesomely stored away. It is important to note that most of the examples presented were intentionally bequeathed (specific things from a specific person). Obviously there are other ways of inheriting and often people are left with collections or an entire house full of things to sort through.

A key area in which problematic tensions emerged owed to the bereaved being unable to understand why they were selected to be the bearer of particular objects. These things came in various forms, ranging from a single silver goblet to an entire wardrobe of clothes. Difficulties also emerged with things specifically bequeathed to participants that made reference to the departed's own death. Considering their nature, these things typically left participants contemplating why they had been selected. Physical things often took the form of final handwritten letters and notes that, at times, included strange or unexpected requests. These objects evoked strong emotional reactions and were hidden away so as to prevent chance encounters.

Several digital examples emerged as well, including hard drive-based diary files, and video wills saved on compact discs (and often stored in drawers or closets to avoid daily contact). For example P6 describes being bequeathed digital files detailing a final correspondence:

> I received an email from her mother saying Susan wanted me to have [them]. It was the transcript of our last chat and a photo of her. ...They were a very odd reminder of her. I often wondered why she wanted me to have them. ...It was extremely painful every time I would see them because it would remind me of her death and our discussion about it and the hole it left behind. ...I didn't want to lose [the files], so I zipped them with a password. ...every once in a while I would check that they were still there but I wouldn't open them. ...The zip was deliberate, because it's passworded, it takes a conscious effort to find those files and look them up. So I have to want to look at it, I can't just accidentally come across it when I'm going through my holiday snaps or something.

P6's reflection illustrates some of the tensions arising from the asymmetric nature of the exchange. Participants felt obligated to hold onto particular objects, despite at times not having a clear understanding of why they were compelled to do so. The act of bequeathing without explaining obligates the receiver to interact with an object that they cannot rationalize in light of previous patterns of communication, complicating the work to deal it and, by consequence, the absence of a loved one.

The Burden of Unfiltered Contents and Collections

Managing and making sense of collections of possessions also appeared to significantly complicate the practices of the bereaved to adapt and move on. While the things we encountered took on both physical and digital forms, they were typically groups of objects that contained things of perceived importance as well as miscellany; a huge archive of paper documents, a large box of miscellaneous items, a computer (hard drive), and mobile phones cluttered with personal and work-related text messages. P10 describes the experience of sorting through a large box her late mother bequeathed to her:

It's full of all kinds [of things] from her life ... photographs from random periods, old train tickets, postcards she never wrote, it's endless really. I feel guilty for not going through it more ...it's a bit overwhelming. ...I'd like to think I will someday, but it will probably sit out in the shed.

In contrast, P11 describes the experience of dealing with a computer left to him by his best friend:

[he] wanted me to have it, the files and all. And, it ended up being horrendous. ...I tried to go through the directories to figure out where things roughly were, but it was disorganized and most of the time made no sense. ...I mean I know there's music and photo files, but there are more important things. ...I came across some text files that were sort of unfinished diary entries ...they were pretty personal ...I feel like he would not have wanted anyone else to see them. That was actually unsettling. They were in a folder with his financial expenses and stuff like that. ...I still haven't copied the hard drive so I don't use the computer.

These examples highlight how the bereaved felt obligated to deal with them, while simultaneously becoming burdened as they worked to cohesively come to terms with a wealth of unfiltered information. In P11's case, the digital seemed to amplify this problem, causing serious, if not paralyzing, trepidation over possible future unexpected encounters as he navigated vast amounts of the departed's personal content with little insight into what might be found.

Across our interviews participants recognized this very issue as they expressed concerns about steadily growing amounts of digital information they wish to pass on, while having no established mechanism to do so. Similar to the photographs and journals inherited by our participants, they themselves conveyed strong interest in passing several kinds of digital objects, such as personal narratives or diaries, archives of blog posts or other digital content posted on social media websites, digital photos and collections, digital artworks, and digital music collections. For example, P2 compares her own archives of twitter and blog data to her extensive collections of family diaries:

I use twitter in a kind of anecdotal way...to document different things from buying a prop for the next rehearsal to more mundane things I do. ...it's all kind of similar stuff really to my family diaries. ...I hope to pass all [my] twitter and blog posts down and even though some of it's boring, when I look back and read diary entries and find my grandmother saying 'I cleaned the bathroom today' in 20, 30, 40, 50 year's time it actually becomes interesting. ...I think there's a lot of potential for my children to look back on this stuff. ...And I'd be delighted if their [children are] reading them. How exactly I'll get that information is another story. Who knows where it really even is!

Coping with Absence: The Doing of Bereavement Through Communication

One emergent theme characterizing the work of the bereaved loss, owed to the participants' continued use of digital communication systems in order to communicate with loved ones. Participants described a range of activities, such as sending private messages to the departed's email account, posting messages on social networking website pages dedicated to the departed, and continuing to call and text their loved one's mobile phone. Returning again to the example of P9 who described sending voice and text messages to her departed husband via a mobile buried in his coffin, she explains:

> ... [I did this] so I could still stay in contact with him. I know it sounds daft, but you cling to things like that, feels important to keep in contact.

However, when asked if she still tries to contact him, P9 reflected:

> ...not as much. I still do sometimes. I want to hang onto him, but I don't do it as much.

In another example, P7 reflects on how his practice of sending emails to the account of his late close friend after his death shifted over time:

> After a while you feel like you need to move on from [doing it]. ...You don't forget them, it's more a moving on if you like.

In the context of these examples, one might say the tapering off of use shows the shifting nature of the social relationship. As the amount of email, text messages and calls to the departed falls, the bereaved perhaps began to feel that they had 'said enough' through these familiar forms of communication.

However, in newer communication systems, such as social networking websites, tensions arose that complicated participants' social relationships with the departed as they worked to move past loss. The core problem across these instances had to do with a lack of established mechanisms to appropriately mark a departed persons' account. For example, over the past 6 years P4 lost a close friend and her boyfriend, both of whom had Facebook accounts. P4 describes tensions of re-encountering their public pages still in operation:

> ...their profiles pop up at me every now and then and I'm not expecting it and it's a bit of a shock. I'd never forget them, but I need them to be somewhere else where I can remember [them] when I want to. ...otherwise it's affecting my life from moving on. I need to be living without being upset about those memories all of the time.

Despite the fact that P4's relationship with her deceased loved ones is shifting, tensions emerge as she comes across their pages within a virtual place conceptualized for the living. In the material world rituals have occurred to mark their passing, whereas online they persist in what could be characterized as a "liminal" space (van Gennup, 1977); neither alive nor treated as dead, but rather lingering on in ways not unlike any other user of the system. These tensions are amplified as P4 describes the disturbing instance of receiving a posthumous Facebook message from her departed boyfriend:

> Someone went onto his account and invited people who were friends with him to an event to remember him, but it was so shocking because it popped up saying 'John invites you to this event' and I just thought 'how could this be happening' ...it just wasn't right.

Conflicts also emerged from internal actions within Facebook as issues of moral appropriateness of behavior came to the forefront when deceased users' pages became ad-hoc memorial sites. For example, P11 describes problems associated with loss of access:

The main problem was that lots of our close friends weren't on Facebook when he died, so they couldn't get added as his 'friends' and see his page you know since no one could get into his account. So it stayed up there and slowly filled up with a lot of random [people leaving] clichéd messages. ...The whole thing ended up feeling insincere.

P11's reflection highlights complexities around issues of entitlement with respect to who ought to be considered 'bereaved', how to support the work of these stakeholders, and the socially and morally appropriate actions that ought to follow suit. What we want to draw attention to in these examples is that emergent tensions ultimately seem rooted in the inability to treat these virtual places differently when a person has passed away. This is not to suggest that they ought to be deleted, but rather a more sophisticated layer of choice should be considered in the system design — a desire highlighted by several of our participants as they prospectively considered their own online accounts.

Despite these problems our participants also pointed toward potentially novel ways these systems might support work associated with bereavement, particularly in instances where virtual places were specifically demarcated for remembrance. P2 compares attending her friend's funeral and later visiting an online memorial website:

I went to Al's funeral, which was ok but I didn't have a chance to talk to many people. So, it was a shared experience in the sense that we were all there, but there was no kind of interaction for me. But, this [memorial] website was more interactive in the sense that I could write what I wanted to say and other people could read it and I could read what they had to say. ...I found that valuable ...to be aware of all the different dimensions of relationships this person had with others.

This example and others suggest rich opportunities for creating socially constructed narratives reflective of the relationships formed throughout a person's life, if adequate measures are taken to mark and negotiate virtual places and possessions owing to the departed.

Putting to Rest: Rituals and Techniques for Managing the Relationships

The diverse practices developed and drawn on by our participants to manage relationships with the departed were largely reflected in the management of material and virtual possessions in the home. In several instances interactions with these things resulted in troubling experiences. Whether through encrypting digital files deep within the directory structure, removing digital files from an often used hard drive and storing them on external media elsewhere in the home, or filing funeral paraphernalia in the confines of desk drawers, significant work was put into simultaneously preserving and hiding these kinds of possessions. P6 compares his behavior of encrypted files to an analogous practice in the material world:

It's the technological equivalent to putting them in the back cupboard. You put [them] away because you need to ...you have to ...you know they're there ...but they get covered up ...life keeps moving on.

Whether virtual or material, these kinds of possessions are visceral markers of the departed's death; they are hidden and become sedimented as papers and miscellany are stacked on top of them or as files grow and the file directory structure expand. While these artefacts are preserved in one form or another, they are increasingly made peripheral in our participants' lives; these acts provide a foundation to work past the biological moment of death and signify an important act in the relationship's transition.

Our participants also drew on inherited possessions as resources to reflect on the departed in diverse and ritualized ways. A key quality of these things was their ability to be invoked and then be put away or simply fade into the background. A sample of material possessions included candles, small trinkets in a jacket, a windup clock, and photo albums. A particularly compelling example was a statue sculpted by P3's late wife, which was now on display on his mantelpiece and beginning to show early signs of decomposition:

> It was my decision to move it out in the garden for a while, which means that it will rot ...[it is] about finding its final resting place.

One might say P3's management of the statue evocatively reflects the shifting nature of his relationship with his wife. P3 describes the statue's peripheral nature:

> So I would say that I still have it around because it brings up thoughts about my wife, but it's not overwhelming. I can see it and think about her or just as easily not do so.

We also encountered several participants in possession of digital archives of text messages received prior to a loved one's passing. P8 reported possessing over 200 text messages sent from her departed husband, which highlighted many momentous and mundane aspects of their relationship. These messages are saved on a flash memory card, which is stored separately in an ornate box only made present during the ritual:

> Now and then I bring them out. ...[I] see things he's written to me, like 'I hope today went ok' and I think about why he sent that and what was going on then. ...I know I can always find them, but it's also important I can put them away.

P8's & P3's reflections are exemplary in their emphasis on the important role possessions play in enabling the bereaved to manage aspects of their relationship with the departed. Once the ritual comes to a close, aspects of the relationship can be put away by the bereaved on their own terms, or potentially put to rest forever.

Design Opportunities, Considerations and Issues

Bereavement and the many issues characterizing the work to adapt to the loss of a loved one are complex. This fieldwork in part illustrates how a better understanding of the experience of bereavement can be reached by understanding how it is related to the effort entailed in the managing of a shifting, asymmetric social relationship – between the still living and the newly departed, the dead. It provides a way of understanding how the bereaved are communicated with and how aspects of these relationships continue to persist, while others are put to rest, and the significant roles material and virtual possessions play in these processes, even as they gradually abate over time.

We found that virtual places and possessions raise new issues of ownership, access and persistence, which together can complicate the work of the bereaved. That people are inheriting vast amounts of unfiltered, unmanaged digital archives makes the inheritance of virtual materials quite different from the inheritance of physical objects. At the same time, we have seen how interactive technologies are opening up new opportunities for continuing and putting to rest relationships, for engaging in rituals, for creating new kinds of treasured virtual possessions, for celebrating the lives of departed loves ones, and ultimately for mending familial structures.

We wish to highlight just three issues here. First, we found inherited possessions and archives were treated in a variety of ways that ultimately worked to put aspects of the relationship to rest. We found that, despite their troubling qualities, maintaining ownership over these things played a significant role in honoring the departed and adapting to loss. While P6 reported encrypting virtual archives to avoid accidental encounters with their contents, the knowledge of how to successfully navigate this process could be beyond many users' skill set. Beyond exploring solutions merely through multiple points of storage, these instances suggest deeper levels of choice ought to be designed into interactive systems that enable people to demarcate particular content for deep storage and explicitly treat it differently from other data stored within the system. While issues of privacy clearly underlie this area, it equally seems important to consider participants' desires to know where these possessions are, be assured of their safety, and perhaps even convey temporal sedimentation as they gather patina and sink deeper within directory structures. Additionally, a range of prior research has detailed the significant role dispossession of material artefacts plays in shaping both personal (Kleine, 2004) and familial (Miller & Parrot 2009) identity to adapt to life changes. P3's treatment of his late wife's statue highlighted decay as an evocative form of remembrance, tribute and, ultimately, dispossession and letting go.

Second, major tensions arose with respect to participants being unable to make sense of why they had received particular objects. These issues appeared amplified in the digital where few tools exist to ascribe rich information that might help the bereaved understand the value assigned to them by the departed and why they were selected to be the receiver. Several researchers, such as Frohlich et al. (2000), Petrelli et al. (2008, 2009) and Nunes et al. (2008), have speculated on the possibilities of using interactive technology to attach narratives or metadata to material and virtual possessions with an eye toward constructing sentimental value.

This body of work has contributed important insights with respect to how interactive tools might better enable people to engage with their possessions (or those they have inherited) in more expressive and, potentially, enduring ways. We imagine this space could be productively extended to explore how collaborative interactions might encourage reminiscing among loved ones and how these stories might be passed down and added to from generation to generation. However, even the mere presence of these tools in everyday life could conjure reflections of one's own mortality in ways that may not be perceived as socially appropriate or beneficial. Would such toolkits and systems enable the bereaved to expressively celebrate the unique social bonds fortified with loved ones, even in their absence? Or, would they create persistent obligations to continually manage growing archives of virtual possessions as the social relationships implicated in them grow, change and dissolve?

Third, we found issues of privacy and social entitlement complicated the work of the bereaved to adapt to loss, which often owed to a lack of established mechanisms to treat online spaces of the departed differently. In particular there were virtually no ways for the bereaved to gain access to the departed's account to intervene. As people continue to expand their practices of storing and presenting virtual possessions on local computing systems to personal and shared online places, new unanticipated issues are resulting in complications for families as a departed loved one's social networking profile(s) — and their attendant content(s) — continue to persist after she or he has passed away. Turning back to our earlier discussion of the crucial role 'letting go' of possessions plays in enabling people to move past painful life experience and work towards a new personal and familial identity (e.g. Miller & Parrot, 2009), it remains unclear how one might dispossess virtual possessions shared in online places, such as Facebook, which owe to the life of the departed. While recent changes have occurred in Facebook to enable deceased users' accounts to be 'pushed' into memorials (Wortham, 2010), there are still no clear mechanisms in place to facilitate the transfer of account ownership (and attendant virtual possessions) to the bereaved. Clearly there may be opportunities in expanding existing privacy tools to support user delineation of future ownership permissions and enable a more fluid and nuanced transfer of online archives of virtual possessions to various family members or other stakeholders. More research is needed to understand the extent to which new interventions would be effective in making the processes of passing on (or dispossessing) online content more transparent. Similar to the caveat mentioned previously, additional research is required to understand to what degree these kinds of interventions are valued, and, importantly, when they themselves may become socially inappropriate or unacceptable.

Conclusion

Whether through the range of issues related to making (or adjusting to) new homes following a divorce, or coming to terms with the loss of a loved one, adapting to new social circumstances and environments is a fact of life that affects all members of a family. These are very real, if not inevitable, experiences families work to transition beyond, and it is the nature of how this work is done that shapes the identity of a family and its members. Even in the field evidence we presented, it was evident that the work to *do family* takes on diverse forms, and that the digital is increasingly becoming a part of how this work gets done. We found that it is doing so in ways that can support as well as significantly complicate families' efforts to adapt to these kinds of shifting circumstances. Moreover, it is clear that absence is only one indicator that family is a constantly evolving system, and the work of meaning construction in this system is equally dynamically changing. Building on both cases, in what follows we present a set of design implications with a critical eye toward the potential roles smart domestic technologies might play in supporting families' work to adapt to shifting circumstances in the future. To support the work of family, these include managing the storage, presentation and construction of identity that happens with virtual possessions. While physical possessions support these activities, increasingly virtual possessions offer new opportunities for supporting family members' work, in addition to complicating these practices in unanticipated ways.

Similar to Kirk and Sellen's (2010) findings related to the *deep storage* of familial artefacts, we encountered a range of instances in which participants held on to possessions that were not directly on display. Several divorced parents, for example, reported still owning memorabilia owning to their ex-spouse, which were often stored away in a basement or on some form of external digital storage. Bereaved participants also maintained possession of large archives of digital artefacts received from the departed; in many instances the simple knowledge of these virtual things' continued preservation worked to construct an important symbol of honoring the departed's life. Across all these cases, the out of sight storage of these things played a significant role in members' work to construct a new identity in the wake of change and absence. There appears to be an opportunity for domestic technologies that might enable owners to demarcate these kinds of digital objects from others within their storage systems, and offer the self-determined possibility to make owners aware of the safety of these things in subtle and unobtrusive ways. We imagine such subtle indicator systems could be valuable to supporting the work of members, whether through enabling the custodian of a bequeathed collection to simply know they are continuing to honor the legacy of a loved one, or through reminding a divorced parent that the positive experiences and memories implicated in their pre-divorce archives remain intact as they continue to move on with their own life in a new home and reality.

However, everyday storage practices are changing as they migrate from local platforms to cloud-computing services. Among other things, elements of online archives are increasingly becoming shared across many different groups, and social metadata accrued in these contexts are emerging as a deeply valued part of digital artefacts (Odom et al. 2011). We found divorced parents' practices of collectively congratulating children were enacted through attributing metadata to children's photographs, and the bereaved found solace in the comments paying tribute to the departed in online places appropriately marked for it, for instance. Nonetheless, there are no current established ways in which this kind of digital content might be stored and preserved in a longitudinal sense. Exploring the social and technical requirements around how these kinds of digital artefacts could be retrieved from the cloud, stored and potentially drawn upon as meaningful resources within the intimate confines of members' homes seems a little considered, yet important area for future research — for families adapting to change, and for enriching family life in general.

Additionally, we found that in some cases the dispossession, destruction and graceful temporal degradation of objects after they had been in storage for some time played essential roles in members' work to move on with their lives following painful events. Similar to how systems could peripherally indicate the safety of preserved artefacts, we imagine technologies could also be designed to delicately present the temporal decay and eventual disappearance of select digital objects. In a world where nearly endless storage capabilities present the very real possibility of creating exacting histories of our digital life, enabling families with such tools may provide a meaningful space to elegantly put to rest certain aspects of their lives as they productively work toward the future.

The presentation of virtual possessions emerged as one of the most diverse ways they were relied on across various social situations in and around the home. We found divorced parents printed out physical copies of digital photographs acquired through email exchanges, which were situated within their homes among their own personal things. Children in part drew on large mobile archives of photographs to present virtual copies of familial artefacts in a parent's home lacking these things, which opened a space for collective reflection on different pre- and post-divorce family events; in other cases they made digital copies of material artefacts present within domestic spaces in a parent's home to exert personal authorship across differing domestic spheres. Bereaved individuals ritualistically invoked social relationships with the departed by making inherited virtual possessions present for a given time and then putting them away as the practice came to a close. While varied, collectively these instances illustrate the roles virtual possessions and archives are playing as they are integrated within members' practices to cope with shifting circumstances.

On a general level, all of these cases suggest that as people's personal and familial digital archives grow, approaches to communicating the size, scale and significance of these collections remains undeveloped. For children of divorce, we imagine technologies enabling them to be peripherally aware of the diversity, breadth and changing status of their virtual things could help further construct a sense of home and personal space across two houses. Enabling the bereaved to more expressively make inherited digital possessions tangibly present, beyond a computer or mobile device display, could open a space to more richly integrate these things into ritual practices, while retaining material-like affordances to fluidly put them away when the act comes to a close. We imagine these artefacts may eventually be moved to deep storage, and possibly evocatively fade away as bits decay with the relationship's evolution, and the family moves on to consider themselves no longer 'bereaved.'

We found that qualities of the digital enabled members to draw upon their vast collections of virtual things despite their location; to extend virtual proxies of significant artefacts across both homes and engage in key familial (and parental) activities; and to reflect on the lives of departed loves ones in expressive and self-determined ways. Collectively, these instances seem to suggest there is a large opportunity area for new domestic technologies that could make family members' personal and shared virtual possessions more present in rich ways to support the work of adapting to absence, and perhaps beyond it. Undoubtedly, one of the largest issues these kinds of technologies will have to reconcile is how the system itself will adapt to the various social audiences and circumstances present within the home and when the presentation of key virtual possessions may or may not be appropriate and beneficial. Understanding these boundaries appears central to exploring how future smart domestic technologies might be designed to provide an elegant resource to members as family structure and organization continues to evolve.

From divorced parents relying on online shared systems to mediate parenting practices, to virtual environments providing the bereaved with new, but at times complicated, outlets for personal and collective tribute, it was clear complex social processes related to *doing family* are expanding to virtual places. Members are fluidly moving between physical and virtual environments, arguably without distinct boundaries between the two. As family life simultaneously unfolds across both places, it is certain that the digital is often neither flexible nor nuanced enough to handle the various social roles that are constitutive of the work that goes on in families, especially when adapting to significant social changes. While technologies have already enabled families of all kinds to engage with each other over large physical distances, what remains uncertain is how they will enable any given member to manage the many social groups and performances associated with family life (and indeed outside of it). The ability to enact various social roles fluidly across virtual and material environments is fundamental to the work of adapting to absence; how this will be affectively and sensitively achieved, in ways that productively strengthen familial bonds as the underlying structures evolve, marks a substantial area for future research. On a general level, there is a clear need for shared online systems and virtual places to evolve their technical architectures to be adaptable to shifting social structures that will support instances in which a family loses one of its members, divides, or even gains a host of new members. Understanding how virtual possessions (and attendant social metadata) shared in online spaces might be made present in and around the home to support the variety of work to adapt to absence covered in this chapter appears to be another rich area for future investigation.

As we critically consider the future of domestic technologies in family life, a larger lesson we can take from these cases is that the 'place' in which the work of *doing family* unfolds is increasingly expanding outside the physical confines of the house. Technologies that enrich the work of families will be those that support the various social roles its members enact, whether divorced or bereaved, on any given day across virtual and material environments as they seek to establish the scaffolding needed to move past absence and presently be a part of family.

References

Amato, P.R. (2001). Children of Divorce in the 1990s. *Journal of Family Psychology*, 15, 3, 355-370.
Amato, P.R. (2004). Parenting Through Family Transitions. *Social Policy Journal of New Zealand*, 23, 31-44.

Arditti, J. A. (1999). Rethinking relationships between divorced mothers and their children: Capitalizing on family strengths. *Family Relations*, 48, 109-119.

Beech, S., Geelhoed, E., Murphy, R., Parker, J., Sellen, A. and Shaw, K. (2003). The Lifestyles of Working Parents: Implications and Opportunities for New Technologies. *HP Technical Report: HPL-2003-88*, 1-114.

Bovil, M., Livingstone, S. (Eds.) (2001). *Children and their changing media environment*. London: Erlbaum.

Brown, B., Taylor, A, Izadi, S., Sellen, A., Kaye, J. (2007). Locating Family Values: A Field Trial of the Whereabouts Clock. In *Proc. of UbiComp '07*, 354-371.

Cowan, P. A. and McHale, J. P. (1996). Coparenting in a Family Context: Emerging Achievements, Current Dilemmas, and Future Directions. *New Directions for Child Development*, 74, 93-106.

Chawla, L. (1992). Childhood Place Attachments. In *Place Attachment*. Altman, I., Low, S. (ed). Plenum Press, 63-86.

Csikszenthmihalyi, M., Rochberg-Halton, E. (1981). *The Meaning of Things: Domestic Symbols and the Self*. Cambridge University Press, Cambridge.

Darrah, C. et al. (2001). *Families and Work: An Ethnography of Dual Career Families. Final Report to Sloan Foundation grant # 95192-0113*.

Davidoff, S., Lee, M. K., Yiu, C., Zimmerman, J. and Dey, A. K. (2006). Principles of Smart Home Control. In *Proc. of UbiComp*, Springer, 19-34.

Davidoff, S., Zimmerman, J., & Dey, A. (2010). How Routine Learners can Support Family Coordination. In *Proc. of CHI '10*, 2461-2470.

Finch, J., Mason, J. (2000). *Passing On: Kinship & Inheritance in England*. Routledge.

Fitzpatrick, M, Vangelisti, A. (Eds.) (1995). *Explaining Family Interactions*. Sage Publications: London.

Frissen, V. A. Icts in the Rush Hour of Life. *The Information Society*, 16 (March 1999), 65-75.

Frohlich, D., Murphy, R. (2000). The Memory Box. *Personal Ubiquitous Comput*. 4, 4 (January 2000), 238-240.

Golden, A., Dalgleish, T., Mackintosh, B. 2007. Levels of Specificity of Autobiographical Memories and of Biographical Memories of the Deceased in Bereaved Individuals With and Without Complicated Grief. *Journal of Abnormal Psychology*, Vol. 116, 4, 786-795.

Hallam, E., Hockey, J. (001). *Death, Memory and Material Culture*, Oxford, Berg.

Harper, R. (2010). *Texture: Human Expression in the Age of Communications Overload*. MIT Press: Cambridge, MA.

Ito, M. et al. (2009). *Hanging Out, Messing Around, Geeking out: Kids Living and Learning with New Media*. MIT Press: Cambridge, MA.

Kelly, J.B. (1997). Children's Living Arrangements Following Separation and Divorce: Insights From Empirical and Clinical Research. *Family Process*, 46, 1, 35-52.

Kim, S., Kim, M., Park, S., Jin, Y., & Choi, W. (2004). Gate Reminder: A Design case of a smart reminder. In Proc. *DIS '04*, 81-90.

Kharfen, M. (1999, March 26). HHS LAUNCHES "BE THEIR DAD" PARENTAL RESPONSIBILITY CAMPAIGN. US Department of Health and Human Services. Retrieved from on 2011, 21 June: http://archive.hhs.gov/news/press/1999pres/990326.html

Kirk, D., Sellen, A. (2010). On human remains: Values and practice in the home archiving of cherished objects. ACM Trans. Comput.-Hum. *Interact*. 17, 3, Article 10 (July 2010).

Kleine, S., Baker, S. 2004. An Integrative Review of Material Possession Attachment. *Academy of Marketing Science Review*. 1-39.

Massimi, M., Odom, W., Kirk, D., Banks, R. (2011). Matters of Life and Death: Locating the End of Life in Lifespan-Oriented HCI Research. In *proceedings of SIGCHI Conference on Human Factors in Computing Systems*. Vancouver, Canada. CHI '11. ACM.

McHale, J.P. (1997). Overt and Covert Coparenting Processes in the Family. *Family Process*, 36, 2, 183-201.

Miller, D., Parrot, F. 2009. Loss and material culture in south London. *Journal of the Royal Anthropological Institute*, Vol 15, 3, 502-519.

Neustaeder, C., Bernheim Brush, A.J., Greenburg, S. (2009). The Calendar is Crucial: Coordination and Awareness through the Family Calendar. *ACM Trans. Comput.-Hum. Interact.* 16, 1, Article 6.

Newman, D., Grauerholz, L. (2002). *Sociology of Families*. Sage publications: London.

Nunes, M., Greenburg, S., Neustaeder, C. 2008. Sharing digital photographs in the home through physical mementos, souvenirs, and keepsakes. In *Proc. of DIS '08*, 250-260.

Odom, W. Zimmerman, J., Forlizzi, J. (2011). Teenagers and Their Virtual Possessions: Design Opportunities and Issues. In *proceedings of SIGCHI Conference on Human Factors in Computing Systems*. Vancouver, Canada. CHI '11. ACM Press.

Odom, W., Harper, R., Sellen, A., Kirk, D., Banks, R. (2010). Passing On & Putting To Rest: Understanding Bereavement in the context of Interactive Technologies. In *proceedings of SIGCHI Conference on Human Factors in Computing Systems*. Atlanta, USA. CHI '10. ACM Press, 1831-1840.

Odom, W. Zimmerman, J., Forlizzi, J. (2010). Designing for Dynamic Family Structures: Divorced Families and Interactive Systems. In proceedings of *Designing Interactive Systems. Aarhus, Denmark. DIS '10*. ACM Press, 151-160.

Park, S.Y., and Zimmerman, J. (2010). Investigating the Opportunity for a Smart Activity Bag. In *Proceedings of the 28th international conference on Human factors in computing systems (CHI '10)*. ACM, New York, NY, USA, 2543-2552.

Petrelli, D. et al. (2008). AutoTopography: what can physical mementos tell us about digital memories? In *Proceedings of CHI '08*, ACM Press 53-62.

Petrelli, D., van den Hoven, E., Whittaker, S. (2009). Making history: intentional capture of future memories. In *Proc. of CHI '09*, ACM Press, 1723-1732.

Prigerson et al. (2009). Prolonged Grief Disorder: Psychometric Validation of Criteria Proposed for DSM-V and ICD-11. *PLoS Med* 6(8): e1000121.

Proshansky, H., Fabian, A. & Kaminoff, R. (1983). Place identity: Physical world socialization of the self. *Journal of Environmental Psychology*, 3, 57-83.

Steele, J.R. & Brown, J.D. (1995) Adolescent room culture: Studying media in the context of everyday life. In *Journal of Youth and Adolescence*, 24, 5, 551-576.

Strain, J. (2003). Households as Morally Ordered Communities: Explorations in the Dynamics of Family Life. In Harper, R. (ed.) *Inside the Smart Home*. Springer.

Strauss, A. and Corbin, J. (1990). *Basics of Qualitative Research: Grounded Theory Procedures and Techniques*. Newbury Park, CA: Sage.

Sudnow, D. 1967. *Passing On: The Social Organization of Dying*. Englewood Cliffs, New Jersey.

Taylor, A. S. and Swan, L. (2005). Artful systems in the home. In *Proc. of CHI '05*, 641-650.

Taylor, A., Harper, R., Swan, L., Izadi, S., Sellen, A., Perry, M. 2007. Homes that make us smart. *Personal Ubiquitous Comput.* 11, 5 (June 2007), 383-393.

United States Census. 2005. Children Under 18 Years Old By Presence Of Parents: 1980, 1990, 1995, 2000 And 2004 [By Race And Marital Status], p. 54.

van Gennep, A. (1977). *The Rites of Passage*. London: Routledge.

Williams, A., Anderson, K., Dourish, P. (2008). Anchored Mobilities: Mobile Technology and Transnational Migration. In *Proc. of DIS 08*, 323-332.

Wortham, J. (2010). As Older Users Join Facebook, Network Grapples With Death. *The New York Times*. http://www.nytimes.com/2010/07/18/technology/18death.html?_r=1%26scp=1%26sq= ghosts%20reach%20out%26st=cse.

Yarosh, S., Chieh, Y., Chew, D., Abowd, G. (2009). Supporting Long-Distance Parent-Child Interaction in Divorced Families. in *International Journal of Human-Computer Studies*, Volume 67, Issue 2, February 2009, 192-20.

Part III
Remaining Aspirations for the Future Home

Chapter 13
Remote Care: Health at Home

James Barlow, Steffen Bayer, and Tiago Cravo Oliveira

Introduction

Faced by rising demand for health and social care at the same time as growing constraints on available resources, governments and healthcare providers in many countries are turning towards information and communications technology (ICT) to help support and enhance existing care services. Various technologies associated with the remote monitoring and support of people in need of care – sensors, information processing, user interfaces – are developing rapidly and costs are falling. Care service providers, and technology and infrastructure suppliers, are increasingly seeing new market opportunities for home-based care and support and monitoring services.

In the UK the basic community alarm service for elderly people is evolving into a home and personal monitoring system. The realization that this can contribute towards the modernization of care services has moved the concept of 'remote care' – often known as 'telecare', 'telehealth' or 'telemedicine' – up the policy agenda. The widespread deployment of remote care is now central to government plans for increasing the options available to those in need of care.

Remote care has also increasingly formed a key part of healthcare policy in other countries. Using innovations in ICT in combination with new models for care provision, it is helping to redefine the role of the home in the delivery of healthcare. In this chapter we explore the reasons why remote care has become so attractive to governments and care providers, the applications that support remote care and reflect on its possible impact on the role of the home within the care system.

J. Barlow (✉)
Imperial College, London, UK

R. Harper (ed.), *The Connected Home: The Future of Domestic Life*,
DOI 10.1007/978-0-85729-476-0_13, © Springer-Verlag London 2011

Changing Demands on Care Provision

A key health policy challenge for most developed countries is the impact of ageing on the demand for health and social care. By 2030 the OECD countries are likely to experience an increase of 3 to 4 years in the life expectancy of their populations (Jacobzone et al., 1998). The projected growth rate in people aged 80 or above is about 70 per cent over the period 1990-91 to 2020-21 (Barlow J et al., 2011). In the UK the number of people aged 100 or over will nearly double over the next 10 years from the current level (12,000) and reach 280,000 in 2050 (Department of Health, 2010b) and the proportion of the population aged 65 and over will increase by 37 percent to 10.8 million people by 2022. By 2022, the number of those with some disability will increase by 40 percent to 3.3 million and the number of disabled older people with informal care (i.e. households) will rise by 39 percent to 2.4 million (Department of Health, 2008). Parallel to these demographic changes there will be a 40 percent rise in the number of people in residential care homes (to 280,000) and a 42 percent increase in those in nursing homes (to 170,000) in the absence of the introduction of care models that focus on care within people's homes.

There are understandable concerns over the impact of these demographic changes on the cost of care delivery, especially since the population over 65 years old accounts for five times the per capita spending on services as people aged 50-64. And this is compounded by the large number of people (currently over 15 million in England) with a long term health condition. The UK Department of Health's best estimate is that treatment and care of those with long term conditions already accounts for 69 percent of the total health and social care budget. Across Europe the situation is similar. In 2005, 60 million Europeans suffered from some form of age-related impairment (Commission of the European Communities, 2007). This number is expected to reach 84 million by 2020 (Commission of the European Communities, 2007). A further problem faced by some countries is the tight labor market for health and social care staff spanning the entire spectrum of personnel, from home care assistants to consultant physicians.

Parallel to the increased demand on health and social care services from an ageing population, consumer expectations are becoming ever more demanding, with patients seeking greater choice over treatment and services. Part of this trend includes a desire by older people to remain independent and live in their own homes for as long as possible. Governments have recognized that successive generations of older people have higher expectations of public services, partly because they have been accustomed to higher quality services over the course of their lives (Department of Health, 2005). This includes a desire to exert greater control and be able to manage their own independence. An estimated 90 percent of older people want to live in their own home, and while the majority of people die in hospitals, surveys suggest they would prefer to die in their own homes (Department of Health, 2005). Governments in the UK have therefore vowed to 'put patients at the heart of the NHS (National Health Service) through an information revolution and greater choice and control' (Department of Health, 2010a).

These trends are combining to create an increasing need for care solutions which enable people to live longer and grow old, independently but safely, at home. Housing is being asked to perform an increasingly important role in the provision of health and social care. Sheltered housing and residential and nursing homes are being replaced by the mainstream housing stock, with appropriate packages of care and physical adaptation, as a location for care provision. In recent years this trend has begun to speed up, with growing interest in the use of ICT to deliver more control over the domestic environment and provide an 'electronic security blanket' for individuals and their carers.

If the number of elderly people living at home is growing, this will result in an increased pressure on the ageing population of informal carers – friends, family and volunteers – in an already tight labor market for care staff. Informal carers represent the principal source of care for the majority of older people living at home (Pickard et al., 2000) and carer stress is a major reason for the admission of an older person to a residential or nursing home. It has been estimated that the cost of replacing informal carers in the UK would amount to £87 billion per year (Buckner and Yeandle, 2007). Pressures on the sustainability of this model are growing as children caring for their parents grow older themselves. It is therefore only possible to move substantially more care into the home environment if this home environment is equipped to support elderly people as well as their carers.

Remote care is seen as a potential solution for meeting the growing demands on care services, giving informal carers more personal freedom, meeting potential shortfalls in the workforce and complementing the work of clinicians and social care providers (Department of Health, 2005). In doing so, the hope is that home-centered care models will help to achieve better health outcomes and improve general well-being. More recently, the need to reduce government expenditure on health and social care within a slowly recovering economy has also led to increased interest in the potential of new technology-enabled health services to address the budgetary challenge of providing as much or more care with fewer resources (Department of Health, 2010b).

In the UK the policy agenda around remote care has evolved considerably over the last decade. Calls for remote care have been made in numerous government and other official documents since the late 1990s and there have been around £175 million made available to support the development of new services over the period 2006-2011 (Barlow and Hendy, 2009, Curtis, 2007). Remote care has become increasingly embedded in health policies for the management of long term conditions aiming to provide people with greater choice over their care pathways, as well as in policies intended to reduce inappropriate hospital admissions and facilitate earlier discharge. This trend has been echoed in the health policies and strategies of other countries.

Making the Home Suitable: From Assistive Technology to Remote Care

Most older people do not live in (and are unlikely to move to) new purpose-built homes specifically designed around their needs. While the concept of 'lifetime homes' – carefully designed residential spaces that cater for people's changing capacities without the need for expensive adaptations – has been incorporated into UK planning policy for over a decade, most new-built homes are not designed as true lifetime homes. Neither private house builders nor typical buyers see incentives to incur the additional costs necessary to make the homes suitable (or at least easily adaptable) for potentially frail occupants in the future. Even if house buyers might benefit from a more suitable home in their own old age, short time horizons, the uncertainty of future needs and of the length of expected tenure make it unrealistic to expect most buyers to pay a premium for a potentially more future proofed home. Demographic trends towards more elderly buyers, an increasing recognition of the needs of elderly people in society, changes in building standards or home automation desired for convenience reasons by younger buyers might have some impact on the housing stock in the future, but this impact is likely to remain small given the size of the overall housing stock and exceptionally slow replacement rate.

The situation in the social housing sector is slightly more positive. Local authorities now require social housing developers to meet lifetime homes standards, including features such as space for the future installation of a stair or through-floor lift which allow for a degree of flexible living over the lifetime of the occupants and the dwelling. While these types of dwellings are relatively easier to adapt to the needs of frail inhabitants, even then building works are likely to be necessary.

To create home environments that are able to facilitate independent living of frail occupants from a housing stock mostly not designed for that purpose often requires extensive and expensive alterations and adaptations. This involves tackling physical design features, introducing 'assistive technology' and creating safe and secure environments that reduce risk for individuals and their carers to an acceptable level.

Improving Functionality in the Home – Assistive Technology

Physical aspects of the domestic living environment can present a fundamental barrier for independent living. The most common problems associated with frailty or disability are to do with baths and showers, the toilet, stairs, access within and to/from the house, risks of falls and accidents and carrying out practical tasks (Heywood, 2005). Measures to overcome these problems involve adapting the design of the home through physical adaptations such as level access showers, door widening, ramps and extensions and installing 'assistive technology'.

The term 'assistive technology' covers simple items such as walking sticks, bath seats and grab rails, as well as electro-mechanical equipment (e.g. powered wheelchairs), electronic aids (e.g. digital hearing aids and environmental controls), or equipment used by carers such as lifting aids. Some forms of assistive technology have been enhanced by ICT. Electronic assistive technology (EAT) is designed for people who have such severe physical disabilities that their needs cannot be met by conventional home adaptations. Functions include control of visitor access, door opening and closing for wheelchair users, control of furniture and beds, control of the ambient environment and operation of home entertainment and communications equipment. Some functions such as electrically powered door opening, curtain control and window opening can be achieved only in conjunction with home adaptations.

Assistive technology aims to provide its users with the ability to control their environment more effectively partly by physical manipulation. While this is an essential part of the basket of measures designed to improve independence, installation costs can be high, especially where major alterations are required in the home. The costs of such alterations might be incurred – depending on the nature of the alterations and various eligibility criteria for public provision – by individuals and their families as well as by statutory services. Waiting times for assessments and alterations in the case of public provision can be long. For private individuals and their families, the challenges include dealing with a fragmented and unfamiliar market of builders and suppliers.

Physical adaptations and assistive technology can improve the functionality of housing and help people remain independent, but not necessarily sufficiently to reduce the risks associated with either discharging vulnerable people from an institutional to a domestic setting or maintaining them within their own home for longer than would conventionally be the case.

Remote Care – Telecare, Telehealth or Telemedicine?

If there is a question as to who might be implicated in assistive care, from builders, governments, local agencies as well as the 'users' themselves, then in remote care, the participants are all the more diverse including different types of providers of care services. This is even reflected in the diversity of terms used: telecare, telehealth and telemedicine (and other terms) are often used interchangeably to describe the remote delivery of health and social care using ICT. This highlights the nature of the field: open, constantly evolving and adapting to new and emerging technologies and changing needs. They all emphasize 'remote care' but there are differences in emphasis depending on the type of end-user and their location.

Telemedicine is essentially a health professional-to-health professional relationship with the patient somewhere in the system but not necessarily physically present. It typically involves consultations with specialists at a distance – there are many variants focused on specific medical specialties such as teleradiology, teleoncology and teledermatology. Telemedicine emphasizes the exchange of information for diagnosis, treatment and prevention of disease and injuries, research and evaluation, and for the continuing education of health care providers (World Health Organization, 2010). It has proved especially useful where there is a geographically dispersed population and there are problems of access to high quality healthcare because patients have to travel large distances for specialist health services. Telemedicine is increasingly common both in developed countries such as Australia and Canada and in the developing world, with India being a prominent case.

Of interest in this chapter are forms of ICT-assisted care provision which are changing the delivery of health and social care services to the home and the role of the home within *care pathways*. The focus of these models is partly on reducing the risks associated with care provision outside formal institutional settings such as hospitals or nursing homes. Providing an 'electronic security blanket' within an individual's home allows the earlier detection of emergencies and faster response than would normally be the case. Risks can therefore be better managed – emerging problems can be predicted, harm can be mitigated or personal safety confirmed. However, the technology is now moving towards much more extensive remote care functionality, embracing individual health monitoring and prevention as well as risk management.

Important for the successful delivery of remote care is the integration with other services. While assistive technology and home adaptations make their impact through their mere presence in the home and do not require anything beyond occasional maintenance, telecare and telehealth are only useful if a permanent service is provided which reacts appropriately to alarms raised or changes in health status detected. Often such appropriate response will require the integration with further services beyond a simple contact center e.g. dedicated response services or the integration with other care services delivered to individuals in their homes.

Risk Minimization – Telecare

The challenge for increasing the role of the home in the care system is to create environments that are not only safer because they are better designed but also help to alleviate the susceptibility to stress, fear and anxiety amongst frail elderly people, their relatives and carers. From its origins as the community alarm service – at its simplest comprising an enhanced telephone, a wearable pendant for triggering an alarm call and a response by a carer or neighbor – telecare has expanded to offer more sophisticated options. There are now a large number of commercially available telecare products including more advanced integrated systems to monitor the home environment, such as smoke, gas, flood, and temperature sensors, and devices to record data on the use of electrical appliances and trigger a human response or shut down equipment (Jarrold and Yeandle, 2009).

In the UK, local authority departments have been providing a telephone-based alarm service since the 1970s. This infrastructure has now grown to include social services departments, voluntary sector organizations and commercial suppliers and there are currently about 300 community alarm systems, serving an estimated 1.6 million people. The most recent estimates suggest that of these around 350,000 have a more sophisticated, telecare system (Barlow J et al., 2011).

Remote Care

Increasing the safety and security of an individual in their home environment is clearly an important component of home-based care models and is now relatively well-established in mainstream social care practice in the UK. The emphasis is now on developing systems for monitoring vital signs (commonly referred to as telehealth) or using passive sensors to build up a picture of activity in the home and detect the early onset of health or social care problems. This requires greatly improved data collection on an individual's changing care needs, as well as reliable data analysis methods and heuristics, to support preventative measures or earlier interventions in the course of an emerging health condition, minimize risk and allow for an appropriate response. Remote care is comprized of three components: safety and security monitoring, individual monitoring of physiological parameters and activities of daily living, and information and communication (Barlow et al., 2006) – see Fig. 13.1. The first two are directed at managing the risks associated with care outside formal care institutions. Personal monitoring of an individual's vital signs or their activities of daily living may be used to detect changes in lifestyle which may indicate an underlying problem or a worsening condition. Electronic assistive technology, designed to improve the functionality of the home and described above, can also provide data which if integrated into activity monitoring, leads to a better picture of how individuals cope with their home environment.

The third component – information and communication – involves delivering care-related information to individuals over appropriate channels depending on their needs, such as the phone, the internet or interactive television. Virtual self-help groups using the internet to bring together patients in a particular locality with a particular health condition have also become more important.

Substantial developments can be expected in coming years in the use of technology to support contact with friends and family and to reduce social isolation. Cheaper and more powerful broadband, wireless and audio-visual technologies have, for example, led to the more widespread availability of video-conferencing. As low cost videoconferencing services have spread in the general population (Skype being here the most prominent example), network effects have increased the usefulness of such services: what was restricted to within a niche community is now available to a large number of potential communication partners. The key here seems to be the development of mainstream use across society, often driven by younger, more technologically minded parts of the population. While the next generation of elderly people will be more used to the use of communication services like email and video-conferencing, the current generation of elderly people is often introduced to such services by their younger relatives.

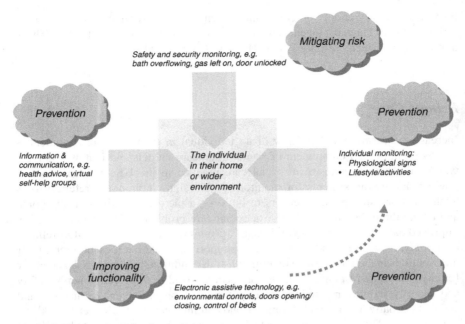

Fig. 13.1 Components of an integrated remote care system
Source: Barlow et al. (2006)

Remote Care and the Changing Role of the Home

Will the widespread introduction of remote care create the true 'lifetime home'? Residential or nursing home care has for a long time been viewed as the housing choice of last resort (Henwood and Waddington, 1998, Smith et al., 1993), yet the typical pathway for many older people is to move from traditional housing to sheltered housing or residential care and eventually to hospital and/or nursing care. This situation was already criticized by the Royal Commission on Long Term Care in 1999, which argued that people are frequently pushed into institutional care too soon because of inadequate alternative services to support people in their own homes. Enabling people to live in the circumstances they choose has therefore been a key principle of health and social care policy for a number of years.

However even "lifetime" homes only represent an incremental approach to designing accessible homes suitable for older people. There is a point in the life of many individuals when physical design solutions can only provide a partial solution to the challenges of ageing. A particular problem is the management of risk, real or perceived, by those formally responsible for an individual's care and by their relatives. Under these circumstances, the principal options have generally involved residential relocation or the use of large amounts of human intervention within the individual's own home.

Remote care is based on the premise that people in need of care should be able to live in the community for as long as possible. It should be able to support them at home, in 'lower intensity' residential care settings or on a mobile basis in the normal daily living environment as appropriate. Because it can potentially transform a previously unsuitable environment into a lower risk one, remote care has important implications for the future location of care delivery and places the home in a much more central position.

The combination of innovation in housing design and care processes supported by remote care could help to reorganize the delivery of care towards a more person-centered and home-based model and reduce the need for relocation to institutional care. This is shown schematically in Fig. 13.2. The figure shows possible housing pathways based on changing levels of dependency and the likelihood of residential relocation. A typical housing pathway for an older person living in a traditional home may involve the installation of adaptations and assistive technology, before the individual moves from their existing home to sheltered housing or residential care and then to a nursing home as their need for assistance rises. However, with the introduction of remote care the likelihood of needing to move reduces.

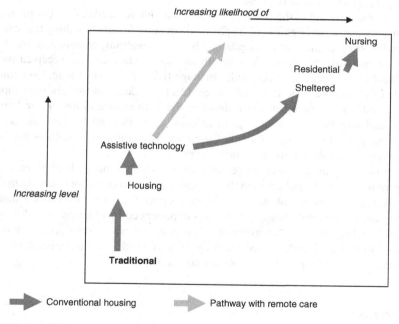

Fig. 13.2   Possible housing pathways with remote care

Over the last decade a great number of pilot projects have been conducted demonstrating the possibility of a shift of the housing pathway. More recently remote care has move towards a more mainstream use in some localities.

Conclusions

Society is changing rapidly, both demographically and socially. Health and social care will face a number of challenges in the coming decades. As the population ages, an increasing number of people require services provided and funded by a decreasing number of people.

Remote care delivered in the home has the potential to meet the growing demand for health and care services, providing end-users and carers with services that meet their needs and allowing them to live more independent and fulfilling lives. In addition it can help doctors and social care workers better manage their patients.

Enhancements to the home at a number of levels can help to support the care needs of older people. First, design innovation is required to create building structures that are capable of accommodating the changing needs of their occupants. Second, the functionality of the home can be increased through the installation of assistive technologies, some of which are electronically enhanced to provide greater control for the user. Third, the risks associated with care at home can be reduced through the use of remote care. Finally, more sophisticated monitoring of individual health can help to alert care providers of emerging changes to their health condition and trigger an appropriate response.

The transformation of the home into a place suitable for frail elderly people using remote care and the adaptation of its physical structure is not something that can be successful in isolation. Unlike standalone home adaptations, remote care needs to be integrated with the set of wider health and social care services received by an individual if it is going to successfully manage risk for elderly people. One consequence of this is the wide range of stakeholders and decision-makers who should be involved – some or all of the following: the individual and his or her family, formal and informal carers, care professionals, assessors and funders, as well as equipment providers and contractors. Coordination of these stakeholders has long proved a major challenge to the statutory services.

Reinforced by the move of successive governments to change health and social care provision models and position the domestic environment more centrally in care delivery, the combination of these developments have the potential to have a significant impact on the future housing pathways experienced by older people. However, if domestic dwellings are to really fulfil their potential new service, business models need to be developed, agreed upon by all stakeholders, and implemented and integrated with existing structures of care provision.

References

Barlow. J., Hendy, J. & Chrysanthaki, T. (2011). Sustaining innovation in remote care – four lessons. International Congress on Telehealth and Telecare. King's Fund, London, 2 March.

Barlow, J. & Venables, T. (2004). Will Technological Innovation Create the True Lifetime Home? Housing Studies, 19, 795-810.

Barlow, J., Bayer, S. & Curry, R. (2006). Implementing complex innovations in fluid multi-stakeholder environments: Experiences of 'telecare'. Technovation, 26, 396-406.

Barlow, J. & Hendy J. (2009). Adopting integrated mainstream telecare services: lessons from the UK. Eurohealth, 15, 8.

Buckner, L. & Yeandle, S. (2007). Valuing carers: calculating the value of unpaid care.

Commision of the European Communities (2007). Ageing well in the information society, An 2010 Initiative, Action plan on information and communication technologies and ageing, Brussels: Commission of the European Communities.

Department of Health (2005). Building telecare in England: London: Department of Health

Department of Health (2008). Raising the profile of long term conditions care: a compendium of information, London: Department of Health.

Department of Health (2010a). Equity and excellence: liberating the NHS, London: Department of Health.

Department of Health (2010b). Research and development work relating to assistive technology 2009-10, London: Department of Health.

Henwodd, M. & Waddington, E. (1998). Expecting the worst? Views on the future of long-term care, Help the Aged, London: Help the Aged.

Heywood, F. (2005). Adaptation: Altering the House to Restore the Home. Housing Studies, 20, 531 - 547.

Jacobzone, S., Cambios, E., Chaplain, E. & J., R. (1998). Long term care services to older people, a perspective on future needs: the impact of improving health of older persons, Paris: OECD.

Jarrold, K. & Yeandle, S. (2009). A weight off my mind: exploring the impact and potential benefits of telecare for unpaid carers in Scotland, CIRCLE - Centre for International Research on Care, Labour and Equalities, University of Leeds.

Pickard, L., Wittenburg, R., Comas-Herrera, A., Davies, B. & Darton, R. (2000). Relying on informal care in the new century? Informal care for elderly people in England to 2031. Ageing & Society, 20, 745-772.

Smith, S., Alexander, A., Hill, S., McGuckin, A. & Walker, C. (1993). Housing provision for people with health problems and mobility difficulties, York, Joseph Rowntree Foundation.

World Health Organisation (2010). Telemedicine: opportunities and developments in Member States, report on the second global survey on eHealth 2009, Geneva: World Health Organisation and Global Observatory for eHealth.

Chapter 14
Energy in the Smart Home

Simon C.R. Lewis

Introduction

Every few years a new wave of information technology finds its way into our homes. The last few decades have seen the arrival of audio and video technology, computers and internet connectivity, home cinema, mobile phones, and other digital technologies. Each wave brings with it new complexity – a new set of concepts to understand, new issues to deal with, and new frustrations to endure in exchange for the benefits that the new technology offers. Eventually, usually, the technology is domesticated and becomes part of everyday life.

In this chapter we'll address the possibility that the next big wave of new technology to arrive in our homes will not be information-related, but energy-related. We're going to explore the likelihood that today's comparatively simple situation, energy-wise, will be replaced with unexpected complexity that ordinary people may struggle to manage. And we're going to suggest that the designers of this technology are making poor assumptions about their users, and using wrong understandings of how ordinary people will react to and interact with these new products. The possibility of these products being poorly designed — at least from the point-of-view of user-interaction — threatens to undermine their adoption, and to reduce the global impact that they're intended to have.

But first let's consider how we've arrived at this state of affairs.

From Complexity to Simplicity...

Energy has long been vital in our homes. Originally in the form of solid fuels for heating and cooking, it had to be scavenged or bought, delivered, stored and managed by hand, separately in every home. It was a laborious and time-consuming task.

S.C.R. Lewis (✉)
Conceptual Simplicity, Cambridgeshire, UK

R. Harper (ed.), *The Connected Home: The Future of Domestic Life*,
DOI 10.1007/978-0-85729-476-0_14, © Springer-Verlag London 2011

The 19th and early 20th centuries brought the great innovation of a network of pipes connecting homes to central energy sources. First locally and then nationally, these allowed gas to be delivered to every home for immediate use. Simple technology allowed its use to be metered and the user to be billed appropriately. This conversion of the energy supply into a utility greatly simplified the demands of interacting with it. Warm homes, hot water, and cooked food became widely available cleanly and efficiently, and as the advertising of the 1970's emphasized, with great simplicity.

Beyond heating and cooking, other domestic uses of energy generally need electricity — whether to power the electric motors in fridges, washing machines, and other white goods, or to energize the electronics in the many audio-visual and information products that now fill our lives. Once again, although early industrial users had to build their own private power plants to generate electricity locally from fuel or running water, the entrepreneurs of the early 20th century soon realized that electricity too could be turned into a utility. Great improvements in efficiency and convenience could be achieved by generating electricity centrally and distributing it via what became a national, and even international, grid of wires into every home.

By the end of the 20th century, energy — whether gas or electricity — had become almost invisible; the ultimate utility. Although never regarded as cheap, its use became largely unconsidered by most of the population, who simply flicked on a switch when it got dark, or turned up the thermostat when it got cold. The technology of the day made things simple and uncontroversial. As a result, domestic energy technology has historically played second fiddle to information technologies when it comes to interest in the smart home.

In the last few years though, things have begun to change. As energy becomes ever-more expensive, homeowners become increasingly minded to use less of it. And because fossil fuels are implicated in climate change, there's a growing imperative to both reduce consumption and to swap to less carbon-intensive sources of energy. This pressure not only motivates individual behavior, but also generates national and international legislation affecting the whole population in significant ways.

...And Back Again

There has recently been a surge of interest in technology intended to both reduce energy waste, and deliver alternative sources of energy in and to the home. Some of this technology is fundamentally "energy" technology: materials and designs for photovoltaic cells; battery chemistry; more thermodynamically efficient boilers, heat pumps, insulation and heat storage techniques. However, just as information technologies have transformed the way a modern car and its engine are managed in comparison with the clockwork technologies of 30 years ago, so information technologies are being introduced into the home with the specific aim of managing domestic energy more efficiently.

Even as our computers start disappearing into the cloud thus turning our information processing into a simple-to-use utility, the reverse is happening to energy. The previously simple, energy-as-utility, "you flick the switch, we do the rest" model that's reigned supreme for the last 50 years is now coming under pressure. Slowly at first, but with increasing speed, we're seeing a slew of new energy technologies introduced into homes. Furthermore, energy is starting to flow both ways through the grid instead of simply being generated centrally, and consumed locally. These changes are creating a whole new industry built around the "smart grid".

Start-up companies are being formed, and industrial giants are piling into this new gold rush. Technology, methods, and people from the world of telecoms and IT are being brought to bear on managing energy in the home, and are rapidly transforming it. It's even possible that domestic energy management will turn out to be the "killer app" for some of the home automation technologies that have been touted for years without significant traction.

But this time, instead of making things simpler, life for domestic users of energy is about to get much more complex. Users of energy at home may soon need to understand much more about where their energy came from and how it was generated. They'll need to know much more about the complex and dynamic energy "marketplace". And they'll have to reason much more about the trade-offs they want to make between comfort, convenience, cost, and carbon. Unless we do something about it, a new wave of technology-led confusion may soon arrive in our homes, just as happened with the waves of consumer electronics and information technologies that arrived over the preceding decades.

Starting with the simple energy monitors that many of us have already acquired, progressing rapidly through new energy technologies like solar panels, heat pumps, and other exotica, and soon arriving at the full-blown domestic energy management systems that are already under development, the idea of "you flick the switch. . ." may soon be replaced with the complexity of opaque technology, incompatible systems and over-specified applications that already characterizes many people's experiences of smart systems in the home.

As we shall see, that process has already begun.

Monitoring Energy

You can't manage what you can't measure, and yet historically, consumers have used energy almost completely blind. They have simply turned on energy-consuming appliances (including space heating and hot-water), with little or no idea of how much energy each consumes, either in absolute terms, or relative to each other. Most will never have bothered to look at the electricity meter hidden under the stairs or outside in the rain, and many will not even look at, let alone understand, their quarterly electricity bill (especially if someone else in the home actually pays it). Worse still, the increasing tendency to pay for energy via a fixed monthly direct-debit further dissociates the point-of-payment from the point-of-use, making the cost/benefit relationship almost completely invisible.

Technically-minded readers may feel that they can judge which appliances consume more energy, but popular concern about trivial loads like mobile-phone chargers, even whilst patio heaters are blasting, should be enough to convince the energy-numerate that their expert judgement is not widely shared.

Even for experts, the truth is sometimes not obvious. Which is more expensive, a kettle of boiling water or a tea bag? What about an evening of TV? It turns out that boiling a kettle is surprisingly cheap.

The situation has been compared by some observers to a family with several cars, some gas-guzzling, others more frugal (Faruqui, Sanem, & Sharif, 2010). In this particular thought-experiment, none of the cars have fuel gauges or odometers. This hypothetical family simply fills them up from petrol pumps that have no displays, and receives one un-itemized financial bill each month. There is no way to tell which car or family member is consuming the bulk of the fuel, which car should be replaced or used less, or which family member needs to change their driving habits. Such a situation would be ludicrous in real-life, and yet this is almost exactly the situation for domestic energy. In the last few years, this has been seen as the "big problem" in need of a simple solution.

The first step in the "digitization" of domestic energy has therefore been the introduction of energy monitors into our homes. Not to be confused with the utility-owned smart meters that will soon replace our existing dumb meters outside or under the stairs, these in-home displays show in real-time how much electricity is being used by the whole home now and in the recent past. Such real-time displays have also been proposed as peripherals to smart-meters when the latter arrive later this decade, and much has been made by governments of how they will enable consumers to understand and reduce their energy consumption.

The last few years have seen a boom in such displays, with a dozen or more models available. Some of these are relatively sophisticated, recording energy use against time, handling complex tariff structures, offering the facility to upload data to a PC or the internet. Others have experimented with unusual industrial designs, and with the idea of the ambient display of consumption magnitude popular in HCI research (for example, a lamp that changes color depending on whether usage is low, medium, or high).

In the UK, government funding has allowed such devices (which retail for £25-£75) to be widely provided unrequested and free-of-charge to consumers. Unfortunately, since these meters were often supplied through the post, we cannot be certain how many recipients actually installed and used them. However, the assumption has been that such meters would make consumers conscious of the energy they're using, and that reductions in use would follow. But this seems not to have proved to be the case in practice, and the industry is now reconsidering the merits of this approach. Research evidence shows that in small scale trials this way of displaying energy consumption does result in reduced usage (Darby, The Effectiveness of Feedback on Energy Consumption, 2006), but the practical experience of utilities supplying the products en-masse appears anecdotally to be the opposite, with many devices reportedly sitting either unused, or falling into disuse once the first set of batteries expire (Hargreaves, Nye, & Burgess, 2010).

There is an absence of clear data on this effect, which merits further research because it may be that there a number of reasons for this apparent lack of consumer interest and engagement. Designing an effective energy monitor is far from simple. For one thing, many people struggle with the abstract physical quantities involved. They may understandably ask, what is energy and how is it different from the more common word in everyday language – power? The answer is obvious to a physicist, but to a consumer these are a difficult concepts to visualize and easy to confuse. Worse still, energy (the billed quantity), is typically measured in kilowatt-hours (which sounds naïvely like a rate), whilst the more familiar kilowatt that we see on electrical appliances is actually the rate of consumption (the power). Unfortunately, the naïvely logical set of units that exist in the automotive world (miles, miles-per-hour, miles-per-gallon, for example) has no easy equivalent in the world of energy.

Some designers have tried to overcome these challenges by replacing energy units with other units they presumably think are easier to understand. Tonnes of carbon dioxide is an option offered by many systems, although human ability to judge whether a particular mass of that gas is a relatively large or small amount is probably limited, and many people may not care anyway.

Money is another obvious and popular choice, but still fraught with difficulty. Tariffs for energy will soon become much more complex, so the amount paid for a given amount of energy will vary regularly by time of day, and in unpredictable ways as renewable energy supplies (which tend to be linked to unpredictable sources like wind and sun) come and go. This effect compromizes the accuracy and relevance of historical energy data based on cost, and makes daily comparisons of energy consumption difficult.

Since the amounts of money involved are small, consumers may also lack the motivation to save what seems to be just a few pence (per day) by turning off a light (Wood & Newborough, 2007). The price that any individual might be willing to pay for energy also depends on what they're doing with it. How important is it to wash clothes versus powering the PC? And can everything be reduced to a financial value anyway? Many consumers report that they are going to leave their lights on, or watch the football, come what may (Pierce, Schiano, & Paulos, 2010).

There is also the likelihood that the kind of savings that might be made using these devices — of the order of 5-15% annually (Darby, The Effectiveness of Feedback on Energy Consumption, 2006) — are masked by a similar annual rise in energy prices, thus potentially nullifying perceived reward and motivation to continue.

Even using more natural human units, there remains the difficulty that what is often measured and displayed in real-time by such systems is a rate of consumption. Given that energy is consumed at a highly variable rate, such measures are not usefully predictive of the total amount of energy likely to be consumed, and thus billed for, over even a short period of a few minutes. Whilst the instantaneous rate (the power) may appear informative and actionable, what really matters, in energy terms, is the summing up or integrating of the rate over time. The display of rate does not, therefore, easily support the budgeting behavior we regularly deploy in other domains to manage our expenditure against the benefit that it brings.

Another important problem is that even accumulated energy usage information is not particularly actionable. One may be able to see that £3.45 worth of electricity was consumed today, and even that £2.98 was used yesterday, but what should one do about it? What changed between yesterday and today that caused this difference (assuming it wasn't just the tariff), and how much of that change was discretionary, such that it could be repeated if desired?

A potential solution to this problem is disaggregation, where the consumption of individual appliances can be reviewed separately, and specific costs can be attached to each occasion of actual usage. One might see that roasting a chicken last night cost £0.59 in addition to the £4.99 spent on the bird, and is thus good value. One might also see that leaving the home PC on all the time is costing £57 per year, and decide therefore to turn it off at night. Evidence from the somewhat analogous field of internet bandwidth (Chetty, et al., 2010) suggests that it might be even better to know who in the home used the energy as well.

Such disaggregation can in principle be achieved by attaching separate monitoring equipment to every appliance (or perhaps every circuit) in the home, but this is an expensive and probably impractical approach. In future, appliances may be able to report their own energy consumption, which would be an elegant and powerful approach. However, in the meantime, a number of organizations (for example, http://www.navetas.com, http://www.sentec.co.uk) report that they are working on inferring the individual energy consumption of different appliances from the overall consumption profile of the home by understanding the typical load characteristics of each type of appliance. This disaggregation technology, although in its infancy at present, may prove to be a powerful tool in motivating reduced consumption.

However, despite all the potential for improving the way energy consumption information is analyzed and displayed, there remains a further problem — an assumption that seems to be inherent in many products — namely that ordinary consumers are interested in, and will act and react rationally to the information being displayed. This may be an inappropriate assumption, given the small amounts of money involved and the ever-rising price of energy. It may be that ordinary consumers (as opposed to the technologists who often conceive of and design these products), simply are not inclined to perform the economic calculations and make the resulting value judgements that these monitoring products appear to be designed to support.

It is also possible that yet another factor limits the success of energy monitoring as a means to promote a reduction in energy use. For those consumers who can afford it, one of the benefits of enjoying a reasonable income is a lifestyle that minimizes the need to think, much less to worry about the cost of things that are consumed as an apparently necessary side-effect of ordinary life. There are significant attractions of unfettered energy-use (the freedom to be as warm as one likes, watch television for as long as one likes, and enjoy clean and dry clothes as a matter of right). To the extent that energy falls into this category of perceived fixed-costs, devices or services which draw attention to this expenditure may be an unwelcome intrusion on an otherwise affluent lifestyle.

Finally, we might even suggest that monitoring energy in this way with the ambition solely of reducing its use is a flawed approach to energy efficiency in the same way that simply reducing one's calorie intake without altering the balance of foodstuffs consumed is a crude and often ultimately fruitless way to lose weight. Many studies have reported short-term gains (that is, reductions in energy use) as a result of the use of energy monitors, but raised questions about how further, bigger, longer-term gains could be achieved (Hargreaves, Nye, & Burgess, 2010).

Reduce, Shift, and Limit

The simplest way to save money and reduce carbon emissions is just to consume less energy, and most of the monitoring technology already in homes today is targeted at that goal. As we've seen though, today's energy monitoring products may not be particularly effective at persuading consumers to do even that apparently simple task, and unfortunately the situation will soon get even more complex, as the energy supply industry seeks to deal with other problems.

With minor exceptions, electrical energy cannot effectively be stored at scale. It must be produced for immediate use, and since the amount of energy being used at any time varies significantly, the electrical generation system must be able to produce more or less energy essentially in real time.

Electricity is generated in a number of ways. Large-scale, financially-efficient production satisfies the always-on base load. Such production, although it is typically fossil-fuelled or nuclear-powered, is actually relatively more environmentally friendly than methods that can be turned on or off quickly to deal with peaks and troughs in demand. This rapidly controllable production is usually also fossil-fuelled, but consists of the older, dirtier, or more expensive power stations. Unfortunately, the cleanest (renewable) forms of energy-production are often not only the least controllable, but also the least predictable (it may or may not be sunny or windy today, although the tides are fairly reliable, if uncontrollable).

Because electricity is generated in these different ways, each of which has a different economic and environmental footprint, reducing economic and environmental costs means considering not only how much energy is used, but also when that energy is consumed, and how rapidly. In other words, for lowest cost and greatest environmental friendliness, we want not only to reduce overall energy consumption, but also to shift some consumption into periods of lower overall use, shift it to times when renewable energy is available, or limit the maximum rate at which energy can be consumed. Such control would allow the utilities to reduce costs and emissions by choosing which generation sources are used, rather than being at the mercy of a somewhat predictable, but largely uncontrollable demand.

In the near future therefore, we are likely to see increased incentives to shift consumption from one time of day to another. Although there are exceptions, today's consumers are generally used to relatively simple forms of tariff in which energy is billed based only on the total amount consumed month-to-month, and not on when it was consumed (by time of day), or how quickly. There is therefore no incentive to manage consumption, other than to reduce it overall. However, we may see the introduction of time-of-use tariffs, which seek to financially motivate consumers to electively move some of their energy consumption to off-peak periods.

In some cases though, this shifting needs to happen dynamically, and very rapidly. Rather than be forced to bring an additional power station on line at short notice (requiring so-called spinning reserve), utilities would prefer to be able rapidly to reduce demand whenever required. In the UK, they already offer incentives to those industrial users of energy who are prepared to reduce their consumption immediately on the receipt of a certain signal. In some cases, this needs to happen within two seconds of the signal being issued. Much has been made of the possibility that this "load-shedding" might be extended to the domestic arena, where the consumer may enter into a standing contract with the utility that would allow domestic load to be shed automatically on demand. Such load would typically be "non-essential". For example, the washing machine (or just its heater) might be turned off for 30 minutes, or the freezer might be powered down for 10 minutes — losses that can easily be made up when power is restored. Appliance manufacturers are considering how to build such capabilities into their appliances, but the big challenge remains how the user might express their preferences about when and under what circumstances such load-shedding is considered acceptable. It is likely that guarantees would have to be provided not to remove power at certain times or in certain circumstances that would adversely affect daily life. A user may therefore want the economic advantage of allowing a third-party (the energy supplier) to turn off his washing machine, but also expect to be given some say in how and when it could happen. This naturally raises the question, what's the nature of the human-machine dialogue that underpins that interaction?

In respect of renewables, there is also the challenge of taking advantage of the unexpected availability of low-cost energy (when, for example, a period of windy weather is forecast). In this case, the challenge is not to delay but to bring forward the use of energy to take advantage of the available low-cost energy, or to make use of certain forms of in-home storage (for example, heating the domestic hot-water more eagerly). Again, the user may expect to participate in these decisions, bringing in all sorts of social and domestic factors into the reasoning process. Again, how is the interaction to be designed so that the system and the user might collaborate effectively in making decisions?

There may also soon be contractual limits on the maximum rate at which electricity can be consumed (the peak power drawn). This latter limit is analogous to the bandwidth limitation that many of us are familiar with in respect of our home internet connections, over which data can be transmitted at up to a certain capped rate depending on our contract with the provider. It may even come to be the case that tariffs offer a different rate for energy depending on what it was used for (heating versus entertainment, for example).

In summary then, we might ask how the ordinary domestic home occupant is going to deal with all this emerging complexity? It can't simply be automated away, because different people have differing preferences. One family might be prepared to leave their washing in the machine to be done tonight if the wind blows, but another might want it done now whatever the cost (except if the sun is going to come out in a couple of hours, in which case they might be prepared to wait). Worse still, different individuals in the same home may have different preferences for the use of a shared appliance.

One might suggest that the human-system interaction challenge is that of allowing users to express their preferred policies for such load management in advance and in ways they understand and are motivated to interact with, so that they may be executed automatically on demand. This is a user-interface problem — that of designing a mechanism through which this expression of preferences can take place.

Alternatively, one could interpret the challenge as a structural one — that of partitioning the problem and its solution in such a way that those parts that are amenable to automation are automated, whilst those parts that need user decision-making are left to users to manage manually.

Either of these approaches may turn out to be very significant challenges, involving as they do a need to talk about some very human-oriented values — something that has historically been hard to achieve in other fields (such as the creation of digital assistants that behave as naturally and with the same finesse and judgement as a human personal assistant). And yet a failure to address these challenges could have at least two negative consequences: a body of users who are frustrated that their automated "smart home" systems behave in ways that are perversely contrary to what they actually, for good reasons, want; and the foregoing of significant potential energy efficiency improvements because the system behaviors required to achieve them couldn't be fitted around the actual (and completely reasonable) expectations of the human users.

Managing Heating and Hot Water

We have so far considered mainly electrical energy, which is simply consumed by many appliances to drive their real value — devices like the television, personal computer, microwave oven, hair-dryer, and so on. For this kind of appliance, it's the responsibility of the manufacturer to design them to be as energy-efficient as appropriate, and for the user (perhaps using an energy monitor), to choose which, when, how much, or how little to use them to balance their benefit with their cost (economic and environmental).

But another kind of appliance has as its primary purpose the transformation of significant amounts of energy from one form to another, usually heat. The gas boiler and immersion heater are examples in almost every UK home today, with more exotic variants coming very soon (see later). In practice, these appliances, which provide space and water heating, consume the bulk of the energy used in a typical home, and are thus legitimately the target for the most impactful energy-efficiency efforts.

In many of these appliances — which are often permanently installed in a building — the core energy transforming function is separate from the control function. For example, a gas boiler may have a separate timer/programer/thermostat that together manage its operation according to declared user preferences and circumstances. Often, the appliance and its controller are designed and made by different companies, and are brought together only in the context of a particular in-home installation. This architecture is the hook for the energy management systems we'll consider later.

Existing control systems for such appliances are usually technically very crude, often being based on simple mechanical clock timers, bi-metallic strip thermostats, and other 19th or 20th century technology. But they're simple to use, offering just a knob that's turned this way or that to make the home warmer or cooler. In contrast, digital technology offers not only a more precise measurement capability, but also — being based on software — an almost unlimited richness and subtly of control. But just as such software-based systems have delivered advantages but burdened us with complexity in other applications (home cinema, for example), they threaten to do exactly the same thing in managing the heating in our homes.

For example, in many homes today the heating is managed via a simple 24-hour timer programmed to fire the boiler twice per day (usually in the morning and the evening), and often at the same times every day even at weekends, all year round. A crude thermostat prevents the boiler firing when it would otherwise do so if the home has reached a preset maximum temperature, and represents almost the only control that a user regularly interacts with. Simple to use, but thermally inefficient, since the crudeness of control means that the heating may well be on (or on higher) when it is not required (at least in some parts of the home).

In contrast, a typical digital heating control might incorporate a multitude of details aimed at extracting the very best from the underlying appliance. Such details can include a subset of:

- Separate electronic air temperature sensors in every room, accurate to +/- 0.5 °C rather than the 1-2 °C of a bimetallic strip thermostat. Such sensors can avoid the regular swings in temperature that would otherwise prompt users to turn up the thermostat when they feel cold;
- Wall temperature sensors, because the perception of warmth in a dwelling is influenced not only by air temperature, but also by radiant heat, which is a result of wall temperature;
- Water temperature sensors to measure usage and availability of domestic hot-water;
- Humidity sensors to allow the heating to be run just enough to avoid condensation when the house is unoccupied, and because humidity also affects the perception of warmth;
- Independent temperature settings for each room, and for different occupancy states of the room or whole home (people at home, asleep, at work, etc.);
- A much richer, occupancy-based schedule, taking into account the planned and unplanned comings and goings of members of the family throughout the week

and year, whether explicitly declared to the system by the users, implicitly indicated via other means (for example smart-phone GPS or proximity detectors), or inferred by the system over a period of time;

- A detailed understanding of the thermodynamic behavior of the boiler and the heating system, allowing it to be fired in the pattern most conducive to efficient conversion of gas into heat (and/or maximum lifetime of the boiler), rather than simply turned on and off according to demand;
- An understanding (potentially learnt automatically) of the heat characteristics of the home, allowing the heating to be fired "just in time" before the occupants return home or get out of bed, such that the house is warm, but not over-heated), and conversely allowing the heating to be turned off as early as possible before the occupants go to bed, saving energy without the occupants suffering a perceptible temperature drop;
- Knowledge of the current and forecast external weather conditions (temperature, wind, and rain) which influence the rate at which the heating system warms the home, the rate at which it cools when the heating stops, and even the occupants' perception of a comfortable temperature;

Given that heating and hot-water represent the majority of domestic energy use (Buildings Research Establishment, 2003), the efficient management of just these two systems is a significantly more impactful contribution to energy efficiency than reduction of electrical appliances on standby, for example.

It's therefore very attractive to design and install such advanced heating controls, but once again efficiency's gain threatens to be usability's loss, as users are potentially-forced to interact in much more complex ways with these new control systems. Increased energy efficiency threatens to require users to relinquish control of their heating systems to automatic black boxes which, whilst they may produce significant energy improvements, may fail to account for the subtle and human-oriented expectations of the home's occupants.

For example, a heating system might traditionally be set to come on at 0630 because the occupants get up at 0700 and want their home to be warm by the time they get up. However, the occupants (being asleep at the time), may not realize that the house is actually warm by 0645, wasting 15 minutes worth of energy — which could be 25% of the morning heating period (in other words, a significant proportion). How much better it appears to be for the occupants to tell the system only that they get up at 0700 and leave the system to decide when to fire the boiler at the last minute based on local conditions of internal and external temperature, boiler efficiency, thermal capacity, and so on. But what if one member of the family gets up significantly earlier than the others? They may not want the house to be warm (preferring economy to comfort). However, when later occupants get up, they may legitimately and rationally prefer comfort to economy. Immediately, an attempt to manage the underlying energy technology more efficiently breaks down. And what if the temperature that's required in the morning is lower than that desired in the evening. Just as in too many PC applications, the designers of such systems can be tempted to add more user options and controls to deal with these exception conditions, and the undesirable result is more complexity for the user.

In addition, because a control system such as this is software-based, it can be designed to be self-learning, monitoring its own performance, and altering its behavior to improve over time. Even better, such advanced control systems can in principle be internet-connected, allowing monitoring, learning, and improvement to happen across a population of homes, delivering best-practice for all instances of a given system (subject, of course, to the recognition and appropriate management of privacy and security concerns). All very attractive from an efficiency point-of-view, but representing yet more complexity for users struggling to decide why their previously predictable system is behaving the way it is. "How do I get the heating on?" could soon replace "How do I get the TV on?" — a question that's become all too familiar in many homes where complex multi-box home cinema systems have replaced old-fashioned television sets with a single on/off button.

It might appear that this complexity could be avoided by making everything, or nearly everything, automatic. But this is no get-out-of-jail card. Consumers have become very used to directly controlling their heating and hot-water, and may be unwilling to relinquish control for the reasons outlined above. Any automatic system gains its advantage by switching such appliances on and off in ways different to those a user would choose — otherwise what's the point? But in practice the user may want to know why his boiler is or isn't running when he thinks it shouldn't or should be (especially if he believes it to be consuming unnecessary energy). In this case, with a fully automatic system, the problem of designing appropriate control and preference interactions is replaced by the problem of designing another form of dialogue, in which the system must explain its automatic behaviors in a way that makes sense to the user — something that's historically been quite difficult to achieve in, for example, expert systems.

My Home, My Power Station

We began our discussion by considering how turning the supply of energy into a utility has been making life simpler for nearly 100 years. During that time, energy has been generated centrally, distributed in one direction over a national network, and consumed locally. Although the management of generation and distribution by the utilities is complex for them, the situation in-home for consumers has been simple. A straightforward consumption meter and a flat tariff have been all that's been required to manage this configuration. But, motivated again by economic and environmental concerns, this simple situation is changing rapidly, and in so doing it's creating yet more control problems and complexity for users.

Energy is increasingly being generated not just centrally, but also directly in homes, where it may either be used locally, or exported to the grid for use elsewhere. Amongst other things, electricity might be generated directly from solar photovoltaic panels (solar PV), hot-water might be generated directly from solar thermal panels, or space heating might be obtained by pumping low-grade heat from the ground or air into the building (a process that allows 3-4 times as much energy to be pumped as is consumed by the pumping). There is also a new generation of combined heat and power ("micro-CHP") boilers that generate electricity from fuel, and provide space-heating and domestic hot-water as a side-effect.

We might ask why such distribution of generation is happening. Why can't all generation, including renewable and alternative sources, stay centralized, keeping things simple? One answer is simply "because we can". Just as the availability of new technologies drove the "PC on every desk and in every home" revolution, so new technologies make it possible to build micro-generation plants at an affordable price. Capital cost and planning permissions are another reason. Why would governments or utilities spend billions and take decades to build a new nuclear power-station, when consumers will spend their own money generating their own electricity on their own premises, starting tomorrow. And of course, as the central energy supply gets more expensive, and as increasing demand makes reliability potentially more uncertain, we may all appreciate the comfort of knowing that we could survive off-grid if we needed to, just as we enjoyed the freedom of having a PC on our desk when it wasn't under the control of the IT department. For all these reasons, local energy generation is likely to grow in ubiquity, adding again to user complexity.

The rollout of local generation is also being encouraged by government incentives including feed-in tariffs (FITs), which offer payments to consumers for generating and exporting their own energy. At the time of writing in the UK, consumers generating electricity locally were paid a tariff worth between around three and four times the price of electricity bought from the grid — a payment that is made even if the electricity is not exported but is instead consumed entirely locally. Ignoring the significant capital cost, locally-generated electricity is not only free, but the consumer is paid more for generating it than it would have cost to buy. A further small payment (less than the cost of electricity bought from the grid) is made if the electricity is actually exported to the grid rather than merely being generated and used locally.

By creating and offering such tariffs, the government seeks to influence energy behaviours for economic and environmental reasons. In effect, they are creating a game (in the mathematical sense), and a consumer can in principle choose to play that game for a potentially useful financial gain.

The complexity of playing the game is considerable though, and dynamic. In addition to straightforward monitoring of local production (for example, are the solar panels working as they should, given local weather conditions and the specific location, orientation, and inclination of the installation?), there are constant optimizations available. For example, can any of the day's electricity consumption (use of the dishwasher, perhaps) be brought forward in the day to take advantage of available free electricity during daylight, which would otherwise have to be exported, and purchased back later at a higher price in order to run the machine in the evening? The technical answer is almost certainly "yes", and the economic calculation is simple to automate. But is that what the user wants? For a variety of reasons (including convenience and expectations of future appliance availability), the answer may be "no", or even worse, "maybe". Perhaps running the dishwasher when it's half-full will mean it needs emptying at an inconvenient time. Again, how is the user to express to the system the complex circumstances under which he does or doesn't want the dishwasher put on? Or is the opportunity to optimize this energy consumption to be foregone simply because it cannot be automated and yet is too laborious for a user to bother reasoning about personally every day?

Worse still (from a complexity point-of-view), homes can also store energy to some extent. This can be implicitly in the form of warmth within the structure (a quite considerable capacity in some buildings, especially those with under-floor heating), or explicitly in the form of a tank full of hot water. In both cases, the storage capacity is limited, and must ideally be kept available to store energy produced in the cheapest possible way (which, depending on the weather, will likely be the solar thermal panels, but may be from surplus electricity from the solar PV panels), or electricity bought off-peak from the grid. But hot-water has a shelf-life of at most 24 hours, and it's not usually very pleasant to run out. How is the system to know how much hot water might be needed later today? It might be thought that a pattern of such expected use could be learnt by the system from monitoring historical usage, or that it could be explicitly set up by the user. But what about the exceptions that happen for reasons far outside the system's knowledge of the world (the unexpected arrival of grandma, for example). How is that to be accounted for?

Finally, the eventual arrival of electric cars may create further complexity. Such cars could be charged from in-home renewable resources if their usage patterns were carefully monitored and understood, and if the availability of free electricity was predictable (via weather forecasts). In addition, the energy stored within an electric car is an important asset, and it's possible that in the future we'll see electric cars used as an enormous distributed battery for the nation. Thus, a car may be charged during the day using locally-generated solar power, or at night using cheap off-peak grid electricity. Then, if it looks likely that it won't be used, the energy in the batteries could later be sold back to the grid at a time of peak demand (and hence, price). In this way, cheap and relatively greener electricity is shifted to a period where more expensive and less environmentally-friendly electricity would otherwise have to be generated, and the shifters (the owners of the electric vehicles) make a profit in the process. This mechanism may be beneficial even when losses associated with conversion and transmission are taken into account. But what about unexpected use of the electric car? Does the user have a way to express the likelihood of this to the system (for example, a user who usually walks to work, but will take the car if it looks like rain is expected), or do we again forgo the chance to optimize energy efficiency because of the inconvenience and frustration that doing it badly creates.

What is in effect happening here is that the complexities of management (and opportunities for optimization) that are already present in the corporately managed national generation and distribution infrastructure are being extended into the home, creating an obligation, or at the very least an opportunity, for every householder to participate in the smart grid. However, just as the benefits of owning and operating your own computer come with a certain burden of complexity, owning and operating your own power-station will carry the same responsibility.

Domestic Energy Management Systems

We have so far discussed ways in which designers are attempting to encourage consumers to reduce energy consumption, and also to shift it, or to take the same total amount of energy more slowly. We have also considered new ways to manage heating and hot-water systems that can squeeze more useful heat out of each unit of fuel than hitherto, provided that users are prepared to interact with the complexity and put up with the potential compromises that are required. We have even explored the opportunity to turn our homes into miniature power generating and storage stations, and to trade energy on the open market with our neighbours near and far, again provided we're prepared to set up and interact with the required systems.

The history of user-interfaces on energy appliances is not a happy one though. Having been designed mostly by expert engineers, and manufactured to a limited budget, they tend to feature low-quality displays, multi-function push-buttons, and a plethora of special modes and press-and-hold features. It is not uncommon, for example, for householders never to reprogram their central-heating timer from one season to the next, and difficulties with user-interface are surely a contributory factor.

As we have seen, houses will soon gain ever more of these energy-transforming appliances, and each may be designed by a different manufacturer. Each will, by default, come with its own user-interface — its own tiny display and set of buttons, and its own obscure behaviour. But we need to ask again, for whatever reason that they might be tempted or coerced into acquiring this new technology, how is the ordinary domestic householder going to deal with all this new complexity?

Many technology companies, utilities, and others believe they have the answer. They are responding to an opportunity to bring together the monitoring and control of all these systems to create a joined-up and even more efficient whole. There is also an opportunity to bring together the user-interfaces to these systems to create a unified and understandable interaction with their human masters. These companies are competing to supply a new generation of home energy management systems for domestic use. Most share the same basic architecture, which consists of:

- A central "black box" installed in the home, sometimes referred to as a hub. This device acts as a gateway to the outside world (usually via the internet), and as a controller for the various peripheral devices disposed around the home. It also acts as a hardware host for the software applications that provide all the various features of the system. The hub is usually self-managing and remotely upgradeable, in the same way that a typical set-top-box or games console acts as the central repository for the provision of its services.
- A set of peripheral sensors, actuators, switches and displays that allow the hub to interact with the real world including the various in-home systems it's managing and the users who control it. These might include air and water temperature sensors, flow sensors, electrical sensors, relays, dedicated displays, and so on. Such peripherals are typically connected using a low-power wireless network standard such as ZigBee or Z-Wave. Different vendors may provide different

peripherals, and work is underway to create and promote standards to allow such interworking. There is the usual debate between proponents of "open" and "closed" systems, whose arguments are familiar from other domains.

- A service proposition "in the cloud" — often subscription-based — that works with the hub to offer extra capabilities like remote access via a smart phone or the web, software upgrades, weather forecasts, community comparisons, and so on.

Such systems deliver a kind of digital nervous system for the home — capable of sensing the state of many variables, reasoning about the conditions that prevail, and then intervening to deliver some desired improvement or optimization. This can apply across the entire broad spectrum of energy use in a home, including space heating, domestic hot water, white goods and information appliances, local generation, and the emerging electric vehicle.

It's also worth noting that whilst our interest here is primarily in energy management, the same platform of hardware and software components can relatively easily be used to offer additional services in the home, including security and assisted-living, and that several vendors of such systems are actively developing these additional applications. It's in this way that energy management may be the killer application that motivates the wide-spread deployment of a more general-purpose home automation infrastructure.

However, the arrival of such whole-home domestic energy management systems where none existed before may once again herald an increase in complexity for users. As we have already discussed, where once there might have been just an electricity meter, a central heating timer, and a thermostat, there may soon be an array of more sophisticated energy technology. Sitting on top of that array will be the domestic energy management system, itself implementing complex whole-home control algorithms, integrating tens of heterogeneous appliances, and dealing with hundreds of variables.

Just as for the individual appliances, it's unlikely that these integrated systems will be fully automatic — needing no user interaction at all. Neither, as we have extensively discussed, would that be particularly desirable since, like all such systems, a domestic energy management system is most usefully a servant, not a dictator. Such a relationship between human and machine cannot be productive without an effective dialogue between the two, or very careful design so that they can live in comfortable symbiosis without any such conversation. This is simultaneously a great opportunity and a significant risk.

We've already considered the challenges inherent in displaying the fundamental quantities involved (energy, power, and so on). These challenges apply to any in-home energy monitoring system. But control brings a new set of challenges around representing and making clear the various metaphorical levers that users can now pull. The user of such a system may struggle to understand such things as:

- What are the energy flows between the systems within my home, and what's the status of the various energy producing, consuming, and storing appliances?

- What choices and preferences are available, what have I currently chosen, what's the effect of those choices, what would be the effect of different choices, and how do I change my mind?
- Much of home life follows a repeating pattern, with exceptions. What's the repeating schedule for my home?
- In general, how is time represented and manipulated? What happened in the past, what's happening now, and what will (or might) happen in the future?
- How do I set up conditional behaviors? If something happens, what should happen as a consequence?
- What is the system doing now, and why did it decide to do that? Can the system explain its reasoning to me?

An additional challenge may be that as we've already observed, homes are shared spaces, so any interaction design must also respect the possibility of there being multiple users, and allow users to manipulate and reason about the impact of control changes on different occupants. Any interaction with a domestic energy management system is also likely to be presented across a variety of interaction surfaces — through dedicated in-home displays, on smart phones and tablets, on the web, and even through good old-fashioned physical buttons and knobs.

Users appear to be highly motivated (or at minimum, prepared) to interact with home entertainment systems and with communication and other smart home infrastructure, perhaps because of the immediate gratification such systems offer in the form of entertainment and social interaction. But is energy management as important as entertainment to most people? Despite the manifest efficiency and economic possibilities, can we really be sure that many people will choose to interact with these systems to the extent that is likely to be required to get the most out of them? The designers of such systems clearly hope the answer is "yes", but is there a risk that they represent only the early adopters of such technology, and that the majority of the population will lack the required motivation to interact that such systems require? Will something different be needed?

This is a big challenge, but the rewards for success (in terms of energy efficiency and economy) are equally large. There is a significant opportunity to create an interaction approach for energy management that addresses these various challenges, and which helps to move advanced energy systems onwards from the domain only of the energy enthusiast, and into the everyday understanding of the ordinary population where the maximum benefit can be delivered.

Conclusion: Co-existing in Peace and Efficiency

In most homes today, energy systems are simple — almost primitive: there is probably a gas boiler warming the home and heating the water; there will also be a variety of more-or-less energy efficient electrical appliances used to turn electricity into heat, sometimes doing something useful along the way (such as storing, transforming, or displaying information). Energy is supplied by utilities that charge a fixed price, or at most a price that changes only slowly and predictably. Today's users are used to operating, or in many cases, ignoring such systems. One might say that for them, life is simple.

Tomorrow, things will be much more complex: As we have seen, solar PV panels on individual roofs will provide electricity during daylight hours, which can be used locally, stored, or exported to the grid; heat-pumps may well provide background warmth in the home, itself potentially powered from the electricity generated by the solar PV panels, or from the grid; air conditioning may be in use where previously it was unnecessary; an immersion heater might also absorb spare daytime electricity from the solar PV to heat water — effectively storing the free energy for a few hours. Meanwhile, a gas boiler will continue to provide backup heat when renewable energy is not available. In the garage, an electric car will need charging from the best available source, depending on the expected pattern of use. Its stored energy can be sold back to the grid if the management system believes it's economic to do so without risk of the car becoming unavailable if required. While this is happening, white goods will be able to shift their consumption — delaying use until energy is cheap from the grid at night, or free from the roof in the day. They may also respond to signals requesting a rapid reduction in demand — if the user has entered into such an agreement with the utility and has specified his preferences about how it is to be enacted. As the same time, energy prices will change dynamically in both scheduled and unexpected ways according to the time-of-day, the weather, and other people's demand and supply patterns. And finally, each of the systems that transform energy in homes will come from a different manufacturer and each, whilst highly optimized in itself, may have little intelligence about how to work in a "joined-up" way with the other systems in the home. Left to their own devices, they could fight: the gas boiler mindlessly filling the tank with hot-water overnight leaving no room for the free hot-water that tomorrow's sunshine will generate. Or the reverse: the standard hot-water schedule could fail to take into account the exceptionally cloudy day that's expected tomorrow. The car might sell its energy back to the grid not knowing that it's needed tonight.

There is a significant opportunity for information technology to be deployed to mediate between these various energy-generating, storing, and consuming systems, and between the human occupants of the home. Such systems could also effectively play the games created by an ever-changing economic and legislative landscape, to maximize — on the user's behalf — the economic benefits of acquiring local renewable energy generation and storage products.

But there is also a possibility that such systems might be conceived and based on overly simple and potentially inappropriate understandings of real human motivations, reasoning patterns, and behaviour. In many cases, people might erroneously be assumed to act according to a form of rational choice theory, for example, and hence thought to be motivated only by the economic (financial) trade-offs offered by different ways of configuring their use of energy. In practice though, ordinary people reason rationally about a series of other, non-economic factors including things related to comfort, luxury, cleanliness, and social propriety. Unless such factors relating to the "moral economy" of the home are taken into account, we may be headed for wholesale rejection by users of this new technology — a scenario explored in detailed in (Strain, 2003). Such an occurrence would represent not just the failure of a technology that's being developed for commercial gain (and therefore presumably subject to the normal acceptance of the largely financial risks of such failure), but in this case also the failure of the technology to address the greater imperatives of planet-wide climate change (for which failure may well have commensurately greater consequences).

Developing this new understanding of users, and even more so expressing and applying it effectively to the process of conceiving, designing, and implementing new energy products and services, is likely to be both complex and difficult. But the obligation to develop such understanding is simultaneously a great challenge for the research community, and a significant commercial opportunity for product suppliers.

References

Wood, G., & Newborough, M. (2007). Energy-use information transfer for intelligent homes: Enabling energy conservation with central and local displays. *Energy and Buildings* 39, 495-503.

Buildings Research Establishment. (2003). *Domestic Energy Factfile*. Farnborough: BRE.

Chetty, M., Banks, R., Harper, R., Regan, T., Sellen, A., Gkantsidis, C., et al. (2010). Who's Hogging the Bandwidth? : The Consequences of Revealing the Invisible in the Home. Proc. *CHI 2011*. ACM.

Eun-ju, L., Ji-nyoung, P., Jae-min, K., & Min-ho, B. (2009). User interface design for changing energy end-users behavior. *International Association of Societies of Design Research (IASDR)*.

Ehrhardt-Martinez, K., Donnelly, K. A., & Laitner, J. A. (2010). *Advanced Metering Initiatives and Residential Feedback Programs: A Meta-Review for Household Electricity-Saving Opportunities*. Washington DC: ACEEE.

Energy Saving Trust, (2009). *The smart way to display*. London, EST.

Darby, S. (2008). Why, What, When, How, Where and Who? *Summer Study on Energy Efficiency in Buildings* (pp. 7-70 - 7-81). *American Council for an Energy Efficient Economy* (ACEEE).

Darby, S. (2006). *The Effectiveness of Feedback on Energy Consumption*. Oxford: Environmental Change Institute - University of Oxford.

Faruqui, A., Sanem, S., & Sharif, A. (2010). The impact of informational feedback on energy consumption - A survey of the experimental evidence. *Energy 35* (pp. 1598-1608), Elsevier: Amsterdam.

Frost & Sullivan. (2010). *The European Home Energy Monitoring Market*. London.

Hargreaves, T., Nye, M., & Burgess, J. (2010). Making Energy Visible: A qualitative field study of how householders interact with feedback from smart energy monitors. *Energy Policy 38*, 6111-6119.

Jackson, T. (2005). *Motivating Sustainable Consumption. University of Surrey, Centre for Environmental Strategy*. Guilford, UK: Sustainable Development Research Network.

Janda, K. B. (2009). Buildings Don't Use Energy: People Do. *PLEA 2009 - 26th Conference on Passive and Low Energy Architec*ture. Quebec City, Canada.

Pierce, J., Schiano, D. J., & Paulos, E. (2010). Home, Habits, and Energy: Examining Domestic Interactions and Energy Consumption. *CHI-2010* (pp. 1985-1994). Atlanta, GA, USA: ACM.

Scott, J., Krumm, J., Meyers, B., Brush, A., & Kapoor, A. (2010). Home Heating Using GPS-Based Arrival Prediction. *MSR Technical Report*, Cambridge, UK: Microsoft Research.

Sentec Ltd, (2006). *Smart Meters for Dumb Markets*. Cambridge, UK: Sentec Ltd.

Strain, J. D. (2003). Households as Morally Ordered Communities. In R. Harper, *Inside the Smart Home* (pp. 41-62). Springer.

The Economist (November 6th 2010). It's a Smart World - Special report on smart systems. London, UK.

Index